PERSONAL FINANCIAL PLANNING FOR GAYS & LESBIANS

Our Guide to Prudent Decision Making

PETER M. BERKERY, JR.

IRWIN
Professional Publishing®
Chicago • London • Singapore

This publication is designed to provide accurate and
authoritative information in regard to the subject matter
covered. It is sold with the understanding that neither the
author, the publisher, or the Human Rights Campaign is
engaged in rendering legal, accounting, or other professional
service. If legal advice or other expert assistance is required,
the services of a competent professional
person should be sought.

*From a Declaration of Principles jointly adopted by a Committee
of the American Bar Association and a Committee of Publishers.*

Library of Congress Cataloging-in-Publication Data
Berkery, Peter M.
    Personal financial planning for gays and lesbians/Peter M.
Berkery, Jr.
      p. cm.
    Includes index.
    ISBN 0-7863-0482-0
    1. Gays—Finance, Personal. 2. Lesbians—Finance, Personal.
I. Title.
HG179.B4572 1996
332.024'0664—dc20   96–16269

Printed in the United States of America
1 2 3 4 5 6 7 8 9 0 QBP 3 2 1 0 9 8 7 6

*To my grandfather Charles F. Leonard
and my father-in-law William A. Diggins, Jr.*

*The latter taught me the importance of saving
money, the former the importance of sharing it.*

INTRODUCTION

Why a book about financial planning for gay people? What special needs does the lesbian and gay community have? Isn't financial planning the same for us as it is for everybody else?

Questions like these cross many minds when they reflect on the topic of this book. They are valid questions at first blush, but, in truth, the lesbian and gay community's unique needs in the financial planning arena are overwhelming. In trying to plan for our financial futures, we are forced to deal with a system that simply wasn't designed with us in mind. For example, it is a system that is still grappling with how to insure our lives and our property. It is a system that presents unique challenges to our ability to plan a secure retirement. And it is a system that is downright hostile to our relationships in every aspect of the financial planning process. There are literally hundreds of consequences that flow from these and related realities. Throughout this book, you will see example after example of the ways in which the entire financial infrastructure— the insurance industry, the investment process, the tax structure, the retirement system, and the probate process—does not accommodate our goals, our priorities, or our relationships. If we fail to take all of this into account when we make financial decisions, we run a real risk of having our efforts thwarted.

As lesbians and gay men, we simply are not able to plan for our financial goals in quite the same ways as the dominant culture. Sometimes we have to take extra steps to get to the same place as our straight counterparts. Other times we are forced to do things differently in order to achieve the same goals. Occasionally, we even have to rewrite the rules as we go along in order to end up where we mean to be. This book is a first-ever attempt to explain the unique challenges we face as lesbians and gay men and to offer solutions to meet our needs. On virtually every page you'll see in excruciating detail just how oblivious the system is to our circumstances. More importantly, you'll see the steps you can take to work around the limitations inherent in the status quo.

How This Book Is Organized

There are at least five distinct "disciplines" that combine to form the financial planning process:

- Risk planning and insurance.
- Investment planning.
- Tax planning.
- Retirement planning.
- Estate planning.

This book is organized along these lines, with each discipline constituting a separate chapter. The topics within each chapter are divided into discrete subject-matter sections, each designed as a self-contained treatment of one particular aspect of the larger discipline. This offers you the option of either reading through an entire chapter (or the entire book) all at once, or zeroing in on specific topics of greatest interest to you at the moment. If it works, this modular approach should enable you to digest the information you need without drowning in detail—or dying of boredom! It also should allow you to use the book as a reference volume and revisit particular issues as they arise for you.

Each topic in each chapter has three parts: (1) The Straight Facts; (2) Our Issues; and (3) Related Topics. There's nothing tricky about the names of these parts, and each part does what its name implies. The Straight Facts discusses the general rules, issues, and strategies for the topic. Our Issues explains how the general rules apply to lesbians and gay men, notes the exceptions that work against—and occasionally for—us, and points out any other "gay angles" to the topic. The cross-references provided in Related Topics are not afterthoughts. They can contain valuable information not repeated elsewhere in the text. They also serve the important purpose of linking a particular topic to the larger financial planning process.

Although it may seem strange to some to separate "Our Issues" from the larger discussion of a given topic, doing so serves three important purposes. First, by drawing attention to the differences and difficulties our community faces, it makes an important political statement. Next, by explaining separately the unique ways in which we are forced to interface with the system, it provides emphasis that may help minimize mistakes or oversights in your financial planning. Finally, on a more practical level, it facilitates the book's modular approach to digesting reams of heady information.

Space has been one of the biggest constraints in writing this book. There simply is not enough room to say everything that could be said. At times you'll find this hard to believe, but throughout the book there has been a conscious effort to economize on words in order to get as much between the covers as possible. You therefore need to keep the following in mind:

1. There has been a deliberate attempt to craft technical sentences as tightly as possible, and when you run across such sentences—and the book is loaded with them—please try to keep in mind that every word in the sentence may have significance. For example, if you see the word *generally* in a sentence, it's there for a reason. There may be exceptions to the rule you're reading, and those exceptions may apply to you; generally, they won't, but they may. (That was a test. Did you get it?) Similarly, technical terms are used with precision throughout the book. If you see a reference to *taxable income* in a discussion of tax planning, it is not the same as *gross income* or *adjusted gross income*. All terms are explained at or near the first time they appear. Go slow and be certain you understand what you're reading. The topics are separated into small, manageable modules. Don't read more than you can absorb at once.

2. The book is liberally peppered with examples. The examples serve both to demonstrate a point as well as to elaborate on it. Examples sometimes can be an important source of additional information; hopefully, they are always a source of clarification. Read the examples carefully.

A final thought regarding the book's structure: Financial planning does not occur in a static universe. Congress regularly tinkers with the tax laws, and the IRS and the courts constantly scramble to interpret them. The insurance industry gradually is learning about the unique needs of our community, and some forward-thinking companies are designing new products to meet our needs as expediently as their actuaries can figure out how to let them. The prices of investments fluctuate daily, and the data used to track the performance of those investments are updated continuously. While the information in this book is accurate and current as of its writing, there's always a chance that a rule will have changed by the time you get around to reading (or revisiting) it. Be open to this possibility, do your best to keep current, and seek competent professional advice when you sense things may have changed.

The Queen's English

Lest the PC Police come calling, a few words about terminology are in order. Three difficult linguistic issues surfaced repeatedly in drafting this text. The first of these was every writer's perennial favorite: gender. One of the most frustrating facts of modern life is that we've proven no more adept at eliminating sexism from the lexicon than we have at eliminating it from the culture. This probably doesn't surprise the anthropologists among us who understand well that language is a reflection of a culture. In any event, the mother tongue is limited in its inclusivity, and the options therefore are similarly limited. This author's admittedly imperfect solution is as follows: Unless doing so made a sentence awkward to the point that inclusivity threatened comprehension, both feminine and masculine pronouns appear ("he and she," "her and his"). When the sentence simply became unmanageable, the gender of pronouns is interchanged at random.

A related grammatical issue concerns the use of *gay* as an adjective. Does *gay* refer only to gay men, or does it refer to both men and women who have a same-sex sexual orientation? Reasonable people disagree on this point. In order to accommodate all points of view, this book uses both *lesbian and gay* wherever possible. However, the topics in this book are very technical, and it sometimes requires a very lengthy sentence to make a point. Where it seems that the reader may be in danger of losing her train of thought, and a few more words are all it would take to precipitate a derailment, the word *gay* is used alone. Wherever this happens, *gay,* of course, is intended to refer to both men and women.

Once we turn to relationships, the taxonomical waters become even muddier. As we all know, there really is not a single acceptable word for defining the parties to our relationships. Among the more widely employed options, *significant other* is a mouthful, *partner* misses some dimensions of the relationship, and *lover* misses a bunch of others. Moreover, one of the wonderful things about our community is the variety of flavors to be found in our relationships: platonic bonds deeper than many marriages, trusted business partners, marriages of convenience, purely physical unions, and many "couples" in the truest Ozzie and Harriet sense. As we'll say many times throughout this book, we're redefining family in myriad ways, and once again the language hasn't caught up with us. This book's solution to the dilemma reflects the variety found in our alternative families: the terms *partner, lover, domestic partner,* and *significant other* are used interchangeably to refer to the person with whom you share your life. It's left to you to define these terms in a way that has meaning for you.

A Final Thought

Our community is not alone in being ill-served by the status quo. Even if the pace appears glacial to us, the current system is crumbling, and the paradigms that have been operative in the past are ceasing to have meaning for more and more people in our society. Something will need to replace the failing status quo. As has happened not infrequently in the history of our culture, in their quest for new, better, more creative, and more just ways of doing things, some of the solutions people adopt will have originated within the lesbian and gay community. Whether it's our approach to risk, our sense of priorities in making investment decisions, our forced self-reliance in retirement planning, or our courageous efforts to redefine *family* in the face of a hostile legal system, our community is once again blazing new trails. And there can be no doubt that, ultimately, where we lead, others once again will choose to follow. Hopefully, this book will serve as a guide along the way.

ACKNOWLEDGMENTS

A book like this is never written by just one person, and I want to express my gratitude to several people.

A number of technical experts provided excellent review and advice on early drafts of the manuscript. The accuracy and comprehensiveness of the text has been aided by the eagle eyes and keen minds of Mandell Winter, E. G. McBroom, Sandra Phillips, Brian Schmitt, Sally Jo Button, Paul Albergo, and Bill Moran. Similarly, Kathleen Nilles provided a critical final review on behalf of the HRC Foundation. My deep appreciation goes to each.

Many people at Irwin Professional Publishing have invested time and energy well "above and beyond" on this project. It's not possible to thank them all by name, but two deserve particular credit. I will always be grateful to Mike Desposito, who has since moved onto new—and I'm told wonderful—opportunities, for his unwavering enthusiasm and commitment to this project from the moment I proposed it to him. Amy Ost, my editor, responded to every challenge the project and I presented with a patience that would make Job seem like a kvetch. To her and everyone else at Irwin who worked so hard on my behalf, many thanks.

The encouragement of people in my "real job" at RIAG made me believe this book was a risk worth taking. I won't embarrass any of my co-workers by naming names; you all know who you are, and now you also know how important your good wishes have been.

I would be remiss if I didn't mention the assistance Bob Witeck and Wes Combs provided, first in encouraging the good people at the Human Rights Campaign to get involved in this project, and second in helping to get the word out on what we're up to here. Thanks, guys!

Finally, most of all I need to acknowledge the unwavering support of my partner in life and business, Greg Diggins. Greg tolerated months of sometimes uninterrupted bitchiness as this project routinely usurped my "free time" and regularly dominated our "us time." Throughout it all, he remained my strength and my rest, and endured with constant (well ... almost constant) good will. In the end, there is as much of Greg in these pages as me.

Again, my deepest thanks to one and all.

CONTENTS

Chapter 3

Investments   101

Chapter 4

Income Tax Planning   161

Chapter 5

Retirement Planning   231

Chapter 6

Estate Planning   287

Chapter 7

Other Planning Issues   347

Conclusion

Ten Key Financial Planning Strategies for Lesbians and Gay Men   367

1

Financial Planning Fundamentals

THE FINANCIAL PLANNING PROCESS

THE STRAIGHT FACTS

Professionals speak of financial planning as a six-step process which includes

1. Establishing financial goals.
2. Gathering data.
3. Processing and analyzing data.
4. Developing a financial plan.
5. Implementing the plan.
6. Monitoring the plan.

Regardless of whether you've engaged the process for a specific goal or for comprehensive planning, it is important to be mindful of all six steps. Let's take a brief look at each one individually.

Establishing Financial Goals

It's essential to quantify your goals for the financial planning process in order for it to succeed. Identify your goals with as much specificity as possible. Goals like "being successful" or "retiring early" can't be quantified and therefore are difficult to plan for. Identify your goals in terms of specific time frames and dollar amounts.

A variety of financial goals drives people to seek financial planners, including the desire to manage money better (establish a budget, reduce debt, increase savings, etc.), the need to establish an emergency fund, the need to save for a major purchase, funding a new business, insuring adequate protection against personal and financial risks, saving for education, saving for a secure retirement, arranging for the orderly distribution of assets at death, and minimizing taxes. Since many of these goals require saving and investing strategies, a critical related goal usually gets identified: structuring an appropriate investment portfolio.

Gathering Data
Financial planners use a number of tools to gather data, and it's likely that you will, too. First, you'll build a balance sheet and a cash flow statement to get a handle on your current financial condition. In order to develop appropriate strategies to meet your financial goals, you'll also need to refer to copies of all insurance policies, your most recent tax returns, summary descriptions of all your pension plans, and wills or trusts you've executed.

Processing and Analyzing Data
In this step of the planning process, you review the data you gathered in the last step in order to determine which of it is necessary to develop a plan to reach your financial goals. More importantly, you also identify missing information you may need in order to proceed with the planning process. Some professional planners combine this step and the previous step into a single function.

Developing a Financial Plan
This step of the process requires you to apply the financial planning principles you'll learn throughout this book to your financial data in order to identify strategies to meet your goals. In developing a plan, you make decisions about how the data you've gathered and how the principles you've learned can be applied to meet your financial goals.

Implementing the Plan
Once you've identified the appropriate strategies for meeting your financial goals, you need to take the necessary steps to turn the plan into reality. The devil is in the details in this part of the process, and it is often

where most plans unravel. Follow-through is essential to your success. If your plan calls for retitling an asset, executing a will, authorizing a mutual fund to directly debit $200 a month from your checking account, or purchasing disability insurance, and you fail to do so, you've wasted a lot of time.

Monitoring the Plan

Laws change, financial products and services evolve, and your personal finances are dynamic, so you need to monitor your plan in order to ensure that it's still on track for achieving your goals. On a more fundamental level, monitoring your plan also requires you to confirm that the goals you initially set remain valid.

As you read the information presented in this book, step back occasionally to get a view of the big picture. Remind yourself that financial planning is a *process,* and make sure you're approaching it that way.

Also remember that financial planning is a multidisciplinary process. Planning for any specific goal may involve any of the following:

- Risk planning and insurance
- Investment planning
- Tax planning
- Retirement planning
- Estate planning

You'll see as you work through this book how these disciplines are often interrelated in significant ways. One purpose of the financial planning process, and thus one function of the financial planner, is to coordinate these interrelationships to ensure that your financial planning is comprehensive and consistent. Financial planning is an integrated discipline, and the whole genuinely is greater than the sum of its parts.

OUR ISSUES

Finding Professional Help

This book is not intended to be a how-to guide for do-it-yourselfers. That is, it cannot and should not be a substitute for competent professional advice. True, when you finish reading this book, you should know much more about various financial planning issues than when you started. You probably will even know enough to make informed decisions regarding many specific matters. However, this knowledge does not make you a financial planner, any more than knowing how to change a tire makes you an auto mechanic. You are ill-served in trying to make major financial decisions without the input of a trained, experienced professional who is equipped to understand both the parts and the whole. This book should make you an educated consumer, not an ignorant practitioner.

These statements are true for anyone, regardless of sexual orientation, who is serious about financial planning. The challenge faced by lesbians and gay men who seek professional help arises in finding a planner who is competent and experienced, and is sensitive to and educated about our unique needs. Many of us assume this means finding assistance within the gay community, and while this often is a sound approach, it may not always be possible or desirable. If you do not live in an area that has a well-organized gay community, or if the special service you require is best performed by someone from outside our community, you need to draw on the most appropriate resource available. This means you have a little extra work to do.

You should be forthright in asking a potential planner what experience he has in serving the gay community. How well does she understand the unique issues we face? Does he have other gay clients who would be willing to serve as a reference? How capable is she in translating or protecting our issues in her dealings with other financial service providers (banks, brokerage houses, insurance companies, government agencies, attorneys, etc.) on your behalf? However awkward it may feel for you to ask these questions, you must remember that failure to ensure up-front that you have a forceful and enlightened advocate could compromise your financial planning results down the road.

RELATED TOPICS

Constructing a Balance Sheet and *Building a Budget* are two of the most important steps in the data gathering stage of the financial planning process, and these will now be covered (respectively).

CONSTRUCTING A BALANCE SHEET

THE STRAIGHT FACTS

Financial statements are important tools in the financial planning process. They enable you and the professionals advising you to understand your financial situation and to measure progress toward achieving your financial goals. The two principal financial statements used in the planning process are the balance sheet and the cash flow statement. We'll learn how to build and use a balance sheet in this section, and cover cash flow statements in the next section.

Constructing A Balance Sheet

The purpose of the *balance sheet* is to provide a uniform presentation of a person's (or, for that matter, a business's) assets, liabilities, and net worth. Your assets are everything you own, your liabilities are everything you owe to others, and your net worth is the difference between the two (i.e., assets – liabilities = net worth). To build an accurate balance sheet, you must be certain that you've captured all your assets and liabilities. The following lists should help you do just that. You may encounter some unfamiliar terms in the lists. Don't let them intimidate you, as they will be explained in due course. Note, too, that the list of assets is divided into three groups: (1) cash/cash equivalents, (2) invested assets, and (3) use assets. You'll see later in this section when we discuss the uses of your balance sheet how these groupings facilitate the financial planning process.

ASSETS
Cash/Cash Equivalents
- Cash in hand. Includes money in your wallet or your safe, in your nightstand, under your mattress, and so on.
- Checking accounts. Includes money in all checking accounts (bank, credit union, and brokerage house cash management accounts).
- Savings accounts. Includes savings accounts balances in your bank or credit union.
- Money market accounts. Includes money market accounts in all financial institutions—banks, credit unions, brokerage houses, mutual fund companies, and so on.
- Certificates of deposit (CDs). Includes the value of CDs you own, with accrued interest, but excludes both future interest and possible penalties for early withdrawal.
- Cash value of life insurance. This is not the amount of the policy death benefit, but rather the built-up cash value of permanent insurance you own.

Invested Assets

- U.S. government bonds. Includes U.S. savings bonds, Treasury bills, Treasury notes, and Treasury bonds, whether they are held by you directly or through a broker.

- Other government bonds. Includes bonds issued by state, local, or foreign governments, whether they are held by you directly or through a broker.

- Corporate bonds. Includes bonds issued by U.S. or foreign corporations, whether are held by you directly or through a broker.

- Corporate stocks. Includes stocks issued by U.S. or foreign corporations, regardless of whether or not they are traded on a public stock exchange and whether you hold the stock directly or through a broker. If you own a small business organized as a corporation, include the value of that stock here.

- Mutual funds. Includes the value of all mutual fund shares you own, regardless of whether you hold them directly or through a broker.

- Investment real estate. Includes residential or commercial real estate you own directly and undeveloped land you own. Do not include your residence or a vacation home. These are reported under Use Assets.

- Partnership interests. Includes the value of your partnership interests, such as real estate, oil and gas, and other limited partnerships. If you are the co-owner of a small business organized as a partnership, include the value of that interest here.

- Limited liability company interests. If you are the owner of a small business organized as a limited liability company (LLC), include the value of that interest here.

- Sole proprietorship interests. If you are the owner of a small business organized as a sole proprietorship, include the net worth of that sole proprietorship here. Technically, you should prepare separate balance sheets for your personal and business finances, but the approach suggested here will serve our purposes as long as you include only the net worth of the proprietorship (i.e., business assets – business liabilities).

- Individual Retirement Accounts (IRAs). Includes the current balances in all your individual retirement accounts. Exclude taxes that may be due if you were to withdraw funds prematurely from the account. Do not include the investments held in your IRA in any other group on your balance sheet.

- Vested portion of pension plan. Includes the current value of all pension benefits in which you are vested (e.g., nonforfeitable 401(k), 403(b), or 457 plan balances). Exclude taxes that may be due if you were to withdraw funds prematurely from the plan. Do not include the investments held in your pension plan in any other group on your balance sheet.

- Other investments. Includes the current value of aggressive investment such as options or futures, real estate investment trusts, and any other investments you own.

Use Assets

- Residence. Includes the current fair market value of your house, townhouse, or condo.

- Vacation home. Includes the current fair market value of a vacation home, condo, or cabin you own.

- Vehicles. Includes the current fair market value of all personal-use vehicles you own, including cars, pick-up trucks, vans, campers, mobile homes, motorcycles, and boats.

- Personal property. Includes the current value of all your personal property, including household furnishings, china, crystal, silverware, appliances, clothing, jewelry, furs, home entertainment equipment, and home office equipment.

- Artwork. List separately from other personal property the current value of artwork, rugs, antiques, or similar items you own if they are of significant value, quality, or rarity.

- Collectibles. List separately from other personal property the value of any coin, stamp, book, porcelain or other collections you own if they are of significant value, quality, or rarity.

LIABILITIES

- Credit card balances. Includes all outstanding balances from all types of credit and charge cards, whether issued by a bank or other financial institution, retail store, or oil company.

- Vehicle loans. Includes the current balance of loans secured by any car, boat, or other personal-use vehicle you own.

- Student loans. Includes the current balance of all student loans.
- Bank loans. Includes the current balance of other nonsecured loans made by a bank or other financial institution.
- Mortgages. Includes the current balance of all mortgage loans (first, second, third, or home equity loans) secured by real estate you own (residence, vacation home, or investment property).
- Other loans. Includes the current balance of debt you owe not covered by other categories listed above. Include loans from family or friends here.

After you've identified your assets and liabilities, you are ready to prepare your balance sheet. Let's take a look at how Joan Q. Public prepared her balance sheet. You can pattern your own after this sample.

JOAN Q. PUBLIC
Balance Sheet
As of December 31, 19XX

Assets		Liabilities and Net Worth	
Cash/cash equivalents		Liabilities	
Cash on hand	$ 500	Credit card balance	$ 3,500
Checking account	3,500	Bank loan balance	2,400
Credit union savings account	11,000	Student loan balance	12,600
Life insurance cash value	3,500	Vehicle loan balance	11,300
Total	$ 18,500	Mortgage balance	124,300
		Total	$ 154,100
Invested assets			
Stocks	$ 4,300		
Bonds	2,000		
Mutual funds	8,400		
Investment real estate	12,000		
IRAs	4,250		
Vested portion of pension plans	17,350		
Total	$ 48,300		
Use assets		Net worth	$ 164,400
Residence	$ 145,000		
Vacation home	49,000		
Vehicles	21,000		
Personal property	38,700		
Total	$ 253,700		
Total assets	$ 320,500	Total liabilities and net worth	$ 320,500

At first glance most balance sheets look the same, with assets in the left column and liabilities and net worth in the right column. Sometimes there can be variations in the presentation of the details for these items. For example, the subtotals for groups of assets (cash, invested assets, use assets) can be omitted. Sometimes no distinction is made between groups of assets, with individual entries flowing from the top of the column to the bottom without a break. The presentation of individual liabilities can be "tweaked" into groupings as well. These variations have significance for financial professionals, but for our purposes the approach we've outlined should meet our needs. An accountant or other financial professional preparing a balance sheet for you likely would use footnotes to clarify certain pieces of information. This is important to remember if you intend to share your balance sheet with anyone else, such as a loan officer.

Using Your Balance Sheet

Most people don't go through the trouble of preparing a balance sheet just because it's a great way to spend a Saturday night. (A few do, of course, but we call these people "accountants"!) The balance sheet is a tool to help you in your financial planning. As we work through the various financial planning topics in this book, we will from time to time refer to our balance sheet, giving you a sense of how important this tool is. Consider the following uses of the balance sheet:

1. Insurance planning tool. Your balance sheet can be an important source of information in risk management and insurance planning. Information about the value of your house can be a guide in letting you know whether your homeowner's insurance is adequate. Information about your personal property, artwork, and collectibles also can provide clues as to whether your coverage is adequate to protect against losses in these areas. Often the basic coverage provided by a homeowner's policy is not adequate to fully insure high-value contents such as antiques and collectibles. You may need to purchase an add-on "rider" to obtain adequate personal property protection. High totals for these items on the balance sheet indicate that you need to investigate this matter further.

Similarly, a high net worth might suggest that you may need liability insurance coverage to protect against the risk of loss resulting from litigation against you.

The balance sheet also can provide a few clues about your need for life insurance. If your balance sheet includes liabilities that would be a burden on a loved one in the event of your premature death, you'll want to be certain your life insurance coverage is sufficient to satisfy the liabilities.

2. Investment planning tool. A quick review of the relative values of your invested assets can give a rough idea of whether your portfolio is properly allocated among the various types of investments. For example, if your balance sheet indicates that you have $80,000 in cash equivalents and $5,000 in invested assets, there's a good chance your portfolio isn't properly allocated.

3. Retirement planning tool. An important part of the retirement planning process requires that you identify how much you should save to meet your retirement income needs. To do this, you need to understand first how much you currently have available to apply toward your goal. The balance sheet allows you to quickly identify this information.

4. Estate planning tool. The balance sheet is crucial to the estate planning process in a number of ways. First, in order to decide how you want your assets disposed of when you die, you need to identify what those assets are. Your balance sheet provides this information. Next, the net worth information from your balance sheet, when combined with the death benefit from any insurance policy you own covering your life, can provide a good clue as to whether or not you have any federal estate tax problems. If these two figures total over $600,000 (or come near that amount if you're young), you may need to do some estate tax planning.

5. Measuring progress toward goals. Many of your financial goals will not be accomplished immediately. Some of them, such as saving for retirement, will require long-term savings and investing strategies. Preparing annual balance sheets and comparing each year's figures with figures from the prior year can help you measure your progress toward your goals. If your total invested assets don't show a steady upward progression, you know something is wrong. You may have to dig further to identify the problem and get yourself back on track, but your balance sheet will provide you with the initial information to chart your results.

The Emergency Fund

One other important use of the balance sheet that deserves special consideration is for identifying an *emergency fund*. The purpose of the emergency fund is to provide a ready source of cash in the event of a financial emergency, thereby avoiding the need to liquidate assets, borrow at unreasonable interest rates, or endure other financial hardship. The loss of a job is the most obvious example of a financial emergency, but other emergencies can arise: the need to replace a major appliance (e.g., a furnace), a catastrophic medical emergency, an emergency involving a friend or relative, and so on.

Most financial planners recommend that an emergency fund contain sufficient resources to fund at least three months, and potentially up to six months, of your fixed and variable expenses. These expenses can be ascertained from your cash flow statement, discussed under "Building a Budget" in the next section of this chapter. If your income is largely dependent on wages and you work in a skilled occupation, most planners would encourage you to establish an emergency fund based on six months of your expenses.

For most people, cash and cash equivalents—checking, savings, and money markets accounts—are the primary source of their emergency fund. A quick look at the total cash/cash equivalents entry on your balance sheet can give you a good sense of whether you have an adequate emergency fund. If your emergency fund is insufficient to cover your living expenses for at least three months, and probably for six months, then saving an adequate emergency fund should be one of your top financial goals.

OUR ISSUES

The Emergency Fund

While the evidence is anecdotal, many financial planners who serve the lesbian and gay community report that, as a group, we're not very good about our emergency funds. Call it a "lifestyle thing" if you want, but it seems as though many of us don't have enough savings to fund our expenses for six weeks, let alone six months. This observation seems consistent with a few other generalizations we'll make about ourselves in the areas of saving and debt management discussed later in this chapter. If your fund is not adequate, you have some work to do.

Balance Sheets for Gay Couples

When financial planners prepare balance sheets for married couples, they generally present one combined document that reflects the assets of both spouses. Where appropriate, the planner makes notations indicating separately owned property. Whether or not this approach is appropriate for lesbian and gay couples is largely a matter of preference but is also influenced by the manner in which a couple manages its finances. Do you share everything? Do you jointly own property? Or are your checking and savings accounts separate? If the financial aspects of your relationship mirror the "Ozzie and Harriet" approach, then it probably makes good sense to prepare a combined balance sheet. But if you and your partner maintain separate finances, individual balance sheets may be more appropriate. The aspects of joint finances are outlined in the discussion of "Domestic Partnership Agreements" section later in this book. Review that discussion if you and your partner are having difficulty with this issue.

Financial planning goals are another critical consideration in deciding whether a couple should have one or two balance sheets. Are the goals joint or individual? If you are planning for individual goals, it may muddy the waters to include your partner's finances in the balance sheet.

If you and your partner prepare a joint balance sheet, be sure to include both your names on it and to identify separately owned assets, especially if you plan to show your balance sheet to a third party, such as a loan officer. If you and your partner prepare individual balance sheets, make sure you account for only your portion of joint assets (and joint liabilities) in preparing the document. Also note joint assets or joint liabilities if your balance sheet will be used by third parties.

RELATED TOPICS

Another financial document that provides an important tool in financial planning is the cash flow statement. Its structure and uses are discussed in the "Building a Budget" section on page 13.

The "Homeowner's Insurance" section on page 86 explains the various personal property coverages that may come into question when reviewing a balance sheet.

If your balance sheet suggests a high net worth, you need to learn about liability insurance, which is discussed in the "Umbrella Coverage" section on page 99.

Your balance sheet may suggest a need for life insurance. The forms and uses are discussed in the "Life Insurance" section on page 37.

If your balance sheet suggests your invested assets may not be properly diversified among the various investment classes, read the "Asset Allocation and Portfolio Structure" section on page 138 to understand the importance of properly diversifying your portfolio.

Your balance sheet is the key to identifying how much you're saving toward retirement. To understand how much you will need for retirement, read the "Computing Retirement Needs and Savings" section on page 231.

Estate planning requires you to determine the size of your gross estate. If the net worth on your balance sheet (plus the death benefit from any life insurance policies you own on your life) approaches or exceeds $600,000, you need to understand estate taxes. See the "Unified Estate and Gift Tax System" section on page 293.

Gay couples trying to decide how to organize and present their financial statements can find a helpful review of the various approaches in the "Domestic Partnership Agreements" section on page 361.

BUILDING A BUDGET

THE STRAIGHT FACTS

Another essential document used in the financial planning process is the cash flow statement, which summarizes where your money came from and where it went in a particular year. A cash flow statement operates much like a personal budget but with one critical distinction. A cash flow statement usually looks back over a one-year period, whereas a budget usually looks forward over a one-year period. This last sentence probably would make an accountant cringe, because there are important technical distinctions between the two documents, but for our purposes, the time period is the only difference that matters. Since most people use their prior year's experience as the basis for building their current year's budget, use whichever approach you prefer. In deciding whether to prepare a budget or a cash flow statement (or both), consider the following:

1. If your goal is to assess your current spending, a personal budget is more appropriate. You can adjust the numbers in a budget to meet your financial goals, but you can't change the numbers in a cash flow statement.

2. Since a cash flow statement captures your past spending habits, it may offer a better "reality check" regarding your spending patterns. If your goal is to improve your habits, you first need to honestly summarize what they've been. A cash flow statement does that.

3. A financial planning professional understands the technical differences between a budget and a cash flow statement and usually is trained to look at the cash flow statement first.

4. If you plan to show your document to a third party, be sure it's an accurate cash flow statement and not a budget. People such as loan officers find what actually happened with your money last year (as represented in your cash flow statement) more informative for their purposes than what you hope will happen with your money this year (as represented in your budget).

In order to try to keep things simple, in this section we discuss how to construct a personal budget. A budget is more flexible than a cash flow statement and allows you to be proactive in managing your money. You use essentially the same process in building a budget as you do in creating a cash flow statement.

Building a Budget

We'll follow an approach for building a personal budget similar to the one we used in learning how to construct a balance sheet: first we'll define all the elements that go into the document, and then we'll look at a sample format in order to see what our own personal budgets should look like.

The personal budget is divided into two main categories: inflows and outflows. Outflows is divided into three subcategories: (1) savings and investments; (2) fixed outflows; and (3) variable outflows. As with the subdivisions among assets on the balance sheet, there is no universal agreement on the subcategories among financial professionals, but they serve several purposes that will be helpful to you. First, stating savings and investments separately emphasizes the critical importance of "paying savings first," which we'll discuss later in this section. Next, dividing expenses between fixed and variable can be helpful if you need to modify your budget either to increase savings or to reduce spending to meet your financial goals. Since you can't really do much in the short term to adjust your fixed outflows, you can hone in first on your variable outflows to find places to trim. We'll talk more about balancing your budget after we build it. Right now, let's define the components of a personal budget.

INFLOWS

- Wages and salaries. Includes all income from all employment sources. If you are a sole proprietor or a partner in a business, include the net earnings from your proprietorship or partnership.
- Interest. Includes interest income from all sources, including government bonds, but excluding interest earned by a tax-deferred retirement account such as a 401(k) or IRA.
- Dividends. Includes dividends paid from all sources, excluding dividends earned by a tax-deferred retirement account such as a 401(k) or IRA.

- Other income. Includes income from all other sources: gifts or inheritances actually received; sales of assets (unless the proceeds from the sale come from and remain in a tax-deferred retirement account such as a 401(k) or IRA); prizes; scholarships; awards; pensions; Social Security; other government benefits, and so on. If any of these items is substantial, you may want to create a separate category of inflow to account for them.

OUTFLOWS

- Savings and investments. Includes all money set aside for savings and investing, regardless of whether the money is saved pretax or posttax.

Fixed Outflows

- Housing expense. Includes the amount of principal and interest payments on all mortgages, rent, mandatory assessments from your mortgage company (e.g., private mortgage insurance), property taxes, and the cost of condominium fees or mandatory homeowners association dues. Do not include any other expenses related to your home here. They are variable outflows and will be included in that category.
- Vehicle expense. Includes the amount of your car loan or lease payment. Do not include any other expenses related to the ownership or operation of your car here, as they are variable outflows.
- Other debts. Includes payments on outstanding credit card balances, student loans, bank loans, or any other debts you owe.
- Insurance premiums. Includes payments on life, health, disability, homeowners, automobile, umbrella, and other insurance policies you own.

Variable Outflows

- Taxes. Includes federal, state, and local income taxes as well as Social Security and Medicare taxes.
- Food. Includes grocery and restaurant expenditures.
- Transportation. Includes gasoline, oil, parking, tolls, repairs, and public transportation expenses. Do not include any of the fixed outflows listed under vehicle expense above.
- Clothing. Includes clothing purchases, dry cleaning, repairs, and alterations.
- Entertainment/vacations. Includes travel, movies, plays, books, recordings and similar expenditures.

- Health care. Includes deductibles on employer-provided health insurance, out-of-pocket expenses for services not covered by health insurance, and similar expenditures. Do not include health insurance premiums; they are fixed outflows.

- Utilities/household expenses. Includes water, gas, electricity, telephone, cable television, household repairs, cleaning services and supplies, and similar expenditures. Do not include housing expenses listed under fixed outflows.

- Contributions. Includes donations made to charitable and tax-exempt organizations, excluding contributions that do not come from current income.

- Other expenses. Includes education, child care, pet care, or any other expense not covered by the fixed and variable outflow definitions above. If any of these items is a substantial amount of money, you may create a separate category of fixed or variable outflow to account for them. The other expense category should be a nominal amount, as it may mask excessive expenditures.

Now let's see how the items of a personal budget fit together. Look at Joan Q. Public's personal budget on the next page to get an idea of how you should construct your budget.

Balancing Your Budget

Our exercise assumes that your inflows will equal your outflows; that is, that your budget will balance. If your budget doesn't balance, you've identified another critical financial goal for yourself! If your outflows exceed your inflows, you must find immediate ways to decrease your outflows, increase your inflows, or both. Anyone serious enough about financial planning to spring for this book cannot possibly be blind to the imminent disaster in continuing to spend in excess of your income (unless, of course, you're a Member of Congress). If your budget doesn't balance, review your variable outflows and make the necessary cuts before you turn another page. If you've made every possible cut in variable outflows and your budget still is out of whack, you'll need to consider ways to reduce your fixed outflows. The first place to look may be your credit card debt. For ideas on how to reduce this debt, read "Managing Consumer Debt" in the next section.

JOAN Q. PUBLIC
Personal Budget
For the Year Ending December 31, 19XX

	Annually	Monthly
Inflows		
Wages and salaries	$ 52,200	$ 4,350
Interest	1,440	120
Dividends	1,200	100
Other	0	0
Total inflows	$ 54,840	$ 4,570
Outflows		
Savings and investments	$ 4,800	$ 400
Fixed outflows		
Housing expense	$ 14,700	$ 1,225
Vehicle expense	3,900	325
Other debts	2,940	245
Insurance premiums	1,500	125
Total	$ 23,040	$ 1,920
Variable outflows		
Taxes	$ 13,200	$ 1,100
Food	3,000	250
Transportation	1,200	100
Clothing	1,500	125
Entertainment/vacations	2,400	200
Health care	1,200	100
Utilities/household expense	2,400	200
Contributions	1,200	100
Other expenses	900	75
Total	$ 27,000	$ 2,250
Total outflows	$ 54,840	$ 4,570

If the above steps aren't enough to bring you back into balance, drastic action is going to be required. (You may want to review again your variable outflows to be certain you've made all possible cuts. For example, is entertainment and vacation at $0? How draconian have you been with clothing? What's really buried underneath the "Other expenses" entry?)

First, consider ways to supplement your inflows, such as part-time work or freelancing. Next, if you rent, investigate the feasibility of moving to smaller, more affordable digs and/or finding a roommate. But keep in mind the costs associated with moving, such as fees to break your old lease, security deposits and prepayment of rent on your new residence, moving expenses, and so on. Third, consider selling your car and buying a less expensive one or, better yet, taking public transportation if it's practical. If after all these steps you're still not back in the black, it's time to call in the pros; contact a financial planner or a state or local credit counseling agency for more specific help.

Pay Savings First

It's no accident that savings and investments is the first outflow financial planners list in preparing budgets or cash flow statements for their clients. It helps emphasize how critically important savings and investing are to achieving your financial goals. The most fundamental rule in financial planning—the Golden Rule, if you will—is "pay savings first." Even if you save only $5 a week, you must get into the habit of paying savings first. That way, when you can afford $50—or $500—a week, it will seem natural to do so.

Throughout this book you'll see specific applications of this Golden Rule: In the chapter on Tax Planning, for example, we'll discuss how essential it is to participate in your employer's 401(k) or similar plan. This is one easy way to pay savings first, but there are others. If your employer offers you the option of direct deposit of your salary, you usually can arrange to have a portion of your pay deposited in one account, such as a savings account, with the balance going to your checking account. Another way to pay savings first is to authorize your bank or brokerage house to electronically debit a fixed amount from your checking account each month for savings or investment purposes.

The advantage of these techniques is that you never actually see the money, so it's less likely you'll get a chance to spend it. If none of these options works for you, you must discipline yourself to write a check each month for saving or investing. In the Investment Planning chapter we discuss where you might put the money you're setting aside, but it's essential that you start doing this now.

OUR ISSUES

Pay Savings First

Financial planners who work with the lesbian and gay community report that too often we're not very good about paying savings first. If you see yourself in these words, you know what the straight facts are, and you know what you have to do about them. Enough said?

Budgeting for Couples

As with the balance sheet, lesbian and gay couples sometimes face the difficult decision of preparing individual or joint personal budgets (or cash flow statements). As with the balance sheet, the decision depends largely on the nature of the relationship. Are your finances combined? Do you own property jointly? Again, reviewing the discussion of joint finances in the "Domestic Partnership Agreements" section may be helpful. Also remember that if you prepare separate budgets, each partner should account for only his or her share of joint inflows and outflows.

RELATED TOPICS

The companion document to the budget (or the cash flow statement) for financial planning purposes is the balance sheet. How to build and use this essential tool is explained in the "Constructing a Balance Sheet" section on page 4.

If your personal budget appears to be out of control, excess consumer debt is often the culprit. Strategies for dealing with this problem are outlined in the "Managing Consumer Debt" section on page 27.

After making the commitment to pay savings first, you face the critical and challenging task of determining where to put the money you're setting aside. The process of constructing a portfolio is outlined in "Understanding the Investment Process" on page 101.

The "Domestic Partnership Agreements" section on page 361 explains the many issues surrounding the joint finances of gay couples.

MANAGING DEBT

THE STRAIGHT FACTS

Buying a House

Home ownership has long been the cornerstone of The American Dream. However, few people start out with the dream fully funded. Most rely on a mortgage loan to help them realize their dream. Let's begin by focusing on what you need to know to make sure that when you decide to buy, your mortgage obligations do not conflict with your overall financial goals.

One quick disclaimer before we dive in: The discussion that follows is not a comprehensive treatment of the home-buying process; such a topic could easily fill its own book. Purchasing a residence is a complicated and daunting task riddled with details and paperwork. Our purpose here is to look at buying a home from a financial planning perspective; that is, to make sure that your purchase is consistent with your financial goals and appropriate for your financial circumstances.

The Mortgage Process

In order to understand how to make smart decisions about mortgage debt, we first need to review briefly the mortgage process. Before you look at a house, you and your real estate agent must determine whether you're qualified to buy and what you can afford (more on this below). Then the house-hunting process begins. Once you identify a house, you submit an offer to the seller through your agent. You and the seller negotiate (through your agents). If all goes well, you reach an agreement and sign a contract. Usually after the contract is signed, you apply for a mortgage. You fill out a standard loan application form, providing the lender with complete information about your finances—employment, assets, liabilities, and so on. The lender also obtains a copy of your credit report and an appraisal on the house you're buying. The lender evaluates all of this information, and, assuming it all meets the lender's standards, your loan is approved. Sometimes you apply for a mortgage before you even find a house. Getting their clients preapproved or prequalified for mortgages is one way real estate professionals streamline the process.

After the paperwork is completed and the loan is approved, you go to settlement on the house. Settlement consists of

- Acquiring title to the house from the seller.
- Paying the seller the purchase price using your down payment and funds advanced on your behalf by the lender.
- Giving a security interest in the house to the lender in exchange for the mortgage amount.
- Purchasing insurance to make sure the title you've acquired from the seller is valid.
- Agreeing to purchase private mortgage insurance designed to make the lender whole in the event you default on your obligation if your lender requires it.
- Paying all the taxes, charges, and professional fees assessed on the transaction.

How Much House Can You Afford?

Your budget can serve as the starting point for determining how much house you can afford. Your current fixed housing expense (e.g., your rent) provides a (very) rough basis for figuring out how much you can afford to pay toward a mortgage each month. Your real estate agent can help you translate the monthly rent payment into a total loan amount. Adding the total loan amount to what you've saved for a down payment indicates what you can afford. There are, however, a few important points to keep in mind that complicate the translation of a monthly payment into a total loan amount.

Mortgages come with a wide variety of repayment terms. You can pay your mortgage off over just about any time frame, but 30 years or 15 years are the most common. You can lock in a fixed interest rate for the term of the loan, or you can allow the interest rate to adjust periodically (e.g., each year) based on market conditions. You can blend both approaches, so that the rate is fixed for a set number of years and then adjusts each year thereafter. When you apply for your mortgage, each option will have a different interest rate. Therefore, you'll need to decide which one makes the most sense for you.

Fixed rate loans tend to come with higher initial rates than do adjustable rate loans, which may at first make adjustable rate loans seem more attractive. However, there is something to be said for the security and predictability that comes with a fixed rate loan. If the difference between fixed and adjustable rates is less than 2 percent, or if overall interest rates are low, it usually makes more sense to lock in the fixed rate. If you can afford the higher monthly payment, a 15-year loan often is preferable to a 30-year loan. Beyond owning your house in half the time, a 15-year loan can save you up to one-third of the total interest you'd pay on a 30-year loan. Remember that the same monthly payment will "purchase" different loan amounts depending on the type of loan you choose. This has a direct bearing on how much house you calculate you can afford. Ask your real estate agent to run the numbers several different ways, so you can understand all your options.

Also keep in mind that if you're currently renting, you probably can afford a monthly mortgage payment higher than your current rent payment. The mortgage interest and property taxes you are allowed to deduct for income tax purposes lower your after-tax cost. This means you can afford to pay more each month. The tax advantages of home ownership are explained in the Tax Planning chapter of this book.

Your mortgage lender also has some ideas about how much house you can afford. The rules your lender uses should give you a good sense of what you can and cannot do in financing a home. First, the lender usually will only lend you an amount equal to either 2.5 or 3 times your annual income.

EXAMPLE

Barbara's income is $50,000. She probably won't qualify for a mortgage in excess of $150,000 ($50,000 × 3). If Barbara has her heart set on a $250,000 dream house, she'd better be able to put down at least $100,000 ($250,000 – $150,000) toward her goal.

Next, the lender will only allow your monthly mortgage payment to equal a certain percentage of your total monthly income. Usually your monthly payment can't be more than 28 percent of your income. Your mortgage plus all your other debts usually can't exceed 36 percent to 38 percent of your income. If your monthly payments exceed these percentage amounts, you probably won't qualify for a loan.

EXAMPLE 1

Tony's monthly income is $5,000. He will not qualify for a mortgage that requires a monthly payment in excess of $1,400 ($5,000 × 28% = $1,400).

EXAMPLE 2

The same facts as above apply, but the monthly payments on Tony's other debts (student loans, credit card payments, and a car loan) total $600. Now he will not qualify for a mortgage payment in excess of $1,300 ($5,000 × 38% = $1,900; $1,900 – $600 = $1,300).

Occasionally, lenders will let these ratios slide by a percent or so (especially if your income or down payment is high and your credit record is clean), but usually not by much more.

A final thought on what you can and cannot afford: Most likely you will be working closely with a real estate agent throughout the house-buying process. Early in the process, the agent will help you calculate what you can afford. Quite likely the agent will focus on the maximum amount you can afford to pay for a house. That's alright, it's his or her job to do that. Keep in mind, however, that you don't have to buy as much house as you can afford. It's okay to buy less, and maybe it's even smart to do so.

Refinancing

Sometimes financial circumstances change during the time you own a house, and it may make sense to refinance an existing mortgage. For example, there can be a significant difference between the interest rate on your loan and current interest rates. Advisors suggest that the difference between your rate and the current market rate needs to be 2 percent for the expenses associated with the process to justify refinancing. But it may not make sense to refinance the mortgage on a house you don't expect to own much longer. Because of the costs associated with refinancing, most experts suggest that you need to stay in your house for at least three and perhaps as many as seven years to realize the full benefits of refinancing.

Sometimes a dip in interest rates causes people to consider swapping their 30-year loans for 15-year loans. This makes sense if the rate approaches the 2 percent rule mentioned above. Another way to achieve the same goal is to calculate the difference in monthly payments between your 30-year loan and the same loan amortized over 15 years and send your current lender the additional amount each month. In fact, you can trim seven to eight years off a 30-year mortgage just by making one additional payment at the beginning of each year. Make certain your mortgage payment coupon allows you to reflect "extra payments" you make, so they are credited to your outstanding balance and not to next month's interest payment. Your lender can answer questions about extra payments.

Buying a Car

In this section, we're going to make two unpopular but completely accurate statements about contemporary American consumer behavior. The first is, with the exception of antiques and collectors items, cars are lousy investments. (If you're wondering whether your car is a collectible, it probably isn't. Collectors know these things about their cars without having to wonder.) Other than our culture's inexplicable love affair with the automobile, there's no reason why the average American would tolerate a so-called investment that depreciates anywhere from 10 percent to 20 percent the instant it is made. Any financial planner worth her salt will tell you that, with a return on investment like this, you should look at your car as a form of transportation—and nothing else! Having said this, however, it's clear this book cannot stop the (financial) insanity, so we'll have to settle for discussing the steps you can take to minimize it.

The Car-Buying Process

The car-buying process is one of the most excruciating and predatory rituals in all of capitalism. The dealer has the deck so stacked against most of us that we can't even recognize the hosing we're getting. The process can be so draining and high-pressure that many of us are worn down well before the deal is closed. Take heart, however—there are steps you can take to fight back!

1. Do your homework. Shopping for a car and buying a car should be two separate tasks. When you shop, compare cars, gather data, and take test drives. In addition to the dealer information about safety features, handling and performance, fuel economy, and so on, you should find out from third parties what the car you want to buy cost the dealer. You can obtain this information from your credit union, or you can buy it for a nominal fee from a consumer's organization such as Consumer's Union, the publisher of *Consumer Reports*. This is the best way to find out how much you should pay and how much you can afford. Car salespeople are trained to get you to sign a sales contract the same day you visit the showroom, so be sure to avoid making a hasty decision while you're still shopping around.

2. Determine a purchase price—and stick to it! After you've finished shopping for a car, your next task is to buy one. Decide for yourself what price you're willing to pay, based on the information you've obtained about the car's cost and what you can afford, and don't exceed it. Car buying requires negotiation, so your initial offer needs to be lower than your final price. If the dealer can't meet your price, go talk to another.

3. Secure financing in advance. If possible, ask your bank or credit union for a preapproved car loan before negotiating a purchase price with the dealer. From shopping, you should know the amount you want to spend, and you can get a loan commitment for that amount that's good for 30 days. When you go to the dealer, tell the salesperson you've already arranged financing through your bank or credit union. Don't give the dealer a chance to muddy the waters—keep the financing discussion out of the purchase price negotiations. If the salesperson thinks you'll be financing your purchase through the dealer, it will affect the negotiation, but not to your benefit. Your goal must be to get the lowest possible price for the car—and nothing else. After the deal is closed, you always can give the dealer a chance to beat your bank's financing. Make sure that the loan terms offered are identical, if not better.

4. Never talk trade-in. Never give a salesperson the opportunity to cloud price negotiations with talk of trading in your old car. Make it clear up-front that you intend to keep your old car or sell it yourself, and keep it off the table while you're talking price. It's easy for a dealership to let you save a few bucks on the new car you're buying from it, only to make it up in spades on the used car it's buying from you. After the deal is complete, you can always inquire how much the dealer is willing to pay you for your car. Make sure you know what your old car is worth. Read the classified ads in your local paper or ask your credit union about its "blue book" value. If the dealer offers a reasonable price, take it. Otherwise, you're probably better off selling your old car elsewhere. Even if your old car is an absolute clunker and you know you're going to take whatever the dealer will give you, do not negotiate this until after the price on the new car is firmly settled.

5. Never talk lease if you intend to buy. Later we'll discuss the pros and cons of leasing versus buying. Keep in mind, however, that salespeople more and more are being trained to persuade customers to lease cars. This is because dealers can either confuse you out of more money with lease agreements or they can talk you into more expensive cars through comparatively lower lease payments. Neither reason benefits you. If you want to buy, avoid lease discussions.

6. Watch out for the last minute add-ons. The car-buying process no longer ends after you have agreed on a price. You have to talk to other people about purchasing add-ons such as an extended service warranty, a car alarm, or rustproofing. Be careful! Most of these add-ons are rip-offs. Your goal should be to blow through this recently added last step as quickly as possible. You can buy a car alarm for much less elsewhere. Few new cars need dealer rustproofing; often this is done at the factory. Reasonable people differ on the value of an extended service warranty, but you usually have up to a year to purchase this protection if you want it. Remember, since you've been negotiating for hours, you are worn down. Go home!

7. Leave. Anytime you think you've lost control of the process, terminate it. Stand up and leave. It's amazing how often people forget they can do this. The salesperson likely will try to intimidate you into staying, but no one can force you to remain someplace against your will.

Financing a Car

The most important aspect of financing a new car is understanding how much you can afford. Unfortunately, too many car buyers find themselves backing into this figure. They know what they can afford to spend each month and then let the dealer arrange the financing to accommodate the payment. These people sometimes never know what they've actually paid for the car. They've negotiated a monthly payment, not a purchase price. You can bet they've probably paid too much for the car. Never, under any circumstances, allow yourself to be in a situation where you are negotiating a monthly payment with a salesperson. Remember that you're buying a car, not a car payment.

There is a way to figure out how much car you can afford without throwing yourself on the (non-existent) mercy of a car dealer to back into it for you. After you determine the amount of the monthly car payment you can afford from your budget, ask your bank, credit union, or financial planning professional to help you figure out the loan amount that corresponds to this payment. This will depend on prevailing interest rates at the time you want to buy. Adding this amount to the down payment you've saved and a reasonable estimate of the value of any old car you're selling should indicate how much car you can afford. Don't let yourself be talked into more than that amount.

You should also know that monthly payments get smaller as the length of a loan gets longer. This explains the increasing popularity of five-year car loans. They enable people to buy more expensive cars for the same monthly payment amount than they could get with a four-year loan. However, five-year loans are a bad idea because you pay too much interest over the life of the loan and don't have enough time to save before the madness has to start again. Never finance a car for more than four years. If you can't pay off a loan in that amount of time, you're probably trying to buy more than you can afford.

Don't become discouraged if you can't afford the car you want or if you don't like any of the cars you can afford. Rather, be creative! First consider a good used car. Some cars hold their value well over time and prove reliable for many years. A solid used car may make more sense than a shoddy new one. The buying process for a used car is much the same as the process for new cars, especially if you buy through a used car dealer. Follow the steps described in the car-buying process.

Another strategy that can work well for flexible car buyers with limited budgets is to scour the newspapers for a used current-year model. Your lender and insurance company will consider the car new, but someone else has taken the hit for the loss in value that occurs whenever a car rolls off a dealer's lot. You may not be able to find the color you want, but the strategy is great for people who want to drive both a new car and a good bargain.

Buying versus Leasing

The popularity of leasing automobiles rather than buying them has grown substantially in recent years. There's a good reason for this. Since you're not actually buying the car, monthly lease payments always are lower than loan repayments. The downside of leasing is that when you get to the end of a lease term, you have to either plunk down a huge chunk of cash to buy the car you've been driving or turn in the keys and start the process all over again. In contrast, at the end of a loan term you own the car.

Leasing allows people to drive more expensive vehicles than they normally could afford. This arrangement is good for the automobile industry and our collective vanity. Car ads are just as likely to quote monthly lease payments as purchase prices. Remember, however, that the rule regarding buying cars also applies to leasing them: Never buy (or lease) a monthly car payment—buy (or lease) a car.

How do you know whether leasing or buying makes better sense for you? It's difficult to make appropriate comparisons in trying to answer this question. There is no uniform format for lease agreements, and only a few states have any sort of disclosure requirements. It's very easy for a dealer to bury important details in fine print, and many do. As a result, comparisons between the cost of leasing and the cost of buying frequently are misleading. As a general rule of thumb, buying is more economical than leasing over the long term. There are two possible exceptions. First, if the car you are buying is intended for bona fide use in your business, the complicated tax rules applicable to business automobiles often are more beneficial for leased cars than for purchased cars. Second, if you're the kind of person who is comfortable with always having a monthly car payment, who always wants to drive a new car, or who never needs to cycle into your annual budgets some "down" time to save up for the next car, leasing allows you to get "more" car for your monthly payment dollar. Of course, you're violating the fundamental assumption underlying this entire discussion: cars are lousy investments. But, if you're going knowingly down that road, you might as well go with style!

Managing Consumer Debt

For most people consumer debt means credit card debt, although the terms are not synonymous. We'll go with this assumption, however, because the rules and strategies discussed in this section apply equally in both cases.

The second unpopular statement about contemporary American consumer behavior is that credit cards are *evil* and you should never carry a balance on them. There are several important reasons why this is true. Credit cards are designed to keep you in debt forever. If you made only the minimum payment required by most credit card companies, it would take you 20 years to pay off your total balance! In the process, the credit card company makes thousands of dollars from the exorbitant interest rates it charges you. Living within the budget you establish will make you—not the credit card companies—rich.

If you already have a balance on your credit cards, you need to eliminate it immediately. Stop using any cards on which you're carrying a balance, and scrub the variable outflows in your budget to see how much cash you can free up to quickly pay off your balance. If you can't pay off your balance quickly, and budget-tweaking can't get you out from under in a reasonable time, you need to take steps to avoid disaster. But before you take any of these steps, you must make a few other, more fundamental changes. Don't just put away your credit cards. Cut them up and throw them away. You've proven you cannot handle them, so you should not keep them. Pay by cash or check only. If an expense is not in your budget, you can't have it. If you can't make these changes, the following strategies will not help you one whit. Within two years, you'll charge your way right back to carrying a balance you can't pay. After you've banished Satan from your wallet, consider the following ways to handle a consumer debt crisis. They are listed in ascending order of severity.

1. Switch your balances to a credit card with a lower interest rate, if possible.

2. Consider refinancing your mortgage, but only if it will lower your monthly payment sufficiently to make doing so worthwhile.

3. Consider consolidating your debt with a home equity loan. If a home equity loan is not an option, ask your bank or credit union about a debt consolidation loan.

4. Add a second job.

5. Contact the credit card companies to see if it is possible to work out an extended repayment schedule.

6. Consider borrowing against other assets (retirement plans, life insurance, brokerage accounts, certificates of deposit) to pay off your credit cards.

7. Contact your mortgage lender to see if your loan can be rescheduled to reduce the payments.

8. Sell assets.

9. Consult an attorney to consider filing for bankruptcy.

This list presents a cursory review of a very serious issue. Keep in mind that there are downsides to each of these options, and, as you work your way down the list, those downsides grow dramatically. If your situation is serious, you should contact a state or local credit counseling agency or a financial planning professional for more specific help.

Home Equity Loans

Tapping into your home's equity can be a great way to borrow money on a tax-advantaged basis. That's because under many circumstances, you can deduct the interest you pay on a home equity loan. With other consumer debt, the interest is not tax-deductible. The rules for tax-deductible interest are explained in the Tax Planning chapter. The deductibility of interest payments, combined with the lower interest that is usually available for a loan secured by your house, can significantly reduce your cost of borrowing. If you have sufficient equity in your house, it often makes good sense to use a home equity loan to finance the purchase of a car, for example.

The process for obtaining a home equity loan is similar to the process described earlier for obtaining a first mortgage. After you've contacted local banks or other lenders and shopped for the best available rate, you submit the same type of loan application used for the initial mortgage. The lender checks your credit, verifies your employment, confirms the other information you provided on the application, and usually orders an appraisal on your property. If all the information checks out, the lender approves the loan. Home equity loans have become a very competitive business in most areas, and lenders are constantly finding ways to streamline the process. It's not uncommon to get a preliminary approval from the bank within two or three business days. After the paperwork is complete, you go to the bank's offices for a streamlined settlement. You give the bank a lien against your house, and they give you a credit line you can tap into on an as-needed basis.

However, using your home's equity as a source of ready cash can be fraught with difficulties. Remember, a home equity loan is in essence another mortgage on your house. For average Americans, the family home is the largest investment they'll ever make. Also, the inflation-fueled build-up in a home's equity over the course of a working life plays a significant role in determining the size of retirement nest eggs. The nest egg dwindles when equity is tapped out by home equity loans. To be certain that you make smart use of your home's equity, consider the following four safeguards.

First, don't get in over your head. Home equity loans frequently can be good ways of consolidating debts (especially high-rate credit card debts) or financing cars, but they should not be viewed as another source of easy credit. If you're inclined to run up large balances on your credit cards, you should think long and hard about a home equity loan. Running up a large balance against your home's equity could be a recipe for disaster. Defaulting on a home equity loan is not like defaulting on a credit card. Because the loan is secured by your house, the lender can take action against it, possibly including foreclosure, if you default. Before you tap into your home's equity, make sure there's a good purpose, a clear and short fixed repayment schedule, and adequate cash flow to make the monthly payments. Smart use of an equity loan should not be confused with a shopping spree you really can't afford!

Second, don't get in over your house's head. Lenders generally will allow you to borrow only a certain percentage of your house's value. Traditionally, the limit has been 80 percent. Recently the limit has been extended to as high as 90 percent or even 100 percent. Remember, this percentage, often referred to in lending shorthand as the *loan-to-value ratio* or *L-T-V ratio,* includes all debts secured by your residence.

EXAMPLE

Your home is worth $100,000, and the balance of your mortgage is $50,000. If your lender has an 80 percent L-T-V limit, you can borrow up to $30,000 through a home equity loan ($100,000 × 80% = $80,000; $80,000 − $50,000 = $30,000).

The idea behind the L-T-V limits is to make sure that the total amount of debt secured by your house doesn't exceed its value. Then, if you default, the equity cushion between the amount your house is worth and the amount of debt outstanding against it assures your lenders of getting all their money back.

In today's climate of fluctuating real estate values, it's a good idea for you to monitor whether your L-T-V limit is consistent with changing market realities. You need to protect your equity cushion at least as much as the bank does. If you had to move, for example, you'd need that equity for a down payment on a new house. If you're approaching retirement, you need equity as part of your nest egg. If you've maxxed out on home equity borrowing and market values in your area drop just a little bit, you may not have enough equity to meet your other needs.

Third, don't get in too long. If you anticipate selling your house and moving in the not-too-distant future, be very careful about using your home's equity. You're going to need that money to buy a new house, but it may not be available if there's still a balance on your home equity loan when it's time to sell. Lenders have rules about repayment schedules, and these rules are usually tied to the size of your loan. Make sure that your repayment schedule fits in with your plans and not just the bank's. Remember, the longer you take to pay back your home equity loan, the more interest the bank earns from you.

Fourth, keep track of the paperwork. A home equity loan is a secured line of credit. This means that the bank files a lien against your house when you take out the loan. Once the loan is paid off, be certain the lender has completed the paperwork to get the lien released. This can save you time and hassles when you sell your house later. Because home equity loans are usually revolving lines of credit (i.e., you can tap into them as needed), be confident that you will have no future need to borrow against your equity before you ask the lender to close out your account. But, remember, just because you pay your loan down to zero does not mean the lender will automatically release its lien against your house. A zero balance is not the same as a closed account.

OUR ISSUES

If the anecdotal evidence offered by financial planning professionals who know and love us is to be believed, as a group, lesbians and gay men are below average when it comes to managing their consumer debt. (Well, we can't be fabulous about everything, can we?) Credit card balances went out of style years ago, darlings; if you're still carrying one, it simply must go.

RELATED TOPICS

Tax deductions associated with mortgages and home equity lines are explained in the "Tax Deductions from Your Home" section on page 180.

After you buy a house, you need to protect it from the risk of loss, which is discussed in the "Homeowner's Insurance" section on page 86.

The "Automobile Insurance" section on page 92 explains various issues for car buyers.

The "Building a Budget" section on page 13 is essential to several aspects of the debt management process, such as figuring out how much you can afford to spend on a mortgage, how much you can afford to spend on a car loan, and how to rein in excessive consumer debt.

If you're considering purchasing a house jointly with another person, read "Joint Ownership of Property" on page 309 and "Domestic Partnership Agreements" on page 361.

2

Risk Management and Insurance

UNDERSTANDING RISK MANAGEMENT

THE STRAIGHT FACTS

Risk management is one of the fundamental goals of the financial planning process. If you don't adequately anticipate and plan to avoid (or at least minimize) the financial losses associated with the various types of risk in life, all of your other financial planning efforts could be for naught. One catastrophic loss could wipe out your life's savings.

This chapter identifies the various sources of risk exposure and discusses the possible techniques for managing those risks. Insurance figures prominently in these discussions because it is such an essential—and potentially expensive—technique for managing risk. Before we dig into the various aspects of risk management and insurance, however, it probably would be helpful to get some "big picture" background. We'll begin with the basic principles of risk management and insurance and also touch briefly upon what to look for in a good insurance company.

Risk Management Theory

An entire discipline is devoted to risk management, and large companies employ people specifically to manage risk. Like any discipline, risk management has principles and rules its practitioners must follow in order to do their jobs effectively. Insurance is the most widely known technique for dealing with certain risks. But it's not the only strategy available. In fact, in some cases it doesn't even make sense to use insurance to manage risk.

Experts talk about risk in terms of its severity (how catastrophic the potential losses are) and its frequency (how likely or how often the risk may become a reality). Different risk management methods are used depending on the severity and the frequency of the risk. Experts usually identify four methods for handling risk.

1. **Risk avoidance.** In this method, an individual does not engage in the activity producing the risk. For example, if the risk is identified as dying in a plane crash, the risk avoidance technique would be not to fly. Avoidance is an appropriate strategy for risks where both the potential severity and the potential frequency are high. This actually would make "not flying" a poor risk management technique because the frequency of plane crashes is very low.

2. **Risk retention.** In this method, the individual exposed to the risk assumes personal financial responsibility for its consequences. The deductible imposed by a health insurance policy is a good example of a risk retention strategy. Risk retention is appropriate where the potential severity of a risk is low, and the individual retaining the risk can easily absorb the loss.

3. **Risk transfer.** In risk transfer, the risk of loss is assumed by another entity. Insurance is the classic example of risk transfer. Risk transfer is most appropriate for risks with the potential for high severity but low frequency. Buying insurance to protect against the risk that your house may burn down is a good example of risk transfer.

4. **Risk reduction.** In risk reduction, affirmative steps are taken to minimize either the severity or the frequency of a potential loss. The installation of sprinklers or smoke detectors to reduce the risk of damage from a fire is a good example of risk reduction.

An important rule for managing risk through the use of insurance is known as the *large loss principle.* This principle holds that you should purchase essential insurance coverages first. It defines *essential* as coverages with potentially catastrophic financial results. For example, under the large loss principle it would be more important for a single person with no dependents to protect his income stream while he's still alive than to insure the continuation of that stream in the event of his premature death. In applying the large loss principle to this person's circumstances, disability insurance becomes a more essential coverage than life insurance.

Choosing an Insurer

Purchasing insurance coverage is the most significant and well-known risk management technique. Regardless of the type of insurance you're going to buy, it's important that you purchase your coverage from a solid insurer. If the company isn't reputable, or if its finances are shaky, you run the risk of significant potential losses—loss of coverage, nonpayment of claims, and perhaps even the inability to find replacement coverage if your circumstances have changed since you first became insured.

Although there are no guarantees in these situations, there are steps you can take to make sure that the company you're dealing with is reputable and financially sound. First, several private companies rate the financial health of insurance companies. Moody's, A. M. Best, and Standard & Poor's are widely known names in the insurance ratings business. Ideally, you should only buy a policy from insurance companies that have received the highest possible rating from all three of these companies. If that's not possible, use the ratings as an indicator of the overall strength of the company you're considering. If you're comparing two or more policies, the one offered by the company with the higher rating has a big plus in its favor.

Next, consider the company's size and age. Large insurers that have been in business for many years tend to offer a higher level of assurance than newer firms. Similarly, find out whether the type of coverage you are considering is a new line of business for the insurance company. If a company has been writing disability insurance for many years, it knows the business and is good at it. But if disability is a new line of coverage for the firm, it may lack the history and experience needed to do the job right.

Finally, you should look at the insurance company's financial performance. Study its operating statistics, balance sheet, and investments performance. Ask your financial planner, broker, and/or agent for help in analyzing the figures.

OUR ISSUES

Insurance companies traditionally have not developed and marketed their products with lesbians and gay men in mind. Thus, whether by design or by default, you'll see in several places throughout this chapter that the insurance industry tends not to give our issues the consideration they require. Fortunately, more insurance companies are beginning to see the benefits—economic and otherwise—in doing the right thing when it comes to serving lesbian and gay customers. The situation is slowly but surely improving.

It is critically important that you work with an insurance broker or agent who understands our issues and, more importantly, understands in advance how the insurance company he or she recommends will respond to those issues. The obvious solution is to work with an insurance professional within our community. This option may not be available to you, or better coverage with a better insurance company may only be available outside the community. If circumstances dictate that you work with an insurance agent or broker outside the lesbian and gay community, be extra sensitive to the possibility of a homophobic reception. You need someone who will be your advocate in dealing with an insurance company, and not someone whose own biases may undermine your efforts and perhaps even compromise your future ability to obtain coverage. Referrals from friends or colleagues satisfied with the service they receive often are the best way to find an agent or broker.

In short, you must find a knowledgeable and experienced insurance professional with whom you can be completely forthright. After you've found this person, it's also imperative that you are in fact forthright about your circumstances. Failure to adequately factor our issues into the insurance decision-making process can lead to serious and expensive oversights.

RELATED TOPICS

One important aspect of risk not covered in this chapter is the sources of risk incident in various investments. Most financial planning professionals view investment risks as qualitatively different from the types of risk discussed in this chapter, but they are risks nonetheless. These risks are explained, along with strategies for minimizing them, in the "Investment Risk and Risk Tolerance" section on page 106.

LIFE INSURANCE

THE STRAIGHT FACTS

Insuring against the risk of financial loss associated with death probably is the most widely recognized of all financial planning tools. The financial planning profession can in part trace its roots to insurance agents and brokers who sought to provide a broader level of service to their clients. Although financial planning now is a mature, independent, and comprehensive discipline, life insurance professionals have been a part of it from the beginning.

Uses of Life Insurance

It is because life insurance can assist in meeting so many financial goals that it is integral to the financial planning process. Consider the following common uses of life insurance.

- Maintaining a standard of living. Perhaps the most traditional use of life insurance is to provide the funds necessary for people who are financially dependent on you to maintain their standard of living in the event you should die prematurely. Remember that the term dependent has a broad meaning. In addition to spouses, children, and significant others, it contemplates parents, other family members, or anyone else who relies on you for economic support.

- Paying estate taxes. For individuals with a high net worth who expect to owe federal estate taxes when they die, life insurance can be an excellent technique for (in effect) "prepaying" those taxes, often for pennies on the dollar.

- Making charitable contributions. For people with philanthropic intentions, life insurance can be an excellent (and potentially tax-advantaged) way to leverage charitable contributions. Depending on your circumstances, insuring your life and naming a charity as the beneficiary on the policy could create significant extra income for the organization.

- Protecting business interests. Life insurance often is used to insure the life of a business partner. If the partner dies prematurely, the insurance proceeds can be used to buy out the partner's interest, providing cash for the partner's survivors and continuity for the business. Similarly, if a business is dependent on the expertise of one person for its financial success, the death of that person could have a significant adverse impact on the business' fortunes. *Key person* life insurance protects a business against this risk.

■ Repaying debt. Life insurance can be used to pay off debts in the event of premature death. Examples of this use of life insurance are the offers you periodically get from your mortgage or credit card company for insurance to cover your outstanding balance. (This does not mean that these offers are a good way to obtain such coverage; in most instances they're not.) In evaluating this use of life insurance, remember that the debt could be a future obligation, such as college tuition.

■ Final expenses. Life insurance can be purchased to defray the cost of a person's final expenses. Funeral arrangements are seldom cheap, and people of limited means often purchase enough insurance to ensure a "decent" burial. For people tending toward the other end of the economic spectrum, life insurance can provide dependents with an important source of interim liquidity when a person with complicated finances dies. Recurring monthly expenses tend not to respect one's death. When an estate's assets are not liquid (i.e, if they are tied up in investments, real estate, a farm, and/or a small business that cannot easily be sold), life insurance can provide an immediate short-term cash flow.

■ Tax-advantaged investing. Some types of insurance build up value over time. The tax law treats this build-up favorably, and insurance companies have developed several products specifically intended to take advantage of this favorable tax treatment. Life insurance can offer people who invest regularly the option of doing so without paying current taxes on their earnings. This use of insurance is particularly suited to saving for long-term investment goals such as retirement.

■ Forced savings. For people who have trouble saving, the types of insurance that build up value over time provide a mechanism that "forces" them to save.

■ Employee benefits. Many workers receive a form of life insurance known as *group term life insurance* as a fringe benefit from their employers.

■ Nonqualified deferred compensation. Some businesses use specialized forms of life insurance to provide a retirement fringe benefit known as *nonqualified deferred compensation* for key executives. This is discussed in more detail in the chapter on Retirement Planning.

Determining Insurance Needs

Determining the right amount of insurance to buy is difficult. Your broker or agent no doubt thinks you need a lot. That's OK. It's his or her job to think that way. Insurance professionals are trained to help their clients minimize all potential risks. While they use basic risk management principles in identifying risks for which insurance is the appropriate strategy, they are taught to err on the side of caution. Nevertheless, the responsibility for this decision rests with you, not your broker or agent.

So, how much life insurance do you really need? First and foremost, that depends on what you're using it for. For the traditional use of insurance—to replace income lost through premature death—financial planners and insurance professionals use a formula to compute your insurance needs (or, more accurately, your dependents' needs). The complex computations take into account your assets, liabilities, other investments and your dependents' other sources of income. This determines the amount of cash needed to generate an income stream sufficient to replace the one lost if you die. To further complicate things, the formula also takes into account how long the income stream will need to last. The formula is too involved to accurately repeat here, so let's instead work with a (very) rough rule of thumb. You should seek professional guidance in computing needs specific to your circumstances. Depending on your age, it usually takes between five and seven times your annual salary to generate a cash stream sufficient to replace your income. If you're very young, have a large family, or earn a very high salary, you may want to go as high as eight to ten times your salary.

For most of the other uses of life insurance listed above, there is a specific sum required to address the need, and this is the amount of insurance you would buy. Some people even use this approach (rather than the income-replacement approach) to compute the amount of insurance needed to maintain financial security for a loved one in the event of an untimely death. This technique usually works well for dual-income couples without children.

EXAMPLE

Carl and Lonn own a house together. The mortgage on the house is $100,000. They both work, have good jobs, and consider themselves reasonably able to support themselves individually. Nevertheless, Carl and Lonn are concerned that, if something should happen to one of them, the mortgage payment would become a burden for the other. Carl and Lonn each purchase a $100,000 life insurance policy so one of them could pay off the mortgage should something happen to the other.

Term Insurance

The two basic types of life insurance are term insurance and cash value insurance. Because the distinction between them is so critical, we'll look at each separately.

Term insurance provides life insurance protection over a specified period of time. If you die during the period of coverage, your beneficiaries collect your death benefit. If you're alive at the end of the term, you get nothing. It's usually the less expensive of the two types of insurance because it provides death protection and nothing else.

You can purchase term life insurance in one of two forms. You can contract for a *level premium* for a period of years (usually five or ten), or you can buy an *annual renewable* policy that allows you to renew the policy at the end of each term (usually one year) for ever-increasing premiums. In the long run, level premium term usually is cheaper and generally is a better insurance buy. If your needs are short-term, annual renewable may make more sense. Just be sure your policy contains a renewability clause. Otherwise, your insurer may have the option not to renew your insurance.

Cash Value Insurance

In contrast to term insurance, which provides only a death benefit, *cash value* insurance allows you to build up tax-deferred savings in your policy. For this reason, cash value life insurance is an important investment vehicle for some people. Of the forms of cash value life insurance, four comprise the majority of the coverage sold: (1) whole life, (2) universal life, (3) variable life, and (4) variable universal life.

Whole life is the traditional form of cash value life insurance. Premiums on whole life policies tend to stay the same for the length of the policy, or at least for long intervals lasting many years. You accumulate cash savings in the policy but have no say in how the money is invested. The insurance company makes that decision, and they usually decide conservatively. This means that the rate of return on the portion of your premium that represents an investment is very low.

Universal life is intended to provide more flexibility than whole life in terms of managing (i.e., adjusting midstream) the policy's terms—premium payments, death benefits, and cash value build-up. For example, after the policy has been in effect for a time, you can lower the amount of your monthly premium by applying a portion of the accumulated cash value to cover part of the premium payments. You also can adjust the amount of the death benefit over time. In exchange for this flexibility, you pay for the insurance company's higher administrative costs. Universal life policies make certain assumptions about interest rates when they're written. If those assumptions prove to be incorrect, there's a small chance you'll have to pay additional premiums in order to continue funding the same death benefit. The insurance company is strongly motivated to avoid this result, but there are no guarantees. As with whole life, the insurance company makes the investment decisions with universal life policies.

Variable life is the most investmentlike of all cash value life insurance options. You—not the insurance company—make the investment decisions. Premiums are fixed and the death benefit is guaranteed, but the cash value of the policy fluctuates with the performance of the investments you choose. Usually you allocate your investment among a family of mutual funds affiliated with or managed by the life insurance company writing your policy. Keep this in mind when considering variable life as an investment. You need to investigate both the carrier's performance as an insurer and how well its funds perform as investments. Remember that the advantages of tax-favored investing can't compensate for inferior returns and limited investment options.

Variable universal life combines the insurance flexibility of universal life with the investment flexibility of variable life in a single insurance product. While it can offer many advantages in the right circumstances, it is an option best reserved for sophisticated investors who grasp its many technicalities.

Cash value life insurance allows you to borrow against the cash value portion (but not against the death benefit), usually at favorable interest rates. In contrast, you can't borrow against a term policy. Borrowing from a policy's cash reserve can be an important debt management technique in the right circumstances. Keep in mind, however, that your cash value is not a credit card or a revolving line of credit. If you die with a loan balance outstanding, the death benefit is reduced by the amount you owe. Borrowing against a policy therefore never should be undertaken lightly. It's best reserved either for strict emergencies or serious, one-time efforts to consolidate debt and get one's finances in order.

What happens to your built-up cash value if you stop making premium payments on permanent insurance? Usually policies offer three choices. First, you can take the cash yourself, but you must pay income tax on the build-up. Second, you can use the value to buy a fully "paid-up" insurance policy for a lower face value. Under this option, the insurance company treats your cash value as a one-time premium payment for a lifetime of death benefit coverage. The amount of your death benefit is determined by the amount of your cash value. Third, you can use the cash value to buy term insurance at the company's then-prevailing rates. Under this option, you buy an amount of term coverage equal to the death benefit of your old cash value policy, and the coverage lasts for as long as your cash value can pay for it. The difference between the second and third options is that under the second option you get a lower death benefit permanently, and under the third option you get the same death benefit for as long as the cash value can afford it.

Term versus Cash Value

How do you know whether term or cash value insurance is right for you? The answer depends on your circumstances. In particular, it depends on the reason you're buying life insurance, the length of time you need the insurance, and your financial resources when you buy the insurance. For example, term insurance usually is appropriate for short-term needs (i.e., for 10 years or less). Cash value insurance may make more sense for long-term needs. If you're in a very high tax bracket, the tax advantages of cash value insurance such as variable life may have appeal. Business, charitable, and estate planning uses of life insurance usually involve term policies.

Some financial planners take the point of view that insurance is an inferior investment and advise clients to buy term insurance to meet death benefit needs and to invest their money elsewhere. Reasonable people can disagree on this point for some uses of insurance. However, one undeniable advantage to cash value insurance as an investment vehicle is its ability to grow on a tax-deferred basis. This feature makes cash value insurance in general, and variable life in particular, an attractive option for regular investors.

What if investing isn't a major factor in your insurance purchase? First, ask yourself why you're willing to give up the tax advantages of investing this way. If you have a good answer for that question, then your time frame and financial resources become the major factors in deciding the right choice for you. If you're just starting out in life and you need to maximize the death benefit coverage from your insurance dollar, term probably is the better choice—for now. If finances force you to go the term insurance route, but you expect things might improve later, make sure your term policy has a *conversion* feature. This way, if you choose to, you can convert your policy to cash value coverage when you're more flush.

Payout Options

When you die, your beneficiaries can receive their money from the insurance company in one of several ways. They can request (1) a lump-sum payment of the cash; (2) a payment of the interest earned by the proceeds, leaving the death benefit untouched until some future point; or (3) a payout in the form of an annuity over a fixed time period or over one or more lifetimes. (Annuity payouts are discussed in detail in the next section of this chapter.) If you have a compelling reason to choose a specific payout option on behalf of your beneficiaries (say, for example, one is a spendthrift), most insurance companies will permit you to do so. Your decision must be in writing to the insurance company (usually on one of their forms) and made before you die. If this issue concerns you, attend to it early on.

Buying Life Insurance

When you shop for life insurance policies, the agent or broker trying to sell the policy will present you with a *policy illustration*. This is the insurance company's best estimate of what will happen to the policy over time. Since it's only an estimate, however, you need to review it carefully. Watch for the following:

- Does the illustration go out to age 95? Although you may not live that long, policy illustrations should be made to age 95. If it stops sooner, it may mean something unpleasant is possible in the final years.
- Are the assumptions regarding interest rates and inflation reasonable?
- Does the policy illustration accurately reflect your age, health status, and smoking status?
- If you're comparing illustrations for two different policies, make sure your comparison is between apples and apples (not between

apples and oranges). If any of the features discussed above (age, interest rates, inflation, health status) vary even slightly between illustrations, there's no way to make a fair comparison. For this reason, be reluctant to show one company the policy illustration prepared by another. While it's unscrupulous, some people aren't above "hiding" a small difference that has a big impact on the price quoted.

OUR ISSUES

Life Insurance and HIV (Part I)—Obtaining Coverage

People who have AIDS or test positive for HIV face a serious challenge finding life insurance coverage. Thus, if you already own a policy, do whatever you can to keep it in force. If it's a policy provided through your employer, investigate the possibility of converting it to individual coverage when and if you leave. This insurance could prove to be a valuable financial asset in helping you meet the high costs of living with HIV.

If you don't have coverage or if you have inadequate coverage, it's probably no surprise to hear that your options are severely limited. Insurers in every state are permitted to perform a blood test for the presence of HIV, and no insurer will write a policy if the test is positive. This means that your only option will be to find legitimate ways of obtaining life insurance coverage without submitting to a physical. The word *legitimate* cannot be emphasized enough. If you try to pull a fast one on the insurance company, it's quite likely that they'll simply cancel the policy or deny the death benefit when it is claimed.

So, how can you find life insurance coverage if you have AIDS or you're HIV positive? First, it may be possible to obtain coverage through an employer. Sometimes, employer-provided insurance covers a large enough risk pool that HIV is already taken into account when the actuaries figure the rates. This can be an option for employees of very large companies or those in the public sector, where group insurance contracts are negotiated to cover tens, or even hundreds, of thousands of people. If you can obtain coverage in this way, find out if you can convert it to individual coverage without submitting to an exam. We're getting into longshots here, but it's worth making discrete enquiries.

Next, watch for life insurance offers from your creditors. Mortgage and credit card companies occasionally offer life insurance coverage that will pay off outstanding debts when you die. While the coverage is small and the rates usually aren't competitive, it's better than nothing. Check the fine print in the promotion to make sure that there are no exclusions for HIV in the policy. If there are exclusions, the coverage has no value for you.

Life Insurance and HIV (Part II)—"Living Benefits"

When you die and your beneficiaries receive proceeds from your life insurance policy, they are not required to pay income tax on that money. (There can be estate tax consequences, however, which are discussed in the Estate Planning chapter of this book.) The income tax exclusion generally does not apply when you receive money from a policy while you are alive. For example, if you cash in a cash value life insurance policy, you must pay tax on the build-up in the policy. The amount you pay tax on generally is equal to the difference between what you get from the insurance company and your investment in the policy (i.e., the amount you've paid in over the life of the policy). Another way in which the taxability of life insurance proceeds received prior to death becomes an issue, and one of particular importance to the lesbian and gay community, is the use of *living benefits* by persons with AIDS.

Several years ago a group of entrepreneurs realized there was a way for them to make money and at the same time provide a valuable service for people whose financial resources were being depleted by the expenses associated with AIDS. In essence, they "bought" the right to receive the death benefit under an insurance policy owned by a person with AIDS. The policyholder received immediate cash based on the amount of the eventual death benefit—usually at a fairly steep discount—in exchange for a guarantee that the death benefit under the policy would be paid to them for advancing the cash. Other entrepreneurs followed suit, resulting in a number of *viatical settlement companies.*

Life insurance companies now offer living benefits of their own to policyholders. Insurance policy living benefits essentially do the same thing that viatical settlement companies do (i.e., offer "advances" on life insurance death benefits to people with AIDS and other "terminal" illnesses). Insurance policy living benefits (also known as accelerated death benefits) usually pay the full policy amount, whereas viatical settlements generally pay only between 60 percent and 80 percent of the policy's death benefit. If your insurance policy doesn't offer accelerated death benefits, a viatical settlement may be your only option.

Insurance companies couch their practices in slightly different legalese than the viatical settlement companies. The difference in terminology may be enough to create different tax results. Under current law viatical settlements or living benefits are taxable regardless of whether they're received from an insurance company or a third-party viatical settlement company. The IRS has proposed rules that would exempt living benefits from taxation, but these rules are not final. A related IRS ruling suggests that the proposed exclusion would apply only to living benefits received from insurance companies and not to payments received from viatical settlement companies. For several years Congress has been considering legislation that would achieve this same result. If the IRS or Congress make this change, people who have a choice will want to get their viatical settlements from their insurers and not from third parties, in order to avoid having the payments taxed. For now, however, you have to pay income tax on any living benefit payments you receive from your life insurance policy (to the extent they exceed your investment in the policy), regardless of who pays them.

Life Insurance and Gay Couples (Part I)—Insurable Interests

In order to purchase insurance, you have to name your intended beneficiaries in your application. If those beneficiaries don't have an insurable interest in your life, the company won't write the policy, even if you otherwise qualify for coverage. The ostensible purpose of this requirement is to prevent people from turning insurance into a lottery, and to prevent other unscrupulous behavior in the same general vein. Traditionally, however, lesbian and gay couples didn't have an insurable interest in each other's lives.

There were (and are) a few exceptions to this application of the insurable interest rule. People who own a house together always have an insurable interest in each other, but only up to the amount of their share of the mortgage. Similarly, people who own a business together can get coverage on each other's lives, but only up to the amount of the economic loss they'd suffer if their co-owner died unexpectedly. But the full range of needs for lesbian and gay couples historically has not been recognized by the insurance industry.

There also was (and is) an awkward way to get around this problem. You can name someone such as a parent or a charity as the beneficiary on your application, as they always have an insurable interest in your life. Then, a few months later, you can change the designation to whomever you wish. Mom or dad comes off the policy and the significant other goes on. Insurance companies don't like this little game, but it's largely their own creation and there's not much they can do about it. Sometimes their agents or brokers even recommend it. The complete success or failure of this strategy depends on how much insurance you're buying, but most often it works. Also, there's always the small risk that a death before the beneficiary is changed could leave a surviving partner without much coverage and a parent or charity with a windfall.

The situation has improved considerably in many areas, and the prognosis for future improvement is good. Insurance companies are learning how to redefine insurable interest in ways that protect their legitimate concerns but still recognize the validity of our relationships. On a more informal basis, agents or brokers in many areas are able to let insurance company underwriters know that an insurable interest exists and that the issue need not be pursued further.

Nevertheless, the insurable interest issue still surfaces. Be sure you're working with a broker who understands not only your circumstances, but also how the insurance company you're applying with will react to them. After all, while you could always play the game we just discussed, why should you demean yourself and give your money to a company that doesn't respect your concerns?

Life Insurance and Gay Couples (Part II)—How Much?

Lesbian and gay couples frequently have difficulty determining how much life insurance to provide for each other. Usually both partners work, and the surviving partner may not be completely dependent on the deceased partner's income stream. In this fairly typical scenario (at least it's typical for our community), the debt repayment approach to life insurance discussed earlier may be a more appropriate way to determine life insurance needs than the more conventional income-replacement model.

Here's the logic of this approach: The mortgage on the house is our most significant debt. If one of us were to die tomorrow, we would want to provide protection for our surviving partner for the burden associated with that debt. Accordingly, the amount of insurance purchased is equal to the amount of money needed to eliminate the debt in the event of one partner's untimely death.

This approach may not make sense if there is a large difference in the partners' income. If the higher-earning partner were to die, the other partner may need more than just a paid-off house in order to remain financially secure. Similarly, if your retirement income planning relies heavily on one partner's noncontributory employer retirement plan or on both partners' Social Security retirement benefits, a premature death could ruin that planning. Life insurance is one appropriate way to manage both these risks.

Since this debt replacement strategy therefore contemplates only one of the many possible uses of life insurance, it can't be viewed as a complete answer to the question, how much do I need? But it offers an alternative approach to the most traditional use of life insurance, and one uniquely suited to the needs of many in our community.

RELATED TOPICS

To the extent that cash value life insurance in general, and variable life in particular, offers an alternative form of tax-advantaged investing, it's important to understand how it fits with your overall investment strategy. For more information see "Asset Allocation and Portfolio Structure" on page 138. The advantages of tax-deferred growth are explained in the "Tax-Favored Investments" section on page 212.

If you own a life insurance policy when you die, the proceeds of that policy are included in the determination of your gross estate for estate tax purposes. Since life insurance death benefits often reach six figures, this can create estate tax problems for more people than might imagine it is. The pitfalls and planning strategies of this issue are detailed in the "Estate Tax Planning Techniques" section on page 328.

Sometimes people use life insurance to "prepay" the estate taxes they know they will owe. This strategy is discussed in the "Estate Tax Planning Techniques" section on page 328.

The use of insurance as a tool for structuring nonqualified deferred compensation plans is discussed in the "Supplemental Retirement Plans" section on page 249.

Although most policies permit their owners to borrow against built-up cash value, doing so makes financial sense under very limited circumstances. How this technique might help you is discussed in the "Managing Debt" section on page 19.

Life insurance benefits can be claimed by beneficiaries in the form of an annuity. See the "Annuities" section on page 49 for applicable payout rules.

Designating a beneficiary on a life insurance policy is an important estate planning strategy for lesbians and gay men. The need for this strategy is detailed in the "Beneficiary Designations" section on page 308.

When you purchase a life insurance policy, you almost always enter a long-term relationship with the company writing it. To understand the appropriate considerations in choosing an insurance company, see "Understanding Risk Management" on page 33.

Couples whose retirement planning relies heavily on an employer's plan or Social Security may need to consider life insurance as a replacement for these sources of retirement income in the event of a premature death. This issue is explored more fully in "Employer-Sponsored Retirement Plans" on page 243, and in "Social Security Retirement Benefits" on page 262.

ANNUITIES

THE STRAIGHT FACTS

Annuities are unique financial products sold by life insurance companies. In exchange for a payment or series of payments, the insurance company provides you with a stream of income for some future period of time. Of even greater potential value, the money contained in an annuity grows on a tax-deferred basis until it is taken out. These features combine to create an important investment strategy that for many may have only incidental significance as a risk management tool. To be fair, some view annuities as an appropriate technique for managing the risk of outliving their assets, which actually is the original intended use of the product.

The best way to understand what annuities are and how they work is to look at the five characteristics that define all annuity contracts. They are:

1. How premiums are paid.
2. When benefits begin.
3. How long benefits are paid out.
4. Who receives the benefits (referred to as "annuitants").
5. How the annuity grows.

Understanding these characteristics and how they combine in various annuity products makes it easier to envision what role annuities might play in your financial planning.

How Premiums Are Paid

Annuity contracts generally are written to require one of three payment options.

1. A *single-premium annuity* requires a payment of one (usually very large) lump sum to fund all future payouts. Single-premium annuities are an appropriate choice for someone who is buying an annuity in order to generate a guaranteed income stream (often in retirement) or for someone who wants existing assets designated for retirement use to grow on a tax-advantaged basis.

2. A *fixed-premium annuity* requires regular periodic payments (monthly, quarterly, or annually) over an extended period of time in order to fund future benefits. Fixed-premium annuities are more desirable for people who want to save on a regular basis.

3. A *flexible-premium annuity* allows you to alter the amount of the periodic premium in order to best meet your saving and investment goals.

When Benefits Begin

When you buy an annuity, you have two choices for when you want your benefits to begin.

1. *Immediate annuities,* as the name suggests, provide for payouts to begin as soon as the premium is received. Thus, this characteristic generally comes in tandem with a single-premium payment. This makes single-premium immediate annuities appropriate for retirees seeking a secure retirement income stream.

2. *Deferred annuities* begin paying out benefits at a future date. Thus, there is an accumulation period (when you pay the insurance company) and a distribution period (when the insurance company pays you) for deferred annuities. Deferred annuities can be used for both investment and retirement income purposes.

How Long Benefits Are Paid Out

The distribution period under an annuity contract can be measured in one of four ways.

1. A pure-life annuity pays out over the life of the annuitant or over joint lives if there's more than one annuitant. When

people buy annuities to secure a retirement income stream, the characteristic they normally look for is guaranteed payments for the rest of their lives. The ways to measure life annuities are discussed below. Keep in mind that the insurance company assumes a risk in paying out benefits with a lifetime guarantee. Therefore, part of your annuity is used to pay the insurance company's mortality costs. This means you receive a lower payment.

2. A life annuity with a refund feature guarantees continued payments for a specified period of time (usually 5, 10, or 20 years), even if the annuitant dies before the payout period ends. Annuities usually represent a significant investment of resources, and the refund feature is intended to protect against the risk of having your entire annuity savings forfeited in the event of an early death. This feature also is often sought when annuities are used to guarantee an income stream for life.

3. An annuity for a certain period guarantees payments for a specified period, usually 5, 10, or 20 years. Regardless of when you die, the contract continues to pay out for the duration of the period, either to other beneficiaries or to your estate if you fail to name other beneficiaries. However, there is no lifetime guarantee. Period certain annuities offer people the ability to plan a retirement income stream while avoiding the need to pay for the insurance company's mortality charges.

4. Most annuities permit the option of withdrawing the entire proceeds in one lump sum. This offers maximum flexibility for those who use annuities primarily as an investment vehicle. They can enjoy the advantages of tax-deferred build-up during the accumulation period but don't have to bear the insurance company's administration and mortality expenses when the time comes for a payout.

Who Receives Benefits

Although you may pay your annuity premiums yourself, you have several choices regarding who gets to receive benefits under the contract.

1. An individual annuity pays benefits over the life of one person. These annuities are appropriate for single people with no

dependents whose primary goal is to guarantee an income stream only for their own lives.

2. A joint-life annuity pays benefits over the joint lives of (usually) two annuitants. After the first of the joint annuitants dies, the payments stop. These annuities generally don't offer the retirement income protection sought by most couples.

3. A joint and survivor annuity also pays benefits over the lives of (usually) two annuitants, but the payments continue until both annuitants die. This feature provides the maximum income security for couples seeking such protection in their retirement years. Remember, however, that promising payments over two lives increases significantly the insurance company's mortality exposure. Joint and survivor annuities therefore offer lower benefits than most other options.

How the Annuity Grows

The money you pay into an annuity, whether all at once (as in an immediate annuity) or over time (as with fixed-premium and flexible-premium annuities), can grow in one of two ways.

1. A fixed-rate annuity grows at a rate of return projected in the contract. Although the return is not guaranteed, the insurance company in a fixed-rate annuity is under tremendous pressure to perform consistent with its projections. Therefore, it's not surprising that insurers behave very conservatively when it comes to fixed-rate annuities. This feature generally makes such annuities inferior growth-investment vehicles but acceptable for generating an income stream, in retirement.

2. A variable-rate annuity grows—or shrinks—based on the return earned by the financial vehicles in which it is invested. Much as with variable life insurance, variable annuities allow you to allocate the cash in the annuity among a family of mutual funds associated with or managed by the insurance company that wrote the annuity contract. Variable annuities therefore offer both the risks and the rewards of participating in market-oriented investments. Consequently, the potential return on a variable annuity generally is greater than the return offered by a fixed-rate annuity.

Uses of Annuities

Although the only real restriction on the use of annuities is your creativity (and the creativity of your financial planner, broker, and/or advisor), our discussion has directed us to the two most common uses of annuities—as investment vehicles and tools for providing a guaranteed income stream (usually in retirement). These uses are not mutually exclusive. In fact, they often are complementary.

The major advantage of annuities as investment vehicles is the lure of tax-deferred build-up of interest, dividends, and capital gains. This lure is far greater with variable annuities than with fixed-rate annuities. For regular investors, then, a fixed-premium deferred variable annuity may be an important part of the overall investment strategy. However, this can only make sense if the commitment to investing—that is, to paying premiums—can be made on a permanent basis.

Using annuities as a means of securing a guaranteed retirement income stream is a less certain strategy. For example, it's often not clear why you wouldn't invest your money as you see fit, enjoying wider investment choices and the probability of higher returns than most annuities appropriate for this purpose can offer. You then either can withdraw the money from your own investment accounts on your own schedule as you need it or annuitize your accounts yourself, making periodic withdrawals over your life expectancy. When you buy an annuity, part of your investment goes to pay the insurance company's administrative costs (and profits!). By managing your own money, you avoid these expenses as well as potential mortality charges. On the other hand, everyone faces the risk of outliving their assets, known as superannuation. So, if you're bad at managing money or if you are concerned about the economic security of someone else, using an annuity to guarantee an income stream can make good sense.

Buying an Annuity

There are several considerations you should keep in mind when buying an annuity contract. Some are consistent with the general advice offered on selecting an insurance company in the "Understanding Risk Management" section of this chapter. Other considerations are the same as those we discussed earlier with regard to purchasing life insurance. For example, with fixed-rate annuities, be skeptical of unrealistic rate projections. Select only a top-rated company. When shopping for an annuity, be certain that the comparisons you make between companies and products are apples to apples so that all of the key assumptions and variables in the projections are identical.

Beyond these general tips, some advice applies specifically to the purchase of an annuity. First, be sure you understand how the insurance company's surrender charges work. If you surrender (i.e., cancel) an annuity too soon after opening it, the company will hit you with a penalty known as a surrender charge. Annuities are supposed to be long-term arrangements, and insurance companies want you to keep your commitments. Surrender charges encourage you to do so. Most annuities impose surrender charges only for the first seven or so years. Usually the surrender charges decrease on a sliding scale over this period. Avoid the rare annuities where the surrender charges never phase out. That's unnecessary and unfair.

Beyond surrender charges, another reason to be certain that you're in annuities for the long haul is taxes. If you enter into an annuity contract and then surrender it prematurely, you have to pay income tax on all the deferred build-up. This is fair, since the taxes were only deferred, not erased, and it's reasonable to ask you to pay them when you take your money out. Indeed, a portion of all annuity withdrawals eventually are taxed. This is explained in the discussion of "Tax-Favored Investments" later in this book. If you surrender an annuity before you reach age 59½, you also have to pay a 10 percent penalty tax on the so-called premature distribution. This is an incentive built into the tax law in order to encourage you to keep on saving. It's the price the government charges for the benefit of tax-deferred accumulation. But it's a price you don't want to and don't have to pay, so make sure you know what you're getting into before you purchase an annuity.

Finally, let's look at some advice specific to variable annuities. First, remember that you must consider both the performance of the insurance company as an insurer and the performance of its mutual funds as investments. Poor investment performance or limited investment options cannot be justified by the lure of tax-deferred savings. Make sure the company's investment results are in line with the benchmarks appropriate to the particular investment type. (Benchmarks are explained in the discussion of "Classes of Investments" in the next chapter.) Next, make sure the annuity offers at least five different investment options, so you can be sure your money is properly diversified. Last, make sure that the total annual fees charged by the insurance company for managing the investments in the variable annuity are reasonable. Generally, fees over 2 percent are too high and should be avoided.

OUR ISSUES

Annuities offer lesbian and gay couples significant added flexibility in their retirement planning, particularly as compared to most traditional pension plans. Annuities allow gay couples to receive distributions that recognize their potential need to plan for income security over two lives. In contrast, most traditional pension plans offer this benefit only to married couples. This is explained in detail in the Retirement Planning chapter. Remember that annuities allow gay couples to program a retirement income stream in ways that most traditional pension plans do not. While the added flexibility offered by annuities will not be necessary in all circumstances, it's reassuring to know it's available. This flexibility makes annuities an important planning tool for lesbian and gay couples, worth longer-than-average consideration.

RELATED TOPICS

Annuities are an important part of many people's retirement planning strategies, but they are seldom a complete answer. To get a sense of the big picture in planning for a secure retirement, review "Computing Retirement Needs and Savings" on page 231.

Annuities offer great flexibility in naming the people who are entitled to receive payouts during the distribution period. This makes annuities an ideal retirement planning and estate planning tool for lesbians and gay men. To understand the retirement planning aspects of this issue, see the "Withdrawals and Distributions of Retirement Savings" section on page 266. The estate planning advantages are detailed in the "Beneficiary Designations" section on page 308.

Annuity payments are generally partly taxable and partly nontaxable. The taxation of annuities is explained in the "Tax-Favored Investments" section on page 217.

If you cash in an annuity prematurely, the tax consequences become more severe. They are the same as those discussed in the "Premature Distributions and Penalties" section on page 268.

Diversification is an essential tool for minimizing investment risk. It also is essential in choosing and working with a variable annuity. The principles of diversification are explained in the "Investment Risk and Risk Tolerance" section on page 106.

Benchmarks and their use in measuring the performance of a particular investment (such as a mutual fund in a variable annuity) are explained in the "Classes of Investments" section on page 114.

When you buy an annuity, you make an important and long-term commitment to a particular insurance company, and vice versa. It's important that you wisely select the company you are going to deal with. Strategies for choosing an insurance company are discussed in "Choosing an Insurer" on page 35.

You need to carefully analyze the illustration provided to you when someone is trying to sell you an annuity. Techniques for doing this are offered in "Buying Life Insurance" on page 43.

Finally, you are making an important investment decision when you buy an annuity, particularly a variable annuity. Criteria for selecting good investments and for allocating your funds among available options are applicable to annuity purchases. These criteria are explained in the "Asset Allocation and Portfolio Structure" section on page 138.

DISABILITY INSURANCE

THE STRAIGHT FACTS

What is your most valuable asset? Your home? Your investment portfolio? A family heirloom or priceless antique? While all of these can be highly valuable, and one of them might be your most valuable asset, there is one item routinely overlooked in considering possible answers to this question: the ability to produce income and earn a living. For most people, their earning capacity is their most valuable asset. Can you honestly say that you own an asset worth more than your lifetime earning potential?

Ironically, this most valuable of your assets is also the one most vulnerable to risk of loss. If you become sick or injured, your ability to earn income could be impaired—permanently or temporarily, partially or totally. Disability probably is one of the greatest risks you face, and statistically one of the risks you are least prepared to bear. A study reported by the American College of Life Underwriters found that at age 35, an individual faces a one-in-three chance of experiencing total disability for at least three months before age 65, and that nearly 30 percent of those cases result in permanent disability. If you are young and in good health, disability is a greater risk for you than any other hazard, including death.

Experts estimate that most people need to replace between 60 percent and 80 percent of their income in the event they become disabled. If this seems high to you, consider that while some expenses go down when you can no longer work, such as clothing and transportation, others tend to go up, such as food and medical care. Moreover, most expenses continue regardless of one's disability, and these tend to be the major ones, such as housing and utilities.

A few fortunate people own sufficient income-producing assets that loss of earning power is not a significant source of risk for them. They can meet their needs through their investment income. For the overwhelming majority of Americans, however, the financial consequences of a serious disruption in income due to disability are enormous. Clearly, with risks this high, insurance is the appropriate risk management technique to protect yourself from financial loss in the event of your disability.

There are three possible sources for insuring against the risk of disability.

1. State workers' compensation insurance for disabilities arising on the job.
2. Social Security disability benefits.
3. Disability insurance policies.

We'll look at the last two options in some detail in this chapter. You should note that, depending on the nature of a particular disability, you may be eligible for coverage under more than one of these three options. Be advised, however, that the people administering each system compare notes regarding the amount you receive, making it unlikely you can earn more disabled than you did working.

Workers' compensation laws vary slightly from state to state, but if you are injured on the job, workers' comp will be part of your disability coverage. Essentially, workers' comp is a mandatory insurance regime imposed by law on all employers in every state. It provides predetermined payments for bodily injury or loss resulting from injuries sustained while working. The laws set fixed dollar values for each injury—so much for each lost arm, leg, and so on. If you are injured on the job, workers' compensation is your exclusive remedy. In theory, you can't sue your employer. The main purpose of workers' comp laws is to prevent litigation by eliminating fault-finding from the equation and to provide for uniform treatment of workplace injuries.

Financial planners do not consider workers' compensation coverage to be sufficient protection against the risk of disability. The reasons for this are

1. Workers' comp sometimes makes only a single, lump-sum payment for injuries (as opposed to monthly payments lasting the length of the disability).

2. In most cases, the amounts authorized by the workers' compensation laws are insufficient to meet ongoing income needs.

3. Most disabilities occur outside the workplace.

You will need to look beyond workers' comp in order to adequately protect yourself against the risk of losing income due to disability.

Social Security

Disability Benefits

A portion of the Social Security taxes you and your employer pay are earmarked to provide benefits in the event you become disabled. Qualifying for those benefits, however, is extremely difficult. As with other Social Security benefits, the amount you actually receive probably won't be sufficient to replace enough of your lost earnings to ensure complete financial security throughout your disability.

To be eligible for disability insurance benefits, you need to have been paying enough taxes into the Social Security system for a sufficient period of time. Meeting this requirement is measured in *quarters of coverage*. You earn a quarter of coverage for about $640 (for 1996) of wages earned in a single calendar quarter. You can only earn four quarters of coverage per year. You need one quarter of coverage for every year after you turn 21, up to a maximum requirement of 40 quarters, in order to qualify for disability benefits. You also must earn 20 of those quarters in the 10 years immediately preceding your disability. These requirements are prorated for workers under 30, who nevertheless must have a minimum of six quarters of coverage.

Even if you meet these eligibility requirements, you still have to satisfy the law's very strict definition of *disability* in order to qualify for Social Security disability benefits. It is irrelevant whether your doctor, employer, or private insurer has concluded you are disabled. Social Security makes its own determination using its own rigid criteria. For example, Social Security does not recognize partial disabilities. In order to receive benefits, you must be unable to perform any work of any sort. In other words, if you are a disabled neurosurgeon who can still say "Do you want fries with that?" you might not get any benefits!

Next, you must be unable to earn over $500 a month in order to qualify. For comparison purposes, $500 per month translates into less than full-time employment at the minimum wage. Your disability also must be expected either to last more than 12 months or to result in death.

Finally, the Social Security Administration will want to review your complete medical history, your insurance history, your tax returns, your employment history for the past 15 years, and proof of your age when evaluating your claim.

As you can see, qualifying for Social Security disability benefits is an arduous task. About half of all initial claims are denied. You can appeal a denial of benefits, and the government's decision to deny benefits is reversed in about half of all appeals. Disability payments don't begin until the sixth month after your disability, but you can't apply until you've been disabled for five months. The determination process can easily last for more than a year before a decision is made.

If you qualify for Social Security disability benefits, the amount of your benefits is calculated using a very complex formula based on your age at the time you're disabled and your annual salary for each year you paid into the system. The formula used to compute your benefits is too complicated to explain here. You should know, however, that Social Security disability benefits almost never replace the 60 percent to 80 percent of predisability income experts say you'll need. If you're really keen to know what you might be eligible to receive, the Social Security Administration can give you an estimate of your benefits. Instructions on how to request a Personal Earnings and Benefit Estimate Statement from the SSA are given in the discussion of Social Security benefits in the chapter on Retirement Planning.

Supplemental Security Income

The Social Security Administration (SSA) also runs a government program known as Supplemental Security Income, or SSI. Unlike the other programs administered by the SSA, SSI is funded through general tax revenues and not payroll taxes.

SSI is intended to provide a safety net for retired or disabled individuals of limited means. In order to qualify for SSI, you must be either 65 or older, blind, or disabled. Also, your total assets must be worth less than $2,000 ($3,000 if you're married). Your house and your car are the only assets excluded from this requirement. In addition, there are income limits you must meet in order to qualify for SSI. The limits vary based on where you live and whether or not you work. They allow for only very modest amounts of outside income. The basic SSI benefit runs slightly under $500 per month (under $700 if you're married), but people living in high cost areas can qualify for additional payments. These benefits increase slightly each year to keep up with inflation.

SSI truly is intended to be a program of last resort. While those eligible for SSI benefits certainly should take advantage of them, in no sense can SSI be considered an appropriate tool in planning for the risk of disability.

Disability Insurance

For most people, neither workers' compensation nor Social Security provides an adequate defense against the financial risk associated with becoming disabled. The benefits they provide are either too modest to serve as an adequate replacement for lost income, too difficult to qualify for, or restricted to only certain injuries. Individual or group disability insurance is needed to ensure that necessary income streams will continue in the event you become incapable of producing them.

Many people receive this insurance coverage as a fringe benefit from their employers. If you are in this category, your work here may be done. But please read on before concluding that it is. In the rest of this section we will review the important components of a good disability insurance plan. You would be well advised to compare your employer's plan against these criteria to see how it stacks up. There's a wide variety of disability coverages available, and you can't assume that your employer's plan is adequate for your needs. If your employer's plan comes up short, you may want to investigate a supplemental plan to bridge the gap(s). Such a plan may even be available through your employer from the insurance company providing your basic coverage. This is frequently the case when the coverage offered by your employer does not replace the recommended 60 percent to 80 percent of your income. You may have the option of purchasing coverage yourself for the 10 percent to 20 percent needed to adequately protect against the risk of disability. If you can't get the protection you need through an employer's plan, you should consider purchasing coverage on your own, especially if the holes in your employer's policy are serious.

If you don't have any disability insurance, there's a serious gap in your financial planning, and you need to purchase a good disability policy from a solid insurance company as soon as possible. The important components of disability insurance follow.

Amount of Coverage

As we've said above, studies show you will need to replace between 60 percent and 80 percent of your predisability income. A few insurers let you go as high as 85 percent, but this is rare. In fact, it probably will be difficult for you to get above the 70 percent mark (but that doesn't mean you shouldn't try). Also keep in mind that if your disability protection is from a number of different sources, they probably all will coordinate payments to ensure you're not getting a windfall.

Definition of Disability

Some insurance policies exclude "occupational disabilities" from the scope of coverage. This means that no benefits are paid if your disability arose from your occupation (i.e., on the job) and if you receive workers' compensation benefits. Since workers' compensation may not be adequate to replace your lost income, be sure your policy pays benefits regardless of whether your disability is occupational or nonoccupational.

Definition of Occupation

In order to receive benefits under a disability policy, the nature of the disability sustained must impair your ability to work. This requirement begs the question: to work as what? In the same line you were in before the disability or in any line of work? This is a critical distinction. If an acclaimed concert violinist sustained a disability that prevented her from playing the violin again, but not from flipping burgers at a fast-food joint, should she receive benefits under her disability policy? She, of course, would think so, but her insurance company might not. Her disability doesn't prevent her from engaging in any occupation, just her own occupation. Because the potential for conflict here is enormous, policies define what kind of loss of occupation will qualify a person for benefits. One of two formulas is used.

Under an *any occupation* (*any occ* in insurance lingo) policy, disability benefits are not paid unless the disability prevents the person insured from engaging in any meaningful employment in any occupation. This is a very strict test from the insured's perspective, and you should not buy any occ disability insurance. Under an *own occ* policy, benefits are paid if the disability prevents the insured from engaging in his or her own occupation. This is a much more appropriate way of insuring against the risk in question, and an own occ policy is always the preferred choice.

Own occ coverage is expensive for insurance companies and policyholders and therefore is becoming more difficult to find. By increasing the situations in which benefits must be paid, own occ policies increase the risk to the insurer and the cost to policyholders. In order to rein in costs, some insurers offer one of two compromises to the own occ/any occ formula. Under a *modified any occ* definition, benefits are paid if the disability prevents the insured from working in "any gainful occupation for which he or she is reasonably fitted by education, training, experience, and prior economic status." Thus, our concert violinist would not be expected to flip burgers before getting any disability benefits. However, she might be expected to give violin lessons if the nature of her disability permitted it. Modified any occ is a commendable effort by the insurance industry to bridge the gap between own occ and any occ, but it still leaves a large area of potential risk exposure for the insured. Since insurance is supposed to reduce risk, why do only part of the job?

The second compromise uses a split definition of occupation. Under this approach, the policy uses an own occ standard for the first x years (usually five years), and then reverts to a modified any occ definition thereafter. This is an improvement over a straight modified any occ policy, but the protection remains incomplete. What happens, for example, if in year six our violinist and her insurer disagree over whether her disability prevents her from teaching the violin? If you are in a skilled trade or profession, you should try to purchase own occ coverage. Having said this, however, it should be reiterated that own occ policies are becoming difficult to find in today's insurance marketplace, and the split definition approach may be all that's available to you.

Renewability

Like most other forms of insurance, disability policies are in force only for specified periods of time, usually one year. At the end of the year, the policy may or may not be renewed by the insurance company, either at the same price or at a different price. As a policyholder, you want some assurances in your policy that you will have the right to renew the policy when it expires, that you will be able to do so at a reasonable price, and that the insurance company cannot decline to renew you (because, for example, your health has deteriorated).

There are several approaches to the issue of policy renewability that insurers may offer, and some of them are not in your best interest. The worst option, from your perspective, is a *cancelable* policy, which the insurance company can terminate at any time. This type of policy is virtually useless to you. The next policy level is *renewable* at the company's option, which also provides you with no guarantee that you will be able to renew the policy at the end of its term. The next approach to renewability is through a policy that is *conditionally renewable.* Here, the insurance company can only decline to renew the policy for another term under a certain set of conditions specified in the insurance contract. At the next level of *guaranteed renewable,* the insurance company must renew the policy if you ask it to, but it is permitted to raise the premium it charges you based on group experience. This means that if the insurance company wants to raise prices for a whole class of insureds, it may do so, but it can't single you out for a rate hike. This is an acceptable approach to renewability. It is becoming the best option available from an increasing number of insurance companies.

The best renewability feature from the policyholder's perspective, is a *noncancelable* policy. This type of policy gives you both the right to renew and a guarantee that your premium won't change for a certain number of years. You might have to pay a lot of money for this high level of protection, and an increasing number of companies don't even offer noncancelable policies. If you can't find or can't afford noncancelable insurance, guaranteed renewable is an acceptable alternative, but don't settle for anything less.

Waiting Period

The *waiting period* before disability benefits begin also is referred to as the *elimination period.* Basically it refers to how long you have to wait after becoming disabled before benefits begin to be paid. Ninety days is a standard waiting period, but the insurance company generally lets you decide how long you want to wait when writing the contract. You can go as low as 30 days, but it probably isn't worth the extra premiums you'd pay. Similarly, by going beyond 90 days you can trim your premium costs a little. However, you need to weigh the premium savings against your ability to keep your cash flow going for more than three months while waiting for benefits to begin. If you've got a solid emergency fund, a longer waiting period may be appropriate.

Inflation

Unless you purchase an inflation adjustment, the amount of your benefit will be the same in your sixtieth month of disability as it was in your sixth month. It is essential that your policy include a cost-of-living adjustment to ensure that your benefits keep pace with inflation. This is additional coverage for which you will have to pay extra, but it is fairly essential to the purpose of disability insurance (replacing your income stream) that your benefits increase for inflation the way your income presumably would have.

Waiver of Premium

Although it may seem illogical, you are required to continue paying monthly premiums for disability insurance even while you are receiving benefits under the policy. For a nominal additional monthly charge (or sometimes no additional charge), the insurance company will agree to waive the premium in the event you become disabled. This is a very smart move at a very low cost. Without it, you could have to use part of your disability benefits to keep up the premium payments on your policy.

Definition of Illness

In most policies, an illness must occur or become known after the policy becomes effective in order to qualify for benefits. This is usually accomplished by language in the policy requiring that the illness become *first manifest* after the insurance's effective date. However, some policies use language that refers to when an illness *is first contracted* or *begins.* Under such a policy, benefits can be denied for an illness contracted before the policy is in force, even if nobody knew of its existence until well after the policy is in effect. This can produce particularly harsh results in the case of illnesses with long dormant periods, such as HIV. Review your policy carefully to be certain that it covers illnesses when they are first manifest and not when they are first contracted or when they begin.

OUR ISSUES

Our risk of financial loss resulting from disability is pretty much the same as everybody else's. The risk of disability is both greater than and more overlooked than virtually any other insurable risk—gay or straight. For some people, disability insurance may even be a higher priority than life insurance. If you're young and healthy, you're likely to need disability insurance sooner than life insurance. This isn't to suggest that life and disability insurance should be an either/or decision. You probably have a need for both.

One aspect of disability that may affect lesbian and gay people slightly differently is that for some, the additional expenses associated with disability may be higher than average. For those of us who have been estranged from our extended families, the ongoing familial care and support (financial and emotional) usually forthcoming in the event of a crisis such as disability isn't likely to be there. If you aren't sure who'd help you were you to become disabled, there's a good chance you might have to pay for some of that help. If this applies to you, you should tend toward the high side of the 60 percent to 80 percent range discussed throughout this chapter.

A final thought: Remember that disability does not always mean HIV. Although we frequently live in a world of red ribbons and purple lesions, it's important to keep in mind that we too can get hit by buses and thrown from horses. Although HIV provides an added dimension of disability risk for part of our community, we also must be mindful of the thousands of other sources of risk we share with the dominant culture.

RELATED TOPICS

If you need to shop for private disability insurance, it's important to know what to look for in a company as well as a policy. The criteria for selecting a good insurance company are discussed in the "Understanding Risk Management" section on page 33.

The procedures for requesting a Personal Earnings and Benefit Estimate Statement from the Social Security Administration are explained in the "Social Security Retirement Benefits" section on page 262. The section also gives you a (very) rough idea of how SSA uses your age and earnings record to compute benefits. Although it treats retirement benefits, the procedure is similar for disability benefits.

HEALTH INSURANCE

THE STRAIGHT FACTS

Health care and the availability of health insurance remain very much on the national agenda. Despite the deserved attention these topics have received, however, the vast majority of Americans receive health insurance coverage as a fringe benefit from their employers. Nevertheless, the significant expenses associated with health care treatment represent a major issue for many Americans. People are either concerned about obtaining health insurance coverage to protect against those risks, the adequacy of their coverage, or maintaining coverage in an increasingly uncertain job market.

The two types of health insurance coverage common in America today are comprehensive major medical plans and managed care plans (such as health maintenance organizations and preferred provider organizations). This section reviews the major features of each plan and discusses ways to minimize the uncertainty of the current environment.

Comprehensive Major Medical Plans

Comprehensive major medical plans are the traditional form of health insurance coverage. There is a wide variety of coverage offered by the various major medical plans. In the absence of a standard policy format, each policyholder must read and understand the terms of his or her policy. The following are the important features you'll want to focus on when evaluating a plan.

Exclusions

Subject to the various payment limitations contained in other parts of the policy, most comprehensive major medical policies cover any medical service they don't specifically list as excluded. The exclusions section of the policy therefore requires careful reading. Health insurers are drafting increasingly expansive lists of exclusions into their policies. For example, almost all policies exclude coverage for experimental treatments.

Pre-Existing Conditions

A pre-existing conditions clause generally excludes coverage for a stated period of time (usually six to twelve months) for medical conditions that are already being treated (or already should be under treatment) when the policy begins. Pre-existing conditions can create real problems for people with chronic illnesses (e.g, asthma) who switch insurance companies—for example, when they switch jobs. Sometimes it makes economic sense for people to continue purchasing coverage under their old plan until the pre-existing conditions period under their new plan passes. This is done by exercising so-called COBRA rights, which are explained later in this section.

Utilization Review

Utilization review is insurance-speak for a requirement that you check with the company before undergoing certain medical procedures. The purpose of utilization review is to help the insurance company control its costs. Utilization reviews take one of two common forms. Under the first form, precertification, the policyholder must obtain prior approval from the insurance company for any hospital stay or surgical procedure. Failure to obtain precertification can result either in a denial of benefits or in benefits being reimbursed at a lower rate. Emergencies usually are excluded from this requirement, although policies containing this form of utilization review generally require policyholders to notify their insurers within 24 hours of an emergency hospital admission. Case management is the second form of utilization review. It involves the assignment of an insurance company employee to "manage" the treatment of cases involving serious and expensive illnesses such as cancer or AIDS.

Reimbursement Amounts
Insurance companies decide how much to reimburse for a given procedure based on their understanding of the average fees charged for the service in the policyholder's area. The insurance company determines these fees through surveys and other forms of research. The fees a company will permit are then set out in its *usual, customary, and reasonable (UCR)* fee table. Any fees a policyholder incurs in excess of the amounts in the UCR table generally are not reimbursed by the company. UCR tables are set at a local level, so reimbursement rates usually are appropriate for a policyholder's geographic location. Reputable insurance companies try to keep their UCR tables current and competitive.

Maximum Benefits and Policy Limits
Many policies specify a lifetime maximum on the amount of benefits they will pay out. Often this figure is very high (e.g., $1 million), but a low limit may be inadequate to meet the full cost of a very serious illness. Some policies also specify lower limits that apply to particular medical treatments. For example, a policy with a $1 million maximum benefit may also specify a separate $50,000 limit on the expenses associated with rehabilitation treatment programs for alcoholism or drug dependency. Some insurance companies also write lower policy limits for specific illnesses such as AIDS.

Deductibles
A *deductible* is the amount an individual policyholder must pay before he or she becomes eligible for any benefits under the policy. For example, benefits might not be paid until after the policyholder has incurred $200 or $500 in covered medical expenses. One purpose of a deductible is to

prevent policyholders from filing small or insignificant claims. A more important purpose of a deductible in the context of health insurance is to encourage policyholders to exercise financial discipline in purchasing medical services. Higher deductibles generally result in lower premiums, so consider a higher deductible if you're looking for ways to keep down the cost of your coverage.

Coinsurance

Coinsurance is perhaps best thought of as the policyholder's "share" of a covered medical expense. Many policies require that the person insured pay 20 percent of the cost of covered services, while the insurance company pays the other 80 percent. Some policies have even lower coinsurance provisions, meaning policyholders have to pay even more out of their own pockets. A few policies do not require any coinsurance payments. However, coinsurance is becoming an increasingly important way for insurance companies to encourage their policyholders to behave like consumers when making health care purchases.

Stop-Loss Limits

Because the point of insurance is to help individual policyholders avoid catastrophic losses, *stop-loss limits* act like "ceilings" on coinsurance requirements. A stop-loss provision basically says that after you incur x dollars in covered annual medical expenses, the insurance company won't require you to pay any more money for the rest of the year. Don't confuse stop-loss limits with maximum benefits provisions. A stop-loss limit specifies when you get to stop paying for the year. Maximum benefits refers to when the insurance company gets to stop paying for good.

Coordination of Benefits

A *coordination of benefits clause* is the insurance company's way of making sure that a policyholder does not come out ahead as a result of receiving benefits from more than one source. If you are covered by more than one health insurance plan (perhaps because a spouse or domestic partner also has coverage), the plans usually compare notes to make sure you don't receive back more than 100 percent of what you paid out.

Supplemental Coverages

Comprehensive major medical policies may or may not cover the cost of prescription drugs. They generally do not cover dental or vision care.

Dental or vision services usually are covered by a major medical plan only if they are required as a result of an accident (e.g., dental work incident to reconstructive surgery to the mouth necessitated by a head injury). Where these coverages are not provided by the policy, supplemental coverages for these benefits may be available for an additional fee.

Cost-conscious health insurance consumers who cannot afford all supplemental coverages should prioritize their needs, keeping in mind the basic principles of risk management—first insure those risks that threaten to result in catastrophic losses. It is not unusual for prescription drugs for certain serious illnesses to cost hundreds, if not thousands, of dollars each month. Dental and vision expenses, while not insignificant, generally are routine and predictable (and therefore budgetable). For many people trying to stretch scarce insurance dollars, prescription drug coverage will represent a better investment than either dental or vision coverage.

Managed Care

As health expenditures continue to account for an increasing share of the country's gross domestic product (i.e., total output of goods and services), employers and other consumers of these services continue to seek ways to control their costs. Managed care options such as HMOs and PPOs are common ways for doing this.

Health Maintenance Organizations

A *health maintenance organization (HMO)* is an increasingly popular way of obtaining health insurance coverage. In exchange for a monthly fee, the HMO promises to provide an array of medical services in a contract that contains many of the same terms and conditions used in comprehensive major medical plans.

There are important differences between HMOs and major medical plans. HMOs offer the services of only the health care providers who participate in their plans. If a policyholder chooses to seek treatment outside the plan, the expenses generally are not reimbursed. (There sometimes can be exceptions to this rule for emergency treatment, treatment outside the policyholder's geographic area, and outside treatment specifically authorized by the HMO.) On the plus side, HMOs frequently provide broader coverage for preventive care (e.g., physical examinations, well baby programs) than do most comprehensive major medical plans. The other major advantage of HMOs is that, since they have a greater ability to control costs, the fees they charge their policyholders can be considerably less than those paid for major medical coverage. On the downside, HMOs limit a policyholder's choice of health care providers to those within its system. Also, some HMOs require you to see a generalist before getting an appointment with a specialist, even when it's painfully apparent that you need specialized treatment.

There are two types of HMOs. Under the first type, the health care professionals are all employees of the organization. This is referred to in the health care field as the *staff model* HMO, and it's the type of organization most of us think of when we hear the acronym HMO. The other type of HMO, the Independent Practice Association (IPA), involves groups or networks of nonaffiliated health care providers who've all agreed to abide by the terms of the HMO contract. IPAs tend to give consumers more flexibility in choosing health care providers than do staff model HMOs.

Preferred Provider Organizations

Preferred provider organizations (PPOs) are seen by some people as the health insurance industry's response to the increasing popularity of HMOs. More so than HMOs, PPOs function largely like major medical policies, containing most of the same features described earlier in this section. There are, however, a few additional features. In a PPO, the insurance company organizes a network of health care providers, much like the IPA-model HMO. Health care providers within the PPO network negotiate reduced fees with the insurance company administering the PPO in exchange for rapid payment and the advantage of being on the preferred provider list. When a policyholder goes to a provider within the PPO network, he or she pays only a nominal coinsurance amount (usually a flat fee of $5 to $15), and is not required to submit any paperwork to the insurance company. In theory, the insurance company benefits from controlled costs, the health care provider benefits from being in the network, and the policyholder benefits from lower premium and coinsurance payments.

One drawback to the PPO arises when the policyholder wants to go outside the network. Usually the coinsurance percentage payable by the policyholder is higher for out-of-network services. For example, a $5 coinsurance requirement for a visit to an in-network physician could turn into a 30 percent copayment for services outside the network. Another drawback is that PPOs, like major medical plans, tend to be less generous with preventive care benefits than HMOs.

OTHER ISSUES

Other Types of Plans

Keep in mind that there are other types of health insurance policies available. While they usually don't offer very good value for the insurance dollar and you'll probably want to avoid them, it's important to know that they exist. Some plans offer less comprehensive coverage than do major medical care, and a few limit their applicability only to specified "dread diseases." Some insurance companies separate their major medical coverage from their basic coverage. These policies present unnecessary risks of gaps in coverage.

Shopping for Insurance

If you're not fortunate enough to receive health insurance coverage through your employer, you can take some steps to find quality, cost-effective insurance. First, contact a trade or professional association that represents your line of work. It can be a good source of cost-effective coverage or at least referrals. If that doesn't work, consider a local civic or business league or fraternal or community organization. Sometimes these groups also sponsor plans. Next, request a high deductible when buying insurance. If you increase the amount of the expense you're willing to bear, the insurance company will decrease the amount of money it charges you. Remember to insure against catastrophic losses first, and prioritize the coverages you want. As we saw above, prescription drug coverage is often a smarter insurance buy than vision or dental care. Finally, if affordable coverage still remains elusive, consider going the HMO route. HMOs generally are more cost-effective than private insurance plans and often will contract directly with the general public.

Supplementing Inadequate Coverage

If you are covered by an employer's health insurance plan but are concerned about the adequacy of your coverage, you can take steps to increase your available coverage or at least to stretch your insurance dollar. (You can take some of these steps even if you buy your own insurance and you're concerned about the adequacy of its coverage.)

First, contact your employee benefits department to find out if it's possible to purchase supplemental coverages yourself. There's a small chance something may be available that you don't know about.

Next, consider the HMO option. Generally, your employer is required to offer you the option of an HMO if it provides a traditional health insurance plan. (This requirement does not apply to employers with fewer than 10 employees.) You probably will find that you are able to get broader coverage from an HMO than through a private insurance plan.

The final strategy, while technically not insurance, is an important way of controlling health care costs. The tax law allows employers to offer employees, through *cafeteria plans,* the option of setting aside a certain amount of their salaries on a pretax basis to be used for out-of-pocket medical expenses. These plans are usually called Flexible Spending Accounts (FSAs) or Medical Spending Accounts (MSAs). (Employers also can offer this type of account for child care expenses.) The advantage of these accounts is that you don't pay income tax on the money you put into them. When you incur unreimbursed out-of-pocket medical expenses, you simply ask the people administering your FSA to reimburse you from your own funds. The expenses paid out of an FSA effectively are subsidized by Uncle Sam, lowering your overall health care costs. The disadvantage of these accounts is that if there's any unspent money left in them at the end of the year, it's forfeited—so plan carefully. Usually forfeited funds go to a charity designated by the employer (for which you cannot claim an income tax deduction). These accounts are an important way to save on heath care. If your employer offers one, you should be participating judiciously. If your employer doesn't offer one, ask why not. They're a great way to provide an attractive, low-cost fringe benefit.

Continuing Benefits When You Leave Your Job—COBRA

When you leave an employer, your health insurance benefits usually terminate. However, a federal law, known by the acronym COBRA requires your employer to permit you to continue purchasing insurance at your own expense for 18 months after you leave, regardless of whose decision it was for you to go. In some instances, the 18 months is extended to 36 months. Your employer must notify you of this right when you leave.

COBRA benefits are important for two reasons. First, they can be an excellent source of interim health insurance coverage for people between jobs or for entrepreneurs striking out on their own. COBRA makes employment transitions smoother and less stressful and increases the availability of health insurance coverage for many people. Second, COBRA benefits are an important way for people with chronic and expensive medical conditions to maintain health insurance coverage when switching jobs. If the economics make sense, people in this situation should elect COBRA coverage through their former employer for the length of the pre-existing conditions period in their new employer's health plan. COBRA can protect some people with pre-existing conditions from feeling trapped in a job just for the sake of retaining insurance coverage.

OUR ISSUES

Domestic Partner Benefits

The lesbian and gay community uses the term *domestic partner benefits* to apply to a wide range of employee fringe benefits that recognize the legitimacy of our alternative family relationships. Bereavement leave on the death of a significant other, inclusion of domestic partners in company-sponsored events open to employees' families, and the granting of leave to provide care for a domestic partner who is ill are examples of such fringe benefits. Of all the fringe benefits available, however, perhaps none has a more immediate and tangible economic impact on lesbian and gay employees than health insurance coverage for their domestic partners.

Most, but not all, employees who receive health insurance as a fringe benefit are also offered coverage for their family members. The definition of "family" until recently never contemplated the alternative family structures established by lesbians and gay men. Indeed, the traditional concept of family creates some important negative tax consequences for lesbian and gay couples who do take advantage of domestic partnership health insurance benefits when they're available. These consequences are explained in the discussion of "Income Tax Basics" in the Tax Planning chapter.

Fortunately, this entire area is one of slow but significant change for our community. Hundreds of employers now provide coverage for the domestic partners of their lesbian and gay employees. Interestingly, many of the employers who offer this coverage do not make it available to the unmarried domestic partners of their heterosexual employees, reasoning that these individuals have the option of marrying if they really wish to receive such benefits. Experts familiar with the employee benefits area expect that the trend toward domestic partner benefits for lesbian and gay employees will grow in the years ahead.

Because coverage for domestic partners is so new, there is no standard procedure to qualify for domestic partner benefits. Most employers require employees seeking domestic partnership benefits to sign a declaration indicating that the person they seek to cover is in fact a "domestic partner" (however the employer chooses to define that term) and provide some tangible evidence of comingled assets, such as a deed to a house or a joint checking account. After these requirements are met, coverage usually begins immediately, subject to much the same terms and conditions as for anyone else.

Many employers and, more importantly, the insurance companies from whom they bought their health insurance coverage, initially were concerned about the potential cost of providing domestic partner benefits. AIDS no doubt fueled this fear. But most employers have experienced lower-than-anticipated costs for providing domestic partner health benefits. First, for a host of reasons, some of which probably are more apparent to our community than to our employers, fewer people than estimated actually have signed up for such benefits. Next, experience shows that those applying for benefits tend to be younger employees, and younger people generally tend to consume fewer health resources than do older people. Third, to the extent that gay men present above-average risks associated with AIDS, the below-average risk in the lesbian community provides an overall balance. Finally, the likelihood that we will take advantage of pregnancy benefits or coverage for dependent children is small. Overall, the experience of employers who've chosen to adopt domestic partner programs has proven to be a win-win one.

A final thought on domestic partner benefits. If both you and your partner have individual health insurance coverage, do the math carefully before signing up for domestic partner benefits. It's possible the tax imposed on these benefits will outweigh the value of the additional coverage. Domestic partner benefits usually make sense only when one partner has no health insurance or has grossly inadequate coverage. The tax considerations of domestic partner benefits are explained in the discussion of "Income Tax Basics" later in this book.

AIDS

AIDS continues to present a significant set of issues for a significant portion of our community. One of the most important of these issues is the affordability of the health care expenses associated with treating both

AIDS and HIV. People who do not have insurance coverage when they are diagnosed either as HIV-positive or as having AIDS are unlikely to obtain it on their own. In addition, even those with health insurance coverage must be concerned about the duration and adequacy of that coverage as the disease progresses.

Unfortunately, there are few good answers for individuals in this situation. For many, government-sponsored programs such as Medicaid become the only option. Still, there are a few strategies people in this difficult situation should be sure to explore.

First, if you have coverage through your employer you should be certain to exercise your COBRA rights, discussed above, and continue coverage for 18 months when AIDS forces you to stop working. You also should investigate the possibility of converting your coverage to individual coverage when your COBRA period expires. This occasionally is an option in plans covering large groups of employees.

HIV-positive individuals should explore fully whether a change in employers will cause them to lose coverage for AIDS-related health expenses under their new employer's health insurance policy, either as a result of a pre-existing conditions clause, a low maximum benefits clause applicable to AIDS, or some other specific exclusion in the plan. Obviously this can be an awkward topic to investigate in the context of interviewing with a prospective employer, especially since seeking this information tends to disclose a huge amount of highly personal information very early in a potential relationship. But there are potentially enormous risks you need to understand before making a move. There are plenty of HIV-positive individuals who would label themselves "slaves" to their employer, or more accurately, to their employer's health benefits.

Also keep in mind the importance of coverage for prescription drug expenses in the HIV context. Some AIDS-related drug therapies cost thousands of dollars each month. To the extent that you're able, you need to factor this into your planning.

Now that we've touched on the down-side of AIDS and health insurance coverage, let's consider briefly a positive possibility. In a few well-orchestrated situations, it may be possible that finding a new employer actually offers the possibility of access to health insurance coverage for people with HIV. Particularly with large employer and public sector plans, the often generous coverage negotiated with insurance carriers may actually allow for people with AIDS or HIV to obtain coverage. Clearly, the plan will determine the nature and scope of any such coverage, but being included with a group through employment-based coverage is a possibility for some. You're probably not going to be able to pull a fast one on any insurance company, and that's not what's being recommended. Certain plans cover such large groups that HIV has already been factored into the actuarial mix. Accordingly, large groups ask no health questions of new employees who sign up for health care benefits in a timely manner.

Let's conclude by stressing that, if you face this difficult situation, the AIDS advocacy organizations in your area are the best sources of information to help you handle the many aspects of living with HIV, including finances and insurance.

RELATED TOPICS

If you're in the market for private health insurance, it's important to know what to look for in an insurance company. Tips for choosing a carrier are offered in the "Understanding Risk Management" section starting on page 33.

The treatment of medical expenses as deductions for income tax purposes is outlined in the "Income Tax Basics" section on page 168.

For lesbian and gay couples who have joint health insurance coverage through one partner's employer, there is a unique income tax twist to this coverage that requires part of the value of the benefit to be included in income. It is explained in the "Health Insurance" section on page 177.

Paying the medical expenses of another person represents an important and underutilized exception to the gift tax rules. The requirements for this strategy are detailed in the "Gifts" section on page 323.

Health insurance changes considerably when an individual turns 65. This is discussed in the "Health Insurance after 65" section, below.

Serious illness may limit or eliminate your ability to earn a living. Disability is a serious and often unacknowledged risk faced by all working people. Insuring against it is explained in the "Disability Insurance" section on page 60.

HEALTH INSURANCE AFTER 65

THE STRAIGHT FACTS

Piecing together adequate coverage to insure against the risk of financial loss from health care expenses after age 65 can be a daunting task. At the same time, health expenses increase as we get older, making the need for insurance coverage as a risk management technique more acute. The four key components of postretirement health insurance are

1. Medicare, the government-sponsored retiree health insurance that provides the basis of all retirement health coverage.
2. Medi-Gap policies, which attempt to fill in some of the gaps in the coverage Medicare provides.
3. Long-term care coverage, specifically excluded from both Medicare and Medi-Gap insurance, which is intended to protect against the high financial costs of nursing home or similar care.
4. Medicaid, which offers public assistance for seniors of limited means who cannot afford to supplement their Medicare coverage.

While no one piece likely will be adequate to meet all your needs, some of these coverages are certain to be in your arsenal. It's important for you to understand the basic functions of each coverage.

Medicare

Medicare is the government-sponsored program providing near-universal health care coverage for Americans over age 65. There are many aspects to this complex program—deductibles, copayments, excluded services, and so on. Entire books have been written on the depth and breadth of the benefits Medicare provides. Here we'll touch on the basic structure of the program and its major features.

Medicare provides health insurance coverage through two separate programs: Part A and Part B. Part A provides hospital insurance coverage, including benefits for in-patient hospital care, skilled nursing care, home health care, and hospice care. There are limits on how much Part A pays for each of these services, as well as for how long they are covered. Hospitalization coverage, for example, starts phasing out once a stay exceeds 60 days and is completely eliminated if you're not discharged within 150 days. Similarly, benefits for services you receive from a skilled nursing facility phase out after 100 days. You are responsible for any costs not covered by Part A. Part A coverage is available to anyone who qualifies for Social Security retirement benefits (as well as the dependents of those who qualify for Social Security retirement benefits). Qualifying for this coverage is explained in the discussion of Social Security retirement benefits in the chapter on Retirement Planning.

Medicare Part B provides supplemental medical insurance for a variety of health-related services.

1. Medical expenses such as doctors' fees, in- and out-patient medical and surgical services and supplies, physical and speech therapy, and diagnostic services.
2. Clinical laboratory services including blood tests and urinalysis.
3. Home health care such as part-time skilled care, home health aides, and medical equipment and supplies (but only if you meet certain conditions imposed by the Medicare laws).
4. Outpatient hospital treatment.
5. Blood.

Again, there are limits on the extent of coverage Medicare will provide for these services. For some services, Part B requires you to pay a 20 percent coinsurance amount. (If the term *coinsurance* seems unfamiliar to you, the concept is explained in the last section's discussion of "Health Insurance.") Part B also requires the payment of a small monthly premium. Part B coverage is optional, and you must enroll with the Social Security Administration (SSA) to participate in the program. Of course, Part B offers an unbeatable deal, and enrollment is nearly universal. You should contact SSA three months before your 65th birthday to enroll.

Services not covered by Medicare include long-term custodial care for people who need help with the so-called activities of daily living such as eating, dressing, and bathing; experimental drugs and medical procedures; treatment outside the country; and any procedure Medicare doesn't consider "reasonable and necessary." You either must obtain additional insurance coverage for these services or pay for them yourself. Of these uncovered services, the expenses associated with long-term care probably represent the most significant risk exposure for most senior citizens.

From a risk management perspective, it's important to note that Medicare provides an important source of health insurance coverage but that it is not a complete solution. You must develop strategies to deal with the costs above the amounts covered by Medicare, as well as the services not covered by Medicare.

Medi-Gap Policies

Medi-Gap policies are privately sold insurance policies intended to fill in the gaps in the health insurance coverage provided by Medicare. Because seniors sometimes can be easy prey for high pressure or misleading sales tactics, the government has become very involved in the design and marketing of Medi-Gap policies. The 10 types of standardized Medi-Gap policies sold are labeled A through J. Each state decides which plans can be sold in its state, but all the plans allowed are the same from every company. This means insurers must compete on price and service alone. Medi-Gap coverage also is available from some HMOs, but you are obligated to use the HMO's services and play by its rules, discussed in the previous section of this chapter.

Medi-Gap Plan A offers basic coverage. The other plans add optional benefits to Plan A coverage. Medi-Gap Plan A picks up the Part A hospital coverage and the Part B coinsurance expenses that Medicare doesn't pay. Plans B through J offer various combinations of optional coverage for expenses, ranging from paying Medicare's deductible requirements where they're imposed and paying the coinsurance on skilled nursing facility expenses to covering foreign travel emergencies and paying for preventive medical care.

Insurers are permitted to deny benefits to their policyholders for services rendered to treat pre-existing conditions, but only through the first six months of coverage.

You should apply for Medi-Gap coverage at the same time you elect coverage under Medicare Part B. If you apply within six months of your Part B eligibility, insurance companies are required to sell you the Plan (A–J) you want, even if you have health problems that put you in a high-risk category. If you wait more than six months, the insurance company can deny you coverage altogether if you have a pre-existing condition.

Long-Term Care Insurance

The most significant risk exposure not covered by either Medicare or Medi-Gap policies is the cost of long-term nursing home care. To help manage this risk, insurance companies several years ago developed and began marketing long-term care insurance policies. Initially, these policies were not very good. Insurers were unsure of the new market they were entering and were unduly restrictive in what they covered and under what conditions they covered it. The situation has improved considerably, but long-term care insurance is still a comparatively new product. Although experts familiar with the industry predict that policies will likely become more standard in the future, currently there is no uniform format for long-term care policies. This means that it is up to you to review carefully the information about a policy you are considering and to ask a lot of questions. Consider engaging some experienced and objective professional assistance. Some of the features you should look for follow.

Benefit Triggers

The *benefit trigger* is the event(s) or condition(s) specified in the policy that must occur before any benefits are payable under the policy. There are two approaches to triggering benefits currently used: the functional model and the medical model. The functional model usually identifies six *activities of daily living (ADLs)*, and allows benefits to be paid once a policyholder can no longer perform a specified number of them without assistance (usually three out of six). The ADLs are (1) bathing; (2) dressing; (3) eating; (4) transferring (the ability to change positions, such as from bed to a chair); (5) toileting; and (6) continence. Make sure the policy you're looking at defines these terms reasonably and that it doesn't require the loss of too many ADLs before it starts paying benefits (four or more is too many). Some policies omit bathing from their definitions, since it's usually the first ADL to go. In these cases the policy should provide benefits when two of the five other ADLs are lost. A few insurers are experimenting with a seventh ADL, mobility, but it's not clear yet how well this can be distinguished from transferring. The medical model for triggering benefits requires care to be "medically necessary" before benefits are paid. It offers an unduly restrictive definition and should not be accepted.

Level of Care

There are essentially three levels of long-term care: (1) custodial (assistance with ADLs); (2) intermediate (a fuzzy level somewhere between custodial and skilled); and (3) skilled (daily care by trained professionals under physician supervision). The lower levels of care may be provided either at home or in an institutional setting. The higher levels are almost always provided in a nursing home. Your policy should provide benefits for all levels of care, and it should cover both home care and institutional care. Finally, be certain the policy does not require you to use one level of care before qualifying to receive another. A good policy will permit direct access to any level of care. Similarly, watch out for a provision that requires prior hospitalization before it will pay any benefits. This is unacceptable.

Daily Benefit Amount

You purchase long-term care coverage based on the amount of benefits you want to receive each day—$75, $100, $125, and so on. While the daily benefit amount provided by your policy largely is decided by you, the consumer, premiums obviously increase as benefits do. Find out the average price of nursing home coverage in the area you plan to use it and make your decision accordingly. (If you live in Texas but your support network is in California, where are you going to go into a home?) State government agencies, private aging organizations, or a good financial planner usually can provide this information for you.

Length of Benefits

Most policies provide benefits for a specified period of time—one, two, three, or five years, or a lifetime. Obviously, the longer the coverage, the more expensive the premium. Since you know you're only going to need long-term care for a certain period of time, it's important not to overbuy in this regard. Many financial planners recommend a benefit length of three years for two reasons. First, the average nursing home stay is only 30 months, and only 10 percent of those in a home stay for over five years. Second, three years gives people just about enough time to plan to qualify for Medicaid if they choose to do so (this is discussed later in this section).

Inflation Adjustment

Long-term care policies generally are written for specified daily benefit amounts. If the policy is written long before the benefits may be needed, the chances are very good that inflation will erode the value of the benefit amount you've selected. For an additional cost, you can add inflation protection to your policy. If you're a number of years away from the likely need for benefits, it's a good idea to do so. On the other hand, if you're purchasing this insurance close to the time you may need it, consider simply contracting for a slightly larger daily benefit amount. This may be less expensive than opting for inflation protection.

Elimination Period

An *elimination period* is a waiting period before a policy begins paying benefits for covered services. For example, under a 90-day elimination period, you need to receive covered care (such as nursing home care) for

91 days before the policy pays any benefits. Since the purpose of long-term care insurance is to protect against catastrophic losses, it's OK to look for a longer elimination period. It also is an appropriate way to lower the cost of insurance premiums—if insurers can wait longer to start paying, they can charge you less. One hundred days is usually an acceptable elimination period. Remember, however, that translates into $9,000 to $24,000 out-of-pocket (in today's dollars) before benefits begin! Of course, this means your other savings need to be sufficient to cover the first 100 days, so review your finances and plan accordingly.

Pre-Existing Conditions and Excluded Impairments
As with other health insurance policies, long-term care policies sometimes exclude benefits for certain pre-existing conditions or other impairments. In the case of an exclusion for pre-existing conditions, the policy does not pay any benefits for health conditions that were in existence at its effective date until a certain period of time lapses (e.g., six months). Pre-existing conditions clauses are a reasonable way for insurance companies to protect themselves against "buying claims," and a six month exclusion period is probably acceptable for most pre-existing conditions. An excluded impairments clause, in contrast, denies any coverage for conditions such as Alzheimer's Disease, senility, or dementia, regardless of how long you've had them. An excluded impairments clause is not an acceptable policy provision.

Waiver of Premium
When you start collecting benefits under a long-term care policy, you still must pay the premium on your policy. In order to stop making payments when your benefits kick in, you need to be sure your policy contains a *waiver of premium* provision. As the name suggests, this provision waives the payment of premiums when you start receiving long-term care.

One thing all long-term care policies have in common is that they are expensive. The premiums on a good policy can cost about $2,000 per year at age 60, and as much as $5,000 per year at age 75. It's difficult to predict what the long-term care picture will look like 20 or 30 years from now, but note that premiums are significantly lower for people in their late forties and early fifties. Long-term care insurance is an evolving product, and the advice of a knowledgeable and up-to-date expert could prove invaluable in making this expensive investment a good one.

Medicaid

Medicaid enters the retirement health insurance picture in two ways. First, individuals of limited means who cannot afford Medi-Gap insurance and who qualify based on their limited resources can receive Medicaid coverage for most of their health care expenses not covered by Medicare. Second, Medicaid pays the skilled nursing facility (i.e., nursing home) expenses not covered by Medicare or Medi-Gap. This is an important coverage, since neither Medicare nor Medi-Gap provides any benefits for nursing home care beyond 100 days—so-called long-term care. Some seniors are discouraged by the high cost or possibly uncertain coverage connected with long-term care insurance. Accordingly, in recent years increasing numbers of older Americans who generally are not candidates for government assistance have sought to rearrange their financial affairs in order to obtain Medicaid coverage for their long-term care expenses.

While Medicaid generally provides an important safety net for those of limited means, and those who qualify for Medicaid benefits should not hesitate to claim them, reliance on the program for the first use just described in no sense can be considered an adequate or appropriate risk management strategy. With regard to the second use, however, an intense debate currently rages within the legal and financial planning communities regarding whether deliberately planning your affairs in order to qualify for Medicaid is an appropriate and ethical technique.

Medicaid is a combined federal and state government program. Generally, in order to qualify both your assets and your income must be below very limited levels set by your state. While this varies by state, the assets Medicaid will permit you to own and still qualify for coverage are likely to be

1. Your house, regardless of its value.
2. Your household goods, up to about $2,000 (although most states don't check too carefully).
3. Your car, up to about $5,000.
4. A burial plot, up to about $2,000.
5. Life insurance, up to about $1,500.
6. Between about $15,000 and $80,000 in other assets, known as *exempt resources* (the exact amount is set by your state and indexed for inflation each year).

If your assets are too high to qualify, you must wait until they've been "spent down" in order to receive Medicaid coverage. In other words, if you aren't already poor, you have to spend yourself into poverty—in the context being discussed here by paying for nursing home expenses—before you can qualify for Medicaid benefits.

Financial advisors realized that their clients could qualify for Medicaid benefits if they artificially spent down their assets; in other words, if they gave them away to family and friends. This is achieved by a document known as a Medicaid Qualifying Trust (MQT). In an MQT, a person essentially gives up control of her assets to the trust in order to qualify for Medicaid, but grants the trustee authority to make payments on her behalf in the event of an emergency. The assets ultimately are distributed much as they would be under her will when she dies. The loss of control over one's property inherent in MQTs makes them a scary option for some people. However, when faced with the grim reality of long-term nursing home costs, increasing numbers are going the MQT route.

As MQTs have become more popular and more middle- and even upper-income seniors have begun taking advantage of them to preserve their assets for the benefit of children and others, legislators worried about the increased expense to the government have taken notice. They've tried to make it harder for people who "artificially" spend down their assets to qualify for Medicaid, with somewhat mixed results. The way the system currently is set up, you need to wait at least three years after "spending down" your assets (to less than your state's Medicaid qualifying levels) before applying for benefits. Otherwise, the government is entitled to "look back" to see what assets you owned and gave away up to five years prior in determining your eligibility for Medicaid. If you apply too soon and the government finds you've transferred assets within this look-back period, it can require you to spend on your own an amount equal to the transferred assets before it will provide any benefits for you.

With regard to the ethics of spending down to qualify for Medicaid, it's hard to say what's "right" and what's "wrong." In fact, these concepts easily get turned upside down in this debate. Generally, most Americans bristle at the notion of turning to government handouts (as a Medicaid Qualifying Trust undeniably does) in order to insure against financial ruin from the cost of long-term nursing home care. At the same time, however, it probably cannot be seen as fair to expect people who've saved all their lives, perhaps denying themselves indulgences that others have not, to deplete their life savings on nursing home expenses while those who were less disciplined in earlier years are taking advantage of the MQT technique.

The root of the problem lies in a flawed system that encourages people to engage in economically rational but ethically ambiguous activities. And, to be sure, the drive to legally preserve one's assets is an economically rational activity. The dilemma cannot be resolved until the underlying policy issues are responsibly addressed. Meanwhile, we all must make and live with our own imperfect decisions. Wherever you come down on this issue, be certain that it's your views being implemented, not someone else's. Many people, including financial planning professionals, have strong feelings about this subject. Be confident that your wishes are respected.

OUR ISSUES

In some respects, the needs of the lesbian and gay community with regard to health insurance coverage after age 65 mirror those of the dominant culture. However, lesbians and gays have two unique considerations. First, some of the strategies discussed apply largely to incapacity planning at any age, not just over age 65. This is an important point for those in our community who must plan for the expenses associated with HIV. Much of the information and several of the planning strategies discussed may be of help to you whether you're 65 or not. Particular attention should be paid to the strategies for managing the risks associated with the cost of long-term care (i.e., long-term care insurance and Medicaid qualifying trusts).

Second, you'll hear often in this book that lesbian and gay people may not have access to the familial and financial support network in their golden years that is available to most other people. Only a few of us will be able to rely on our children for help. Without such resources, we have extra planning to do, and we may need to plan to pay for more care than most people. If this rings true for you, take a harder-than-average look at the long-term care insurance option. Although the product is fairly new, it may well be coverage particularly suited to the needs of our community.

RELATED TOPICS

If you are considering long-term care insurance, it's critical that you pick a financially strong and reputable insurance company. Tips for selecting an insurer appear in the "Understanding Risk Management" section on page 35.

While disability insurance is an important part of the Social Security program, most people tend to think of retirement when they hear the words social security. See the "Social Security Retirement Benefits" section on page 262.

Some provisions of long-term care policies are similar to the provisions in standard major medical insurance policies. Review the "Health Insurance" section on page 65 for detail on some of the terminology used in this section.

In some respects, long-term care insurance can be viewed as a component of incapacity planning. For another key aspect of this planning see "Advance Directives (Living Wills) and Health Care Powers" on page 354.

Understanding how trusts work is important to making an informed decision about whether or not to use a Medicaid qualifying trust. See the "Trusts" section on page 311.

HOMEOWNER'S INSURANCE

THE STRAIGHT FACTS

In the aggregate, your home and its contents are likely to represent your single most important investment. Loss to that investment as a result of damage from one or more sources of risk could be emotionally and financially devastating. The insurance industry offers six separate forms of homeowners insurance for six separate risks. The risks are

1. Damage to your dwelling.
2. Damage to other structures on the property (e.g., a shed).
3. Damage to contents.
4. Damage for loss of use.
5. Liability for injuries to others.
6. Medical expenses of others and damage to property of others arising on your property.

The six forms of homeowner's insurance are tailored to different sets of needs and provide different levels of coverage (or sometimes no coverage at all) for each of these risks. For convenience, we'll group the six forms into three categories: homeowner's insurance, condominium owner's insurance, and renter's insurance.

Homeowner's Insurance

There are four forms of homeowner's insurance for the traditional single-family home, each designed to serve a different need. In about half the states, each comes with its own name and special insurance industry code number beginning with the letters HO. The code number appears prominently on your policy and can help you quickly identify what you're buying. We'll note the code number for each of the policies we discuss.

The first three types of homeowner's insurance provide protection against increasingly broad categories of damage to your dwelling. Basic coverage (HO-1) protects against damage to your property from ten specific perils.

1. Fire and lightning.

2. Windstorm and hail.

3. Explosion.

4. Riot and civil commotion.

5. Vehicles.

6. Aircraft.

7. Smoke.

8. Vandalism and malicious mischief.

9. Breakage of glass.

10. Theft.

Broad Form coverage (HO-2) adds the following seven perils to the HO-1 list.

1. Falling objects.

2. Weight of ice, snow, or sleet.

3. Collapse of buildings.

4. Accidental discharge or overflow of water or steam.

5. Explosion of steam or hot water system.

6. Freezing of plumbing systems, heating and air conditioning systems, and appliances.

7. Damage from artificially-generated electrical currents.

Open Perils coverage (HO-3) insures you against damage from any source not specifically excluded in writing in the insurance contract. Floods and earthquakes are the two most common exclusions from open perils coverage (although, for an additional premium, you usually can obtain special endorsements, sometimes known as riders, to insure against these risks). There should be no question in your mind that HO-3 offers the best protection and is the type of coverage you should be looking for. Anyone who's serious enough about financial planning to be reading this book cannot believe that homeowner's insurance is a good place to cut corners—can they?

The fourth form of homeowner's insurance (HO-8) provides a basic level of protection for people with older residences where the cost to rebuild or replace the dwelling far exceeds its fair market value. This sometimes happens with older homes in rural areas where property values haven't kept up with building costs. It also happens in inner-city houses where the oak molding, marble window sills, and lathe and plaster walls that characterized construction from an earlier era would cost more to replace than the overall market value of the house. Under HO-8 coverage, the insured receives only the actual cash value of the property damaged or destroyed, rather than the usual replacement value. Coverage also is limited to the 10 perils named in HO-1 policies. While this coverage may seem unduly limited, insurance companies cannot be in the business of creating situations where people are able to collect more through insurance than a property is worth undamaged. If you think about this, you'll see how it might encourage certain inappropriate behaviors. Before the availability of HO-8, homeowners in these situations often were unable to obtain any insurance at all, so HO-8 is something of an improvement.

How much coverage do you need? You should insure your home for a minimum of 80 percent of its replacement cost, but preferably for its full replacement cost (i.e., 100 percent). Discuss this carefully with your financial planner, broker, and/or agent, and make certain you see in writing that your coverage is for replacement cost. Remember that even if your house were to burn to the ground, the land would still be worth something. If you're using the amount you paid for your house as a gauge for deciding how much insurance coverage you need, be sure only to insure the value of the structure. Also, if you make any additions or improvements to your house, be sure to increase the amount of your coverage to reflect the value of those changes.

Keep in mind, too, that the coverage provided for damage to other structures, damage to contents, and damage from loss of use are all expressed as a percentage of the coverage you purchase for damage to your dwelling.

EXAMPLE
Under an Open Perils (HO-3), policy, your coverage for loss of use is equal to 20 percent of your coverage for damage to the dwelling. Thus, if you insure your house under an Open Perils policy for $100,000, you will be reimbursed for up to $20,000 in temporary living expenses should damage to your home render it uninhabitable while being repaired.

Damage to other structures usually is covered for 10 percent of the amount covered for damage to the dwelling. Damage to contents usually is covered for up to 50 percent of the amount covered for damage to the dwelling. However, much lower limits apply to specified types of property such as jewelry, furs, silver, coin collections, and electronics. If additional coverage for these items is required—and it often is—it can and should be obtained at additional cost through a special endorsement or rider, discussed below.

Condominium Owner's Insurance

When you own a condominium, you need to insure its contents (i.e., your personal property) for loss or damage. But did you know that you—not the condo association—are responsible for damage or loss to the fixtures in your condo and its interior walls? If a fire destroys your kitchen, you're not just buying new dishes, you're also buying new cabinets to keep them in and a new dishwasher to clean them in. If the fire destroys a wall between your kitchen and your dining room, you're also buying a new wall and everything inside it like electrical wires and ventilation ducts. Your condo association is responsible for purchasing insurance to protect against all damage occurring outside your unit. However, you are responsible for insuring everything inside your unit. The risks a condo owner needs to insure against may be steeper than they first appear. Condominium owner's insurance (HO-6) protects against these risks. If you own a condo, you are foolish not to have this insurance. Sometimes it's even a condition of your mortgage that you purchase it.

Renter's Insurance

Renters can insure the contents of their homes through renter's insurance (HO-4). Renter's insurance operates much like condo insurance, except that fixtures, walls, and interior systems like plumbing and wiring aren't covered. They're the landlord's problem, not yours. Renter's insurance usually is surprisingly affordable and provides good value for the money. Far too many renters overlook this important coverage. Don't be one of them.

Inflation Guard

When you buy homeowner's insurance, you specify the amount of coverage you want based on your home's value. But what happens five years from now when your home has gone up 15 percent or 20 percent in value and your insurance coverage has stayed the same? Loss or damage to your property could force you to make up that difference out of your own pocket. To protect against this risk, be certain your homeowner's insurance policy includes an inflation guard to automatically boost the amount of your coverage annually.

Personal Property

Most homeowner's policies include dollar limits on the amount of coverage provided for items such as furs, jewelry, electronic equipment, musical instruments, coin collections, and the like. The dollar limits tend to be fairly low (usually only a small portion of your total personal property coverage), and it's quite likely that they will not provide adequate protection if you own valuable property in any of these categories. Ask your broker or agent about buying extra coverage for these items through a *Scheduled Personal Property Endorsement* (sometimes referred to as a policy *rider*). Be sure to cover these items for their full replacement value, and be sure your inflation guard applies to them, too.

Also note that motor vehicles are not considered personal property and must be insured separately through an auto insurance policy.

Inventory

It's a good idea to prepare an inventory of what's in your house. With an inventory, it's easy to outline for the insurance company what you lost, should you ever have to. Receipts for unusually expensive items should be kept with the inventory, preferably in a fireproof strong box or a safety deposit box. Using a video camera is a great way to make an inventory. Simply take a slow walking tour through your entire house, describing the contents room by room, wall by wall, and closet by closet. Provide extra detail for items of unusual value. Keep the tape in a safe place, and update the video inventory once every couple of years. If you don't have a video camera, rent one from the local video store; this actually can be an entertaining rainy day project!

Liability Insurance

The other important aspect of homeowner's insurance is the protection it provides in the event someone is injured on your property, or if you are accused of causing a loss or emotional trauma. You decide the amount of this coverage in consultation with your financial planner, agent, and/or broker. Generally, you should purchase at least $300,000 in coverage for this risk. If you live in an affluent or high-cost area, even this amount may be low.

OUR ISSUES

If you own a home jointly with a significant other or another alternative family member, be certain that everybody's protected under your home-owner's policy. The names of both owners should be on the policy. To ensure proper coverage, you may need an extra endorsement or renter's insurance if one partner (or roommate) is a nonowner. Be sure you're dealing with a sensitive, well-informed broker or agent, and candidly explain your situation. He or she is in the best position to tell you what you need to do to protect everybody.

RELATED TOPICS

Before insuring a home, you have to buy it. The home-buying process is explained in the "Buying a House" section on page 19.

Owning a home offers several important tax-saving opportunities. They are explained in the "Tax Deductions from Your Home" section on page 180.

When selling your home, there can be ways to defer or eliminate taxes on the gain from the sale. You need to understand how the rules governing these strategies work before you sell. They are detailed in the "Tax Planning When Selling a Home" section on page 225.

If you own a home with a friend or loved one, how you both hold title to the home can have an important impact on how easy it is for him or her to inherit it when you die. Minimizing the headaches that can arise in this difficult situation is explained in the "Joint Ownership of Property" section on page 309.

If you are well off, the liability coverage provided by your home-owner's policy may not be sufficient to protect you against someone who's been injured on your property and decided to sue you. To help protect against such a risk, see the "Umbrella Coverage" section on page 99.

AUTOMOBILE INSURANCE

THE STRAIGHT FACTS

The insurance industry has divided the risks associated with the owner-ship or operation of an automobile into three categories:

1. Legal liability to others.
2. Physical injury to oneself or other family members in the auto-mobile.
3. Damage to or loss of your vehicle.

Each of these risks can and should be covered by an automobile insur-ance policy.

Car insurance varies widely from state to state. Some states require their resident drivers to obtain no fault insurance. Under this system, all drivers essentially insure themselves, but only for the first risk listed above. In the event of an accident, each insured files a claim against his or her own insurance policy for damages. No fault laws usually specify a minimum amount of liability insurance coverage each driver must pur-chase. In states without no fault laws, minimum coverage amounts vary widely and may not exist at all. In all states, whatever requirements do exist truly emphasize the "minimum" part of the term minimum cover-age. Note that none of these requirements apply to the second or third risks identified at the beginning of this section.

Liability

Liability insurance coverage is designed to protect you against the risk of loss arising from injuries to other people or damages to other automobiles resulting from an accident caused by you. The insurance company also agrees to pay for your litigation expenses under this coverage, but in doing so it reserves the right to settle a case whether you think it should or not.

The minimum liability coverage available in most states is about $25,000 per accident. You usually can "buy up" this limit to $50,000, $100,000, $200,000, $300,000, $500,000, or even $1 million. Clearly, the $25,000 minimum probably isn't enough to protect you against the full risk of loss in a catastrophic accident. If you total another driver's brand new car, you could easily exceed that amount in property damage alone, leaving you personally liable for any injuries the other driver sustained. While $1 million in coverage may be excessive, the lower amounts are inadequate. Liability coverage of $300,000 generally is a prudent minimum.

Physical Injury (Medical Payments)

Physical injury (also known as medical payment) coverage provides protection against the expenses associated with medical care needed by you, your family members, or anyone else in your vehicle when you are in an automobile accident. The standard coverage is $1,000 per person, but for a small additional premium this coverage can be increased to $5,000 or $10,000. Although these benefits are coordinated with any health insurance coverage you or your family might have (i.e., you can't get reimbursed above 100 percent of your expenses), it's not hard to imagine reaching $10,000 in qualifying expenses in the event of a serious accident. Therefore, this is one area in which it makes sense to purchase the maximum coverage. This coverage also applies if you are hit by a car while you are a pedestrian, and it also can help pay funeral expenses.

Physical Damage to the Vehicle

Physical damage insurance covers you for any losses sustained as a result of damage to your vehicle. There are usually two components to such coverage. The first is *collision,* for when another object collides with your car. The second is noncollision, also known as *comprehensive,* for when your car is damaged for some other reason—for example, if a tree limb falls on it or it is stolen. Such insurance usually covers you for the actual amount of your losses, but not beyond the total value of your car. In order to discourage people from making small or frivolous claims, insurance companies require that the insured pay for the first X amount of dollars in physical damage. The dollar amount is usually between $50 and $500. This is known as a *deductible.* It is common for policies to have different deductibles for collision and comprehensive coverage.

Most policies provide only nominal coverage for transportation expenses you incur as a result of losing the use of a damaged car while it is being repaired, or a totalled car while you are in the process of replacing it. For an additional charge, you can obtain coverage that will reimburse you for the expense of renting a car while yours is being repaired or replaced. Such coverage may be a good idea for someone without access to another car who is dependent on a vehicle to get to and from work. However, if the coverage works out to more than a couple of dollars a month, the protection offered may not be worth the price paid.

Uninsured Motorist Coverage

What happens if your car is hit by an uninsured driver? People who forgo buying auto insurance usually do so because they are of very limited means. What are the odds that you will collect money directly from such a person to compensate you for your losses? Or what if the other driver's insurance company becomes insolvent three days before he hits you? To guard against these risks, most insurance policies provide uninsured motorist coverage. Generally, the limit of such coverage is as low as state law allows, but you can buy additional coverage up to the amount of your regular liability coverage. You probably don't need quite as much uninsured motorist coverage as you need liability coverage, but you certainly will need more than any state law minimum for liability. Remember, the risk being insured against here is injury to yourself or other occupants of your car and damage to your car caused by an uninsured motorist. Find a comfortable middle ground somewhere between the minimum and the maximum.

A related problem arises when a person is hit by an underinsured motorist. Because such a driver has insurance (just not enough), uninsured motorist coverage won't pay any benefits if you're hit by a driver who lacks adequate insurance. Since the minimum coverage required by most states usually isn't enough to fully cover injuries sustained in a serious accident, underinsured motorists pose a real risk. Underinsured motorist coverage protects against this risk. This optional coverage, usually available only when you've purchased increased uninsured motorist coverage, provides important protection at comparatively nominal costs. Be sure it's included in your policy.

Trimming Auto Insurance Costs

Factors that determine your automobile rates include where you live (and drive your car); your age, sex, and marital status; how you use your car (business, pleasure, commuting); your driving record; what other insurance you have with the same company (multicar discounts and discounts for insuring your car and home with the same company); whether or not you smoke; whether or not your car has an antitheft device; and the amount of coverage you require. While some of these factors are beyond your control (where you live, your age, and your sex), others are not (your driving record, the coverages you require). If you are concerned about the overall cost of your automobile insurance, you can take some steps to keep the price tag down. Be advised, however, that these are not "one-size-fits-all" suggestions. Measure them against your own circumstances to see if they make sense for you. In no particular order, here are some things you might consider doing.

- Shop around. Auto insurance is probably the most competitive of all insurance coverages, and there can be a wide difference in prices. Be sure that you compare identical policy quotes. Also, before switching just to save a couple of dollars, consider the value of maintaining a long relationship with one company that may be less likely to cancel your insurance or boost your rates if you have an accident.

- Consider dropping the physical damage coverage on older cars. The cost of this coverage might be disproportionate to the benefit you'd receive if an old clunker were damaged. You can't get reimbursed for more than the value of your car, even if it would cost more than that amount to get it repaired. This may be a good place to adopt the self-insurance principle, assuming you have sufficient resources to get behind a new set of wheels if your old car is totalled. Obviously, this advice does not apply to antiques or collector's cars, which should always be insured for damage.

- Make sure your insurance company knows if you're a nonsmoker, as some companies give nonsmoker discounts.

- Make sure your insurance company knows if your car has an antitheft device. Some companies give discounts for this, depending on the type of device.

- If you own more than one car, they all should be insured with the same carrier to take advantage of multicar discounts.

- Consider insuring both your house and your car through the same insurance company. Sometimes this can result in a discount.

- Pay attention to your driving record—your insurance company does. If you receive too many citations for speeding or other moving violations, your rates will go up. If you've racked up a few "points" in your state, go easy on the gas pedal; it could save you money, and more . . .

- Consider leaving the car in the driveway and using public transportation to get to work. If you change the use of your car from "commuting" to "pleasure," there's a good chance you'll see a dramatic change in your rates. Don't fudge on this, though. You can't tell your insurer one thing and then do another.
- Consider carpooling. If public transportation isn't an option for you, try carpooling. Some insurance companies give discounts to bona fide carpoolers.
- Ask your insurance company if it has any "safe driving plans" or "good driver discounts." A clean driving record for three to five years usually means a slight decrease in rates. If your record is good, make sure you're getting credit for it. Similarly, sometimes attending an approved "defensive driving" course qualifies you for a small discount.
- Keep track of your mileage. The less you drive each year, the lower your premiums will be. This is especially true if there are two cars in your household. If one of those cars logs under 10,000 miles per year, the savings could be significant.

OUR ISSUES

Gay Couples and Cars

In any relationship the automobile seems to be the last asset to be titled jointly. Houses, bank accounts, and most everything else goes joint before the car does. It's not clear if there's a deeply psychological reason for this—"our cars, like our clothes, are an extension of ourselves"—or if it's just the way things work out, but it does tend to happen this way. In fact, couples in general, and gay couples in particular, should *never* title their automobiles jointly.

There are several reasons for this. First, joint ownership of an automobile by an unmarried couple may make it harder to obtain automobile insurance, or it may require you to purchase insurance at higher rates. The most common form of auto insurance written, the Personal Automobile

Policy (PAP), generally is not available to unmarried co-owners of a car (married couples, of course, qualify). Things are slowly changing. As of this writing, at least one insurance company is preparing to market its homeowner's and auto policies to same-sex couples.

Nevertheless the alternatives most likely available to you will be more limited and more expensive than the PAP. If only one partner owns the car, he or she qualifies for the PAP, and this potential problem is avoided. This isn't an invitation to try to do an end run around your insurance company, however. Be sure the nonowner partner is listed as an "occasional driver" on the policy, or the insurance company may try to deny coverage in the event he or she is responsible for an accident.

Another reason not to own a car jointly is that there is no point in putting two names on an asset that is essentially a rolling invitation to be sued. If both partners own a car and one of them causes an accident while driving it, it is virtually guaranteed that both will be named as defendants if the matter ends up in court. In contrast, if only one person is titled on the car and that person is the one who has the accident, only he or she liable. Moreover, depending on your state's laws, if the liability exposure is catastrophic, this arrangement may even protect other jointly owned assets such as your house or savings from being seized to satisfy a liability.

Although joint ownership is an important estate planning tool for gay couples, automobiles are one instance in which the risks don't outweigh the benefits. Keep each car in one person's name.

RELATED TOPICS

For information about purchasing a car, review the "Buying a Car" section on page 23.

If you have a high net worth, the liability coverage provided by your automobile policy may not be sufficient to protect you against someone you've hit who plans to sue. Read the "Umbrella Coverage" section on page 99 to protect against such a risk.

The recommendation that gay couples not title a car jointly is a rare exception to the general rule that joint ownership is an important estate planning tool for our community. To place this exception in the broader context of its general rule, review the "Joint Ownership of Property" section on page 309.

OTHER TYPES OF INSURANCE

THE STRAIGHT FACTS

There are a few other types of insurance you may run across—or may need to run across—depending on the activities in which you engage. Space limitations of this book prevent detailed discussion of them, but you should be aware of their existence and basic features. If any of these coverages may be appropriate for you, consult a knowledgeable financial planner, agent, and/or broker for more details.

Commercial Insurance

If you own a business, you will need to insure it against loss resulting both from damage to your business property as well as injury to customers or people on your business premises. There are standard forms for such insurance, and a good policy with a well-respected company should protect you against financial loss due to property damage or personal injury. If you are concerned about risks specific to your business or your area, consult a trade association or local business league, which are a source of both good information and good referrals for obtaining coverage. Business insurance is critical if you're self-employed or a partner in a partnership. Your other policies don't cover you against these risks.

One frequently overlooked aspect of insuring your business: If your business premises were damaged by fire, flood, or storm, and you were unable to open, how long could you survive without any sales? Business interruption insurance is available to replace the profits you would lose in the event your business has to shut down as a result of property damage. Most small businesses can't last long when their cash flow is interrupted, and business interruption insurance protects against this risk. Don't overlook this important additional coverage when shopping for commercial insurance.

Liability Insurance

Liability insurance protects you from the risk of loss resulting from legal liability attaching to mistakes you make, usually in your line of work. Doctors' malpractice insurance and lawyers' errors and omissions insurance are examples of liability insurance. Given the litigious nature of our society, virtually every professional and skilled tradesperson should be adequately insured for errors they may make on the job. Architects, plumbers, electricians, landscapers—nobody is immune from being sued anymore. One lawsuit could wipe out your life savings. Even if the suit is frivolous, the legal fees to defend it could seriously erode your net worth. The exposure is sufficiently great that insurance often is the only suitable risk management technique for dealing with it. Your commercial insurance may provide liability coverage, but for many professions, liability coverage is specifically excluded from the commercial policy. If you're concerned or unsure about the exposure you may face or need advice on where to find a good policy for your line of work, consult a trade or professional association affiliated with your industry. They're often a valuable source of information on the risks that apply to you and the resources available to insure against those risks. Liability insurance is particularly important for unincorporated business owners (i.e., sole proprietors and partners).

There is one other source of liability exposure you should be aware of. If you serve as an officer or director of a nonprofit organization, or sometimes even as a volunteer, you risk being sued for the actions the board takes (or fails to take) or for your actions as an officer or volunteer. Any nonprofit you are affiliated with (other than as a contributor) should maintain adequate liability insurance. This insurance is often called *errors and omissions* insurance, or *E&O* insurance. As a director, officer, or involved volunteer, you could be named as a party in a lawsuit, even if your liability is remote or contingent. If the organization doesn't have E&O insurance, there's a good chance it will go broke trying to make everybody whole. This risk is real, and you shouldn't ignore it. If your organization does not have E&O insurance covering its directors, officers, and volunteers, insist that they obtain it, or donate your time to another nonprofit.

Umbrella Coverage

Because insurance companies like to know the total amount of their potential exposure, almost all insurance policies today have lifetime caps on the amount they will pay on your behalf. Regardless of whether it's an auto policy, your homeowner's policy, or your professional liability insurance, there is likely to be a limit as to your liability coverage. While these limits often are extremely high, jury awards for liability claims also tend to be extremely high, perhaps even higher than your policy limits.

To protect against this risk, you can obtain what is known as personal *umbrella liability coverage.* This coverage applies only to liability claims above your base policy limits. You must exhaust your regular insurance coverage before your umbrella policy kicks in. Because the level of coverage is so high, umbrella policies usually are only an issue for people in liability-prone professions (e.g., medicine) or people with very high net worths to protect. There is no standard form for umbrella coverage, so each insurer draws up its own contract. Umbrella policies also tend to provide coverage against a broader set of risks than their underlying basic contracts. For example, an umbrella policy may provide worldwide coverage for personal injury arising from the operation of an automobile, whereas your auto insurance might only apply while driving in the United States. Umbrella coverage also might protect you from litigation arising out of your activities with community or nonprofit organizations, whereas such coverage generally is beyond the scope of your homeowner's policy. You usually have to purchase your umbrella policy from the same company that issued your basic liability policies (e.g., homeowner's and automobile insurance). Talking to the agent or broker who sold you those policies may be a good place to start if you think you may need this form of insurance protection.

OUR ISSUES

As with other forms of liability insurance, it is important that an umbrella policy cover all members of your household and not just family members as that term is traditionally defined. Be certain you're working with an agent or broker who is sensitive to the needs of the lesbian and gay community, who knows your alternative family status (whatever its configuration), and who can find you coverage that protects all the people important in your life.

RELATED TOPICS

Umbrella coverage provides liability protection beyond base coverage from your homeowner's and automobile policies. If you want umbrella coverage, you need to understand the basic coverages discussed in the "Automobile Insurance" section on page 92 and "Homeowner's Insurance" section on page 86.

3

CHAPTER

Investments*

UNDERSTANDING THE INVESTMENT PROCESS

THE STRAIGHT FACTS

The Investment Process

People tend to think of "investors" as rich, high-rolling, jet-set types. However, the truth is that just about everybody is an investor. If you own any assets or receive any income, you make investment decisions about those assets and that income whenever you do something with them—whether or not you think of your choices as investment decisions. Whatever you do with your income or your assets constitutes a decision about how to invest them. Whether it's good or bad, made consciously or by default, it's still an investment decision.

> **EXAMPLE**
> Your semimonthly paycheck is automatically deposited into your checking account. From your checking account you pay your rent, monthly bills, and pocket money for each week. If there's any money left at the end of the month, you leave it in your checking account to help pay next month's bills and expenses. Whether you realize it or not, you've made decisions about

---

* Historical data information on average annual returns for certain asset classes described in this chapter was obtained from © *Stocks, Bonds, Bills and Inflation 1996 Yearbook™*, Ibbotson Associates, Chicago (annually updates work by Roger G. Ibbotson and Rex A. Sinquefield). Used with permission. All rights reserved.

your investment goals (an emergency fund), your time horizon (short), your risk tolerance (low), your desired rate of return (even lower), and your portfolio structure (a checking account).

Notice the reference to "your portfolio structure." Nearly everyone has a portfolio, whether or not we recognize it as such. Your portfolio consists of all the items on the asset side of the balance sheet you constructed in Chapter 1, other than Use Assets.

The value of your portfolio will change over time. This can be caused by one of three factors:

1. The net surplus or shortfall in your cash flow.
2. Assets you give away and assets given to you.
3. Increases or decreases in the value of your assets.

We all want the value of our portfolios to increase. For many of us, the third factor—increases or decreases in the value of assets—is becoming an increasingly important determinant of whether or not this actually happens. This is particularly true for invested assets. Of the factors listed above, knowing how to positively influence the value of invested assets often is the most difficult to grasp.

One important purpose of the investment process is to make investment decisions—that is, to create a portfolio structure—that will have an optimal impact on a portfolio's value. The process of structuring a portfolio is different for everyone because it depends on variables unique to each person. These variables, alluded to in the example above, include

1. Your investment goals.
2. The time frame for realizing your goals.
3. The level of risk you are willing to assume to reach those goals.
4. The different types of investments available to help you meet
   your goals within your time frame and given your risk tolerance.

These variables, combined with some basic investment principles, will help you define an appropriate portfolio structure.

Identifying Investment Goals

The first step in the investment process is identifying your goals. In other words, what are you saving for—an emergency fund, a new house, retirement, a college education, a special vacation? Because different goals require different strategies, you need to identify your ends before you can select the most appropriate means. In thinking about your goals, keep in mind that you probably will be working toward several goals simultaneously. That's OK. While goals can be fluid and some will change over time, it is essential that you honestly and fully articulate your goals every time you engage in the investment process. Remember, too, it is important to quantify your goals in specific dollar amounts and time frames.

Time Frames

After you've identified your goals, your time frame for achieving them will follow logically. If the goal is saving for a newborn's college education, you know you've got about 18 years. Keep in mind that some time frames are more rigid than others. For example, because college generally follows high school, you are more or less locked into that time frame. But if your goal is an around-the-world cruise, it may not matter if you take the trip in ten years instead of eight. Also keep in mind that the longer your time frame, the greater will be the risk you'll likely be willing and able to assume.

Risk and Return

There is a fairly direct correlation between risk and return: the greater the degree of an investment's risk, the higher is the expected rate of return.

> **EXAMPLE**
>
> A corporate bond issued by a start-up company usually involves a higher risk than a bond issued by a blue-chip manufacturer. To attract investors, the start-up must offer a higher interest rate on its bond than does the blue-chip.

Because understanding risk and risk tolerance is critical to the investment process, we'll discuss it in detail in the next section.

Investment Suitability

After you know your goals, time frames, and risk tolerance, you can begin to identify types of appropriate investments. To be suitable for your portfolio, an investment must satisfy each criterion. However, before you can determine which types of investments are suitable for your goals, time frames, and risk tolerance, you must become familiar with the features of different classes of investments. The most common classes of investments are described in a later section of this chapter.

> **EXAMPLE**
>
> You have $25,000 that you intend to use for an addition to your home in two years. A five-year certificate of deposit is not a suitable investment for this goal.

What If It Won't Work?

People tend to gloss over this important question because it's unpleasant. What if there are no suitable investment vehicles that will allow you to meet your investment goals within your time frame and given your risk tolerance? The answer is simply that something must give. You either have to adjust your goals, lengthen your time frame, or increase your risk tolerance to make the investment process work for you.

EXAMPLE 1

You are 45 years old. Your investment goal is to retire at age 60 with $40,000 per year in retirement income. After taking into account Social Security and your employer's pension, you determine you will need to save an additional $100,000 by age 60 to meet your goal. You can afford to invest $250 per month toward this goal. However, you project that the only investments suitable to your risk tolerance and time frame will produce $85,000, leaving you $15,000 short of your goal. The $85,000 figure would allow for retirement income of $38,000 per year, and you decide to alter your retirement income goal accordingly.

EXAMPLE 2

The same facts in Example 1 apply, but you conclude that you will need the full $40,000 per year in retirement. You decide to increase your monthly investment from $250 to $300 by reallocating $50 from your monthly entertainment/vacation expenditures to reach your goal.

EXAMPLE 3

The same facts in Example 1 apply, but you decide to alter your time frame and continue working until age 62 to reach your $100,000 retirement savings goal.

EXAMPLE 4

The same facts in Example 1 apply, but you conclude that if you accept slightly more risk, you can find investments that will enable you to meet your $100,000 retirement savings goal by age 60 by investing only $250 per month.

Of the variables you can change to achieve your investment goals, the risk tolerance adjustment in Example 4 will prove the most difficult. If you're old enough to make investment decisions, this personalty trait is already well set. It may be possible to tweak the edges of your risk tolerance, but you cannot fundamentally change it. As Example 4 illustrates, you might endure a slightly riskier investment by keeping your eye on the relatively long time frame. However, it's foolish to think that you can deviate significantly in your risk tolerance. It's even more foolish for someone else to try to persuade you to fundamentally alter your risk tolerance. If your financial adviser is doing this, alarms should be going off in your head.

OUR ISSUES

In many ways the investment process for lesbians and gays is similar to the general investment process. Our investment goals may differ from those of the dominant culture. For example, only a few of us might identify saving for a child's college education as an investment goal. But for many of us, an early retirement goal is feasible, if we properly plan for it. Those of us touched by HIV or another life-threatening illness may want to create a nest egg for a surviving partner. Overall, however, the differences in how we approach the investment process lie more in style than in substance. For example, from our life experiences we are likely to form a unique approach to risk and risk tolerance. Nevertheless, we'll use the same basic principles as everyone else in identifying goals, assessing and accommodating risk tolerance, and selecting investments.

RELATED TOPICS

Your balance sheet is the key to understanding your current portfolio structure (or lack of structure, as the case may be), as well as the starting point for analyzing whether or not the structure is appropriate for your goals, time frames, and risk tolerance. See the "Constructing a Balance Sheet" section on page 4.

Similarly, your budget (or your cash flow statement) can help you get a handle on how much money you're saving and where to make spending changes if you need to increase the amount you're investing in order to reach your goals. See the "Building a Budget" section on page 13.

Once you've established your investment goals, specified your time frames, defined your risk tolerance, and identified the classes of assets from which you should choose to invest, you're ready to construct your portfolio. The techniques are explained in the "Asset Allocation and Portfolio Structure" section on page 138.

Understanding the nature of risk and your tolerance for the various sources of risk inherent in investments is essential to the investment process. You'll find an explanation of these issues in the "Investment Risk and Risk Tolerance" section below.

Diversification is one of the basic principles of portfolio construction. Because it is an essential technique for minimizing risk, it is also discussed in the "Investment Risk and Risk Tolerance" section on page xxx.

With the increasing popularity of IRAs, 401(k)s, and similar deferred compensation vehicles, retirement assets are becoming a large part of many middle-class portfolios. To understand why you need to maximize the value of these assets, see the "Computing Retirement Needs and Savings" section on page 231.

Techniques to deal with investing for multiple goals are explained in the "Asset Allocation and Portfolio Structure" section on page 138.

INVESTMENT RISK AND RISK TOLERANCE

THE STRAIGHT FACTS

Before choosing investment vehicles, you need to understand risk and your risk tolerance. Most people are surprised to learn that every investment carries some form of risk—even investments for which the U.S. government guarantees the security of the principal. Before selecting an investment, it is critical that you first understand the types of risk involved and then honestly evaluate your ability to tolerate those risks.

Sources of Risk

Financial planners generally identify nine possible sources of risk. A brief explanation of each follows. In the next section where we describe classes of investments, we identify the sources of risk usually associated with each investment.

Market Risk

This risk refers to the possibility that the value of a particular stock investment will decrease as a result of changes in the overall level of major stock markets, even though the individual investment does not change. Broad market levels sometimes rise and fall unexpectedly as a result of unanticipated economic or political changes such as inflation reports, unemployment claims, or tax law changes.

EXAMPLE
In the mid-1980s, the stock market took a brief dive when it was announced that then-President Reagan was undergoing cosmetic surgery on his colon

(i.e., polyp removal). Clearly, the condition of President Reagan's innards had very little to do with, say, the financial status of a particular china manufacturer in which his wife Nancy was invested. Nevertheless, the possibility that economic uncertainty might result from a change in leadership if things did not go well for the president's tummy caused apprehension in the market. That apprehension translated into a slightly lower price for the china stock, and perhaps a small capital loss for Nancy.

Interest Rate Risk

Interest rate risk involves the chance that an investment's overall return will be affected by a change in interest rates.

EXAMPLE 1

You purchase a $10,000 Treasury bond paying an annual interest rate of 8 percent. A year later you decide to sell the bond. At that time Treasury bonds are paying 9 percent interest. To induce a buyer to purchase your 8 percent bond instead of the new 9 percent bond, you must discount the $10,000 by an amount sufficient to compensate for the lower interest payments your buyer will receive over the life of your bond.

EXAMPLE 2

You purchase the same $10,000 bond paying 8 percent annual interest. This time interest rates drop. A year later when you decide to sell, Treasury bonds are only paying 7 percent. Now you can charge a premium price (i.e., above $10,000) for your bond to account for the additional interest your buyer will earn over the life of the bond.

Reinvestment Risk

Reinvestment risk arises when the interest and dividends you receive from an investment cannot be reinvested to provide the same rate of return as your initial investment. This situation occurs because market conditions change between the time of your initial investment and the time you try to reinvest the earnings from that investment. Reinvestment risk also applies to the principal of an investment with a fixed maturity, such as a bond or a certificate of deposit.

EXAMPLE

You purchase a three-year certificate of deposit at your local bank. The CD pays 6 percent interest. You also had the option of purchasing a five-year CD paying 6.5 percent interest. By the time your three-year CD matures, interest rates have fallen, and you are only able to purchase a new CD paying 4.5 percent interest.

Purchasing Power Risk

Inflation risk is another way of thinking about purchasing power risk. It refers to the possibility that the rate of return earned by your investment will not keep pace with the rate of inflation, effectively eroding the value of your investment's principal.

EXAMPLE

In the early 1990s, most bank savings accounts were paying interest rates of 2 percent or 3 percent. At the same time, inflation was running between 3 percent and 4 percent. In a very real sense, investors who kept all their assets in savings accounts lost money during this period.

Exchange Rate Risk

Exchange rate risk is the possibility that a change in the value of foreign currency relative to the value of the U.S. dollar (or whatever your domestic currency may be) will negatively affect the return on your investment. This risk comes into play whenever average folks invest internationally, or when high rollers invest in foreign currency transactions.

EXAMPLE

You decide to purchase $1,000 worth of stock in a French company trading at 10 francs per share. On the day you invest, French francs are trading at 5 to the dollar. Therefore, your $1,000 is worth 5,000 francs, and you are able to purchase 500 shares (5,000 francs/10 francs per share = 500 shares). One month later, you decide to sell the stock. The value of the stock remains 10 francs per share. However, francs are now trading at 6 to the dollar. This means that, when you sell your 500 shares for 5,000 francs and convert the money back into dollars, the change in exchange rates will have reduced the value of your investment from $1,000 to $833.33 (5,000 francs/6 francs per dollar = $833.33), even though the value of the stock has not changed.

Business Risk

Business risk refers to the risk associated with investing in a particular firm or industry. The sources of business risk can include everything from environmental regulation or the availability of skilled labor to the firm's ability to generate a profit in its industry and the competence of its management.

EXAMPLE

In a rapidly evolving industry like technology, innovation by competitors can be a source of business risk, since it threatens to make products obsolete.

Financial Risk

Financial risk is the risk associated with the mix of debt and equity used to finance a firm or property. When a business needs to raise money, it can do so in one of two ways. It can borrow from others, thereby creating debt, or it can sell ownership interests in the company (for corporations, in the form of stock), thereby creating equity for its owners. Most corporations use a mix of debt and equity financing to meet their capital needs. A company that uses a lot of debt is said to be highly leveraged. Generally, the greater the leverage, the higher the financial risk will be.

EXAMPLE

A department store chain raises money by borrowing. Before it can make dividend payments to its shareholders, it must first make the required payments on its debt obligations. If the debt repayments consume too much of the chain's profits, there might not be any money to pay dividends to its shareholders.

Default Risk

Default risk refers to the possibility that the financial condition of an entity issuing an investment security may render it unable to honor its obligations. For example, a corporation in financial difficulty may be unable to make required interest payments to its bondholders, technically placing it in default. Securities issued by the federal government are widely regarded as free of default risk, as they are backed by the full faith and credit of the U.S. government. Generally, investments that present a high default risk must offer higher returns to attract investors.

EXAMPLE

A department store chain raises money by incurring a significant amount of debt. Although the chain's earnings and profits are comparable to its competitors', the monthly payments on the debt prove more than its cash flow can support, and the chain is forced out of business.

Liquidity Risk

Liquidity risk refers to an owner's ability to quickly convert an investment to cash when needed. The greater the possibility that a quick liquidation will result in a loss of value, the higher the investment's liquidity risk.

EXAMPLE

Throughout the 1980s, real estate was considered a "hot" investment. But the climate for real estate has changed markedly in the 1990s, and many owners are learning that the long time frames required to sell real estate can create significant liquidity risk.

Risk Tolerance

Now that you've learned about the different forms of risk, it's time to give a little thought to how you feel about them. No investment is worth the return if it's going to cause you to lie awake worrying every night. However, it's also important to remember that every investment involves one or more of the forms of risk discussed above. The key is to decide how much of which type of risk you can accept for how long.

It's important to understand that, as with most things in life, risk is directly related to reward. In investment terms, the higher the potential return, the greater the potential risk. Different types of investments have greater or lesser risk than other investments. The risk differences among investments are frequently depicted in terms of an investment risk pyramid as shown in Figure 3–1. Low-risk (and low-return) investments are at the base of the pyramid, and the levels of risk (and return) increase as the pyramid rises.

Although it's a bad idea to choose an investment that is too high on the risk pyramid for your risk tolerance, it's just as important not to underestimate your risk tolerance. Remember, there's no such thing as a "safe" investment. Even savings accounts are subject to interest rate risk, reinvestment risk, and inflation risk.

The most intelligent way to deal with risk is to employ techniques that can help you minimize it. These techniques include selecting the right investments, using dividend reinvestment or dollar cost averaging plans, making proper asset allocations, and, most importantly, diversifying. We'll examine each of these tools throughout the chapter.

Diversification

The most important thing you can do to minimize your overall risk is to make sure your portfolio is properly diversified. Financial planners and investment advisers spend years studying the ways in which diversification can minimize risk while maximizing returns. Here's what you need to know: Proper diversification lowers risk.

EXAMPLE 1
Maria has $1,000 to invest. If she invests it all in stock A, the entire $1,000 is subject to the business risk of that company. If she invests $500 in stock A and $500 in stock B (a different company), she has lowered her business risk. If stocks A and B are in different industries, she has lowered her risk even more.

FIGURE 3–1

The Investment Risk Pyramid

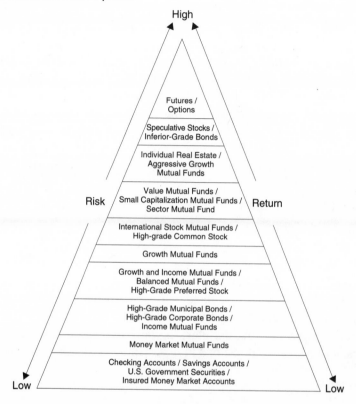

EXAMPLE 2

If Maria puts her $1,000 in a mutual fund, she has spread her risk literally among hundreds of different businesses and probably dozens of different industries.

One other nice thing about diversifying your investments is that when one investment is down and the others are doing OK, you'll tend to focus on the big picture—the total return of your portfolio. This should add to your peace of mind.

Time Heals Some Wounds

Another important aspect of evaluating an investment's risk and your own risk tolerance is the time frame for your investment. Generally, the longer the time frame for an investment, the greater a person's risk tolerance toward that investment.

EXAMPLE

Stefan, age 25, invests $2,000 per year in an Individual Retirement Account and $1,000 per year in building his emergency fund. While his overall risk tolerance is very low, Stefan is likely to be more aggressive in investing in the retirement fund than in the emergency fund.

The reason Stefan is more aggressive with his retirement fund is that he knows time will compensate for some of the risk he has assumed. This is not to suggest that his retirement investments will be inconsistent with his overall risk tolerance. Rather, the risk tolerance for his retirement funds is likely to be different than the risk tolerance for his emergency fund. This is a very important consideration to keep in mind when evaluating your risk tolerance.

A Final Thought about Risk

Risk is a game of probabilities. There are no guarantees that any investment will be free of every form of risk or that the probabilities will play out the way they're expected to. If at this point you're tempted to throw up your hands in disgust and stash your money under the mattress, remember that you've just decided to assume the risk that inflation might erode the purchasing power of your hoard (i.e., inflation risk). Since risk is an integral part of life, darlings, the best we can do is understand its causes, know how we'll respond to it, and make well-informed decisions.

OUR ISSUES

"PC" Risk

Lesbian and gay investors face one other form of risk—the risk that we will invest our hard-earned money in organizations or institutions hostile to our cause. In a broad sense, the issue raised by this risk is referred to as *socially responsible investing.* (Cynics might refer to it as "politically correct" (PC) investing.) A small but growing number of mutual funds and investment advisers screen out companies that discriminate against employees or customers, treat their workers poorly, harm the environment, and/or produce harmful products or services. There is even a school of thought suggesting that socially responsible investing can produce superior returns because in the process of screening investments for social criteria, the overall picture receives heightened scrutiny. While there is compelling logic to this theory, it has not been tested by many financial planners.

Another way of looking at this issue is to consider whether lesbians and gays should give extra consideration to investing in organizations that have made an extra effort to advance our causes. A communications company that bans antigay discrimination, a software developer that offers its employees domestic partner benefits, or a rental car company that does not charge domestic partner renters an "additional driver" fee are examples of companies doing right by us. Shouldn't the lesbian and gay community support these companies by investing in them?

While this question is highly personal, most professional advisers are likely to give a yes and no response. It is certainly appropriate to make social responsibility a consideration in investment decisions, but it is not in your best interest to make it the determining factor. In addition, it probably is considerably less risky to reject homophobic investments than it is to require that all your investments be gay-friendly. The universe of potential investment choices is much more diverse in the former approach than in the latter. Finally, social responsibility should never be an excuse for inferior financial performance. Only after an investment makes good financial sense should social criteria come into play.

The nature of an investment may also influence the degree to which you consider the social responsibility issue. For example, it is fairly easy to avoid buying the stock of a family-restaurant chain that has publicly affirmed a policy of firing openly gay workers. But it's much more difficult to find a garden-variety mutual fund that does not contain the stock of some offending company in its portfolio. A number of socially responsible mutual funds have been established to address this problem. Before you decide to invest in such a fund, however, go back and re-read the last sentence of the preceding paragraph.

For some people, including some gays and lesbians, socially responsible investing is not an issue. They invest for optimal return—period. However, most investors for whom social issues are a consideration find themselves striving for a comfortable middle ground. Regardless of your level of "PC" risk, be sure you communicate your feelings clearly to the financial professionals with whom you are working.

RELATED TOPICS

Mutual funds can be an excellent way for the average investor to minimize risk by gaining exposure to a large number of different investments. They are explained in the "Classes of Investments" section on page 114.

For most people, asset allocation is a critical component of constructing a diverse portfolio. The process is detailed in the "Asset Allocation and Portfolio Structure" section on page 138.

Investing through the use of dollar cost averaging can be an effective way to reduce risk while establishing responsible saving patterns. This technique is discussed in the "Asset Allocation and Portfolio Structure" section on page 138.

Automatic dividend reinvestment plans can serve as a form of dollar cost averaging. They also are explained in the "Asset Allocation and Portfolio Structure" section on page 138.

Recent studies have found that many people have not properly diversified their retirement investments and actually own investments that are too conservative to provide returns sufficient to meet their retirement needs. Review the discussion of long-term goals in the "Asset Allocation and Portfolio Structure" section on page 138 to understand how to avoid this trap. Then see the discussion in the "Computing Retirement Needs and Savings" section on page 231 to round out your understanding of the issue.

CLASSES OF INVESTMENTS

THE STRAIGHT FACTS

In spite of all the hoopla, there are only two ways to earn investment income in our society: You can either be an owner or a creditor. All investments represent either an equity interest or a debt interest. Some sophisticated investments are a hybrid, but, as a general rule, the premise holds. In some respects, then, investing is easy: You either invest for growth (through ownership) or for income (through being paid for the use of your money). The rest, as they say, is details.

If only it were that easy. Those details have undone of millions of investors over the years. The problem is that there are hundreds of ways to be an owner and thousands of different things to own. The choices are almost as broad for income investments, too. The options even can be mind-numbing for investing in cash equivalents! Before we begin the process of structuring the "right" portfolio, we first must understand the different types of investments—called *investment classes* by many investment pros—available to us.

This section describes in detail the various classes of investments commonly considered by average investors. For each class there will be

1. A *description* explaining what the investment class is and how it works.

2. A statement about the vehicle's *investment style* (i.e., growth, income, or cash/cash equivalent).

3. The *sources of risk* (discussed in the previous section) for the class of investment.

4. The appropriate *return benchmark* that can be used to measure the current performance of a particular asset against the average performance of all assets in the class.

5. The average *historical rate of return* the class of investment has earned over time.

At the end of this section, we also will review some of the more esoteric investments.

We will identify as many helpful benchmark figures as possible and also suggest where you can find the most current figures for each. The benchmark will usually be a figure published by an analytical service or brokerage house. Because they facilitate comparative evaluations of individual investments, the benchmarks and historical returns provided for each asset class will help you construct your portfolio in the next section. Try to keep some historical context as you use benchmarks and historical return data, however. Remember what was going on in the economy during the period covered by the data, and make sure it is still a realistic guideline for what to expect in the future. Also, remember that past performance is no guarantee of future returns. As we'll see in the next section, benchmarks and historical rates of return can be useful tools for measuring how a particular investment stacks up against its class, but they are not reliable in predicting future returns.

Savings Accounts

Description Savings accounts probably are the most conservative form of investment available. The bank (or credit union) holding your funds pays you interest, usually each month, based on your account balance. The interest rate varies monthly or quarterly based on market conditions. Usually, up to $100,000 of the principal in these accounts is insured through an agency of the federal government, such as the Federal Deposit Insurance Corporation.

Investment Style A savings account is a form of cash equivalent investing.

Sources of Risk Purchasing power risk is the main form of risk associated with savings accounts. It is quite possible, if not likely, that over time the interest earned on a savings account will be insufficient to enable the principal in the account to keep pace with inflation.

Return Benchmark There is no universal agreement on a single appropriate benchmark for savings accounts, although some experts use the inflation rate as a benchmark. After all, there's probably no place in your portfolio for any investment that fails to keep pace with inflation. Some general circulation publications, as well as most business publications, report the most competitive interest rates quoted by local (or even national) institutions.

Historical Rate of Return The research firm of Ibbotson Associates, Inc., reports that the annual inflation rate from 1926 through 1994 averaged 3.1 percent. The U.S. Department of Labor has calculated average annual inflation rates of 3.5 percent over the 5-year period ending in 1994 and 3.4 percent over the 10-year period ending in 1994.

Money Market Accounts or Funds

Description A money market account is a form of savings account that provides limited check writing ability. In exchange for a minimum balance requirement (often $1,000 or $2,000), money markets provide better interest rates than savings accounts. Traditionally offered by banks, many brokerage houses and other financial services providers have branched into the money market business. Generally, banks offer money market accounts and brokerage houses offer money market funds. If you open a money market at someplace other than a bank, your account may not be federally insured. While most nonbanks have found creative solutions to the insurance issue, make intelligent inquiries about the safety of your principal before opening an account. Because of the insurance issue, you can expect to earn a slightly better rate of interest from a nonbank money market fund. If the minimum balance is not a problem for you, money markets are preferable to traditional savings accounts.

Investment Style Money markets are cash equivalents.

Sources of Risk As with savings accounts, purchasing power risk is the chief source of risk for money markets.

Return Benchmark Money markets probably are best compared to short-term Treasury securities (i.e., 90-day T-bills). Keep in mind, however, that most money markets invest in T-bills. This means that the money market managers must pay their expenses and make their profits before passing any earnings on to you. Money markets therefore generally offer slightly lower interest rates than T-bills. Many business publications provide competitive figures on current money market rates.

Historical Rate of Return The Federal Reserve Board reports that 90-day T-bills have returned an average of 5.0 percent over the 5-year period ending in 1994, and 6.1 percent over the 10-year period ending in 1994.

Certificates of Deposit

Description Certificates of deposit (CDs) are somewhat similar to savings accounts, except that you and the bank agree ahead of time how long they will keep your money and what the rate of interest will be for the entire term of the investment. CDs usually offer the highest interest rate of any traditional bank or credit union product. Usually, there are hefty penalties if you break your agreement—for example, by withdrawing funds prematurely. Typically, these penalties involve forfeiting some or all of the interest you have earned. Because banks and other institutions that offer CDs know they are competing against higher-returning alternative investments, many of them have begun putting fancy bells and whistles on their CD products. For example, it is common to find CDs that allow one or occasionally even two penalty-free withdrawals. Some banks even offer long-term CDs that permit you to "bump up" the interest rate once over the investment's term.

When your CD matures, you will have a certain amount of time to withdraw the funds from the account, or the bank will automatically reinvest the principal plus any accrued interest for the same length of time as the matured CD, at the bank's current market rate for that time period. This is known as *rolling over* the CD. You will need to notify the bank shortly before the maturity date if you do not wish to roll over the CD.

When shopping for CDs, be sure to compare apples to apples when it comes to interest rates. You need to know how often interest is compounded in order to know your real rate of return. *Compounding* refers to how often interest is actually paid on an account. Once interest is paid, it starts earning interest of its own. Thus, the interest is compounding. (It might help to think of all those little interest payments as sitting in your account and breeding!) The more often interest is compounded, the higher the *yield*. Thus, depending on compounding, two different CDs that offer the same rate may provide very different *yields*. Interest can be compounded daily, monthly, quarterly, or even semiannually. You need to determine a CD's yield, expressed as its annual percentage rate (APR), in order to accurately compare competing products.

EXAMPLE
EZ Bank and MT Bank advertise one-year CDs paying 7 percent interest. EZ Bank compounds its interest monthly, while MT Bank compounds semiannually. After a year, the total interest earned from EZ Bank is 7.23 percent, whereas at MT Bank it is only 7.17 percent. Another way to say this is that EZ bank's APR is 7.23 percent, whereas MT Bank's APR is only 7.17 percent.

Investment Style CDs are almost always cash equivalent investments, although very long-term CDs (e.g., 60-month certificates) sometimes can be considered income investments.

Sources of Risk As with other cash equivalent investments, purchasing power risk is the chief source of risk for CDs. However, for longer-term CDs, reinvestment risk also may arise if rates have changed significantly since the original investment.

Return Benchmark Because interest rates on CDs vary with the length of the investment, it is not possible to point to a single appropriate benchmark. A good indicator might be a comparable investment in U.S. Treasury Department securities, which generally pay a fraction of a percentage point more than CDs. Some general circulation business publications report the most competitive CD interest rates quoted by banks. These figures are probably the most helpful in comparison shopping for CDs.

Historical Rate of Return Since returns for CDs vary with the length of the certificate, historical data can get complicated. It might be helpful to review the return information for a comparable-length Treasury investment and then come down a fraction.

Treasury Bills

Description Treasury bills are the short-term debt (less than 52 weeks) of the federal government. They are backed by the full faith and credit of the U.S. government, making them (theoretically) risk-free investments. T-bills would be the ideal place to invest the cash portion of any investor's portfolio, except for one small problem: They are sold in $1,000 increments, with a minimum investment of $10,000. Consequently, they often are purchased by large financial institutions, although it is possible (with some effort, unless you live near an office of the Federal Reserve Bank) for individuals to invest directly in T-bills. For those who cannot work in $10,000 minimums, money markets are the next best thing. States cannot impose income taxes on interest paid by the federal government. So, if you live in a high-tax state, there's an added bonus to investing in T-bills.

Investment Style T-bills are the ultimate form of cash equivalent investing.

Sources of Risk Theoretically, purchasing power risk applies as equally to T-bills as to any other cash equivalent investment. However, because of their short duration, as a practical matter this risk exists only for investors who roll over their T-bills year after year.

Return Benchmark T-bill rates are published in most daily newspapers.

Historical Rate of Return The 90-day T-bills have returned an average of 5.0 percent over the 5-year period ending in 1994 and 6.1 percent over the 10-year period ending in 1994, according to the Federal Reserve Board.

Treasury Notes and Bonds

Description Treasury notes are the intermediate-term debt (2 to 10 years) of the federal government. Treasury bonds are its long-term debt (10 to 30 years). Like T-bills, Treasury notes and bonds are backed by the full faith and credit of the U.S. government. Because of the nominal risk to principal, notes and bonds offer the lowest return of any income-style investment. They are available in increments of $1,000 (with a $5,000 minimum for two- and three-year notes) and can be acquired directly from the Federal Reserve or (more conveniently) through a broker. As with T-bills, states cannot impose their income taxes on interest earned from Treasury notes and bonds.

Investment Style Treasury notes and bonds are generally considered to be income investments.

Sources of Risk Interest rate risk is the chief source of risk for intermediate- and long-term Treasuries, with reinvestment risk a close second. Purchasing power risk also is a significant issue for Treasuries with long maturities.

Return Benchmark Treasury note and bond rates are reported in most major business publications. The rate on the 30-year Treasury bond (sometimes referred to as the *long bond*) is published in the business section of virtually every daily newspaper.

Historical Rate of Return According to Ibbotson Associates, Inc., intermediate-term government bonds returned 5.3 percent from 1926 through 1994, whereas long-term bonds returned only 5.0 percent over the same period.

Corporate Bonds

Description Corporate bonds are the debt instruments of private enterprises. A bond essentially is a form of loan agreement between the issuing corporation and the bondholder. In exchange for the receipt of a principal sum, the corporation promises to pay interest semiannually (usually) for the term of the bond and to return to the bondholder the principal at the end of the bond's term. Many bonds are backed only by the assets and creditworthiness of the issuing corporation. Some bonds, called asset-backed bonds, are secured by specific assets of the corporation. These bonds often present slightly less risk since there are specific assets pledged by the corporation as collateral to secure them. Because of the increased risk, corporations must offer a higher rate of return than government securities to attract investors to their debt.

Since creditworthiness is so critical in determining the value of corporate bonds, several large organizations make handsome profits measuring the financial stability of corporations and publishing ratings of corporate debt. Moody's and Standard & Poor's are the two most widely known rating services. The ratings can range from AAA to D. *Investment grade* securities are generally thought to carry the least risk. They require a rating of BBB or above from Standard & Poor's and a rating of Baa or above from Moody's. Bonds with lower ratings usually are referred to as *junk bonds,* and they have no place in the portfolio of average investors.

Investment Style Corporate bonds are income investments.

Sources of Risk Interest rate risk is a significant source of risk for corporate bonds. Reinvestment risk is another source of risk for many bonds, especially for those with a *call* feature that allows the issuing corporation to redeem the bond prior to its stated maturity. Corporations tend to exercise this feature when interest rates fall in order to refinance their debt. Holders of such debt would be forced to reinvest their principal at the same lower rates the bond issuer seeks to take advantage of. Many corporate bonds contain a call feature. Default risk also is a very significant source of risk for corporate bonds. They are the reason Moody's, Standard & Poor's, and others are in business. Liquidity risk may be a minor consideration for some small corporate issues.

Return Benchmark Most of the major brokerage houses publish indexes of corporate bond performance. Lehman Brothers and Merrill Lynch are two of the more widely used. The indexes are printed in most major business publications. Remember, however, that return rates for corporate bonds are directly related to creditworthiness, length to maturity, and prevailing market interest rates. Figures from the brokerage houses cover only investment grade bonds.

Historical Rate of Return Ibbotson Associates, Inc., reports that the annual rate of return for corporate bonds from 1926 through 1994 was 5.4 percent. For a less historical (and perhaps more relevant) perspective, Lehman Brothers reports the 5- and 10-year averages for such investments through 1994 as 8.3 percent and 10.6 percent, respectively.

Municipal Bonds

Description Municipal bonds are the debt instruments of state and local governments. *General obligation* municipal bonds are backed by the full faith and credit of the issuing government. However, a few of these governments have been known to declare bankruptcy, so the creditworthiness of various "munis" is rated by Moody's, Standard & Poor's, and the like. *Revenue bonds* are secured by the income from a particular project that they are issued to finance (e.g., an airport, a sports arena, or a highway). The federal government does not tax the interest paid on municipal bonds. The state in which the bond is issued usually doesn't, either (although most states tax the interest on munis issued by *other* states). These tax advantages can make municipal bonds a very attractive investment. However, because the issuing governments understand these tax advantages at least as well as we do, they generally get away with offering lower interest rates than Treasury or corporate bonds. An example of the effect of these tax advantages is included in the "Tax-Favored Investments" section in the Tax Planning chapter.

Investment Style Munis are income investments.

Sources of Risk The sources of risk for municipal bonds are similar to those for corporate bonds. Interest rate risk is the major concern, followed by reinvestment risk and then default risk. Purchasing power risk also is a concern for municipal bonds with long maturities. Liquidity risk can be a concern for the bonds of some smaller municipalities.

Return Benchmark Lehman Brothers and Merrill Lynch publish widely used indexes of municipal bond returns. They generally can be found in business publications. As with corporate bonds, keep in mind that return on munis is a function of creditworthiness, length to maturity, overall interest rates prevailing in the market, and the size and stature of the issuing state. Lehman Brothers also issues indexes specific to New York and California munis.

Historical Rate of Return According to Lehman Brothers, for periods ending in 1994, municipal bonds returned 6.8 percent annually for the preceding 5 years and 9.4 percent for the preceding 10 years. Remember that these returns usually are not subject to federal (and issuing state) income tax.

Common Stock

Description   Common stock represents an ownership interest in the company that issued it. For example, if Mega Industries, Inc., has issued one million shares of stock, and you own one share of Mega stock, you own one one-millionth of Mega Industries. The underlying value of your ownership interest increases or decreases with the value of Mega itself. This in turn depends on Mega's financial performance, the goods or services it produces, the industries it competes in, the countries it sells in, the wisdom and experience of its managers, and a host of other factors. Of course, investors hope that the value of their ownership interest will increase over time. Growth is one of the most important reasons people invest in stock.

In addition to growth, there is another way to make money through stock: The board of directors of a company can vote to distribute to each owner his or her proportionate share of the company's net earnings in the form of dividends. As we will see shortly, certain stocks with long histories of healthy dividends work as excellent income investments.

Because there is such an overwhelming variety of stocks from which to choose—domestic stocks, international stocks, preferred stocks, stocks in companies that pay regular dividends, stocks in companies that are expected to grow substantially in the future—financial experts have attempted to classify stocks into manageable categories. These "classes" can be defined by the type of goods or services sold, what countries they are sold in, the size of the company, its growth potential, its income potential, and so on. Stock mutual funds in particular may attempt to focus on only certain classes of stocks. At different places throughout the rest of this chapter, we'll focus on those classes of stocks important to the construction of most portfolios. Where it's more appropriate, we'll do so in the context of mutual funds that invest within a given class.

Investment Style   Most stocks are growth investments, although some preferred and high-dividend common stocks may be considered income investments.

Sources of Risk   Virtually every form of risk presents itself to some degree or another when investing in stock. Therefore, it is important to focus on whether the source of risk is significant or insignificant. Yes, it's possible that some day the whole system could come crashing down, making even the most blue-chip of stocks worthless. If this happens, however, you'll probably have bigger worries than your portfolio. No investment would survive the apocalypse, including those guaranteed by the U.S. government.

Some risks are of greater concern only for specific classes of stock; we'll mention them when we cover those classes. In general, significant sources of risk for common stock investments are market risk, business risk, and financial risk. In addition, there may be liquidity risk in the stock of very small companies. Sometimes it can be a problem if you try to sell all at once a large block of the stock of even a not-so-small company.

Return Benchmark There is no universal agreement on the appropriate benchmark for establishing the overall performance of the stock market. There is fairly widespread agreement that the most recognized benchmark, the Dow Jones Industrial Average, is not a good way to measure broad performance of common stocks. The Dow tracks the performance of only 30 of the nation's largest industrial corporations trading on the New York Stock Exchange. There currently are more than 34,000 publicly traded stocks in the overall marketplace. Additionally, only very large issues of very large companies trade on the New York Stock Exchange. Many stocks are bought and sold elsewhere, either on other exchanges or "over-the-counter." Accordingly, the Dow does not offer a very broad reading of the nation's stock portfolio.

We will encounter some specialized benchmarks that track the performance of particular classes of stocks as we discuss those classes. They are by definition too specialized to provide a reading of the overall market. Two widely recognized benchmarks that seem to offer a broad reading of how stocks in general are performing are the Standard & Poor's 500 and the Wilshire 5000. As the names imply, these indexes track the performance of 500 and well over 5,000 different stocks, respectively. While professionals have valid reasons for preferring one index over the other (the Wilshire 5000 provides more breadth, but the S&P 500 may be more representative of the "typical" portfolio), the broader reading offered by either of these indexes is appropriate for most general purposes. If you want to check the performance of a diverse common stock mutual fund, comparing its five-year return to that of the S&P 500 or the Wilshire 5000 is an excellent place to start. The S&P 500 is reported in the business section of most daily newspapers. The Wilshire 5000 can be just a little harder to find, and you may have to turn to a business publication to get current figures.

Historical Rate of Return Ibbotson Associates, Inc., reports that from 1926 through 1994, the U.S. equities market posted an average annual return of 10.2 percent. More recently, for periods ending in 1994, the S&P 500 averaged annual returns of 8.7 percent going back 5 years and 14.4 percent going back 10 years. Similarly, the Wilshire 5000 returned an annual average of 8.9 percent for the 5 years ending in 1994 and 13.9 percent for the 10 years ending in 1994.

Preferred Stock

Description Preferred stock is similar to common stock in that it represents an ownership interest in a corporation. However, unlike common stock, it has a "preferred" right to receive proceeds in the event the corporation is liquidated. Usually this preferential right also extends to the payment of fixed dividends. Shareholders of so-called cumulative preferred get paid before common shareholders. To be sure, a company weathering difficult economic times may suspend dividend payments even on preferred stock, but it cannot later resume dividend payments for common stock until all preferred arrearages are made up. Companies don't have to issue preferred stock, and many don't. The good news for investors in preferred stock is that the full stated dividend gets paid before investors holding common stock get anything. The bad news for investors in preferred stock is that only the stated dividend gets paid even if the company's performance is spectacular.

Investment Style Because of the "guaranteed" dividend stream and the minimal potential for growth in value, preferred stock is a form of income investing.

Sources of Risk Interest rate, purchasing power, and business risk are the chief sources of risk for preferred stock.

Return Benchmark There is no widely available index that measures the performance of preferred stock. It may be appropriate either to rely on a benchmark for corporate bonds or on one of the benchmarks for broader fixed-income investments issued by brokerage houses such as Lehman Brothers and Merrill Lynch. Some of these figures may be available in specialty business publications.

Historical Rate of Return Ibbotson Associates, Inc., reports that the annual rate of return for broad fixed-income investments was 5.4 percent from 1926 through 1994. More currently, Lehman Brothers reports that through 1994 the fixed-income market returned 7.7 percent going back 5 years and 9.8 percent going back 10 years.

Income Stock

Description Income stocks are common stocks that consistently pay superior dividends. Occasionally, this may be the function of the corporation's deft management. Generally, however, it is a function of the industry in which the corporation operates. Utilities are a classic example of income stocks. Because utility consumption does not ebb and flow much with the economic cycle, utilities generally earn money in any economic environment. Moreover, since they usually are regulated, the rate of return for most utilities is more or less assured. Because of their lack of relationship to the economic cycle, income stocks are sometimes referred to as *defensive* stocks. They can help a portfolio defend itself against the inevitable downturns in the economic cycle.

Investment Style Although it is reasonable to expect modest annual growth from income stocks, they are generally thought of as income investments.

Sources of Risk Income stocks bear most of the risks of common stocks (market, business, and financial), although perhaps to a lesser degree. Investors in income stocks also need to consider interest rate risk.

Return Benchmark There is no single benchmark for income stocks. As with preferred stock, it may be appropriate to compare returns to those posted by corporate bonds. It also may be appropriate to use a utility stock benchmark, since utilities are the bellwether of income stocks. Dow-Jones and Standard & Poor's both publish such indexes; again,

S&P's is quite a bit broader than Dow-Jones'. Both are available in most business publications.

Historical Rate of Return Morningstar analytical service reports that through 1994, utility stocks posted a 6.9 percent annual return going back 5 years and an 11 percent return going back 10 years.

International Stock

Description International stocks represent ownership interests in foreign corporations. In most industrialized countries, stocks and stock markets work comparably to the U.S. domestic market. In emerging market economies, however, the rules are sometimes a bit looser and less predictable. Usually, international stocks are traded on foreign exchanges, although a few foreign companies list their stocks on U.S. exchanges in the form of American Depository Receipts (ADRs).

Investment Style International stocks usually are growth investments.

Sources of Risk In addition to the sources of risk inherent in domestic stocks (market, business, and financial risk), international stocks pose some unique risks. The most important of these is exchange rate risk. Unless you're able to invest in ADRs, converting the earnings from your foreign investment is always subject to the ebbs and flows of currency exchange rates. A particular form of business risk may exist in some foreign countries: the risk that a government may nationalize (i.e., take over) an industry or corporation, decimating the value of your investment. Presumably, this is less of a risk in Western democracies than in countries where market economies are a new concept. Finally, there are liquidity risks associated with obscure foreign stocks, as there may not be a buyer when you want to sell an esoteric issue.

Return Benchmark Morgan Stanley publishes a widely recognized benchmark for international stocks: the MSCI EAFE (EAFE stands for Europe, Australia, and the Far East). It measures the performance of international stocks in the developed countries (more on emerging markets shortly). The MSCI EAFE is published in most major business publications.

Historical Rate of Return The average annual return of the MSCI EAFE for the 5 years ending in 1994 was 1.5 percent and for the 10 years ending in 1994 it was 17.6 percent.

Mutual Funds

Mutual funds are an excellent way for investors with modest portfolios to enjoy the benefits of diversification and professional management. Mutual funds own anywhere from several dozen to several hundred different investments. When you buy shares of a mutual fund, you are in essence buying a proportional interest in all the investments the fund owns. It would be difficult if not impossible for average investors to achieve this level of diversification if they attempted to construct a comparable portfolio through direct purchases.

Of course, a fund's holdings will change over time, but in theory that's one of the advantages of this form of investing. Investment experts are constantly managing the fund's portfolio, fine-tuning the investment mix in an attempt to maximize returns. These pros are far more knowledgeable about trends in industries, markets, and investing than most of us ever could hope to be. Their expertise can add value to a mutual fund investment. In fact, professional management is such an important part of mutual funds' appeal that investment advisers keep track of the comings and goings of fund managers. Good managers attract more investors to a fund. Similarly, a change in managers sometimes causes some advisers to recommend delaying an investment until the new management has a chance to prove itself. You'll want to keep these points in mind when we get to the portfolio construction process in the next section.

You can earn money from mutual fund investments in one of four ways, each of which parallels the way you earn money in direct investments:

1. The fund can distribute to you your share of its earnings from debt in the form of interest.
2. The fund can distribute to you your share of its dividend earnings from equity investments.
3. The fund can distribute to you your share of the capital gain it earns on the investments it sells.
4. The value of your fund shares can increase as the value of the fund's holdings appreciates.

Note that, with this last method, your earnings are only actually realized when you receive them by selling shares. Also note that, as with direct investment in stocks or bonds, the value of your shares can decrease if the value of the portfolio's holdings goes down.

One important tip to keep in mind when considering stock mutual funds is that most stock funds distribute earnings to their owners annually, usually in December. Be sure to avoid buying into a stock fund—unless it's part of a systematic investing plan (discussed in the next section)—just before it makes its annual distribution. Since the fund's share price goes down by the amount of the distribution, and the distribution is taxable to you, you pay tax on the money you've just invested if you buy right before the distribution is made. This concern doesn't apply in the case of funds held through tax-advantaged vehicles like retirement plans.

The advantages of mutual fund investing don't come free, of course. Discussions among investment professionals as to how mutual funds—and the advisers who recommend them to clients like you—make their money can become quite heated. It's important to understand all the fees a fund charges because they will lower your total return. The basic rules of capitalism apply here: The less a fund charges, the more you keep. When building your portfolio, you'll need to be sure that you evaluate fees when you evaluate funds. There are three broad categories of fees a fund may charge: sales fees, management fees, and so-called 12(b)(1) fees. Different funds charge these fees in different combinations, so read the prospectus (the descriptive literature the fund provides you) carefully. The applicable fees are spelled out in the beginning.

Sales fees, also called *loads,* can be charged when you buy into the fund (front-end loads) or when you withdraw from it prematurely (redemption fees). Funds usually phase out the redemption fee gradually over a period of five to seven years. Sales fees usually range from 2 percent to 6 percent, but there is nothing (except competition) to limit the fees a fund charges. There are a few loads as high as 8.5 percent. A significant number of funds don't charge any sales fees. These *no-load* funds are obviously very popular with many investors, and a vocal minority of professional advisers advocates the exclusive use of no-load funds. While loads are an important consideration, don't let them become a siren's song. If a load fund meets all your investment needs and it performs well after the fees are factored in, there is no reason not to invest in it. Also keep in mind that loads are a one-time charge. Thus, the longer you hold an investment, the less significant the load's impact on your annual return. Finally, understand that if you're working through an investment professional, there's a good chance that part of any sales fee you pay will go into his or her pocket in the form of a sales commission. It would be nice to think that the person you're trusting with your finances doesn't have split loyalties, but it's also appropriate to have full disclosure and filter the recommendations you're getting appropriately. In short, remember that high fees can only be justified by high returns.

Management fees are paid out of a fund's income to cover investment adviser, custodian, accounting, and legal costs. They generally run from 0.5 percent to 1 percent per year, but can go even higher. The 12(b)(1) fees, named for the section of the federal law that authorizes them, pay for the cost of marketing the fund and distributing its shares to owners. They also are charged annually and usually average less than 1 percent. It should be noted that no-load funds may have higher management and 12(b)(1) fees than load funds. Again, pay careful attention to the fees your fund charges.

Identifying the right benchmark for a mutual fund is not always as easy as for direct investments. This is partly because some funds are highly specialized, making appropriate benchmarks more difficult to find, but also because some funds may not live up to their stated investment objectives. This phenomenon, known as *style slippage,* is discussed in the next section. For funds that claim to focus on any of the investment classes we've covered so far, the benchmark for that class would be appropriate to apply to the fund. Thus, for example, the S&P 500 or the Wilshire 5000 is an excellent benchmark for a garden-variety stock growth fund. Next we consider some funds with very specific investment objectives and note more specific benchmarks for each.

Value Funds

Description Value funds seek growth by investing in common stocks that the fund's analysts have identified as undervalued by the market. The analysts may have determined that a company's earning potential is higher than it appears, that a new development in the company's industry will have an advantageous impact on it, that a firm is a likely takeover target, or that significant consolidation is expected within a particular industry.

Whatever the reason, the fund's managers try to provide superior returns by identifying and investing in undervalued companies.

Investment Style Value funds are a growth investment.

Sources of Risk The sources of risk are those typical to stock funds— market, business, and financial risk. Given the nature of value investing, the level of these risks may be above average.

Return Benchmark There is no identifiable benchmark for value stocks or value funds. It therefore might be appropriate to consider the benchmarks applicable to general stock mutual funds and then to add a premium for the additional risk involved.

Historical Rate of Return As with benchmarks, there is no historical return data specific to value stocks. Again, in the absence of such information, it may be appropriate to use broader market returns as a very rough guide.

Aggressive Growth Funds

Description As the name suggests, aggressive growth funds are basically stock funds on a testosterone binge. In search of superior returns, they may invest in start-up companies, companies selling stock publicly for the first time, or companies in emerging industries. Sometimes, in pursuit of high returns, they may take higher diversification risks, concentrating their holdings in a particular industry they've identified as having above-average growth potential.

Investment Style Aggressive growth funds are a form of growth investing.

Sources of Risk The sources of risk are those typical to stock funds— market, business, and financial risk. However, each of these risks is magnified by the nature of aggressive growth investing.

Return Benchmark There is no widely available benchmark for aggressive growth stocks. Morningstar provides benchmark performance information based on 81 aggressive growth mutual funds it monitors, but this generally is available only to subscribers. Similar information is available from Lipper Analytical Services and Value-Line. You might ask your investment professional for this information or try to find it in a local public library.

Historical Rate of Return Morningstar reports that, for the 5 years ending in 1994, aggressive growth funds had an average annual return of 11.1 percent, and for the 10 years ending in 1994 the return was 13.4 percent.

Small Capitalization Funds

Description Small capitalization funds invest in new ventures under the theory that therein lies the greatest potential for long-term growth. Microsoft once was a fledgling young enterprise, right? The problem, of course, is that there's a broken investor for every light on Wall Street, and it's hard at the small cap stage to distinguish the Microsofts from the Edsels. Because small cap companies are usually start-up ventures, it's highly unlikely they'll pay dividends for many years.

Investment Style Small cap funds are growth investments.

Sources of Risk The sources of risk are those typical to stock funds— business, financial, and market risk. However, each of these risks is magnified by the nature of small cap investing.

Return Benchmark Although a precise benchmark for small caps is hard to find, three contenders come very close: the NASDAQ Composite Index, the Wilshire 4500, and the Russell 2000. The NASDAQ Composite Index tracks the performance of the small cap stocks traded over-the-counter through the National Association of Securities Dealers. The Wilshire 4500 removes the S&P 500 from the Wilshire 5000 and measures the performance of the remaining 4,500 issues in the Wilshire index. Perhaps most indicative, the Russell 2000 subtracts the largest 1,000 listings from its broader index (called the Russell 3000) and reports on the performance of the remaining smaller issues.

Historical Rate of Return Through 1994, the Wilshire 4500 posted 9.1 percent annual returns going back 5 years and 12.6 percent returns going back 10 years. During the same periods, the Russell 2000 averaged 10.2 percent over 5 years and 11.5 percent over 10 years.

International Stock Funds

Description International stock mutual funds offer average investors exposure to a wide variety of foreign investment options. These can range from diversified global funds to funds that limit their investments to a particular region or country, such as Europe funds, Pacific Rim funds, or emerging market funds.

Investment Style International stock funds usually are growth investments.

Sources of Risk The sources of risk for diversified international funds are the same as those for direct international investments (discussed above under international stocks). For country and regional funds, the risks are these and more. Your investment is captive to the overall economic performance of a given country or region. Moreover, in emerging markets, significant political risk and other forms of business risk not familiar to U.S. investors are a source of concern.

Return Benchmark The MSCI EAFE discussed above is an appropriate benchmark for diversified international funds. Morgan Stanley also publishes more specialized indexes appropriate to regional or country funds. These include the MSCI Europe, MSCI Pacific, and MSCI Emerging Market indexes.

Historical Rate of Return The MSCI EAFE return data is provided above in the discussion of international stocks. For periods ending in 1994, the MSCI Europe Index averaged returns of 6.6 percent over 5 years and 18.5 percent over 10 years. For the same periods, the MSCI Pacific Index recorded returns of –1.8 percent going back 5 years and 16.8 percent going back 10 years. The MSCI Emerging Markets Index is not 10 years old yet, but its 5-year annual returns through 1994 averaged 7.5 percent.

Sector Funds

Description Sector funds concentrate their investments in a particular industry. The majority of the fund's portfolio is limited to securities related to that industry. There are hundreds of sector funds investing in industries such as utilities, banking, biotechnology, computers, health care, media, leisure, and dozens of other areas. Sector funds allow investors who believe a particular industry offers the opportunity for superior growth to concentrate their investments within that industry.

Investment Style Sector funds usually are growth investments. However, some sector funds (e.g., utility funds) have an income element to them.

Sources of Risk All the sources of risk common to stock investments (market, business, and financial) apply to sector funds. However, the business risk is intensified by confining investments to a particular industry. Moreover, sector fund investors assume an added risk from limited diversification. The sector portfolio is more tied to the fortunes of a particular industry than is a broad market portfolio.

Return Benchmark Benchmark information by sector is very hard to come by. The major analytical services (Morningstar, Lipper, and Value-Line) compile data for some of the more popular sectors. You might consult your investment professional or local public library for this information. Presumably, however, you are investing in a sector fund because you expect that sector to outperform the overall market. Accordingly, broad market returns ought to be your minimum benchmark, with a premium added for the lack of diversification you are accepting.

Historical Rate of Return Again, the broad market returns provided above may be a good starting point for gauging the performance of sector funds.

Real Estate

Description Investors can own real estate either directly or indirectly. Forms of direct ownership include a primary residence, a vacation home, vacant land, residential rental property, and commercial property. Most people don't usually think of their homes or their vacation homes as investments, and for purposes of investment portfolio construction, they're probably not. Nevertheless, your house is an investment, and some of the information we consider may apply to it. Indirect ownership of real estate usually comes in the form of either a real estate investment trust (REIT) or a real estate limited partnership. As a portfolio investment, indirect investments are a more practical alternative for average investors. The large sums required for direct ownership of investment real estate put it out of reach for many.

The appeal of owning real estate is its ability—usually—to provide an effective hedge against inflation, and that appeal has proven considerable over time. On the other hand, direct owners assume all the costs and headaches incident to ownership, the risk that investment property will not appreciate, and the risk that property intended to produce income will not do so. In the right circumstances, direct ownership of investment real estate can generate helpful tax deductions. These are explained in the "Tax-Favored Investments" section in the chapter on Tax Planning.

REITs are real estate investments that trade like stocks and work somewhat like mutual funds (in that they're "pooled" investments). An equity REIT invests in property it thinks will produce a steady income stream and/or appreciate in value. A mortgage REIT invests in mortgages secured by real estate. The comparatively nominal dollar amounts required to invest in a REIT, combined with the professional property management they offer (in the case of equity REITs), provide an excellent way for average investors to participate in the advantages of real estate investing in a practical manner.

Real estate limited partnerships allow a small group of investors to band together and directly own a particular property or small number of properties, such as a shopping center. The properties owned by the partnership usually are managed professionally. The advantage of these arrangements is that the pooled resources of the limited partners enable them to purchase much larger investments than they could alone. The drawbacks are that such partnerships require large fees and often are difficult to resell. Moreover, the days when these partnerships served as significant tax shelters are long gone.

Investment Style Real estate investments are growth vehicles, except for mortgage REITs, which are income investments.

Sources of Risk The chief sources of risk for real estate are significant liquidity risk and market risk. In the past five years, it has become painfully clear how hard it can be to sell real estate at any price in a down market. Financial risk also can be an issue if too much debt is incurred in purchasing a property.

Return Benchmark Because performance for direct ownership investments is so location-specific, it is almost meaningless to attempt to find an appropriate national benchmark. Some helpful information might be available from a knowledgeable real estate professional or public library in the area where the property is located.

Historical Rate of Return Again, real estate returns for direct investments are very location-specific. However, the advisory firm of Callan Associates, Inc., reports that, through 1994, the composite return on real estate investments of all types was 8.1 percent over 20 years, 3.6 percent over 10 years, and –0.6 percent over 5 years.

Aggressive Investments

There is an ever-increasing number of aggressive or high-risk vehicles for investors to choose from. For average investors, some of them are tantamount to playing the lottery with our portfolios. There are others, however, with which we need at least a passing familiarity. We may want to respond with an intelligent no when someone tries to recommend them, or they may constitute a small percentage of the portfolio of a mutual fund we are considering. Or, for a very few of us with deep pockets and nerves of steel, they may be minor players in our own portfolios. The most widely traded of these aggressive investments are commodities futures and options.

Futures A futures contract is an agreement made in the present to buy and sell specific commodities (rice, wheat, soybeans, etc.) at a stated price on a stated date in the future. The producers of these commodities (i.e., farmers) make good use of futures contracts to ensure level prices for their products. They avoid the risk that their year's harvest will have to be sold on a "down" day in the market their commodity trades in. For the rest of us, however, futures contracts are a form of speculating on what the underlying commodity will be trading at on the day we have to buy or sell it. For professional speculators, futures trading can be a lucrative business. For the rest of us, they can be an enormous risk.

Options   Options give the holder the right to decide whether or not to buy or sell a specified stock (or futures contract) at a specified price (called the *strike price*) before the option expires. A *call* is the right to buy a specific stock at the strike price. A *put* is the right to sell the stock at the strike price. Speculators who expect the price of a stock to change can make handsome profits if they are right. They can lose their shirts if they are wrong.

OUR ISSUES

In a Class of Our Own?

There probably is no such thing as a gay investment, a class of gay assets, or special considerations for us when discussing classes of investments. Interestingly, however, at least according to one benchmark produced by an Atlanta-based investment adviser, companies that adopt gay-friendly employment policies generally outperform the overall market. While there's no Lambda Index published in *The Wall Street Journal* just yet, perhaps the time is ripe.

RELATED TOPICS

How to make smart choices among various growth, income and cash equivalent investments is discussed in the "Asset Allocation and Portfolio Structure" section on page 138.

If an investment has increased in value between the time you buy it and the time you sell it, you will realize a capital gain on the sale. If it decreases, you will realize a capital loss. Gains and losses are explained in the "Capital Gains Tax" section on page 201.

Certain annuities allow you to invest in a wide selection of mutual funds, offering a great way to engage in systematic investing on a tax-advantaged basis. The fundamentals of how annuities work is explained in the "Annuities" section on page 49. Their tax aspects are discussed in the "Tax-Favored Investments" section on page 217.

The tax advantages of municipal bonds are explained in the "Tax-Favored Investments" section on page 213.

Investors in high tax brackets may do well to favor vehicles (like growth mutual funds) that generate capital gains rather than interest or dividends. The advantage of this approach also is explained in the "Tax-Favored Investments" section on page 212.

Similarly, certain real estate investments can qualify for special tax treatment. These tax considerations are analyzed in the "Tax-Favored Investments" section on page 214.

Because retirement savings are such an important goal for so many investors and because there are special rules applicable to investments held in retirement plans, these matters are discussed beginning with the "Computing Retirement Needs and Savings" section on page 231.

ASSET ALLOCATION AND PORTFOLIO STRUCTURE

THE STRAIGHT FACTS

Now that you have some understanding of the various classes of investments available to you, we've reached the critical phase of the investment process: selecting the investment vehicles appropriate for your goals, time frames, and risk tolerance(s). Generally, if you have any significant amount of money to invest, you are well-advised to make these selections with the help of a professional. The task is daunting, and the truth is that you simply do not have the same ability to sift through reams of investment data as financial planners, investment advisers, brokers, or other professionals. For many of us, the main purpose here should be to become educated consumers of these professionals' services.

On the other hand, at times you will feel compelled to make investment decisions by yourself. For example, a young investor just starting out may not be in a financial position to engage professional services. Similarly, most investors who participate in an employer's 401(k) or similar plan make investment allocations on their own from among the (usually limited) options presented to them. How to handle these kinds of situations and what to know before you bring in the experts is the focus of this section.

Asset Allocation

By now you should understand that portfolio diversification is one of the cornerstones of the investment process. You also know that diversification doesn't just mean putting your eggs in several baskets. In terms of constructing your portfolio, it means putting them in several kinds of baskets by investing in more than one class of asset.

EXAMPLE

You have determined that your investment goal is current income, that your time frame is relatively short, and that your risk tolerance is moderate. For you, diversification doesn't just mean investing in several different municipal bonds offering high current yields. It may mean putting some of your assets in municipal bonds, some in corporate bonds, and the remainder in high-dividend stocks such as public utilities.

The method by which these investment decisions are made is commonly referred to as *asset allocation*. Asset allocation actually has a slightly different, and much more technical, meaning among many financial and investment professionals. They use the term to refer to the analytical process by which investments are combined in a portfolio to produce an optimum return for a given level of risk. These pros spend hours with computer models to determine how different combinations of investments will interact in order to choose the best mix possible. The more general understanding of asset allocation, however, merely contemplates the division of an investment portfolio into the appropriate investment classes. Investments are usually allocated first among the three broad investment styles—growth, income, and cash equivalents. Then further investment allocations are made within each style.

Asset allocation strategies are a function of goals, risk tolerance, and time frame, but they also can be influenced by market conditions. Many of the nation's large investment institutions periodically issue recommended asset allocations based on risk tolerance and time frame, and they consider current market conditions when developing their recommendations. Accordingly, these recommendations change over time.

Since a book like this can't take current market variables into account, we'll confine our consideration of asset allocation to goals, time frame, and risk tolerance. You'll learn how to alter the allocation percentages suggested here in order to accommodate differing factors such as changes in time frame or risk tolerance. When you start thinking about how you're going to allocate your portfolio, also be sure to consider how you should adjust your allocations from those presented here in order to account for current market conditions, or ask a professional to help you do so.

There are several ways to develop asset allocation strategies, but perhaps the most appropriate is by it time frame. After all, every investment time frame changes with . . . well, with the passage of the time in which you wish to achieve financial goals.

EXAMPLE
Allocation of your retirement portfolio will reflect long-term goals at age 30. At age 50, your time frame will have changed, and so should your asset allocation. Once you're in retirement, your asset allocation strategies will be different again.

Let's consider several possible allocations based on the time horizon for the underlying investment goals.

Long-Term Investment Goals

If your time frame for investing involves long-term goals, you need to focus first on growth, next on income, and finally on what is traditionally referred to as security of principal. We know from the historical return information for various asset classes provided in the previous section that, over time, growth investments generally outperform all others. Since your time horizon is long, you can afford to abide the short-term ups and downs in the market for growth vehicles. For our purposes, long-term generally means over 20 years. Retirement portfolios are the most common examples of long-term investments—at least for those of us under 50. An investor with long-term goals and average risk tolerance might consider allocating about 60 percent of her portfolio to growth vehicles, about 30 percent to income vehicles, and about 10 percent to cash and cash equivalents. Because opinions about these matters vary, it is common to see recommended allocations vary from these figures by 5 percent to 15 percent.

Intermediate-Term Investment Goals

Intermediate-term goals range from 5 to 20 years. Saving for a child's college education is a common example of an intermediate-term goal. For more and more baby boomers, however, retirement saving is shifting to an intermediate-term objective. An investor with intermediate-term goals and *average* risk tolerance might consider allocating 40 percent of his portfolio to growth vehicles, 40 percent to income vehicles, and 20 percent to cash and cash equivalents. Again, variations of plus or minus 5 percent to 15 percent are common.

Short-Term Investment Goals

Short-term investment goals usually have a time frame of less than five years. Saving for the down payment on a house, a new car, or a special vacation are good examples of short-term investment goals. Building the emergency fund discussed in the "Constructing a Balance Sheet" section in Chapter 1 is a critical short-term goal for many new investors. An investor with short-term investment goals and an *average* risk tolerance might consider allocating 30 percent of his portfolio to conservative growth vehicles, 40 percent to income vehicles, and 30 percent to cash or cash equivalents. Again, alternative recommendations may vary by 5 percent to 15 percent.

Market influences become more important as time frames decrease, so for short-term investments they are downright critical. A short-term investment may not be around long enough to enjoy the highs that help average out the lows. Allocation of your short-term investments therefore must be made with current market conditions in mind.

Current Income Goals

If your investment goals and time frame require current income rather than future growth, your asset allocation strategies will be somewhat different from what we've seen so far. People living in retirement are a common example of investors with current income goals, although anyone who must rely on their investments for a current income stream has goals in this category. Your asset allocation strategy must balance two competing demands. On the one hand, you can't afford to have market shifts result in a loss of principal. On the other, you can't afford to let inflation erode your principal's earning power. The solution is to create a balanced portfolio that accommodates both concerns. Thus, an investor with current income goals and *average* risk tolerance ought to consider allocating 20 percent of her portfolio to conservative growth vehicles, 50 percent to income vehicles, and 30 percent to cash or cash equivalents. Allocation recommendations can vary by plus or minus 5 percent to 15 percent.

Allocating Retirement Savings

Several recent studies suggest that most people have grossly underallocated the assets in their retirement savings account (e.g., 401(k)s). That is, they've allocated too much to income and cash equivalents and not enough to growth investments. Consider carefully whether you fall within this unfortunate majority. Asset allocation principles apply with equal force to retirement savings. A good rule of thumb to follow is this: regardless of whether your goal for retirement savings is long-, intermediate-, or short-term, the percentage of your retirement assets allocated to income and cash (combined) shouldn't exceed your age.

EXAMPLE

You are 35 years old. No more than about 35 percent of your 401(k) or IRA account should be allocated to cash or income investments. The remaining 65 percent should be allocated to growth investments.

Figuring Risk into the Mix

Now that you've seen how an *average* investor would allocate his portfolio given various time frames, it's time to think about which lane you travel in. If your risk tolerance is average, the allocations described above may be appropriate for you. As a general rule, if your risk tolerance is high, you'll want to adjust the allocations to favor growth more and both income and cash less. If your risk tolerance is low, you'll want to do the reverse—increase the allocations to both cash and income and decrease the allocation to growth. Sometimes, if an adjustment from cash to growth (or vice versa) seems too extreme, allocation adjustments to favor income can be a good compromise.

EXAMPLE 1

Your investment time frame is long term, but you consider yourself highly risk averse. Therefore, the 60 percent growth, 30 percent income, and 10 percent cash allocation suggested above is not appropriate for you. After considering your situation carefully, you decide to adjust the allocation so that your portfolio will be invested 40 percent in growth, 30 percent in income, and 30 percent in cash or cash equivalents.

EXAMPLE 2

The same facts as above apply, except you also are concerned that such a heavy weighting toward cash will impede your portfolio's ability to outpace inflation over the long run. Accordingly, instead of making the allocation adjustments in the last example, you decide to adjust the income allocation so that your final mix is 40 percent growth, 50 percent income, and 10 percent cash.

In Example 2, note that you might not have made quite the same adjustments to the "model" allocation if your time frame were different. It's important to know that once you have a firm understanding of your goals, their time frames, your risk tolerance, the classes of investments available to you, and the general allocation percentages, making the allocation "right" for your situation will be almost intuitive.

Generally we've seen allocations in 10 percent increments. There's nothing magical about 10 percent. You should make your allocations using whatever figures work best for you. If, for example, you're torn between allocating 30 percent and 40 percent of your portfolio to growth, don't agonize over it. Compromise on 35 percent.

Accommodating Multiple Goals

Many investors intend for their portfolio to achieve more than one investment goal. For example, you may be trying simultaneously to save for retirement and for the down payment on a house. If you find yourself in this common situation, it may be helpful to think of your portfolio in separate segments. In this way, you will create one set of allocations for your long-term goals, another for your short-term goals, and so on.

> **EXAMPLE**
>
> Tom, age 37, currently has two principal investment goals: the down payment on a vacation home (a short-term goal) and adequate retirement savings (a long-term goal). Tom participates in his employer's 401(k) plan, contributing the maximum amount allowed. In addition, he can invest up to $500 each month toward the down payment on his vacation home. Tom's employer has made it easy for him to segment his portfolio. The 401(k) savings are earmarked for retirement and allocated (consistent with his risk tolerance) among the plan's investment options in accordance with the long-term percentages discussed above. The $500 per month Tom saves toward the down payment on the vacation home he then allocates (consistent with his risk tolerance) in accordance with the short-term percentages discussed above.

As this example suggests, segmenting or earmarking your investments simplifies the process of allocating your portfolio for multiple goals.

Allocating within Each Investment Style

Now it's time to start thinking about allocating within each investment style. Before we begin, however, heed this warning: Since you are beginning to approach the final stages of the investment process, it becomes increasingly necessary that you filter general advice through the prism of your own particular circumstances. If you're uncomfortable doing this, or if you're working with large sums of money, you've reached the point where expert assistance quickly will pay for itself.

To prepare for this next step, we need to review the investment styles of the various investment classes we will eventually choose from. Here's a quick review of the information presented in the previous section's discussion of investment classes (excluding the aggressive investment).

- Growth Investments. These include common stocks, (most) international stocks, directly owned real estate, equity REITs, real estate limited partnerships, and mutual funds whose holdings are comprised of growth investments (including value funds, aggressive growth funds, small cap funds, international and emerging market funds, and sector funds).
- Income Investments. These include certain long-term certificates of deposit, corporate bonds, municipal bonds, Treasury notes and bonds, preferred stocks, some high-dividend stocks (e.g., utility company stock), mortgage REITs, and mutual funds whose holdings are comprised of income investments.
- Cash and Cash Equivalents. These include savings accounts, most certificates of deposit, money markets, and Treasury bills.

These lists are long, and it's highly unlikely you'll be able (or inclined) to make allocations to every investment class within each style. In fact, one of the chief difficulties many investors face as they try to build a portfolio is getting a handle on how many different investments is too many and how many is not enough. While these are highly subjective questions and the answers vary with each investor's circumstances, there are some guidelines that may assist you. For mutual funds, an *average* investor probably should try to diversify her overall portfolio among a minimum of 4 mutual funds and a maximum of 10 funds. For individual investments (i.e., stocks and bonds), a good range would be between 12 and 30. If you're investing in both mutual funds and individual securities, you'll need to find an appropriate way to split the difference. The reason for these ranges is simple: Realistically, you can't keep tabs on more, and you're not properly diversified with any fewer.

These ranges probably constitute the most sweeping of all the investment generalities offered in this book, so a few qualifiers are in order. First, these ranges apply to *average* investors. If your total portfolio is very large, say, over a hundred thousand dollars, these guidelines could quickly become meaningless for you. Next, on the other end of the spectrum, it probably never makes sense to diversify in increments of less than $1,000. Accordingly, if you're just starting out as an investor, it may take you a couple of years to work your way into these ranges. (The one significant exception to the $1,000 minimum applies to systematic investing discussed below.) Finally, if you're a participant in an employer plan, you may not be able to diversify your investments within the ranges indicated. Simply muddle through as best you can, and try to compensate for any lack of diversification with the rest of your portfolio.

Now that we have some sense of how many investments there will be in our completed portfolio, we are in a good position to decide which investment classes belong there. To keep the process manageable, we'll consider how to do this by investment style. To begin, however, take another look at the investment risk pyramid. Note the dispersion of the various growth and income investments on the pyramid in the section on "Investment Risk and Risk Tolerance." As you allocate within each investment style, you'll want to keep the various risk levels in mind. You'll probably allocate a small portion to the lower-risk investment classes within each style, a small portion to higher risk classes, and the balance to those in the middle—all consistent with your overall risk tolerance.

Let's look at some specific strategies when allocating within each investment style.

Allocating among Growth Investments

Clearly, the bedrock of any growth portfolio should be high-grade common stocks (or stock mutual funds), and the majority of your allocation within this style should be to this investment class. Depending on your risk tolerance, you should allocate between 50 percent and 70 percent of your growth portfolio to a diversified selection of these stock investments (with lower risk tolerances tending toward the higher end of this range). As the list above suggests, however, there are other classes of growth investments to choose from. In small to moderate amounts, they are appropriate considerations for most portfolios. They include small cap, aggressive growth, and/or value stocks, international stocks, and real estate. *Average* investors should avoid allocating any more than 15 percent of their growth portfolios to any one of these investment classes.

Portfolios with long time horizons should have at least a small portion of their growth assets invested in small cap and aggressive growth stocks, and, unless your portfolio is very large, probably through mutual funds. These are the areas where, over time, the greatest appreciation in equity investments is likely to be found. For short-term goals, a value fund can serve this same purpose for investors with high risk tolerances—if the fund is rock solid and if the timing makes sense.

International stocks should be a part of every growth portfolio for a number of reasons. First, the economic cycles in many foreign countries don't track that of the U.S. economy, so foreign markets don't always follow the domestic markets' ups and downs. This can provide some important balance to your growth portfolio as it weathers downturns in the U.S. market. High-grade international investments are appropriate, and even desirable, for virtually all growth portfolios.

There has been considerable interest in emerging market stocks in recent years, in part because the fundamental economic indicators for these markets are so attractive. Emerging market economies, including most of Latin America, Eastern Europe, and many parts of Asia, are poised for significant economic growth in the years ahead. One estimate suggests that gross domestic product (GDP) for emerging markets will be 6.4 percent in 1995, compared to a maximum of 3 percent in the United States. The reason for this phenomenal growth is that as the emerging economies modernize, the demand for goods and services is expected to explode. For investors, this means the growth opportunities for investments in emerging economies may be greater. Time frame is key here. Although the expansion of the emerging markets will outpace mature economies over time, the expansion will not occur evenly, as anyone who invested in Mexico before the 1994 meltdown of the peso can attest. Therefore, while emerging market investing should be an important consideration for most growth portfolios, it is appropriate only for long time frames and moderate to high risk tolerances.

Investing in real estate also should be a part of most growth portfolios. Real estate is thought to be a good long-term hedge against inflation, and some real estate investments offer the possibility of superior returns. As a practical matter, however, it is difficult for average investors to directly own real estate. The investment costs, transaction costs, and carrying costs place it out of reach. Accordingly, direct ownership of investment real estate is only appropriate for large portfolios. For average investors, equity REITs can offer an attractive alternative, and a small allocation to a well-researched REIT is appropriate for most risk tolerances.

Allocating among Income Investments

Yield and creditworthiness are the keys to most income investing, and these factors should largely determine how you allocate and ultimately structure your income portfolio. Here's the steps you'll probably want to follow. First, the majority—again, 60 percent to 80 percent—of your income portfolio should be allocated to a diversified mix of investment-grade corporate bonds, municipal bonds, Treasury notes and bonds, and blue-chip preferred stocks. Next, don't underestimate the value of high-dividend stocks like utilities in structuring your income portfolio. The risk of these investments is just a little higher, and you often receive the added benefit of modest growth in the value of the underlying stock. Unless your risk tolerance is super low, some of your remaining income portfolio should be allocated to these investments. Finally, only a small portion of your income portfolio should be allocated to riskier bonds (i.e., those with lower credit ratings). Mortgage REITs and low-grade preferred stocks probably only make sense in a limited set of circumstances.

The special characteristics of municipal bonds merit a brief discussion. As you learned in the discussion of this investment class in the previous section, munis can be a very attractive tax-favored investment. Don't let yourself be oversold, however, when it comes to the perks of investing in munis. If you're in the 15 percent tax bracket, the tax break isn't worth as much to you, and the aftertax rate may not be impressive. Before you invest in munis, be sure you know the aftertax return for *your* bracket, be sure the return is competitive with other income investments, and be sure the creditworthiness of the issuer is top-notch. In short, don't let the tax tail wag the return dog when it comes to investing in munis.

A general word of caution about investing in bonds also is in order. More than a few investors have seen changing interest rates erode the value of their bonds. The discussion of interest rate risk earlier in this chapter explains why. If you find yourself facing this issue at decision-making time, consider investing in debt instruments of shorter duration. This can reduce—but not eliminate—the risk to your principal, since long-term debt is more vulnerable to the effects of interest rate changes than short-term debt. Of course, if you plan to hold the bond until maturity, this concern does not apply to you.

One last thought about income investing: If you don't currently need the earnings from your income investments, you ought to plow them right back into the investment. It's a great way to grow your portfolio and compound the investment's return. For stocks, this technique is called *dividend reinvestment,* which is discussed later in this chapter.

Allocating among Cash or Cash Equivalents

Allocations are made to cash for two main reasons: security of principal and liquidity. We've already addressed the security of principal issue in the process of determining the amount to allocate to cash equivalents. Now we need to focus on your potential liquidity needs. Here's why. Investing in cash equivalents is largely a matter of seeking the highest available interest rate. The interest rate you are paid usually will increase with the length of time you agree to invest your money. This is why three-year CDs pay higher interest than six-month CDs. Thus, it usually works out that the longer you can safely commit to a cash or cash equivalent investment, the higher the interest you will earn.

Did you notice the word "usually" in the last sentence? On occasion, it doesn't work out that longer deposits result in higher earnings. In a time of rapidly rising interest rates, it may actually be counterproductive to commit your money to a long-term investment.

EXAMPLE

You currently have a choice of investing in a one-year CD paying 5 percent, a three-year CD paying 5.5 percent, or a five-year CD paying 6.2 percent. Right now, the five-year rate seems like the best deal. However, would you still feel that way if one-year CDs were paying 7 percent two years from now?

This is an excellent example of the point made earlier about how important it is for you to factor changing market conditions into your decision-making process.

Also remember that, as we saw in the description of this investment class in the previous section, there can be fairly hefty penalties if you attempt to liquidate a time investment (like a CD) before it matures—the "substantial penalties for early withdrawal" of advertising fame.

To know how long you can commit to a cash investment, you need to think about your liquidity needs. At the risk of being circular, this means you need to refer back to your investment goals. If your goals are long term, then your cash equivalents can be invested long term as well; a three- or five-year CD may be appropriate. If, however, you're a new investor and your goal is to build up your emergency fund, then at least part of your investment must go in a very short-term vehicle; for example, a money market. Once you've decided how much of your cash should go in liquid investments and how much can go in time investments, the only work left in constructing this part of your portfolio is to shop for the best interest rates possible.

It should be pointed out that our entire discussion of investing in cash equivalents assumes that the security of the underlying financial institution is not in question. Historically, federal deposit insurance has been the gold standard for making cash investments. In recent years, however, a variety of non-federally-insured financial institutions, including major brokerage houses, have begun offering comparatively safe and highly competitive alternatives for cash investments. If you're confident in the size and security of the alternative, it's probably OK. Just try to avoid putting your cash in the First Bank of Fred.

One final thought on cash investing: If your cash equivalent portfolio is large enough (i.e., greater than $10,000), it would make good sense to allocate as much as is practical to Treasury bills.

Choosing Individual Investments

Up to this point, we've spent a considerable amount of time and effort whittling your investment decisions down into manageable categories. You've decided how to allocate your assets by style, determined how to allocate by class within each style, and segmented your portfolio to accommodate multiple investment goals where appropriate. Now you're ready for the tricky part: actually choosing specific investments.

If the previous warnings about flying solo in this stage of the investment process didn't give you pause for thought, now may be a good time to reconsider them. It is impossible for a book intended for mass consumption to guide individual investors to precise conclusions. The variables—*your* variables—are too numerous. The most we can hope for in this format is to establish some ground rules to guide and inform your individual choices. We will have accomplished our purpose here if you, alone or with an investment professional, are equipped with the tools you need to make the optimum decisions about your portfolio.

Your final task may not be as daunting as it seems. As you proceed, you should discover that all the work you've done thus far has paid off in

another way: You now have a lot of criteria for choosing particular investments. If you need an income fund and the prospectus indicates it's a
growth fund, put it in the recycling pile! You've used the investment
process to identify which investment classes are right for you, so now you
only have to look within the classes you've identified.

Generally, your individual investment decisions will require you to
choose one or two investments from among a small number of preidenti-
fied alternatives. In other words, you likely will be comparison shopping
to choose the investment(s) in each class most suitable for you. Your
401(k) plan will offer you only so many alternative investment options,
your broker will present you with only so many prospectuses, and so on.
If you're not already in this situation, you'll need to get there before you
can go on. As we read earlier, you want to make your selections from a
manageable number of alternatives. So, if someone hasn't already nar-
rowed your options for you, now's the time to do it yourself.

Make a rough cut by using anecdotal information you've gathered
from colleagues and advisers, newspapers and magazines. Just be sure to
limit yourself to the investment classes you've settled on. If it turns out
none of the contenders in your rough cut is right for you, you can always
start again with another group. Don't be afraid to use this same logic with
an investment professional: If you don't think any of the options he or she
has presented is right for you, ask for another slate of candidates.

There is no single set of uniform rules for choosing individual
investments, and investors over time all tend to develop their own styles.
However, every prudent investor will consider the following in making
investment decisions.

1. Gather Data. There is no substitute for doing your homework in
the investment process. Obtain and read the prospectus for any investment you're considering. Also dig up whatever analytical information
you can on an investment. Many private companies compile data on how
various investments have performed. If it's a mutual fund, read what one
of the ratings services like Morningstar, Value-Line, or Lipper has to say
about it. For stocks and bonds, try to get a copy of the company's annual
report or the analysis done by Moody's, Value-Line, or Standard &
Poor's. You should be able to locate these information services in one of
three places: your local library, your investment professional, or on-line.
You'll gain valuable statistical data about financial performance and

transaction costs, which will be helpful in comparing the results of two different investments. However, you'll also get insight into what changes may be brewing that could affect the company's future performance—management changes, changes in the industry, the economy, and so on.

2. Compare Numbers. Once you've got the financial data you need about an investment's past performance, compare it to (1) the other investments you're considering; (2) the historical rate of return for that class of investment (provided in the discussion of investment classes in the previous section); and (3) the current benchmark return for that class of investment (also provided in the previous section). Certainly, when comparing two investments, you are probably going to opt for the one with superior returns (unless your research has unearthed some indication that the historical return pattern is going to change). Beyond that, there are fewer hard and fast rules, but you're generally advised to look for an investment that has at least some history of beating its benchmark.

Be sure that your number comparisons are apples to apples. Prospectuses, analysts, brokers, and other professionals use financial jargon to discuss return: average return, total return, compound return, annual return, year-to-date return, and so on. Don't fall into the trap of, say, comparing one investment's year-to-date return with another investment's annual return. Many professionals recommend reviewing an investment's 3-year, 5-year, and 10-year average returns in order to make a proper evaluation.

3. Transaction Costs. It costs money to buy and sell most investments—brokerage commissions, mutual fund loads, sales charges, and so on. Many investments also charge annual maintenance fees—custodial fees at banks and brokerage houses or so-called 12(b)(1) fees charged by mutual funds. The money you pay for transaction costs eats into your total return. The proliferation of these commissions and fees has prompted many investment professionals to suggest that average investors should limit their investment selections to no-load mutual funds wherever possible. To some this point of view may be extreme. But there is at least one infallible aspect to it: Transaction costs can turn superior returns into inferior ones.

EXAMPLE
Investment A has an average annual return of 7.9 percent for the past three years; investment B's three-year average is 8.5 percent. At first blush, B appears to be the better investment. However, on closer inspection you

realize that B also imposes various transaction fees totaling 1 percent per year; A has no such fees. Now which is the better investment?

Make sure that the figures you use to compare investments account for all transaction costs associated with the investment.

4. Past Performance Is No Guide. While most investors and many investment professionals spend a great deal of time analyzing an investment's past performance, doing so can be misleading. After all, we're not investing for the past, we're investing for the future. Merely because something was performing well in 1990 doesn't mean it's going to do so today. The truth is that we look to the past because it's where most of the analyzable data are, and the data usually tell us some of what we need to know. But the data do not tell us everything, so we have to turn to what professionals call *fundamental analysis* to finish the job.

Fundamental analysis simply means taking a hard look at the economic fundamentals of an investment. Beyond comparing numbers and looking for solid returns, fundamental analysis requires you to get to know a lot about your potential investment and the environment in which it operates. Pertinent questions include:

(a) What is the current economic environment, and what impact is it likely to have on the investment?

(b) What is the current political/regulatory climate, and what impact is it likely to have on the investment?

(c) What changes are occurring in the industry in which the investment operates that might have an impact on its financial performance?

(d) For stocks, is the current price supported by the company's earnings?

(e) For bonds, what is the investment's creditworthiness?

(f) For mutual funds, what recent changes have occurred (or are rumored to shortly occur) in the fund's management?

If these questions sound vaguely familiar, they should. They mirror the discussions of sources of risk discussed earlier in this chapter. Fundamental analysis attempts to identify what impact the various sources of risk may have on the future return of a potential investment.

EXAMPLE
MBI is a company in the computer industry. Its stock has performed at least 6 percent above its appropriate benchmark for the last 15 years. If you

base your decision on MBI's past performance, this stock would sound like a sure thing. However, through fundamental analysis, you learn that a competitor is about to launch a product that will make MBI's flagship product obsolete. Worse yet, you discover that MBI does not have any products in development to meet the competition. Do you still want to buy MBI stock?

In the end, fundamental analysis says, don't just look at an investment's past performance, look at its fundamentals as well.

5. Mutual Funds or Individual Issues?   One difficult decision average investors often face is whether to directly purchase individual securities (i.e., stocks and bonds) or to invest indirectly in such securities through buying shares in mutual funds. There is a breadth of opinion on this issue, and probably no single right answer that works for everybody. Keep this in mind, though: Unless you have a significant amount of money to invest—probably into six figures—you very likely cannot match the diversification offered to you by a mutual fund. Whereas it might not make sense to spread $25,000 over more than five or six individual stocks, that same $25,000 in one mutual fund can expose you literally to hundreds of issues. This diversification alone has made mutual funds the vehicle of choice for many average investors.

There is one potential pitfall, however, that asset allocators should be aware of when they invest through mutual funds: Sometimes a fund's actual investments won't match its stated investment style. Investment pros refer to this as *style slippage.* In other words, just because a fund is called the ABC Growth Fund doesn't mean its portfolio is invested 100 percent in growth vehicles. As a practical matter, it can't be completely invested that way. All mutual funds need to retain a portion of their assets in cash equivalents for a number of reasons, from paying bills to redeeming exiting shareholders. However, difficulties arise for asset allocators when a fund's holdings stray too much from its stated objective. If you've relied on the stated objective rather than on the actual holdings in selecting the funds for your portfolio, your own asset allocations will be thrown off. There are some very good funds for which this is a real issue. At least one major brokerage house, for example, has a high-performing "global allocation" fund that, as of this writing, holds over 70 percent of its portfolio in U.S. investments!

EXAMPLE

Had you decided to allocate 10 percent of your portfolio to international investments and chosen the fund just mentioned for that purpose, you in fact only would have been investing 3 percent of your portfolio abroad.

To reduce the possibility of having your asset allocation decisions thwarted by situations like this, read a fund's prospectus or the analytical information provided by one of the ratings services in order to determine its true class. In short, don't judge a book by its cover.

On the other hand, it is possible to go overboard in trying to achieve your target allocations. The real world is never as pure as the laboratory, and in life your investment choices will never be as clean as they are on paper. If you can come within 5 percent of your target allocations, you've done well.

6. Balanced Funds. So-called balanced mutual funds attempt to do the asset allocating for you. They invest some of their portfolio in growth and some in income. If you've done all your homework and found a balanced fund that you think works well for you—great! Just be certain that you square its allocation strategy with yours to be sure that your overall allocation decisions aren't undercut by the fund's.

EXAMPLE
You've decided to allocate your portfolio 30 percent to growth, 50 percent to income, and 20 percent to cash equivalents. You've selected a balanced fund that is allocated 40 percent to growth, 40 percent to income, and 20 percent to cash. If you invest 25 percent of your portfolio in the fund, you will have allocated 10 percent (25 percent × 40 percent) of your total portfolio to growth, 10 percent (25 percent × 40 percent) to income, and 5 percent (25 percent × 20 percent) to cash. You still must identify appropriate growth investments for 20 percent (30 percent – 10 percent) of your total portfolio, income investments for 40 percent (50 percent – 10 percent) of your total portfolio, and cash equivalents for 15 percent (20 percent – 5 percent) of your total portfolio.

Also remember that investing in a balanced fund is not a substitute for the diversification strategies emphasized throughout this chapter. You still should be investing in several different funds, even if you decide to go the balanced fund route.

7. Index Funds. Index funds attempt to provide returns that match exactly the performance of a given benchmark index; for example, the S&P 500. Because the funds only try to match an index, they tend to have slightly lower management expenses than other mutual funds. They also tend to sell their investments less frequently, which means owners have to report fewer capital gains on their tax returns than with some other mutual funds. To some, index funds may seem like a good way to avoid most of the headaches incident to the investment process. There may even be a place for them in your portfolio. However, they are not the panacea some suggest.

By investing in an index fund, you are precluding the possibility of superior returns, and there are many investments that over time *do* outperform the market. If you're a very conservative investor, a solid index fund may be a good way to expand the limits of your risk tolerance. However, if you're considering an index fund as a way of abdicating responsibility for taking charge of your investments, you're really not doing your portfolio any favors. If you decide to go the index fund route, it's critical that you fully research the fund's managers, track record, and management style. By agreeing to limit your expectations to a market rate of return, you're trusting them with a lot. Again, also remember that index fund investing does not absolve you from the diversification rules.

8. Systematic Investing. For most people, investing is an ongoing process, not a one-time affair. They may have a lump sum they start out with, but then they add a little to it each month. Systematic techniques allow you to add to your portfolio in nominal increments. Remember, it's likely that, in order to achieve your goals, your portfolio has to grow through what you add to it, and not just as a result of its own earnings. Two particular forms of systematic investing are discussed below: dollar-cost averaging and dividend reinvesting. Both techniques help you live up to the Golden Rule from Chapter 1: pay savings first.

For our purposes in the selection process, be sure the vehicles you choose allow you to make systematic investments in increments that work for you. For example, if you budget $250 per month to add to your mutual fund, you might have a problem if the fund requires a $1,000 minimum for additional investments.

Dollar-Cost Averaging

The price of most investments changes over time. Dollar-cost averaging is an investment technique wherein you invest a fixed amount at regular intervals. Doing so allows you to minimize the impact of price changes on your overall investment strategy.

EXAMPLE
You invest $200 per month in the ABC growth fund. In January, ABC sells for $10 per share, so you purchase 20 shares. In February, it is down to $8

per share, so you are able to purchase 25 shares. In March, it is back at $10, so you acquire another 20 shares. You now own 65 shares of the ABC fund at an average cost of $9.27 per share. Had you invested all $600 in January, you would have owned only 60 shares ($600/$10 per share = 60 shares) at an average cost per share of $10.

Of course, this is a simplified—and happy—example of how dollar-cost averaging can work; you came out five shares ahead over three months' time. In reality, though, you might just as easily have come out five shares behind over the same short period. The important thing that can be gleaned from the thrust of this simplified example is that, over time, dollar-cost averaging will allow you to minimize the impact of price fluctuations on your investment purchases. If you think about this example, you'll see that anyone who participates in a regular savings plan does dollar-cost averaging, by default. The technique should be a conscious part of your investment strategy.

Dividend Reinvestment Programs

Dividend reinvesting is a painless way to increase your holdings in an asset. The technique is fairly straightforward: You instruct the entity paying you dividends (usually your stock brokerage or mutual fund) to reinvest the payments in additional shares of the investment.

EXAMPLE
You own 100 shares of XYZ stock, which currently trades for $50 per share. XYZ stock pays semiannual dividends of $1 per share. This means that you receive a $100 dividend payment every six months. If you opted to participate in XYZ's dividend reinvestment plan, the company would simply add two shares of stock to your portfolio when it pays dividends ($100 payment/$50 per share = 2 shares).

In some respects, then, dividend reinvesting is a way for you to convert an income investment into a growth investment. More importantly, it's a simple way to increase the size of your portfolio without making additional changes in the budget you built earlier in this book.

Two considerations need to be made before you opt for dividend reinvesting, however. First, this technique obviously can't work if you're planning to rely on the dividends to meet your current income needs. Second, and more importantly, unless your investment is in a tax-advantaged vehicle such as a 401(k), IRA, or annuity, you must pay tax on the dividends in the year you receive them, regardless of whether you opt for dividend reinvestment. Some people mistakenly believe that they only owe tax if they receive cash; not so—you receive an economic benefit either way, so the government wants its share either way. In order to participate in dividend reinvestment, then, the taxes you pay on your dividends must come from another source.If neither of these considerations creates a problem for you, dividend reinvesting is a no-brainer and ought to be a part of your investment strategy.

Y'all Come Back Now, Hear?

Now that you've decided on the proper allocation of your investment portfolio, your work is done, right? Wrong! The investment process is cyclical, and for a prudent investor it should never end. You must periodically review your allocations to ensure that they are still appropriate to your goals, time frames, and risk tolerance. You also must review your portfolio to ensure that the investments you own actually reflect the allocations you've decided on. For a variety of reasons, the assets in your portfolio will grow at different rates, and occasionally you may need to adjust the composition of your portfolio to be sure it tracks the allocation you've settled on. You don't need to be obsessive about your reviews; more than once-a-year can be counterproductive. On the other hand, if you let your review slide for more than two years, you're probably slacking off.

A Final Word

We've spent all of our discussion of investment strategies focusing on asset allocation. Before leaving this topic, you should know that not all investment pros consider asset allocation an appropriate investment strategy. In fact, a few don't even worry at all about the portfolio diversification we've harped on throughout this chapter. They attempt to make their fortune by anticipating changes in the market or in a particular investment—a technique referred to as *market timing*. It's important to understand two things about these people: (1) they are all professional investors who live—sometimes lavishly—off their investment income; and (2) there are very, very, few such people. You also must understand this: Unless you live and breathe investments for all your waking hours, over the long haul you will not profit from trying to time the market. For the overwhelming majority of average investors—and this probably includes you—asset allocation is the best way to structure a portfolio. For average investors, trying to time the market is tantamount to gambling with our portfolios. No matter how much we may fancy ourselves as high rollers or shrewd market watchers, timing techniques are not right for us.

OUR ISSUES

Until the government comes to its senses and issues currency in a variety of tasteful colors, gay money is every bit as green as straight money. Therefore, our investment strategies are likely to be remarkably similar to what's been described above. Our life experiences will influence how we approach risk, and we may want to steer clear of homophobic investments. But beyond that, the dominant culture's approach should work for us.

RELATED TOPICS

If you're still a little unsure about the difference between growth investments and income investments, review the "Classes of Investments" section on page 114.

For many individuals, retirement savings constitute the lion's share of their invested portfolios. Ironically, several recent studies have found that people are underallocating their retirement portfolios; that is, they have allocated too much to cash equivalents and not enough to growth. If you fear you may be in this situation, re-read the information above on allocating for retirement. Then read the "Computing Retirement Needs and Savings" section on page 231 to be certain you understand how to prepare for retirement.

Certain annuities allow you to invest in a wide selection of mutual funds, offering a great way to systematically invest on a tax-advantaged basis. Read the "Annuities" section on page 49. The tax treatment of annuities is outlined in the "Tax-Favored Investments" section on page 217.

The tax advantages of municipal bonds are discussed in the "Tax-Favored Investments" section on page 213.

For lesbian and gay couples, ownership of investment accounts is not always an easy issue. Unfortunately, the law can add several legal pitfalls to the personal ones. If a partner's name is added to an account, gift taxes may become an issue. See the "Gifts" section on page 321. On the other hand, joint ownership of property can be an effective way to keep assets out of the probate system. This technique is discussed in the "Wills and Will Substitutes" section on page 302.

4

C H A P T E R

Income Tax Planning

INCOME TAX BASICS

THE STRAIGHT FACTS

Despite the angst tax preparation engenders, there is a very straightforward formula for computing federal individual income taxes. Perhaps the simplest way to explain how the math works is through an equation that tracks how the numbers flow on your tax return.

Total Income
– Adjustments
Adjusted Gross Income
– Deductions
– Personal Exemptions
Taxable Income
× Rates from Rate Table
Tax Liability
+ Other Taxes
– Credits
– Payments
Refund or Balance Due

Easy, right? As with most things in life, however, the devil is in the details, and what goes into each component of this formula has been the undoing of countless frustrated taxpayers. In part, that's because each of the items in the equation is a term of art in the tax law. In this section we'll get an overview of what each term means. Then, throughout the rest of the chapter we'll drill down to get the particulars on many of the deductions, credits, and planning strategies applicable to most taxpayers.

Filing Status

When completing your tax return, the tax laws require you to use one of four possible filing statuses, which roughly parallel your familial status: single, married filing jointly, married filing separately, or head of household. Unless you are legally married, you may not use either of the married filing statuses. If you are legally married, you may use whichever married filing status you and your spouse agree to. Generally, joint filers have lower tax bills than separate filers, but if both spouses are high earners, it pays to check the math each way. More often, the separate filing status is used because one party, for whatever reason—often, but not always, an impending divorce—wishes to insulate him- or herself from the other spouse's liability. With limited exceptions, joint filers are each completely liable for the entire tax debt of the couple (this is called *joint and several liability* in legalese).

The rules for head of household status are a little tricky. Head of household is intended to provide tax relief for unmarried people who are the main source of support for children or certain other dependents. Head of household generally is available to single individuals (and certain divorcing spouses) who either (1) pay over half the cost of keeping up the main home of a parent they are eligible to claim as a dependent; or (2) pay over half the cost of keeping up the main home of themselves and a child, foster child, or related dependent who lived with them for more than half the year.

If you're not married and you don't qualify as a head of household, you must use the single filing status.

Your filing status is the key to determining several important components of your tax liability. First, filing status determines which table you use to compute the tax due on your *taxable income*. The tax brackets change at different thresholds for each filing status, making some more "desirable" than others (assuming one can qualify).

EXAMPLE

In 1996, a single filer with $35,000 in taxable income is in the 28 percent tax bracket, whereas a taxpayer with identical income qualifying as a head of household remains in the 15 percent bracket.

Additionally, the amount and availability of many deductions and credits varies with filing status. Some get phased out as income exceeds certain levels; these levels, too, vary by filing status. We'll encounter many such deductions and credits in the following pages.

Total Income

The tax law takes a very broad view of the definition of *income.* Generally, income includes any money or property you receive from any source, unless it is either (1) a gift or (2) specifically excluded from income by the tax law. Stop and reflect for a moment on how sweeping this definition really is. It includes anything you receive for the services you render—from jury duty pay to the fringe benefits provided by your employer. It also includes such diverse items as any prizes, awards, gambling income, or lottery winnings you may receive. Unless there is a section of the law that excludes something, it's income, and it has to be reported as such.

EXAMPLE

If your employer provides you with health insurance coverage, there's a special provision in the Internal Revenue Code that specifically excludes that coverage from your income. Otherwise, you would be required to include in income the premiums your employer paid for you.

If you receive compensation in cash, the amount of your income is equal to the amount of the cash. If you receive property, your income is equal to the fair market value of the property.

These rules are easy to understand when applied to the compensation you receive for the work you do. However, for more complicated transactions, the rules quickly can become equally complicated. Most of these subjects are worthy of their own books, and indeed many fine books have been written on them, but detail just isn't possible here. Nevertheless, so you can get a sense of what's involved, here's a rough summary of some important components of your *total income* for federal tax purposes.

1. Any interest you receive or is accrued on your behalf from any source except

   a. Interest on qualified municipal bonds.

   b. Interest from EE U.S. savings bonds you choose to defer paying tax on until they mature.

2. Dividends from any source, even if you choose to reinvest the dividends in additional shares of the issuing security rather than to receive the cash.

3. Any state income tax refund you receive, but only if you claimed an itemized deduction for the tax when it was paid to the state.

4. If you sell property, your net gain or loss on the sale. (This can get tricky, but your net proceeds generally are equal to the amount of cash and property you receive from the sale minus your *adjusted cost basis* in the property minus the expenses of selling the property. Your cost basis is equal to what you paid to buy the property plus what you paid for capital improvements to the property minus any deduction you claimed for depreciation on the property.) There are limits on your ability to claim some losses from a sale of property all in one year. These are explained later in the discussion of capital gains taxes.

5. If you are a sole proprietor, the net profit or loss from your business.

6. If you are an unincorporated farmer, the net profit or loss from your farm.

7. If you own rental property, your net rents. In limited circumstances, you can claim a net loss from rental property. These circumstances are explained later in the discussion of rental real estate.

8. Alimony you receive (but not child support).

9. Unemployment benefits you receive. This sometimes causes big headaches around April 15th, since tax is not withheld from unemployment checks. You're nevertheless responsible for paying the tax on your benefits.

10. Retirement benefits you receive in excess of the amount of *after-tax dollars* you paid into your retirement plan. This applies to all types of retirement plans, including individual retirement

accounts, Keogh plans, simplified employee pensions (SEPs), 401(k) plans, 403(b) plans, and traditional company pension plans. When you receive payments from any of these plans, there is a formula that determines what percentage of that payment is attributable to your after-tax contributions and hence is not taxable; the remainder is included in your total income. If you receive your payment in the form of an annuity, the formula more or less gives you credit for your after-tax contributions evenly over your life expectancy. If the payment takes any other form, the formula gives you credit for a percentage of your after-tax contributions that is roughly equal to whatever percentage of the total value of your plan the year's payments represent.

EXAMPLE
Your IRA account is worth $10,000. Your total nondeductible (i.e., after-tax) contributions to the account were $4,000. You withdraw $5,000 from the account this year. So 40% ($4,000/$10,000) of that $5,000, or $2,000 ($5,000 × 40%), is excludible from your income, and $3,000 ($5,000 – $2,000) is includible.

If you made no contributions toward the plan, the entire amount you receive is included in income.

11. Part of your Social Security benefits if your *provisional income* is above certain amounts. Provisional income consists of

   a. All taxable sources of income other than Social Security benefits.

   b. Tax-exempt interest income (e.g., municipal bond interest).

   c. Certain foreign income.

   d. 50 percent of all Social Security benefits received.

   The formula for computing how much of your Social Security benefits actually get taxed is very complex, but essentially, up to 50% of your benefits can be taxed if your provisional income is above $32,000 for joint filers and $25,000 for most others. Moreover, up to 85% of your benefits can be taxed if your provisional income is above $44,000 for joint filers and $34,000 for most others.

Other common sources of income include gambling and lottery winnings, prize money, jury duty pay, election worker pay, the value of bartered property, and money generated from a hobby.

A quick word is needed about whether what you receive is a gift or income. If you get money or other property in exchange for services you perform or property you surrender, you have received income, not a gift. It doesn't matter if it came from your heart's true love or as the result of a barter transaction—it's still income. There's no clever way around this, and people caught trying to find such a way can face charges of criminal tax fraud. In order to be a gift, there must be no exchange of value between the parties. Court cases in this area say the motive must be strictly "affection" and "generosity." Also keep in mind that, as a general tax principle, the person giving you money or other property has no hope of claiming a deduction for it unless you include it in income. This principle can have tremendous influence over whether or not a transaction is characterized as a gift.

Of course, if you really do receive a gift, it is not subject to income tax. This means there are no income tax consequences to you for any inheritances you receive. Note that you may have to pay tax on income the inheritance earns during the period of estate administration, but paying tax on the income is not the same as paying tax on the gift itself. Also note that there may be estate or gift tax consequences to the person who gave you the gift. These gift tax issues merit serious consideration when large sums are involved. They are discussed in the Estate Planning chapter.

Adjustments and AGI

Adjustments to income are deductions you may claim for several important categories of expenses. They include

- Alimony you pay.
- Some contributions to retirement plans.
- 30 percent of the health insurance premiums paid by S corporation owner-employees, partners, and sole proprietors.
- Part of the Social Security taxes paid by partners and sole proprietors.
- Penalties paid on early withdrawals of savings.
- Some unreimbursed moving expenses (if the move is over 50 miles and is because of your job).

As shown in the equation at the beginning of this section, to compute your taxable income you first must compute something called your

Adjusted Gross Income (AGI). The tax law uses your AGI to determine your eligibility for a number of other deductions. Not surprisingly, the higher your AGI, the more likely you are to be ineligible for these deductions.

Later in this section we'll discuss other deductions available to individual taxpayers. In contrasting these other deductions with the adjustments we consider here, it's important to remember that adjustments get claimed before computing AGI (*above the line* in tax lingo), while other deductions get claimed after computing AGI (*below the line*).

This distinction is important for two reasons. First, it means that adjustments are slightly more valuable than below-the-line deductions. Since adjustments are subtracted from total income in reaching AGI, they have the effect of lowering your AGI. Thus, while below-the-line deductions only help you lower your taxable income, adjustments both help you lower your taxable income and help you qualify for other tax breaks.

Beyond adjustments, the only other way to lower your AGI is by lowering your total income. This was alluded to briefly in the discussion of total income above. We'll review some ways to do this later in the chapter and other ways in the chapter on Retirement Planning.

The other reason it's important to distinguish between adjustments and below-the-line deductions is that you can claim adjustments regardless of whether you itemize your below-the-line deductions or claim the standard deduction. If you feel lost in the terminology, read on. The next several paragraphs explain the difference between the standard deduction and itemized deductions. The point to remember here is that you can always claim your adjustments, whereas other deductions will only be of value to you if you have enough of them to itemize.

Deductions

Below-the-line deductions include most of the items we commonly think of as tax deductions: some medical expenses, mortgage interest, state income and property taxes, charitable contributions, unreimbursed business expenses, and so on. But, in fact, not every taxpayer claims these deductions. The tax law gives you two choices for claiming below-the-line deductions: you either can claim a preset amount (called the *standard deduction*), or you can claim the actual amount of your total eligible expenses (called *itemizing your deductions*). The advantage of the standard deduction is that you don't have to prove anything; you get to claim the standard amount regardless of your actual expenses. The advantage of itemizing is that, as long as your actual expenses are higher, you can claim amounts in excess of the standard deduction, resulting in a lower bottom line. There are different standard deduction amounts for each filing status, and the amount of the standard deduction is raised slightly each year for inflation.

Taxpayers who are over 65 or blind are entitled to claim a slightly higher standard deduction. Again, the amount of this "additional standard deduction" depends on filing status and changes slightly each year to account for inflation.

The tax law requires some taxpayers with very high incomes (i.e., well above $100,000) to reduce the amount of the itemized deductions they are entitled to claim. The purpose of this requirement is to increase the amount of tax paid by high earners. Unfortunately, the formula used to compute this *phase-out* is extremely complex. To make things worse, some itemized deductions (e.g., mortgage interest, charitable contributions) are subject to phase-out while a few others (e.g., medical expenses) are not. If your income is within the phase-out range, seriously consider getting professional tax assistance. It's likely your tax situation is complicated in other ways as well, and a pro may help you avoid expensive mistakes.

The IRS has grouped itemized deductions into the following categories. Explanations for some categories follow the list.

1. Medical and dental expenses (if they exceed 7.5 percent of your AGI).
2. Certain state and local income and property taxes, as well as certain foreign taxes.
3. Mortgage interest on up to two houses, home equity interest on loans up to $100,000, points you pay to acquire your primary residence, and investment interest.
4. Charitable contributions of cash or other property.
5. Qualifying casualty and theft losses.
6. Job expenses and certain "miscellaneous deductions" like investment fees and tax preparation fees (if in total they exceed 2 percent of your AGI).
7. Other "miscellaneous deductions."

Medical and dental expenses can only be claimed if the amount you spent exceeds 7.5 percent of your AGI. In tax lingo, this is called the *7½ percent floor.* In practical terms, it means your medical expenses are only deductible if you had a very rough year.

EXAMPLE

Your AGI for 19X1 is $40,000; 7.5 percent of your AGI is $3,000. If you had medical expenses of $2,800 in 19X1, the amount you can deduct is $0, because $2,800 is less than your $3,000 floor. Moreover, if your medical expenses for 19X1 were $3,500, the amount of your deduction would only be $500, because that is the amount by which your medical expenses exceed 7.5 percent of your income ($3,500 − $3,000 = $500).

Miscellaneous itemized deductions generally arise from expenses that produce taxable income that you are not entitled to claim anywhere else on your tax return. They come in two varieties: those subject to a *2 percent floor* (that works pretty much like the 7½ percent floor for medical expenses) and those not subject to the 2 percent floor. It's easy to know which ones are which. The IRS publishes a list of those miscellaneous itemized deductions not subject to the 2 percent floor each year. If a category of expense is not on the list, it is subject to the floor. The list is very short, and gambling expenses probably are the only common item on it (this deduction cannot exceed your total gambling income).

Common examples of itemized deductions that are subject to the 2 percent floor include:

1. Job expenses for which your employer did not reimburse you.
2. Tax return preparation fees.
3. Safe deposit box rentals.
4. Legal and accounting fees related to the production of income (e.g., if you sue your employer for back wages).
5. Fees paid for custodial or trust accounts (such as IRAs).
6. Union or professional association dues.
7. Expenses related to a hobby, up to the amount of any income you earn from the hobby.

It seems to be a widely held belief that deducting job-related expenses remains one of the last great tax planning opportunities for average folks. For several reasons, this simply isn't so. First, there's the 2 percent floor; unless your expenses are significant, you're probably not going to get over it. Next, the expenses have to be required by your employer to be deductible; they must be a condition of your employment. Unless your employer specifically requires you to set up a home office or to purchase a computer, you cannot claim a deduction for these items. Regular commuting expenses are never deductible, and expenses for clothing are only deductible in those rare instances where your togs cannot be used anywhere but on the job. In fact, Liberace was probably the last person not wearing a uniform to successfully deduct his clothing expenses! Finally, IRS takes a dim view of this deduction, and high claims in this area often can be audit flags. While some employees, frequently sales professionals, legitimately can claim a deduction for unreimbursed employee business expenses, for more of the rest of us than would like to admit it, our tax planning efforts can be put to more productive use elsewhere.

A number of the other itemized deductions mentioned in this section (mortgage interest, charitable contributions) are widely used and can provide significant tax planning opportunities. We'll examine them in detail later in this chapter.

Personal Exemptions

The law allows you to claim one *personal exemption* deduction for yourself, one for your spouse (if you file jointly), and one for each of your qualifying dependents. It's important to keep in mind that the test for determining whether you qualify to claim a personal exemption for a dependent is not the same test used to determine whether a dependent qualifies you to claim the head of household filing status. In order to claim someone as a dependent for purposes of the personal exemption, the person you are trying to claim must satisfy all of the following criteria:

1. He or she must either be a relative or live with you for the entire year.

2. Unless he or she is your child, his or her total income must be less than the amount of the personal exemption for the year (this is a very low figure—$2,550 for 1996).

3. Unless you and an ex-spouse agree otherwise, you must provide him or her with at least 50 percent of his or her total support for the year.

4. If he or she has a spouse, they must not use the joint filing status when filing their returns.

5. They must be either a U.S. citizen or a resident of the United States, Canada, or Mexico.

Many divorcing parents determine the "custody" of their children's exemptions as part of the property settlement. The IRS usually respects such decisions, provided the parents comply with its paperwork requirements.

As with itemized deductions, the tax law requires some high-income taxpayers to reduce the amount of their personal exemptions. The income levels at which this phase-out begins vary by filing status and rise slightly each year for inflation, but generally they begin when AGI is well over $100,000. The formula used to compute this phase-out is complex, although it's important to note that, for very high incomes (i.e., well above $200,000), personal exemptions can be phased-out completely. Again, if you're in phase-out territory, you should be thinking about calling in the pros.

Other Taxes

In addition to the regular income tax, there are several other taxes you may or may not have to pay when you file your return. First, when you sell a capital asset, such as a house or stock, technically you are subject to capital gains tax—and not regular income tax—on any gain you realize. If you are self-employed, you must pay both the employer's and the employee's shares of Social Security taxes. These are known as self-employment taxes. If you have very high income and numerous deductions, you also may be subject to what is known as the alternative minimum tax (AMT). As its name implies, the purpose of AMT is to ensure that everyone pays a minimum amount of income tax. In order to achieve this purpose, however, Congress created a very complex system in the AMT. Later we'll look at these other taxes in closer detail. A number of penalty taxes that apply if you mishandle your retirement savings are covered in the Retirement Planning chapter.

Credits

As you read through this chapter and try to find ways to lower your tax bill, be mindful of the difference between a tax deduction and a tax credit. In a nutshell, a deduction is used to offset the income that you ultimately pay taxes on, while a credit is used to provide a dollar-for-dollar offset against the taxes you would otherwise owe. If you think about this statement for a minute, it should become clear that credits are more valuable than deductions.

EXAMPLE

You are in the 28 percent tax bracket. A $1,000 deduction will enable you to reduce your tax bill by $280 ($1,000 × 28% = $280). A $1,000 credit, on the other hand, will enable you to reduce your tax bill by $1,000.

Important credits for many taxpayers include the foreign tax credit, child and dependent care credit, and the credit for the elderly and disabled. In addition, the earned income tax credit is an important tax-related incentive for many of the nation's moderate-income workers. We discuss these credits later in this chapter.

Tax Rates

Many tools available to reduce taxes require a knowledge of tax brackets in general, your own tax bracket in particular, and the difference between marginal and effective tax rates. The federal income tax system uses a progressive rate structure. The current tax brackets are 15 percent, 28 percent, 31 percent, 36 percent, and 39.6 percent. Brackets change at different income levels for each filing status. The levels are adjusted each year for inflation. The 1996 tax rates are shown in Table 4–1.

The progressive rate structure has two important implications for our tax system and, more importantly, for your tax planning. First, people with higher incomes will have a greater percentage of their income subject to tax than people in lower brackets.

EXAMPLE

A person with $20,000 in income will pay a lower rate of tax on her last dollar of income than a person with $60,000 in income.

Second, people whose income exceeds the lower bracket will have different amounts of their income subject to tax at different rates.

EXAMPLE

If the person earning $60,000 in the example above is single, in 1996 she will have the first $24,000 of her income taxed at 15 percent, the amount between $24,000 and $48,150 taxed at 28 percent, and any amount above that taxed at 31 percent.

A person's *marginal tax rate* is the rate they pay on their last dollar of taxable income (i.e., the dollar "at the margin"). Note that we're going to use taxable income, and not total income or AGI, to determine our marginal rate. Since taxable income is what you pay tax on, it's the most appropriate point for measuring your marginal tax rate.

EXAMPLE

Consider again the person in the last example whose income was $60,000. Because of her deductions and personal exemptions, her taxable income probably will be under $48,150, in which case her marginal tax rate would be 28 percent.

Your marginal tax rate is important because it helps you understand how much you will lower your taxes if you use a given tax planning technique to lower your income.

T A B L E 4–1

Tax Rates for 1996

For Single Filers	
If Taxable Income Is	**The Tax Is**
Not over $24,000	15% of taxable income
Over $24,000 but not over $58,150	$3,600 plus 28% of the amount over $24,000
Over $58,150 but not over $121,300	$13,162 plus 31% of the amount over $58,150
Over $121,300 but not over $263,750	$32,738.50 plus 36% of the amount over $121,300
Over $263,750	$84,020.50 plus 39.6% of the amount over $263,750
For Joint Filers	
If Taxable Income Is	**The Tax Is**
Not over $40,100	15% of taxable income
Over $40,100 but not over $96,900	$6,015 plus 28% of the amount over $40,100
Over $96,900 but not over $147,700	$21,919 plus 31% of the amount over $96,900
Over $147,700 but not over $263,750	$37,667 plus 36% of the amount over $147,700
Over $263,750	$79,445 plus 39.6% of the amount over $263,750
For Married Filing Separately	
If Taxable Income Is	**The Tax Is**
Not over $20,050	15% of taxable income
Over $20,050 but not over $48,450	$3,007.50 plus 28% of the amount over $20,050
Over $48,450 but not over $73,850	$10,959.50 plus 31% of the amount over $48,450
Over $73,850 but not over $131,875	$18,833.50 plus 36% of the amount over $73,850
Over $131,875	$39,722.50 plus 39.6% of the amount over $131,875
For Heads of Household	
If Taxable Income Is	**The Tax Is**
Not over $32,150	15% of taxable income
Over $32,150 but not over $83,050	$4,822.50 plus 28% of the amount over $32,150
Over $83,050 but not over $134,500	$19,074.50 plus 31% of the amount over $83,050
Over $134,500 but not over $263,750	$35,024 plus 36% of the amount over $134,500
Over $263,750	$81,554 plus 39.6% of the amount over $263,750

EXAMPLE

You are eligible to make the maximum $2,000 tax-deductible contribution to an individual retirement account (IRA). You are squeezed for cash when it's time to make the contribution, so you want to understand how much you'll save in taxes by making the contribution. You need to know your marginal tax rate to do this. If you're in the 15 percent bracket, for example, your savings will be $300 ($2,000 × 15%). If you're in the 28 percent bracket, the savings increase to $560 ($2,000 × 28%).

By contrast, your *effective tax rate* is the overall amount of income that you pay in taxes.

EXAMPLE

Your taxable income is $50,000, and you paid $8,000 in taxes in year 19X1. Your effective tax rate for that year is 16 percent ($8,000/$50,000). (Note that, in contrast, your marginal rate probably is 28 percent.)

Your marginal and effective tax rates will vary depending on which taxes you take into account when computing them. If you use just federal income taxes, your rate will be lower than if you include Social Security taxes. Your rate goes up even more when you throw in other taxes, such as state and local income taxes, property taxes, or sales taxes. Keep this in mind the next time you read about high tax rates—it's important to know *which* taxes went into the equation.

The difference between marginal and effective tax rates can be very confusing. When evaluating a tax strategy, you'll want to use your marginal rate to understand how the savings will affect you. To get a sense of your overall tax burden, however, you'll want to look at your effective tax rate.

OUR ISSUES

The Big Picture

While the framers of our nation's tax laws probably never contemplated the impact of the system on lesbians and gays, there are a host of tax considerations unique to our community. While many of these affect lesbian and gay couples, some are not limited to those of us who have paired off. Moreover, as we've noted in several places throughout this book, lesbian and gay households come in a wonderful variety of shapes and sizes, so the "couples issues" are not limited to our variation on the Ozzie and Harriet theme.

When reviewing how lesbians and gays interface with the nation's tax system overall, the results are mixed. There are places where we're clearly disadvantaged. For example, some gay couples can't take advantage of the lower rates that may be afforded them by filing jointly. However, to the surprise of some, there also are some places where being gay actually works to produce a lower tax bill. Continuing the example, other gay couples may not have to pay the so-called marriage penalty that results when both spouses hold high-income jobs. (The phrase *marriage penalty* refers to the situation where dual-income married couples pay more in tax jointly than they would if they were single filers. Of course, for some married couples, especially those with a stay-at-home spouse, there actually can be a marriage "bonus," but social conservatives seldom mention this phenomenon.)

We'll examine the uniquely gay angles of tax planning—both the good and the bad—in the places they arise throughout the chapter. Let's begin by looking at a few issues that relate to the straight facts we've already covered.

Claiming a Partner as a Dependent

In reading about personal exemption deductions for dependents, it may have occurred to you that it would be neat if you could claim your partner as a dependent on your return. You're right, it would be, but it's extremely hard to do. Remember, your partner *must* meet *all five* of the tests described in the discussion of personal exemptions in order to qualify as your dependent. This means he or she must earn less than the amount of the personal exemption for the year. While this figure is indexed for inflation each year, it's currently less than $2,600. If your partner earned any more than this small amount, he or she cannot be claimed as your dependent. It also may be a problem in jurisdictions with laws restricting cohabitation by people of the same gender. There is potentially analogous case law on the books for this issue, so check with your tax advisor if you think it may apply.

In addition to meeting the five qualifying tests for a dependency exemption, there is one other relevant restriction contained in the tax law: The relationship between a taxpayer and the person he or she wishes to claim as a dependent cannot violate local law. While the premise has never been tested, it is at least theoretically possible that this could be a problem in states with sodomy statutes.

There also are tax consequences to your partner if you claim him or her as a dependent. Your partner cannot claim his or her own personal exemption when he or she files a return. Additionally, if your partner claims the standard deduction, it will be limited to the greater of his or her actual wages or $650.

On the other hand, there are a limited number of circumstances when it may be advantageous (at least taxwise) to claim your partner as a dependent. If your partner has very high medical expenses and qualifies as your dependent, you can claim as an itemized deduction any of those expenses you actually pay. This strategy is beneficial if you are in a higher marginal bracket than your significant other (which you presumably are if he or she qualifies as your dependent). Also remember that you still must meet the 7½ percent floor to actually deduct any medical expenses. If you think this technique might make sense for you, consult with a knowledgeable tax adviser.

Using a Partner to Qualify as Head of Household

While in some cases it may be possible to claim a partner as a dependent for purposes of the personal exemption deduction, (and desirable to do so in even fewer cases), it is extremely rare that supporting a partner will enable you to qualify to file as a head of household. As we learned earlier, this is because the dependency test for the personal exemption is not the same as the dependency test for filing status. In order to be a head of household, you must be related to the dependent by blood, adoption, or marriage. Thus, except in those rare cases where one partner has adopted the other—a strategy for gay couples that has largely fallen out of favor and is no longer legal in some states—supporting a partner will not qualify you to file as a head of household.

Married Filing Separately during a Divorce

For those of us who come out late in life, and sometimes end a heterosexual union in doing so, for a year or so you probably will experience the joys of the married filing separate filing status. In order to keep explanations workable, throughout this chapter we'll generally talk only in terms of single filers, with an occasional reference to married filing jointly. If you're currently using the married filing separate filing status, be aware that the rules often are different for you. When you see numbers given by filing status, remember that the numbers for married filing separately will be different. Nine times out of ten, the applicable married filing separate figure is one-half of the joint filing figure. The other time, the tax law sticks it to separate filers, and the applicable figure is zero.

Health Insurance

In discussing what constitutes income, we in essence said that everything is income unless the tax law says it isn't. We gave the health insurance benefits you receive from your employer as an example of something that would be included in income except that the tax law specifically excludes it. That exclusion only applies to insurance provided for you and your family. Unless she happens to qualify as your dependent, your significant other is not your family as far as the tax law is concerned. Therefore, if you are lucky enough to work for a company that offers health insurance coverage to domestic partners, the value of that additional coverage will have to be included in your total income for the year. Your employer will calculate the difference between the value of single coverage (which is not taxable to you) and the value of the combined coverage you and your partner are receiving. Your employer will report the amount of that difference as income on the W-2 form it issues to you at the end of the year, and you will pay tax on it.

EXAMPLE 1

Moira and Roberta are partners. Roberta is a self-employed animal sitter. Moira works for the Progressive Soup Company. Progressive provides health insurance coverage to the domestic partners of its employees. Since Roberta is self-employed, and would therefore have to buy her own insurance, she and Moira opt to take advantage of Progressive's domestic partner benefits. Progressive pays $290 per month to cover Moira and Roberta; individual coverage for Moira alone would cost Progressive $140 per month. Progressive is required to report as income on Moira's W-2 the $150 per month difference in cost between the dual coverage and the individual coverage ($290 – $140). Accordingly, as a result of this benefit, Moira has to pay tax on an extra $1,800 ($150 × 12) of income for that year.

This situation sometimes can produce unusual results. Employers often use the difference between family coverage and individual coverage to determine the value of the insurance to include in its employee's income. However, family coverage usually contemplates a traditional nuclear family and therefore is priced to provide for a number of medical treatments that are not likely to arise in many gay families, such as childhood illnesses and pregnancies. Thus, family coverage often is significantly more expensive than individual coverage. Depending on the partner's tax brackets, it actually may be more expensive for the covered partner to pay taxes on family coverage than for the noncovered partner to buy an individual health insurance policy.

EXAMPLE 2

The same facts apply as in Example 1, but assume that the difference between individual and family coverage is $275 per month (or $3,300 per year). Further assume that Moira's combined federal and state marginal tax bracket is 40 percent. Moira will pay $1,320 in federal and state taxes in order to have her employer provide health insurance coverage for Roberta.

EXAMPLE 3

The same facts apply as in Example 2, but assume that, as a member of the Professional Animal Watchers Society (PAWS), Roberta can join an HMO for $95 a month, or $1,140 per year. Before taking into account any tax deductions Roberta may be entitled to, Roberta and Moira can save $180 if Roberta buys coverage through PAWS.

EXAMPLE 4

The same facts apply as in Example 2, but the best Roberta can do through PAWS is $150 per month. Now the couple likely is better off if Roberta is covered by Progressive.

You and your partner need to run the numbers like Moira and Roberta did to determine which approach makes the most economic sense. You also may need to consider some noneconomic factors such as, Do both partners have at least some employer-provided coverage? How long is the covered partner's employment likely to continue? What alternative sources of health insurance coverage are available to the noncovered partner? How do the benefits provided by various policies compare to each other? Does the noncovered partner face the risk of serious health problems that may preclude him or her from qualifying for coverage outside of an employer's group?

If you find yourself frustrated by the convoluted machinations required by what is supposed to be this fringe *benefit,* remember not to take it out on your employer. They're just trying to do the right thing. It's up to Congress to change the law in this area.

Deducting a Partner's Medical Expenses

Generally the tax law only allows you to claim an itemized deduction for the medical expenses you pay for yourself, your legal spouse, or your dependents. This usually precludes you from claiming any medical expenses you pay on behalf of your partner. However, there is a special exception that permits you to claim a deduction for medical expenses you pay on behalf of another person who would have qualified as your dependent except that he or she failed the gross income test.

EXAMPLE

Jeff and Tran have been partners for 10 years. Jeff is in the 31 percent tax bracket and Tran is in the 15 percent bracket. Jeff itemizes his deductions, whereas Tran claims the standard deduction. Tran has AIDS, and Jeff is his primary caregiver. After insurance reimbursements, Tran spends $11,000 per year on medical expenses. Tran receives annual disability income totaling $6,000. If he did not receive this income, Jeff would be able to claim Tran as a dependent. If Jeff pays directly the $11,000 in unreimbursed medical expenses, he will be able to deduct them on his return (subject, of course, to the 7½ percent floor).

But remember that the other four tests for qualifying as a dependent still must be met, and the relationship cannot violate local law. Nevertheless, this special rule could provide important relief for some members of our community.

RELATED TOPICS

As we learned in the discussion of total income, when something's not income, it's a gift. Lesbian and gay couples face unique concerns when it comes to gift taxes. These concerns are explored in the "Gifts" section on page 321.

Ways to minimize the tax bite when you tap into your retirement savings are explained in the "Withdrawals and Distributions of Retirement Income" section on page 266.

If you and your partner are in different marginal tax brackets, you may find some helpful suggestions for lowering your overall tax bill in the discussion of bracket arbitrage in the "Basic Tax Planning Strategies" section on page 206.

If you're usually on the border between claiming the standard deduction and itemizing, you might be able to benefit from the tax planning strategy of deduction arbitrage discussed in the "Basic Tax Planning Strategies" section on page 206.

The tax law imposes a number of excise taxes on those who don't jump through the right hoops when it comes to dealing with their various retirement savings plans. These other taxes are outlined in the "Other Retirement Penalty Taxes" section on page 278.

There is a special exception to the usual gift tax rules for medical expense payments you make directly to a health care provider on behalf of another person. This important exception is explained in the "Gifts" section on page 321.

TAX DEDUCTIONS FROM YOUR HOME

THE STRAIGHT FACTS

Home ownership is one of the greatest tax planning opportunities available to the average American. Many of the most significant expenses associated with home ownership are often tax deductible—points, mortgage interest, property taxes, and often home equity interest. These deductions translate into a huge government subsidy to help finance the American dream. As we review the rules for claiming these deductions, remember that they apply only to a primary residence. Vacation homes and rental property are treated differently and are discussed later.

Closing Costs

When you buy a primary residence, some of the expenses involved in getting to settlement can create a current-year deduction. Watch for two particular items: points and prepaid expenses.

Points are the up-front amounts a lender charges a borrower in connection with a mortgage. They usually are expressed as a percentage of the loan amount, and they generally run from zero to three percent of the loan. However, if your credit is bad or your loan represents a substantial risk for some other reason, the amount of points a lender decides to charge can run much higher. If it is customary for a lender to charge points in your area, and the amount of points the lender charges is reasonable, you can claim those points as an itemized deduction in the year you pay them. Lenders are required to report the points you pay on Form 1098 along with your mortgage interest. If your lender hasn't done this, or the amount reported doesn't seem right to you, look for the terms *loan discount fee* or *loan points* on your settlement sheet to confirm how much you paid in points.

Two other points about points. First, the current-year deduction is only available for a loan used to construct, acquire, or substantially improve your house. Thus, if you refinanced your mortgage, you cannot deduct the points charged by the new lender all at once. Instead, you must amortize them over the life of the loan. If thereafter the loan gets paid off early for any reason—you sell the house, you refinance again, you hit the lottery—you are entitled to a current deduction for the balance of the points. Second, you are entitled to deduct points whether you pay them or the seller of the house pays them for you. For example, in a depressed real estate market, you may have convinced the seller to pay your points. If this is the case, the seller-paid points are considered to be a reduction in the purchase price of the house. You are entitled to claim a current-year deduction for the full amount of the seller-paid points, but you must reduce your cost basis in your house by the amount of the deduction.

Prepaid expenses are the amounts collected from a buyer at the settlement table for the first month or so of home ownership. When you go to settlement on a house, the settlement agent usually will collect the mortgage interest for the rest of the month (and sometimes for the next month, too). This gives the lender time to process the settlement paperwork and get your loan into its computer before you send in your first payment. The settlement agent also must apportion any property taxes, condo fees, and so on between the buyer and the seller up to the day of settlement. It therefore is possible that you paid some deductible property taxes or mortgage interest at the settlement table. These items may or may not be reported to you on Form 1098, so it's a good idea to check your settlement sheet for information. Remember, however, that you're looking for prepaid items, not escrowed items. Amounts you escrow for property taxes or the like cannot be deducted until the escrow agent actually pays them out on your behalf.

Mortgage Interest

A taxpayer who itemizes his or her deductions may claim the interest paid on up to $1 million dollars of mortgage debt. Usually your lender will send you a Form 1098 indicating how much interest you have paid each year. However, if it's the first year you've owned your house, or if at the end of the year you've accelerated your January mortgage payment to get an extra deduction in the current year, doublecheck the lender's math. If the lender "sold" your loan to another financial institution, there's a good chance the 1098 you receive from the new lender will not include any of the interest you paid at settlement. Similarly, the interest component of any accelerated payment may not have made it onto the 1098 if you sent it late in the year. (Also remember that, when you accelerate the January mortgage payment, the 1098 for the following year could be off.)

In order to qualify as deductible mortgage interest, the loan must be for the construction, acquisition, or substantial improvement of your primary residence. That is, the mortgage proceeds must be used to build, buy, or renovate your primary residence. Thus, the money you spent for a weekend at the spa because the contractor has worked your last nerve does not qualify!

Property Taxes

A homeowner is allowed an itemized deduction for the property taxes paid on his or her residence. Often, mortgage lenders require borrowers to make monthly escrow payments to ensure that property taxes are paid on a timely basis. If this is the case, the lender usually includes on the 1098 the amount of property taxes paid on a borrower's behalf during the year. If you do not escrow property taxes through a lender, but pay them directly yourself, consult your property tax bills and canceled checks to determine the amount of your deduction. One trap for the unwary: If your taxing authority separately states the cost of a particular service, you may not deduct the amount charged for that service from your taxes. This often happens when a taxing authority issues a property tax bill that separately lists the charges for trash collection or sewer service.

> **EXAMPLE**
> Ramon receives a property tax bill from San Anselmo County. The bill indicates that his property taxes are $1,800 annually, including $180 for trash collection. Ramon may claim a property tax deduction of $1,620 ($1,800 − $180 = $1,620).

Regardless of whether you escrow property taxes through a lender or pay them directly yourself, you cannot deduct payments for specific services.

Home Equity Loans

A taxpayer's residence can be an ideal source of tax-favored borrowing. In certain circumstances, the tax law allows you to deduct the interest you pay on a *home equity loan* (i.e., a second mortgage secured by your primary residence), regardless of what the borrowed funds are used for. This is a unique exception to the general rule requiring loans secured by your residence to be used to purchase, build, or improve it in order to be deductible. However, home equity loans are a double-edged sword. People who aren't careful in how they use their home's equity can find themselves facing unexpected and expensive problems. Here's how to be tax-smart and street-smart with your home's equity.

First, let's review the basic rules governing the deductibility of interest payments. Since the tax laws were reformed in 1986, interest paid on credit card debts, student loans, car loans, and just about all other forms of unsecured consumer credit are no longer deductible as personal interest.

Some other types of interest, however, are still deductible (usually within certain limits). Mortgages on your first and second home, investment interest (certain interest on loans used to purchase income-producing investments), and business-related interest fall within the deductible category. So does one other type of interest: home equity interest.

In order to deduct the home equity interest you've paid, you must meet the following criteria:

1. You must itemize your deductions (i.e., file Schedule A).

2. The loan on which you paid interest must be secured by your primary residence or vacation home—the lender must have a lien against your house.

3. The total outstanding home equity indebtedness for which you claim an interest deduction cannot exceed $100,000.

Using your home's equity to meet your borrowing needs can provide some serious tax advantages. That's because interest you couldn't otherwise deduct can be claimed on your return if it's paid to satisfy a debt secured by your house. The planning opportunities are almost limitless. Consider just a few common possibilities.

EXAMPLE 1

You want to purchase a new car. You can finance the car either through a car loan from your credit union or a home equity line from a local bank. Assuming the interest rates on both loans are about the same, your monthly payments will be about the same. You estimate the payments will be about $300 per month, and that in the first year you will pay $2,700 in interest (the rest will go to paying down the principal on the loan). The critical difference: Interest on the credit union car loan isn't deductible. By opting for the tax-advantaged home equity loan, you can save $405 in federal taxes if you are in the 15 percent tax bracket ($2,700 × 15% = $405) and over $750 if you're in the 28 percent bracket ($2,700 × 28% = $756).

EXAMPLE 2

You have a $4,000 balance on your credit cards, and the interest rate is 19 percent. You can get a home equity loan that would bring the interest rate down to 8 percent, and your minimum required monthly payment down from $150 to $125. On top of this savings, however, the interest on your debt repayment becomes tax deductible, and you save about $180 in taxes for the first year if you're in the 15 percent bracket and $336 if you're in the 28 percent bracket.

Clearly, there can be some pleasant tax (and nontax) advantages to borrowing against your home's equity: usually lower taxes and sometimes lower monthly loan payments. There are also risks if you misuse your home equity—risks that can leave you caught short further down the road. We explored these risks, along with techniques for avoiding them, in the "Managing Consumer Debt" section in the chapter on Financial Planning.

Vacation Homes

If you are fortunate enough to own a second home, the tax law offers a number of advantages to you, although there are a few differences from how the law treats your primary residence. Mortgage interest on a second home is deductible in the same manner as with a primary residence, as are property taxes. Points, however, must be amortized (i.e., deducted proportionally) over the life of the loan in all instances, even on the initial purchase of the property. You may recall this is different from how the law treats points paid in acquiring a primary residence.

It's worth noting here that a *residence* has a surprisingly broad definition under the tax law. As long as a structure has sleeping, cooking, and bathroom facilities, it's a residence; the white picket fence is strictly optional. Thus boats and mobile homes that have these facilities qualify, as of course do houses, townhouses, condos, and co-ops.

OUR ISSUES

Just Paying the Bills Isn't Enough

Frequently, more than one person is contributing toward the payment of monthly expenses in lesbian and gay households. This usually occurs in the context of a couple, but sometimes nonromantic relationships evolve around home ownership. It is important to understand that, regardless of the nature of your relationship, only individuals who (1) own a house *and* (2) who are obligated on the mortgage secured against it are entitled to claim a tax deduction for mortgage interest.

EXAMPLE

John and Paul have been in a committed relationship for seven years. John is a financially secure partner in an architectural firm; Paul is a stand-up comedian/waiter. Three years ago, they decided that Paul would move into John's home. John contributes about 80 percent of the household expenses, with Paul picking up the other 20 percent. John and Paul would like to be able to deduct the mortgage interest in proportion to their respective contributions. However, because the house is legally owned only by John, and because only John is obligated on the mortgage, only he can claim a deduction for the mortgage interest.

Similar restrictions apply to the deductibility of property taxes (i.e., only a person who legally owns property is entitled to claim a property tax deduction for it).

In contrast, a straight married couple filing a joint return would be able to claim a deduction for mortgage interest and property taxes even if the property and mortgage were only in one spouse's name.

Nominee Reporting

Once a lesbian or gay couple determines that both partners are entitled to claim a deduction for mortgage interest, there's one more hurdle they must overcome: making sure that they reconcile the amounts they deduct with the amounts reported to the IRS on the Form 1098 they receive. Typically, a lender reports the entire amount of mortgage interest in just one owner's name and Social Security number, even if there is more than one name on the deed and the note.

When this happens, the following steps must be taken. First, calculate what portion of the total mortgage interest each partner is entitled to claim. This can be done by determining how much each partner contributed toward the mortgage payments that year and allocating the mortgage interest deduction accordingly.

EXAMPLE
Renee and Fran own a home together. They pay the mortgage each month from a joint household checking account. Over the course of the year, Fran and Renee each contributed $6,000 to the account. Each should deduct half of the mortgage interest expense on their own tax return.

Next, the partner in whose Social Security number the mortgage interest has been reported claims only his or her portion of the mortgage interest as an itemized deduction. This amount is reported on the line of Schedule A captioned "home mortgage interest reported to you on Form 1098" (or words to that effect).

Finally, the other partner (i.e., the one in whose name and Social Security number the mortgage interest has not been reported) claims his or her portion of the mortgage interest as an itemized deduction on the Schedule A line captioned "home mortgage interest not reported on Form 1098" (or words to that effect). The legend "See Attachment X" is written in next to this line, and the statement shown in Figure 4–1 then is attached to this partner's tax return:

FIGURE 4–1

Mortgage Income Attachment

ATTACHMENT X

LINE XX—HOME MORTGAGE INTEREST NOT REPORTED ON FORM 1098

TAX YEAR 19XX

Taxpayer's Name
Taxpayer's Social Security Number

The following person received Form 1098 for deductible home mortgage interest on a jointly-owned property.

  Partner's Name
  Couple's Address
  City, State, Zip

  Partner's Social Security Number

The amount of the mortgage interest deduction claimed on this return has been allocated to this taxpayer as follows:

Total Interest Reported on Form 1098	X
Interest Claimed by Taxpayer	Y
Interest Claimed by Partner	$(X - Y)$

This allocation is based on the taxpayer's contributions to the payment of the mortgage.

Tax Planning for Three Homes

The tax structure actually provides an interesting planning opportunity for well-heeled gay couples who, in addition to their primary residence, wish to own more than one vacation home (or, for example, a vacation home and a boat). The limit on deducting loan interest from just one second home applies to each person in a gay couple individually.

> **EXAMPLE**
>
> You and your partner co-own a townhouse in the city. You also maintain a condo at the beach for weekend getaways. You and your partner recently have begun contemplating the purchase of a sailboat to keep near the beach condo. You own the townhouse jointly, and you both contribute equally to the expenses of owning it, including the mortgage and property taxes. You own the beach condo yourself, paying the mortgage and property taxes on it alone. If you purchase the sailboat, you could not deduct any interest you would pay if you financed it. However, if your partner purchases the sailboat, he can treat it as his second home (assuming it has a head and a galley) and deduct the interest on the loan.

In effect, gay couples may be eligible to deduct the interest on up to one more house than married straight couples. Ask your tax adviser if this can work for you.

RELATED TOPICS

The very serious gift tax consequences if you add or remove a person's name from the deed to a house are discussed in the "Gifts" section on page 321.

For some lesbian and gay couples, titling property jointly with a right of survivorship often can be an effective way to keep a house out of probate court. However, this technique is not for everybody, and often not for those with large taxable estates. To understand when joint tenancy makes sense, see the "Joint Ownership of Property" section on page 309.

Your house probably will be one of the most valuable items in your estate when you die. It may increase the chances that your assets will be subject to the federal estate tax. If you think your estate (or the combined estates of you and your partner) might be worth more than $600,000 when you die, read the "Estate Tax Planning Techniques" section on page 328.

Lesbian and gay couples who cannot document that each contributed equally to the payments on a jointly-owned home may find part of their home is subject to federal estate tax more than once. To understand and avoid this trap, see the "Estate Planning Basics" section on page 287.

If you rent out one of the homes you own, there are a host of important tax and financial implications. Read the "Rental Real Estate" discussion on page 214 for more details.

To defer taxes when you sell your primary residence, see the discussion of rollover of gain in the "Tax Planning When Selling a Home" section on page 225. To eliminate taxes when you sell your primary residence after age 55, see the discussion of exclusion of gain in the same section.

Your house represents a major investment. To understand how best to protect that investment, see the "Homeowner's Insurance" section on page 86.

There can be nontax pitfalls in the misuse of your home's equity. These traps, along with strategies for avoiding them, are covered in the "Buying a House" section on page 19.

If you own a home with a friend or lover, seriously consider spelling out the rights and obligations of each party. This is discussed in the "Domestic Partnership Agreements" section on page 361.

CHARITABLE CONTRIBUTIONS

THE STRAIGHT FACTS

The Deduction

Taxpayers who itemize are entitled to claim a deduction for the contributions they make to recognized charities. The deduction can be claimed for the full amount contributed, up to 50 percent of your income. This 50 percent limit can be lower—only 30 percent or even 20 percent of your income—if your donation consists of property rather than cash. If the amount of your donation exceeds the applicable income limit, you generally can carry the excess forward to use in the next tax year (again subject to the applicable income limit). There is a five-year limit on these carry-forwards.

Also keep in mind that your contribution must be to a recognized charity. A contribution that you make directly to individuals—for example, the quarter you give every day to the homeless person in front of your office building—does not qualify for the deduction.

Proving It

As with any deduction a taxpayer claims, the IRS may ask for proof of the contribution. Historically a canceled check usually sufficed. However, in 1993 the rules changed for contributions over $250, and the law now imposes very specific substantiation requirements on taxpayers who claim deductions for large contributions. You must obtain written substantiation from a charity to which you donate more than $250 in a single contribution in order to claim a deduction. Moreover, since the "single contribution" requirement created the possibility that some people could game the system (by writing multiple checks), Congress included in the new law what's called an antiabuse provision to help keep people honest. The best way to understand these new rules is to look at a few examples.

EXAMPLE 1
You place a $10 check in the collection basket at church each week. Even though the total amount you've contributed for the year exceeds $250 ($10 × 52 weeks = $520), you will not need a receipt from the church to claim a deduction, because each contribution is counted separately.

EXAMPLE 2
On December 31, 1994, you decided to contribute $300 to your church's building fund. You wrote two checks for $150 each. You must obtain a receipt or acknowledgment before you file your 1994 tax return in order to claim the deduction. Even though neither check exceeded the limit, your intention was to make a contribution in excess of $250.

Canceled checks do not satisfy the new substantiation rules for contributions over $250. You will need some sort of receipt, acknowledgment, or computer printout from the charity to be able to claim your deduction. The law places the legal burden on you, the donor, to obtain the receipt in order to claim the deduction. Most charities are geared up to help you comply with the new rules. It's likely that your charity will be as helpful as possible. After all, they want more of your money next year!

Donating Property

In addition to cash, you can claim contributions for the market value of property—such as clothes, household items, or stock—you donate to a recognized charity. However, if you make charitable contributions of property worth more than $500, you are required to attach a form to your tax return giving the IRS the details of the transaction. Also, donations of property worth $5,000 or more require verification from the recipient. All this helps the IRS to verify the real value of certain large contributions that in the past have tempted some taxpayers to "exaggerate" a little.

The amount of the deduction for donated property is equal to its fair market value on the date of the contribution. If you paid more for the property than it is worth when you donate it, your contribution still is limited to its fair market value. As you might imagine, taxpayers and the IRS sometimes battle over how to value donated property. If you're contributing something very expensive, you certainly should engage the services of a qualified appraiser in order to help substantiate your deduction. Also keep in mind that, for donations of clothing and household goods, the IRS considers the fair market value to be equal to what similar items sell for at local thrift stores.

EXAMPLE

Philipe purchases a $275 Armani polo shirt. After wearing it to a party one evening, he concludes that the style is horrible and Giorgio has taken leave of his senses. Because he has worn it, Philipe is reluctant to return the shirt for a refund. Instead, he donates the shirt to the Salvation Army, where polo shirts sell for $9. Philipe's charitable contribution deduction for the shirt is $9, not $275.

Most IRS auditors have something akin to a price list from the local thrift shop they use in deciding how much to allow for charitable contributions of clothing and household goods.

As we saw earlier, sometimes when you donate property, the annual limit on the amount of your charitable contributions deduction is lowered from 50 percent of your income to 30 percent (or even 20 percent). The rules get terribly tricky here for three reasons.

1. If your contributions for the year are both cash and property, you have to deal with multiple limits simultaneously.
2. The nature of the property you donate has an impact on which limit applies.
3. The type of organization you donate the property to and how they intend to use it has an impact on which limit applies.

Although you may want to seek professional assistance if you're donating expensive property, here's a few general rules to keep in mind.

- If you contribute property to a veterans' organization, fraternal order, cemetery, or (often) a private foundation, the annual income limit for the deduction is reduced from 50 percent to 30 percent.
- If you contribute property that has appreciated in value, the annual income limit for the deduction is reduced from 50 percent to 30 percent.
- If you contribute property that has appreciated in value to a veterans' organization, fraternal order, cemetery, or (often) a private foundation, the annual income limit for the deduction is further reduced from 30 percent to 20 percent.
- If you contribute property to any charity for its own use, the annual income limit for the deduction is reduced from 50 percent to 30 percent.

A few final technicalities regarding donations of property are worth mentioning. First, if you donate property for which you have previously claimed a depreciation deduction (usually this means business property), you may have to "recapture" in income the amount of any accelerated depreciation you claimed. Next, if you sell property to a charity at a bargain price, the "bargain" element is treated as a charitable contribution, but the remainder of the transaction is considered a sale, which may result in a taxable gain if the property has appreciated in value. Third, you generally have to donate your entire interest in property before you are entitled to claim a deduction for the contribution.

EXAMPLE
You own an office building. You donate rent-free use of a portion of the building to a qualified charity. Since you still own the building, you have contributed a partial interest and are not entitled to claim a deduction.

Lastly, in the midst of this mumbo jumbo, a possible tax planning opportunity exists: When you donate appreciated property, you avoid any capital gains tax you otherwise would have paid if you sold the property. The tax savings offered by this strategy has motivated the donation of countless works of art, jewelry, books, historic relics, and buildings.

By now you should have a strong sense that, if you are contributing valuable property to a charity, good tax advice is well worth the investment.

Quid Pro Quo

Remember, too, that if you receive anything from a charity in return for your contribution, you must reduce your deduction by the value of the property received. Tax geeks call these *quid pro quo* contributions. In order to help you figure out the correct amount to deduct, the law generally requires charities to tell you how much the item they're giving you is worth.

EXAMPLE

You send the local public television station a $75 contribution and they send you a $15 compact disc in return. You can only claim $60 ($75 − $15 = $60) as a deduction on your tax return.

Volunteer Work

You cannot claim a deduction for the value of your time when you do volunteer work or perform complimentary services for a charity. You are entitled to deduct the reasonable out-of-pocket expenses you incur while performing volunteer work at the behest of a charity, including a deduction for reasonable mileage you accrue while doing charity work (12 cents per mile as of this writing). In most situations, the deduction for out-of-pocket expenses does not extend to meals purchased while performing charitable work.

EXAMPLE

Min works as an attorney for a large law firm. Min's firm bills his time at $250 per hour. He volunteers four hours every other Saturday morning at the local gay men's health clinic drafting wills for people with AIDS. Notwithstanding the fair market value of Min's legal services, his charitable contribution deduction is limited to the cost of any out-of-pocket expenses he incurs. Examples of allowable out-of-pocket expenses might include the mileage he accrues driving to the clinic, and the costs of paper or photocopies he pays for.

OUR ISSUES

Advocacy Groups Aren't Always Charities

An organization that qualifies to receive tax-deductible charitable contributions is known in tax parlance as a *501(c)(3) organization*. However, there are over 20 categories of 501(c) organizations discussed in the Internal Revenue Code, and only the (c)(3)'s are recognized as charities. While there are many lesbian and gay groups working toward important goals for our community, not all of them qualify as charities under the law. Generally, for example, organizations that endorse candidates for public office do not qualify. Thus, a contribution you give to such a group probably would not be deductible. Nonprofit organizations are required to tell you whether or not they qualify as tax-deductible charities, so read your receipts carefully. If you're not sure about the status of a donee organization, ask whether it's a 501(c)(3).

Joint Gifts

When lesbian and gay couples make charitable contributions, a question usually arises as to who is entitled to claim a deduction for the contribution. It may be easiest to answer this question by first considering who can't claim the deduction. If one partner (partner A) makes a contribution using cash or funds from a nonjoint account, the law probably will presume the deduction for that contribution to belong entirely to that partner (partner A). In other words, partner B probably is not entitled to claim a portion of the deduction. If partner B were able to prove that she reimbursed partner A for all or a portion of the contribution, the presumption probably would be overcome and the deduction would be allowed. In the end, a couple probably is more audit-proof if they make joint contributions from a joint account. In the absence of a joint account, each partner should write a separate check to the charity from his or her own account for the portion of the total contribution he or she intends to deduct.

Once you've crossed this initial paperwork hurdle, the law may actually present a planning opportunity for gay couples who make joint gifts. If two partners are in different tax brackets, it may be possible to allocate the contribution in such a way as to increase tax savings, as long as the allocation is reasonable. Consider the following three examples of how this technique can and cannot work.

EXAMPLE 1

Pat is a doctor at the county hospital. Her income is $170,000 per year, and she is in the 36 percent federal tax bracket. Her partner, Fran, is a counselor at the local office of Planned Parenthood. Fran's income is $30,000 per year, and she is in the 15 percent bracket. All income is deposited into a joint checking account. Fran and Pat make a $10,000 contribution to Catholics for Choice, a recognized 501(c)(3) organization, from their joint account. If they each claim one-half of the contribution as an itemized deduction, it will save Pat $1,800 in taxes ($5,000 × 0.36) and Fran $750 ($5,000 × 0.15). The couple's total tax savings as a result of the contribution is $2,550 ($1,800 + $750).

EXAMPLE 2

The same facts apply as in Example 1, except that Fran and Pat allocate the deduction based on how much each contributes to their joint account. Since Pat contributes 85 percent of the funds in the account [$170,000/($170,000 + $30,000)], she reasonably can deduct 85 percent of the contribution made from that account, or $8,500. In doing so, she increases her tax savings from $1,800 to $3,060 ($8,500 × 0.36). Of course, the tax benefit of Fran's contribution is reduced from $750 to $225 ($1,500 × 0.15 = $225). Nevertheless, the total tax savings for this couple has increased by $735, from $2,550 to $3,285 ($3,060 + $225).

EXAMPLE 3

The same facts apply as in Example 1, but Pat wants to deduct the entire $10,000 contribution. It is likely that the IRS would not deem this a reasonable allocation and would limit Pat to the 85 percent figure computed in Example 2.

There are several things for lesbian and gay couples to keep in mind when considering how these examples might apply to their own tax planning. First, there is a dramatic difference in Fran and Pat's tax brackets— 15 percent versus 36 percent. If one partner is in the 28 percent bracket and the other is in the 31 percent bracket, much of the value of this planning is lost. Next, while Fran and Pat's single $10,000 contribution may seem exceptional to most middle-income couples, keep in mind that, over the course of the year, it is likely that a couple will make numerous smaller contributions that amount to similarly substantial sums. By consistently applying the allocation techniques explained herein, some lesbian and gay couples can achieve tax savings on the same order of magnitude as Fran and Pat's. Finally, if the degree of a couple's income discrepancy is as substantial as Pat and Fran's, it might be advisable for the high-income partner to maintain a separate checking account to maximize the value of charitable contributions—and indeed all itemized deductions. If Pat had contributed the $10,000 from her own account, the entire amount would have been deductible at her 36 percent bracket, saving the couple another $315 in taxes ($3,600 – $3,285).

RELATED TOPICS

Charitable contributions can be an important part of any estate plan, and they are particularly significant ways for lesbians and gay men to perpetuate the important work of community-building. Charitable contributions also can lower federal estate taxes and state inheritance taxes and sometimes generate a current income tax deduction. To understand these possibilities, read the "Charitable Contributions" section on page 188.

To learn more about how couples can maximize the tax value of all itemized deductions, including charitable contributions, see the "Bracket Arbitrage" section on page 206.

Charitable contributions can be an important part of tax planning for any high-income taxpayer. However, the law limits the amount of itemized deductions—including charitable contributions—a high earner can deduct each year. This "phase-out" is discussed in "Charitable Contributions" section on page 188.

TAX CREDITS

THE STRAIGHT FACTS

The tax law provides for a number of personal credits that may be taken against an individual's tax liability. Some of these credits are refundable; that is, they can be used to reduce a person's tax liability below zero, thereby creating a tax refund, even when no tax was paid in. Other credits are nonrefundable; they can be used to reduce a person's tax liability to zero, but not to create a refund greater than any tax paid in.

The following refundable credits may be available to you:

- The earned income tax credit.
- A credit when excess Social Security taxes are withheld from your salary (eligibility for this credit usually arises when a high-wage earner switches jobs midyear).
- The credit for federal excise taxes paid on non-taxable uses of fuels.
- The credit for the original purchase of a qualified lightweight diesel vehicle, if purchased before 1999.

The following nonrefundable credits may be available to you:

- The foreign tax credit.
- The credit for child and dependent care expenses.
- The credit for the elderly or the disabled.
- The credit under a state or local qualified mortgage credit certificate program.

- The credit for the original purchase of a qualified electric vehicle, if purchased before 2005.
- The credit for certain alternative minimum tax amounts paid in prior years.

In the rest of this section, we'll take a more detailed look at four of the more widely used tax credits.

Earned Income Tax Credit

The tax law provides a refundable credit known as the earned income tax credit to assist low- and moderate-income workers. The amount of the credit varies based on a complex formula that uses a taxpayer's earned income and the number of his or her qualified children. The relevant figures increase slightly each year for inflation, but to give you a sense of the ranges involved, for 1996 they are

1. For an individual with no qualifying children, the maximum credit is $306. This maximum credit is available on earned income of $4,220, after which the credit begins to phase out and is reduced to $0 by the time earned income reaches $9,500.

2. For an individual with one qualifying child, the maximum credit is $2,152. This maximum credit is available on earned income of $6,330, after which the credit begins to phase out gradually and is reduced to $0 by the time earned income reaches $25,070.

3. For an individual with more than one qualifying child, the maximum credit is $3,556. This maximum credit is available on earned income of $8,890, after which the credit begins to phase out gradually and is reduced to $0 by the time earned income reaches $28,490.

The term *earned income* refers to your wages, salaries, tips, bonuses, and all other forms of compensation. It also includes disability income and the net profits from your business if you are a sole proprietor. It does not include pensions, annuities, unemployment compensation, or workers' compensation. Earned income also usually doesn't include interest and dividends. However, if you receive more than $2,350 in unearned income such as interest, dividends, rents, and royalties, you may not claim the credit.

A *qualified child* is your child, grandchild, great-grandchild, stepchild, or a foster child who lives with you the entire year. To qualify, the child must either be under age 19 (24 if a full-time student) or permanently and totally disabled. Finally, the qualifying child must live with you for at least half the year, and that residence must be within the United States.

If you have no qualifying children but meet the income test, in order to claim the earned income tax credit you must live in the United States for at least half the year, be over 24 but under 65, and not be claimed as a dependent on anybody else's return.

If you know you are going to be eligible for the earned income tax credit, you can file paperwork with your employer to have a portion of the credit included in each paycheck you receive. If you think you are eligible for this benefit, check with your payroll or human resources department about completing IRS Form W-5.

Foreign Tax Credit

If you pay taxes to a foreign government, the tax law gives you the choice each year of claiming the amounts you pay either as a nonrefundable credit or an itemized deduction. If you recall the earlier discussion of the difference between a credit and a deduction, at first blush opting for the credit would appear to be a no-brainer. However, the tax law imposes some limits on your ability to claim the credit, so some taxpayers opt to claim the deduction.

One of the most important limitations on the credit is the numbingly complex formula used to compute it. The formula requires you to separate your foreign income into categories based on what type of income it is.

1. Passive income.
2. Interest from a country with high withholding taxes.
3. Income from a financial services company.
4. Certain dividends from U.S. international sales companies.
5. Certain payments from foreign sales companies.
6. Dividends from companies where a minority of the owners are Americans.
7. Income from shipping activities.
8. Income from taxable foreign trade activities.
9. Foreign income that does not fall within any of the above categories.

Once you've divided your income by category, your foreign tax credit for that category is limited to the lesser of (1) the foreign taxes you paid or (2) the portion of your total U.S. income tax attributable to your income from that category.

Many people pay foreign taxes because of their investments. Ironically, average investors with only a small percentage of their portfolios invested abroad who go to the trouble of jumping through all these hoops usually find that all of their foreign taxes are eligible for the credit. The problem, of course, is that if you've only had nominal amounts of foreign taxes withheld from your foreign-source income, this effort may be more trouble than it's worth. If you find yourself in such a situation, in the long run it may be easier to claim foreign taxes as an itemized deduction, assuming that you itemize. A good rule of thumb is: If you've paid less than $25 in foreign taxes, go for the deduction. If your foreign taxes are between $25 and $50, it's a toss-up. If they're over $50, it probably makes sense to grind out the paperwork to claim the credit.

Child and Dependent Care Expense Credit

You may be eligible for the child and dependent care expense credit if you pay another person to care for either (1) your child under age 13 or (2) your spouse or another dependent who was unable to care for him- or herself. You must have paid for the care in order to enable you (and your nondisabled spouse if you're married) to earn a salary or look for work.

The amount of the credit you can claim is based on three things.

1. How much you pay for child and dependent care services.
2. How many children or dependents receive those services.
3. Your AGI.

The credit is equal to 30 percent of your employment-related expenses (discussed below) if your AGI is under $10,000. Above $10,000, the percentage decreases by 1 percent for every additional $2,000 in AGI until it reaches a minimum of 20 percent for AGIs of $28,000 and above.

Employment-related expenses are the payments you make to the people who provide child or dependent care for you so you can work. If you have only one child or dependent, the maximum amount of your actual employment-related expenses that can be taken into account is $2,400. If you have more than one child, this figure is doubled to $4,800. Thus, for one child or dependent, the maximum credit cannot exceed $720 ($2,400 × 30%) for taxpayers with AGI at or under $10,000, and $480 ($2,400 × 20%) for taxpayers with AGI at or above $28,000. Again, if you have more than one child or dependent, these maximum credits double to $1,440 and

$960, respectively. If your AGI is between $10,000 and $28,000, your maximum credit will fall somewhere between these figures.

In certain circumstances, you can claim the credit if you hire a relative to perform child or dependent care services for you. To do so, the relative you hire cannot be a dependent and must be over 19. Of course, your relative will be expected to include in his or her income the payments you make. In fact, regardless of whether they're your relatives, you must give the IRS the name, address, and Social Security number of the people you pay in order to claim the credit.

Credit for the Elderly or Disabled

The tax law provides a nonrefundable credit to senior citizens age 65 and older and to disabled persons regardless of age. The credit is available to U.S. citizens below specified income levels. In order to qualify for this credit as a result of disability, your disability must be total and permanent, you must be younger than your employer's mandatory retirement age, and you must receive taxable disability benefits.

The credit is equal to 15 percent of a base amount (discussed below) minus any nontaxable Social Security benefits minus any excess AGI (discussed below).

The *base amount* is $5,000 for a single person over 65 ($7,500 if filing jointly and both spouses are over 65). For a person under 65 qualifying for the credit as a result of disability, the base amount is limited to the lesser of $5,000 or the disability income for the year. Taxpayers claiming the credit based on disability also must file a physician's statement with their tax returns.

Excess AGI is one-half of the amount by which a single taxpayer's AGI exceeds $7,500 ($10,000 for joint filers). This means that the credit is eliminated for single taxpayers with AGI of at least $17,500 ($20,000 or $25,000 for joint filers, depending on whether one or both are over 65).

You can see from this simplified explanation that the amount of an individual's credit is highly fact-specific and that a lot of math goes into computing it. It is important to keep in mind that the maximum credit a single filer can claim is $750 ($1,125 for joint filers who both are over 65) and that for most taxpayers the credit is usually a much lower amount. Consider the following example:

EXAMPLE

Dave is a single 49-year-old who was diagnosed with HIV/AIDS seven years ago. Two years ago he retired on permanent and total disability. He received the following income for the year: nontaxable Social Security benefits of $3,000, $100 in interest from a bank account, and taxable disability income of $8,400. This means that Dave's AGI is $8,500 ($8,400 + $100). His credit is 15 percent of: (base amount − nontaxable Social Security Benefits excess AGI) = [$5,000 − $3,000 − ($8,500 − $7,5000/2)] = ($5,000 − $3,000 − $500) = $1,500. Thus, Dave's credit is $225 (15% × $500). Note that, since Dave's disability income was $8,400, he used the lower $5,000 figure for his base amount.

OUR ISSUES

Credits That Can Help People with AIDS

Two of the credits discussed in this section may be of value to people dealing with HIV/AIDS or other serious illness. First, if you are in a relationship and are financially supporting a partner who is ill, you may be eligible for the dependent care credit discussed above. In order to claim the credit, your partner would need to qualify as your dependent on your tax return. As we discussed in the "Income Tax Basics" section, this means that he would not be eligible to claim his own personal exemption when filing his tax return and that his deductions would be limited to the greater of $650 or his actual wages. However, if you paid for someone to stay with your dependent partner so you could go to work, the amount of the credit is significant, and it might be worth running the numbers to see if you and your partner will come out ahead.

Similarly, an individual with HIV/AIDS or other serious illness who has gone on disability should remember that the credit for the disabled outlined above may be available to help lower his or her tax bill.

RELATED TOPICS

If you're confused about the difference between a credit and a deduction, see the explanation in the "Income Tax Basics" section on page 161.

If you have employed someone to work in your home, such as a caregiver for a person with AIDS, you may be subject to the domestic employment tax rules, which are detailed in the "Nanny Tax" section on page 203.

OTHER TAXES

THE STRAIGHT FACTS

Capital Gains Tax

When you sell certain assets such as stocks, bonds, and real estate—classified by the tax law as capital assets—the gain or loss from the sale is taxed under the capital gains tax rules (as opposed to the regular tax rules applicable to ordinary income). The tax law slightly favors capital assets in order to encourage certain economic activity.

There are two important features of the capital gains regime. First, the maximum rate of taxation on capital gains is 28 percent. If you're in the 15 percent bracket, your capital gains are taxed at 15 percent. Your capital gains are treated on your tax return the same as other items of income. Ditto for the 28 percent bracket. However, if you are in the 31 percent, 36 percent, or 39.6 percent brackets, your capital gains are taxed at only 28 percent. This creates some planning opportunities for taxpayers in the upper brackets, which are discussed in the "Basic Tax Planning Strategies" section later in the chapter.

There is a second tax benefit contained in the capital gains rules. At the end of the year, once you tally the gains and losses from each of your transactions, the tax law allows you to claim up to $3,000 in net capital losses to lower your total income. This rule is meant to help soften the financial blow from an investment that's gone south. Because of it, investors sometimes consider selling stocks or bonds they know will generate capital losses around the end of the year as a way to help reduce their total income for the year. The advantages of this tax planning opportunity must be weighed carefully against the investment's overall performance, what its fundamentals suggest about likely performance in the future, your investment goals, and your overall tax situation.

If your net capital losses for the year exceed $3,000, you can carry the excess forward to next year's return to offset that year's capital gains. If you still have carry-forward losses after you've offset all of that year's gains, you can use up to another $3,000 to reduce that year's total income. You can keep doing this indefinitely until your losses get used up.

Self-Employment Tax

If you are a sole proprietor or a partner in a partnership, you must pay Social Security taxes along with income taxes when you file your return.

What's worse, the tax law considers you to be *self-employed,* which means you have to pay both the employer's and the employee's portions of Social Security. This adds up to 15.3 percent of your net self-employment income on the first $62,700 in wages; this 1996 figure is indexed for inflation. Above that amount, you only have to pay the Medicare portion of the self-employment tax, or 2.9 percent. You are entitled to deduct half of your self-employment taxes as an adjustment when computing AGI.

Alternative Minimum Tax

Congress devised the alternative minimum tax (AMT) system as a way to ensure that taxpayers with very high income and many deductions and tax shelters—called *preferences* in AMT jargon—pay at least some income tax. The AMT system runs parallel to the regular income tax system. In theory, you pay Uncle Sam the higher of your regular tax or your alternative minimum tax.

To compute your AMT, you start with your regular taxable income and add back the following preference items:

1. Personal exemptions you deducted.
2. The standard deduction if you claimed it.
3. Itemized deductions you claimed for state and local taxes, some mortgage and home equity interest, most miscellaneous deductions, and a portion of medical expenses.
4. A portion of some depreciation deductions.
5. A portion of the gain or loss on some property sales.
6. Any gain the regular tax rules allowed you to avoid on the exercise of qualified incentive stock options you received from your employer.
7. A portion of some income recognized under an installment sale.
8. A portion of some *passive activity losses* (such as rental real estate losses) you claimed.
9. A portion of any deductions you claimed for depletion or drilling activities associated with oil and gas investments.
10. The tax-exempt interest income generated by so-called private activity municipal bonds.

After you've added these items back to your regular taxable income, you subtract out a hefty $33,750 AMT personal exemption ($45,000 if filing jointly) to reach your alternative minimum taxable income (AMTI).

You then pay tax at a flat 26 percent on AMTI up to $175,000. The rate increases to 28 percent when AMTI exceeds this amount.

The good news about the AMT is that only a very small number of taxpayers are subject to it. Even then, it tends to be a one-time affair, triggered by an unusual receipt of income, and not an annual event. The bad news is that when the AMT hits, it can hit hard. If you are one of the unfortunate few subject to the AMT, here are a few things you can do to minimize its impact:

1. Defer itemized deductions. Where possible, itemized deductions that are treated as AMT preference items (e.g., medical expenses, home equity interest) should be deferred to the next (i.e., non-AMT) tax year.

2. Delay incentive stock options. If you can, you should delay the exercise of any incentive stock options until the next (i.e., non-AMT) tax year.

3. Re-evaluate investment decisions. If you are a high-income taxpayer regularly subject to the AMT, it may make sense to switch out of tax-free investments. Your after-tax return on taxable investments may actually be superior once the AMT is taken into account. Consult a tax adviser if the sums involved are substantial.

4. Accelerate income. If you are in the 36 percent or 39.6 percent marginal tax brackets for regular tax purposes and know you will be subject to the AMT, it actually may make sense to accelerate income into the current year. In doing so, the income will be taxed at the lower AMT rates (26 percent or 28 percent) in the earlier year, rather than at the higher regular tax rates (36 percent or 39.6 percent) in the later (i.e., non-AMT) year. Again, check with a tax pro for details. You should not be trying to fly solo when it comes to the AMT!

"Nanny" Tax

If you employ someone to work in your home, such as a maid, babysitter, nurse, gardener, cook, or chauffeur, you may be a domestic employer, subject to special rules regarding the reporting and paying of domestic employment taxes—also known as *"nanny"* taxes. If you have domestic employees, you must comply with all the nanny tax rules relating to

1. Withholding your employee's Social Security and Medicare taxes (FICA).
2. Paying your share of FICA and federal unemployment taxes (FUTA).
3. Reporting and paying to the Internal Revenue Service all taxes.
4. Keeping proper records.

You must withhold FICA taxes from the wages of any domestic employee you pay more than $1,000 per year. FICA should be deducted starting with the first paycheck, rather than waiting to see if the $1,000 threshold will be reached. If the threshold is not reached, you must refund the tax withheld. A separate rule applies for FUTA taxes. If the sum of all wages paid to all domestic employees equals or exceeds $1,000 in any calendar quarter, then you owe unemployment taxes. You're not required to withhold federal income tax from your employee's pay unless he or she asks you to and gives you a completed Form W-4, Employee's Withholding Allowance Certificate.

There also are several reporting requirements you must satisfy if you are a household employer. You must furnish a Form W-2 to your employee by January 31st each year. The W-2 must be filed with the Social Security Administration by the last day of February. You also have to report to the IRS all FICA and FUTA taxes, as well as any income tax withheld at your employee's request. The IRS has devised a new Schedule H, Household Employment Taxes, you can attach to your tax return for this purpose.

Currently, you may pay to the IRS the taxes you have withheld from your domestic employee's wages, as well as the FICA and FUTA taxes you are responsible for, annually when you file your own tax return. However, starting in 1998, domestic employers will be required to pay domestic employment taxes either through quarterly estimated payments or by increasing the tax withheld from their own wages.

Finally, there are recordkeeping requirements that apply to household employers. If you withhold FICA or income tax, you must keep a record of the name and Social Security number of each household employee. As an employer, you must apply to IRS for an employer identification number (EIN) in order to file Form W-2 and Schedule H. Every employer is required to verify that an employee is either a U.S. citizen or legal alien eligible to work in this country. Your employee must complete Part I of the Immigration and Naturalization Service Form I-9, Employment Eligibility Verification. You must complete Part II. Adequate earnings records must be kept for at least four years, along with copies of all employment tax returns, Forms W-2 and W-4, and other relevant information pertaining to household employees.

One of the most difficult aspects of the nanny tax is knowing whether a household worker is an employee subject to the rules or an independent contractor exempt from them. A worker is an employee if you have control over the type and manner of the work done. It doesn't matter if he was hired through an agency or whether he works full- or part-time. If you have the right to tell him where, when, and how to work, he probably is an employee. Also, if you provide him with the tools and materials he needs to do his job, then he is your employee.

EXAMPLE
Someone who cuts your lawn once a week, uses her own tools, and decides when to do the job based on her schedule is an independent contractor, not an employee.

Anyone 18 or under who is a full-time student and not working principally as a household employee is excluded from the definition of domestic employee for purposes of the nanny tax rules. This exception is intended to cover the high school student who babysits on weekends.

OUR ISSUES

Hiring a Significant Other to Reduce the SE Tax

Self-employment taxes can impose a tremendous burden on small business owners, many of whom find themselves paying more in SE tax than in income tax. Accordingly, there is a strong incentive to do everything possible to lower the amount of your self-employment income through the use of legitimate business deductions. One excellent strategy for this involves hiring your partner as an employee of your business, a technique detailed in the "Basic Tax Planning Strategies" section later in this chapter.

RELATED TOPICS

Because of the comparatively favorable treatment of capital gains under our tax system, investors who pay tax in the higher brackets should consider structuring their portfolios to favor capital gains rather than current income. This technique is explained in the "Tax-Favored Investments" section on page 212.

If you're considering selling a capital asset in order to generate a capital loss to lower your total income, be certain your decision makes good investment sense. Review the "Asset Allocation and Portfolio Structure" section on page 138.

If you own a business, the many tax planning opportunities from hiring your partner as an employee are detailed in the "Basic Tax Planning Strategies" section on page 206.

If you aren't quite sure how your taxable income—the starting point for figuring out if you owe AMT—is computed, review the explanation given in the "Income Tax Basics" section on page 161.

BASIC TAX PLANNING STRATEGIES

THE STRAIGHT FACTS

In earlier sections of this chapter we reviewed some specific tax planning strategies that were closely linked to the particular exemption, deduction, tax, or credit being explained. In this section, we discuss some basic tax planning strategies with broader applicability.

Bracket Arbitrage

Arbitrage is a fancy word that refers to the ability to time financial transactions in order to maximize their overall return. In the stock market, arbitrage might mean buying securities on one exchange where they're trading for a lower price while at the same time selling the same securities on another exchange where they're trading at a higher price. In an age of instant communications, this sort of basic arbitrage opportunity rarely arises anymore, but there are individuals who make very handsome incomes by engaging in more sophisticated forms of market arbitrage.

Tax bracket arbitrage involves a similar shifting on the taxpayer's part. It involves legally moving income from a higher bracket to a lower bracket. There are two ways you can engage in tax bracket arbitrage: (1) shift income to a lower-bracket taxpayer (usually a family member or someone else with whom you have both an emotional and economic relationship) or (2) shift income to a lower-bracket year of your own.

At first blush, shifting income to a lower-bracket taxpayer seems like a straightforward affair: transfer title to the assets producing the income to a relative or friend in a lower tax bracket. Of course, once you transfer title to an asset, you no longer have control over it. Not surprisingly, therefore, most people are very cautious about to whom they choose to transfer their assets. A spouse, who normally would be a logical choice for such a transfer, will not be of much help in this instance. He or she (presumably) is filing joint returns with you, which means you haven't successfully shifted income out of your bracket.

Children may be the next logical choice for transferring assets. However, the effectiveness of shifting income to one's children is limited by a part of the law known as the *kiddie tax*. The restrictions, which apply to the "unearned" (i.e., investment) income of children under age 14, work as follows: A child's first $650 in income is tax-free, the next $650 is taxed at 15 percent, and the remainder is taxed at his or her parent's marginal tax rate. These figures are indexed each year for inflation.

> **EXAMPLE**
>
> Your daughter, age 12, earns $1,500 in taxable interest income each year. The first $650 of that income is tax-free to her. The next $650 is taxed at 15 percent, or $97.50. The last $200 will be taxed at your marginal rate—$56 if you're in the 28 percent bracket, for a total tax of $153.50.

This $153.50 compares favorably to the $420.00 in income tax you'd pay on the interest if the account were in your name ($1,500 × 28%, assuming you're in the 28 percent bracket), so there is still some potential for tax bracket arbitrage by titling income-producing assets in your children's names. While the kiddie tax rules don't eliminate this tax savings strategy, they do limit its utility.

The kiddie tax rules don't apply to a child's earned income (e.g., wages from part-time jobs, etc.), and they don't apply once a child reaches age 14. Parents can elect to report and pay kiddie tax on their own returns, or they can file separate returns for their children.

Other relatives also can be good "partners" for tax bracket arbitrage. Elderly parents often can fill this bill.

> **EXAMPLE**
>
> Your mother is a widow in her early 60s. She is in the 15 percent tax bracket, and you are in the 31 percent bracket. Although you do not claim her as a dependent, you do provide your mother with about $2,000 in financial assistance annually. If you and your spouse transfer into your mother's name a brokerage account valued at $20,000 and returning about 11 percent (or $2,200) annually, she will still receive about the same amount of money from you after she pays taxes. You, however, will have reduced a $682 tax bill ($2,200 × 31%) to $330 ($2,200 × 15%).

Also remember that there can be gift tax consequences when you change the ownership of income-producing assets. Make sure that your arbitrage efforts don't collide with the gift tax rules, discussed in the Estate Planning chapter.

The other form of tax bracket arbitrage involves timing your own items of income or deduction in order to ensure they provide the maximum tax benefit to you. In general, where you have the ability to control the timing, you should try to recognize income in a year where you expect to be taxed in a lower bracket and pay deductible expenses in a year in which you will be taxed at a higher bracket. To do this, you need to compare your tax bracket for two years in order to determine which year is more advantageous for you. Usually opportunities for this kind of tax planning occur toward the end of the calendar year, sometimes in connection with a pending change in employment status.

EXAMPLE 1

In December of 19X1, you decide to sell some of your stock for a $10,000 gain. You expect to be in the 28 percent tax bracket that year, which means you will pay $2,800 in income tax on the gain. However, you also expect to be in the 15 percent bracket in 19X2, which means you would pay only $1,500 in tax on the gain. By waiting until January to sell your stock, you could save $1,300 in taxes ($2,800 – $1,500).

EXAMPLE 2

Your property tax bill ($2,500) is due in February of 19X2. However, you will be retiring in that year, and expect that your tax bracket will go down from 28 percent in 19X1 to 15 percent in 19X2. If you pay the bill in December of 19X1, you will generate an extra $325 in tax savings for yourself, assuming you itemize your deductions in both 19X1 and 19X2 [($2,500 × 28%) – ($2,500 × 15%)].

Also remember that this technique works regardless of which way your brackets are shifting from one year to the next.

EXAMPLE

Your property tax bill ($2,500) is due in January of each year, so you usually pay it in December. However, you know that you will be receiving a promotion in the first quarter of 19X2, which will move you from the 15 percent to the 28 percent tax bracket. By waiting until January to pay your taxes this year, you will generate an extra $325 in tax savings in 19X2.

The hard part about this kind of tax bracket arbitrage is figuring out what tax bracket you're going to be in for each of the years you are comparing. You need to have a good sense of your finances for two years in order to be successful at it. If you feel confident about your projections, a few hours with a calculator in December could be advantageous. On the other hand, if your income and expenses fluctuate widely, this strategy may not be for you.

It is critical that you understand some important limits on your ability to engage in this form of arbitrage before you try it. First, with regard to the timing of income, once you have control of the money, you no longer have the ability to defer taxation of it until the next year. This concept is called *constructive receipt* in tax jargon. Once you have constructive receipt of income, you must pay tax on it.

EXAMPLE
You receive a $3,000 dividend check on December 29th. You know you will be in a lower bracket the following year, so you wait until January 2nd to deposit the check. You are in constructive receipt of the income on December 29th so you must pay tax on it in the earlier year and in the higher bracket.

If you are a salaried employee, you have constructive receipt of your wages once you are entitled to receive them, so you can't ask your employer to hold your paycheck until January.

Also, with regard to the timing of deductions, while prepaying certain expenses (e.g., property taxes, charitable contributions) in December can help generate some extra deductions for the current year, there is a limit to what the IRS tolerates. While the IRS will consider your individual facts and circumstances if it audits you, a helpful rule of thumb is that you should not try to prepay deductible expenses more than one year in advance, absent compeling or unusual circumstances. (Some tax pros even consider this too aggressive and would be more comfortable with an outer limit of six months.)

Finally, tax bracket arbitrage only makes sense if there is a big jump in rates. For example, if you can shift a deduction from a 15 percent rate in 19X1 to a 28 percent rate in 19X2, it is a good idea to wait to January to pay the expense. However, if the shift is only from the 28 percent bracket in 19X1 to the 31 percent bracket in 19X2, it probably makes more economic sense to take advantage of the deduction in the earlier year. The small (i.e., 3 percent) tax advantage in the later year is more than offset by the time value of the money saved lowering your taxes in the earlier year. (The *time value of money* considers what *x* amount of money received at some specified point in the future is worth today because of that money's ability to earn income over the time interval from today to that specified future point.)

One of the most significant opportunities to engage in bracket arbitrage arises in many workplaces, and the tax law actually encourages you to engage in it. If your employer offers any form of tax-deferred savings, such as a 401(k) plan or a 403(b) plan, by participating in that plan you are using arbitrage techniques. You presumably will be in a lower bracket when you retire than you are while you're working (although some futurists question the validity of this assumption), so by putting money in the plan you defer taxes on it until you withdraw the funds in retirement. You also enjoy the advantages of deferring taxes on the interest, dividends, and capital gains your contributions earn, in effect multiplying your arbitrage opportunities. We'll look at this in more detail in the Retirement Planning chapter.

Deduction Arbitrage

If your deductions routinely put you on the border between itemizing and claiming the standard deduction, you may be able to benefit from *deduction arbitrage*. Like bracket arbitrage, this technique requires you to time the payment of your deductions in order to maximize their (tax) effectiveness. However, instead of accelerating or deferring expenses in order to take advantage of a rate change between years, you're going to "batch" your deductions in order to take advantage of the value of the standard deduction.

This strategy isn't for everyone. It's only for people whose deductions hover around the standard deduction threshold each year. If you're always above that amount, or always below it, you can't profit from this technique. Thus, for example, if you own a home and pay mortgage interest each year, you probably have too many itemized deductions to profit from deduction arbitrage.

While these figures are adjusted slightly each year for inflation, the standard deductions for 1996 are

Single	$4,000
Married Filing Jointly	$6,700
Married Filing Separately	$3,350
Head of Household	$5,900

If your deductions are on the applicable border, consider this example of how the technique works.

EXAMPLE

You are a single taxpayer with a salary of $45,000, putting you in the 28 percent bracket. You have $2,000 withheld annually in state income tax, make annual charitable contributions of $2,000, and pay $300 annually (in two semiannual installments) in personal property tax on your automobile. Your total deductions are $4,300, and you qualify to itemize. However, you are only $300 over the 1996 standard deduction amount ($4,300 – $4,000), so these deductions are only worth $84 more in tax savings beyond what the government was going to give you anyway ($300 × 28%).

There is a way to restructure your deductions, however, to increase your tax savings. Try paying them this way.

Expense	Year 1	Year 2
State tax	$2,000	$2,000
Contributions	3,000	1,000
Personal property tax	450	150
Total Itemized Deductions	$5,450	$3,150

This payment pattern recognizes the following nontax realities: You cannot control the timing of your state tax withholding, you probably would not forgo charitable contributions altogether every other year, and you can only partially prepay your personal property taxes. However, if you maintain this alternating payment pattern, you will save $238 over every two-year cycle.

Here's how that figure is computed. Assume that year 1 is 1996. The value of your itemized deductions for year 1 increases from $84 to $406 ($5,450 – $4,000 = $1,450; $1,450 × 28% = $406). That's an additional year 1 savings of $322 ($406 – $84). Meanwhile, in year 2 (1997), you've lost that extra $84, because in that year deductions—$3,150—won't be enough to enable you to itemize. This leaves a net savings of $238 ($322 – $84).

The payment pattern you need to use to make this strategy work can vary widely depending on personal circumstances, so your actual tax savings will be different. Moreover, it is not always going to be possible to control the timing of all your deductions. However, if you're on the itemizing border, it's likely this strategy can pay off for you.

Remember, as with bracket arbitrage, you can only prepay expenses so far in advance before the IRS takes an interest in your tax planning. In the example above, you only prepaid personal property taxes six months out. Also remember that the standard deduction is indexed for inflation every year, so you need to be sharp with figures in order to use this strategy. If you are, it's a nice way to shave a couple hundred dollars off your tax bill.

There's one other possible downside to be aware of with this technique: state income taxes. If you're in a state that requires you to itemize deductions on its return when you itemize them on the federal return (and vice versa when you don't), this strategy may leave you paying more in state taxes than you save in federal taxes. Here's the issue: Your federal itemized deductions include state income taxes you paid during the year; your state won't let you claim a deduction for these amounts. As a result, your state itemized deductions are almost always lower than your federal itemized deductions. When you do the arbitrage outlined here, there's a chance you might lower your state deductions too much. Whether this will spoil your arbitrage opportunity depends on four things.

1. How big your state's standard deduction is.
2. Whether your state does in fact makes you treat your deductions the same way you do on your federal returns (a few states don't).
3. Your state's income tax rates.
4. How much of your itemized deductions consist of state income tax withholdings.

Because these factors vary widely from state to state and taxpayer to taxpayer, it's hard to generalize. But if you live in a state with a high tax rate, do the math for both federal and state returns before you engage in deduction arbitrage.

Tax-Favored Investments

Changes in the tax law are making it increasingly difficult to shelter your income from taxes—the first time around. However, there are ways to invest your after-tax dollars to ensure that the income they earn takes maximum advantage of the incentives ("loopholes" if you're a cynic!) remaining in the law. This section explores several of the more time-tested approaches to tax-smart investing.

Remember that none of these investments alone is the answer to all your troubles. In fact, some of these investments may be inappropriate for your financial situation or risk tolerance. Direct ownership of real estate, for example, is not for new investors or for those with only a small amount to invest. Always seek competent professional advice in constructing a balanced and diversified portfolio that fits your individual needs. And never let the tail wag the dog. An investment needs to make financial sense before taxes or it's not likely to make sense after taxes.

Municipal Bonds

Municipal bonds are one of the most popular forms of tax-advantaged investing. That's because, under almost all circumstances, income generated by the bonds is exempt from federal income tax. And, in most states, if you purchase in-state municipal bonds, they're free of state and local taxes as well. For people who derive a substantial percentage of their income from interest on their assets, this can mean huge tax savings.

> **EXAMPLE**
>
> You have $10,000 to invest. As a conservative investor, you want to avoid as much as possible any risk to your principal. You could invest your funds in a corporate bond earning 8 percent or a municipal bond paying 6.5 percent. While the corporate bond sounds like a better deal at first blush, a closer look at the after-tax numbers shows this isn't so. The municipal bond will pay you $650 in interest, but, assuming it's been issued by the state in which you reside, it's completely tax-free. With regard to the corporate bond, in the 15 percent bracket, you would pay $120 in federal income tax on your $800 interest income, leaving you with a return of $680 before state income taxes. If you live in a state with at least a 4 percent income tax rate (and most states are higher), the municipal bond is a better deal ($800 × 4% = $32; $680 − $32 = $648).
>
> The situation is even more compeling in the 28 percent bracket. The municipal bond still earns you $650, but the corporate bond now costs you $224 in federal income tax ($800 × 28%), leaving you with a return of $576 before state income taxes ($800 − $224). In the 31 percent bracket, the difference becomes substantial. The federal income tax on the corporate bond rises to $248 ($800 × 31%), and the net return shrinks to $552 ($800 − $248). The municipal bond leaves you with about $100 more in your pocket—and that's before state and local taxes are figured in!

As you can see, the higher your tax bracket, the more valuable municipal bonds are to you.

Rental Real Estate

Investing directly in real estate is one of the few remaining ways to generate tax losses; that is, paper (i.e., noneconomic) losses that can be used
to offset other sources of current income and thereby reduce taxes. It also
can be terribly risky. The difficulties of owning real estate—finding tenants, collecting rent, evicting tenants, making repairs, market fluctuations, and potential illiquidity—suggest it's not for the squeamish.

The tax law allows you to deduct up to $25,000 in excess rental real
estate losses (i.e., losses in excess of your rental income) if you meet several requirements. First, you must own the real estate directly (e.g., you
cannot own it through a limited partnership; if you are a partner in a general partnership, however, you qualify). Next, if you own the property
jointly with others, your ownership interest must be greater than 10 percent. Additionally, you must "actively participate" in the management of
the property (more on this shortly). Finally, the amount of your deduction
gets phased out as your income rises. If your AGI is under $100,000, you
can deduct up to the full $25,000. Above $100,000, the $25,000 limit gets
reduced until it reaches zero at $150,000 in AGI. Thus, this technique is
not available to you for any year in which your AGI exceeds $150,000.

If your income consistently exceeds $150,000, you should only con-
sider investing in rental real estate from the perspective of its potential
appreciation. Under current law, it can't offer you the special tax write-
offs being discussed here. If you're a high-income earner who has been
bitten by the real estate bug, a vacation home may be a better bet.
Although it can't generate the tax losses that rental property can, a vacation home still allows you to deduct mortgage interest and property taxes.
Again, though, in order for such an investment to make financial sense,
you should have some indication that the property will appreciate sufficiently to make up for its negative cash flow—or you better enjoy the
place a lot!

A quick word about *active participation:* The IRS actually interprets
this requirement fairly broadly. You can still employ a management company or rental agent to assist you in running your real estate activities.
You don't have to hammer the nails or screw the screws yourself. You do
have to be a part of management decisions, however, like selecting tenants or setting rents. When it's time for capital improvements, you should
be the one calling the shots. You also should keep good records to prove
that you participated in the management of your rental real estate.

We've already briefly touched on the rewards of qualifying for this deduction—deducting excess losses against other sources of income, such as wages, interest, dividends, or business income.

EXAMPLE

You own a condo that you rent for $500 per month ($6,000 per year). However, after you pay the mortgage, condo fees, and property taxes and claim depreciation, the property costs you $7,000 per year. Assuming that your income is under $100,000, the $1,000 loss ($6,000 – $7,000 = $1,000) can be used to offset your other income. If you are in the 15 percent bracket, this will reduce your federal taxes by $150, or $280 if you are in the 28 percent bracket.

Clearly, these rules give rental real estate the potential to be a singularly attractive investment from a tax perspective. However, how you generate these excess losses without also having to spend a lot of out-of-pocket money can be tricky, and it highlights one of the risks involved in direct investment in real estate.

It is not always easy to find a real estate investment that will generate tax losses without also generating real out-of-pocket losses, but it can be done. The key is to consider the value of the depreciation deduction in determining whether a loss is a real loss or just a tax loss. The tax law allows you to recover the cost of your real estate investment over its *useful life*. The tax law specifies what the useful life for real estate is—27.5 years for residential property, 39 years otherwise. Note this deduction applies only to the cost of buildings and improvements; you can't depreciate land. Each year you can deduct about 3.6 percent of the cost of your investment residential real estate.

EXAMPLE

Consider the example above. Of your $7,000 in expenses, suppose $4,500 was for mortgage interest, $1,000 was for condo fees, and $1,500 was for depreciation. Since that $1,500 didn't really come out of your pocket (at least not the same way the mortgage interest and condo fees did), it is not a cash flow loss. It is, however, a tax deduction. Moreover, since you only spent $5,500 out of pocket ($4,500 + $1,000), you've earned $500 more in rent than you've laid out in expenses that year. The net result: a $1,000 deduction for excess losses and $500 in "tax-free" income!

Sounds too good to be true? That's because sometimes it can be. In the example above, what would happen if the condo sat vacant for one month? Or two? What if your tenant didn't pay rent for a month, or if major repairs were required? Expenses associated with real estate are not always as predictable as with other investments, and cash flow can vary significantly from year to year.

Small economic losses aren't always a sign that you've made a bad investment. If the property appreciates by more than the amount of the loss, it still is possible to come out ahead. But situations like these quickly become speculative and are best left to investors who can afford to lose the money involved. Although appreciation may help you through a dry patch, it's clearly not a guarantee anymore.

There are steps you can take to minimize the nontax financial risks, both before and after you buy. First, spend a lot of time going over the numbers before you buy. Hire a number-cruncher if you have to; a good one is worth her weight in gold. She can help you determine whether your cash flow is going to be negative just on your tax return, or also in your bank account. She also should be able to tell you whether the deal you propose makes economic sense or whether it would be more profitable to park your money elsewhere.

Next, be slow and deliberate when selecting a property. Don't let anyone pressure you into buying before you've done a thorough analysis. In the current market, there's no deal so hot that it can't wait until you're good and ready. Consider the pros and cons of residential versus commercial property. Commercial property can have a higher vacancy rate, but being a residential landlord can cause lots of headaches. Also, screen your tenants carefully; bad tenants are guaranteed to be your single biggest source of trouble. References and credit reports are a must, along with as much in security deposits and rental deposits as your local law allows.

Finally, make sure your budget for the investment sets aside a little each month to cover unforeseen contingencies—repairs, late rent, and vacancies all should be planned for.

There's one last thing to know about investing in rental real estate. Lest you be fooled into thinking the government is giving money away, you should know that all the depreciation you claim while you own your property gets added to your gain when you sell it. This can increase the size of your tax bill when you sell your property.

A final reminder: These rules only apply to investment property and not to your residence or a vacation home. Many of the things you can deduct for investment purposes (e.g., depreciation, condo fees, repairs) are not deductible when spent on your primary or secondary home.

Annuities

In Chapter 2 we learned about the different types of annuities. They are classified based on how they are purchased (single premium versus periodic premiums), how they earn income (fixed rate or variable rate), when they begin paying benefits (immediate versus deferred), and to whom those benefits are paid (individual versus joint).

Annuities allow you to save money on a tax-advantaged basis. When you purchase an annuity, the income it earns usually is not taxed to you until you take it out. This means that the interest—and dividends and capital gains if your annuity invests in mutual funds—grow tax deferred. Moreover, since annuity withdrawals usually are made in the form of periodic payments at some future date, they generally permit your money to grow this way over many years.

When you withdraw money from an annuity, usually part of it is taxable and part of it is nontaxable. The money you put into the annuity does not get taxed coming out; only the growth on that money does. If for some reason you receive your annuity payment in a lump sum, you simply subtract the total payments you made from the gross proceeds you received to determine what portion is taxable. (If you receive this before age 59½, you also owe a 10 percent penalty tax, as explained in the discussion of annuities in Chapter 2.) In the more common situation where you receive periodic distributions, however, you would exclude from income a proportionate share of each payment until your entire investment in the contract is accounted for. The exact computation depends on several complex factors. The insurance company that sold you the annuity will provide you with the information you need to compute your exclusion ratio.

Capital Gains

If you are in the top income tax brackets, you have an incentive to seek investment vehicles that emphasize capital gains (as opposed to interest or dividends). The top income tax rate is 39.6 percent, but the top rate on capital gains is 28 percent. This differential makes investments that declare capital gains (such as some growth mutual funds) more attractive to taxpayers in higher brackets.

EXAMPLE

You are in the 36 percent tax bracket. You are considering investing $10,000 in two different mutual funds. One offers a 10 percent return, usually in the form of dividends. The other offers a similar return, but through capital gains distributions. If both investments provide a $1,000 pretax return, the "dividend fund" will net you only $640 ($1,000 – 36%), whereas the "capital gains fund" will leave you with $720 ($1,000 – 28%). The investment returning capital gains distributions provides a superior after-tax return.

Note that the example above does not consider the state tax consequences of your transaction. If you live in a state that still differentiates between capital gains and ordinary income, the advantage of capital-gains-oriented investing could be even greater. Of course, as always, your investments should make nontax sense and fit in consistently with your overall portfolio structure.

EE Bonds

Series EE U.S. government savings bonds offer smart investors several tax-saving opportunities. They also offer at least one seeming opportunity that can actually turn out to be a tax trap for the unwary. EE bonds offer these planning opportunities because they give you the option of either paying tax on interest income as it is earned or deferring the tax until the bond matures.

You generally would benefit by electing to defer recognition of the interest income on a bond until it matures. However, there can be some situations, particularly when the bond is titled in a child's name, where the kiddie tax rules discussed earlier make it advantageous for you to recognize the interest income in the year it is earned.

EXAMPLE

Your 7-year old son owns $7,000 in EE bonds. He earns $400 in interest on them annually. If they are his only source of income, he would pay no tax on the $400 he earns each year. However, if he defers recognition of the interest income until the bonds mature, he very likely would be required to pay tax on at least some of the income. Assume, for example, that he was given the bonds at birth and owns them until age 20. That would give him $8,000 in deferred interest income ($400 × 20), some of which almost certainly would be taxable.

As long as the amount of interest income is beneath the kiddie tax limits, you (or, technically, your child) probably are better off recognizing it in the year it is earned than deferring it. This is certainly the case if the interest income falls below the $650 limit, and may also be the case even for the $1,300 limit. In essence, you are using the lower kiddie tax brackets to your advantage. Just remember that, above $1,300 (indexed for inflation) in interest income, this benefit is lost and the additional amount is taxed at your marginal rate.

One good use of EE bonds is for financing a child's college education. Under certain circumstances, not only can the interest earned on EE bonds be deferred for tax purposes, but it can be eliminated altogether when the bonds are redeemed. In order to qualify for excluding EE bond interest from your taxable income, you must meet the following restrictions:

1. The bonds must be issued after 1989.
2. You must be at least age 24 when you purchase the bond, and the bond must be registered in your name (it can be registered jointly with a spouse). This means the bonds will have to be titled in your name, not your child's.
3. The bonds won't qualify for the exclusion if they are transferred to you by someone else.
4. They also won't qualify if you transfer them to the educational institution; you must redeem them.
5. The expenses must be paid by you for yourself, your spouse, or your dependent child.
6. Eligible expenses include only tuition and fees (i.e., not room, board, or club dues).
7. If the total amount you redeem exceeds your eligible expenses, you must include a portion of the excess in income for the year you redeem the bonds.
8. If your AGI is over $43,500 ($65,250 for joint filers), the exclusion begins to phase out; these 1996 figures are indexed for inflation.

Although these rules may seem like a lot of trouble, the tax advantage can be significant. Excluding 15 or 20 years of accumulated interest from income can be a tremendous help in meeting the high cost of a college education. EE bonds should be a part of most parents' savings program for their younger children's college expenses.

One final word of advice: Make sure that savings bonds are a good economic investment before buying them. As of this writing, EE bonds are only paying about 5 percent interest. That may make them an inferior investment for you, even with their tax advantages. Always remember that your decisions have to make good financial sense and not just good tax sense.

OUR ISSUES

Bracket Arbitrage for Gay Couples

Within the confines of the gift tax rules, the tax law creates an opportunity for lesbian and gay couples to engage in bracket arbitrage. Ironically, the system has numerous barriers intended to thwart the efforts of straight couples to move money to lower-bracket relatives (most significantly, in the form of the kiddie tax rules), but for us the door remains slightly more open. If there is a significant and fairly permanent difference between the tax brackets of you and your partner, and if you have significant income-producing assets, you might consider moving some of those assets to the lower-bracket partner.

EXAMPLE 1

Greg and Wes have been in a relationship for 15 years. Greg is a vice president for a Fortune 500 company; Wes is a waiter/actor/musician. Greg is in the 36 percent tax bracket, and Wes is in the 15 percent bracket. Greg earns about $12,000 in taxable income annually from an investment portfolio valued at $100,000; he pays tax of $4,320 ($12,000 × 36%) on this investment income. Assuming he has made no other gifts to Wes in the current tax year, Greg and Wes can shave $252 from their combined income tax bills if Greg gives Wes $10,000 from his portfolio. Here's how: by giving Wes $10,000, $1,200 of the income earned by the portfolio will be taxable to Wes, not Greg. Since Wes is in the 15 percent bracket, his tax of $180 ($1,200 × 15%) is $252 lower than Greg's tax of $432 ($1,200 × 36%). The savings could be even higher if Wes and Greg live in a state with high income taxes.

EXAMPLE 2

If Greg continues to transfer $10,000 from his portfolio each year, the total tax savings to him and Wes combined will multiply. The couple will need to keep an eye on Wes' tax bracket, to make sure it doesn't change as a result of the increasing investment income.

Of course, there are tremendous nontax considerations for gay couples when it comes to using bracket arbitrage. For one thing, the relationship needs to be on very solid ground; the partner transferring the property had better trust the receiving partner implicitly. In order for this technique to work, the transferring partner gives up all control of the income-producing property. Next, if assets from a brokerage or similar account are going to be transferred, make sure that transaction costs don't override the tax savings. In the example, above, for instance, Greg may need to maintain a $100,000 balance in his account in order to avoid fees or qualify for some higher level of service. Third, if you've got complicated estate plans, keep in mind that moving assets may undermine those plans. Check with your estate planner before using this technique. Finally, be ever-mindful of the gift tax rules when planning to use this strategy.

Hiring Your Partner

If you own a business, whether it's a sole proprietorship, partnership, or corporation, there can be several tax planning opportunities available to you if you hire your significant other. Although the income tax issues surrounding the ownership of a business generally are beyond the scope of this chapter, because your business may give you and your partner an opportunity to do some personal tax planning, it's important to briefly touch on the subject here. Also note that many of these techniques are of no value to married straight couples, who generally file joint returns and therefore share the same tax bracket.

First, hiring your partner may give you another opportunity to engage in bracket arbitrage. Moreover, when your partner is an employee of your business, the gift tax limits on your ability to use the arbitrage strategy won't apply. Of course, in order for this technique to make sense, you and your partner need to be in different tax brackets.

EXAMPLE 1

Donna is a psychotherapist with a very successful practice. She is in the 31 percent income bracket. Marilyn, her life partner of 20 years, retired last year from a teaching career, and her modest income puts her squarely in the 15 percent bracket. Donna's practice has grown in recent months, and she can no longer keep up the scheduling, filing, and processing of insurance claims by herself. She hires Marilyn as an office assistant at an annual salary of $18,000. Donna can deduct the compensation she pays Marilyn, which means she has successfully shifted this money from her 31 percent bracket to Marilyn's 15 percent bracket. Donna would have paid $5,580 ($18,000 × 31%) in tax on this amount; Marilyn will pay only $2,700 ($18,000 × 15%), for a tax savings to the couple of $2,880 ($5,580 – $2,700).

If Donna is a sole proprietor, the $18,000 in salary she pays to Marilyn also will reduce the amount of Donna's income subject to self-employment tax.

Other aspects of an employment relationship beyond salary include payroll taxes and fringe benefits, which must be factored into the equation. Marilyn and Donna each would have to pay their share of the Social Security taxes on Marilyn's wages. Donna also will have to pay unemployment insurance, workers' compensation, and, in a few states, disability insurance for Marilyn. In addition, any fringe benefits (e.g., a retirement plan, health insurance) Donna provides for Marilyn affect in important ways how the numbers will shake out with this strategy. While some of these expenses can lower the couple's tax savings, others (e.g., Social Security taxes) Donna likely would incur anyway. Moreover, some of these payments provide important benefits to Marilyn (e.g., Social Security, unemployment insurance, retirement savings), making them money well spent. Even for the expenditures that prove to be a drag on the cash flow aspects of the arrangement, it's some consolation to know that they're deductible to Donna. It's hard to make generalities in this area, but it's virtually certain that there are significant tax planning opportunities available here.

In fact, the fringe benefits an employer-partner provides for his or her employee-partner can create important planning opportunities in and of themselves.

EXAMPLE 2

Continuing with Example 1, assume that Donna provides Marilyn with coverage under a simplified employer pension (SEP), contributing 15 percent of Marilyn's salary to the plan each year. Not only has Donna reduced her own taxable income by another $2,700 ($18,000 × 15%), but the couple gets several other benefits as well. Marilyn doesn't have to pay tax on Donna's contributions to the SEP until Marilyn starts withdrawing them. Similarly, the interest, dividends, and capital gains Marilyn's SEP earns accumulate on a tax-deferred basis. And, most importantly, Donna and Marilyn have taken an important step in preparing for a financially secure retirement.

When it comes to another important fringe benefit—health insurance—the tax law provides lesbian and gay couples with a unique opportunity for some creative planning. There can be several significant advantages to providing health insurance to an employee-partner. This topic is important enough that we'll cover it separately below.

You need to understand that there are restrictions on your ability to use a partner-employee to shift taxes. This strategy should not be viewed fundamentally as a way to scam the system. First, this means that the employment relationship must be bona fide. The employee-partner must actually do the work he or she is being paid for. Next, the salary paid to the employee-partner must be "reasonable." While there can be some wiggle room in what constitutes reasonable compensation, the IRS would not let Donna get away with paying Marilyn $100,000 as an office assistant (or at least they wouldn't let her deduct it all). Finally, the employer-partner generally can't give the employee-partner fringe benefits unless they are provided to all other employees.

This tax planning strategy also raises a few very important nontax considerations. It is necessary that the relationship be that of employer-employee, and not one of co-owners. While co-owning a business offers its own tax planning opportunities, including the possibility of its own form of bracket arbitrage, the technique under consideration here contemplates an employer-employee arrangement. This implies, of course, that one-half of the couple earns more than the other. This could raise many issues both within and beyond the office setting: who gets to tell whom what to do, who's work is undervalued, who really pulls the weight at work, who *isn't* the boss at home. These issues should be fully and forthrightly explored before the (employment) relationship is consummated.

Providing Health Insurance for an Employee-Partner

If you are able to hire your partner as an employee, the tax law provides some important incentives for you to offer health insurance coverage for him or her—and maybe even a way to save some money on the coverage you buy for yourself.

You can deduct the amount you pay to provide health insurance for your employee-partner as a fringe benefit, provided your plan is in writing and you don't discriminate against other employees. This in turn reduces your income for income tax purposes, as well as for self-employment tax purposes if you are a sole proprietor. In contrast, if your partner-employee had to buy her own health insurance, she would only be able to deduct it as a miscellaneous itemized deduction, and then only if it exceeds 7½ percent of her AGI.

There may be a way to increase even more your overall tax savings. Presumably, if you offer health insurance as a fringe benefit, you also are buying coverage for yourself. If you are a sole proprietor, partner, or owner of a so-called S corporation, you only can claim an above-the-line deduction for 30 percent of your own health insurance premiums; the remainder must be claimed as an itemized deduction subject to the 7½ percent floor. However, if your business adopts a policy of providing health insurance coverage for the domestic partners of its employees, you can obtain coverage for yourself through the domestic partnership coverage you provide to your employee-partner, and your business can deduct the full amount it pays. Of course, as we learned earlier in this chapter in the "Income Tax Basics" section, your partner will have to include the value of the domestic partner benefits in his or her income. Whether you will benefit from this technique depends on your tax bracket, the cost of domestic partner coverage, and whether you will have to cover the domestic partners of any other employees. However, if you and your tax adviser run the math, there's a good chance in the end you'll come out ahead.

RELATED TOPICS

One form of bracket arbitrage requires you to transfer assets to another person. You will need to be careful not to trigger any gift taxes in doing so. See the "Gifts" section on page 321 for an explanation of how to avoid this.

The nontax aspects of municipal bonds are explained in the "Classes of Investments" section on page 114.

While real estate investments can generate important tax advantages, it is equally important that you keep a perspective on their proper place in your overall portfolio. Help with this can be found in the "Asset Allocation and Portfolio Structure" section on page 138.

The various nontax aspects and diverse uses of annuities are detailed in the "Annuities" section on page 49.

The significant tax advantages associated with owning a primary residence or a vacation home are reviewed in the "Tax Deductions from Your Home" section on page 180.

The mechanics and numerous tax advantages associated with simplified employer pensions (SEPs) are explained in the "Employer-Sponsored Retirement Plans" section on page 243.

TAX PLANNING WHEN SELLING A HOME

THE STRAIGHT FACTS

When you sell your primary residence, the tax law generally requires you to pay tax on any gain you recognize from the sale. The gain is computed by subtracting the amount you paid for the property (its *cost basis*) from its sales price. You can use the cost of any improvements you made to the home (adjustments to its cost basis)—but not repairs—and most of the expenses of selling your home (broker's commissions, transfer taxes you pay, etc.) to reduce the gain.

EXAMPLE 1
You purchased your home 10 years ago for $100,000. You sell it today for $150,000, paying $10,000 in broker's commissions, transfer taxes, and settlement charges. Your gain is $40,000 ($150,000 – $10,000 – $100,000).

EXAMPLE 2
The same facts apply as above, except that you also put a $15,000 addition on your house a few years ago. Now your gain is $25,000 ($150,000 – $10,000 – $100,000 – $15,000).

If you've lived in your house for a number of years, inflation alone will probably leave you with a substantial gain when you sell. There are two important tax breaks you can use, however, to postpone or even eliminate some of this gain.

Deferring Gain

Under certain circumstances, you can defer the gain you recognize when selling your old home by rolling it over into a new one. Here's the catch: You must pay at least as much for the new home as the adjusted sales price of the old one. When you roll over the gain into a new home, you postpone paying the tax on it until you sell your new home. Be aware, however, that this special provision has a funny wrinkle: If you qualify to roll over your gain, it is mandatory that you do so.

EXAMPLE 1
You sell your primary residence for $140,000 and immediately buy a new one for $145,000. Any gain you may have on the sale of the old residence can be rolled over into the new home.

EXAMPLE 2
You sell your primary residence for $140,000, and pay a broker's commission
of $5,000. You immediately buy a new home for $138,000. You still qualify
to roll over your gain because your adjusted sales price ($140,000 – $5,000 =
$135,000) is lower than your purchase price ($138,000).

There is one other important restriction on your ability to use this
tax-deferral technique: Settlement on the sale of your old home and on the
purchase of your new home must occur within two years of each other.
The law gives you more time if you are in the military or move overseas.

You can use one additional strategy to help you qualify for rollover
treatment. Normally, fix-up expenses—minor landscaping, painting,
wallpapering, and so on—are not deductible when spent on your primary
residence. However, if you incur these fix-up expenses within 90 days of
entering into a contract to sell your home, you can use those expenses in
computing the gain you qualify to postpone.

EXAMPLE 1
You paid $100,000 for your primary residence 10 years ago. You sell it for
$140,000, and pay a broker's commission of $5,000. Thirty days before the
sales contract is signed, you pay $4,000 to have the exterior of your home
painted. Your adjusted sales price is $131,000 ($140,000 – $5,000 –
$4,000), and as long as your new home costs at least this much, you qual-
ify to roll over your gain.

Note, however, that while fix-up expenses can be used to help you
qualify for a rollover, they cannot be used to lower the amount of your
gain, whether you defer that gain by doing a rollover or not.

EXAMPLE 2
The same facts apply as above. The gain you can qualify to rollover is
$35,000 ($140,000 – $5,000 – $100,000). No reduction in gain can be
made for your $4,000 fix-up expenses.

Remember, by rolling over the gain, you don't eliminate the tax;
you only defer it. When you sell your new home, you'll either have to do
another rollover or pay tax on all the gain from the sale of both residences. In some situations, however, you may qualify to completely eliminate some of that gain.

Excluding Gain

Once you reach age 55, it is possible to completely exclude from tax up to
$125,000 in gain on the sale of your primary residence. Not surprisingly,

however, there are several important restrictions on this major tax break, and you are only allowed to claim it once in your life. Therefore, it is very important to consider carefully when to claim the exclusion in order to maximize your tax savings.

First, the home you sell must be your primary residence. Vacation homes and rental property are not eligible for the exclusion. Next, the home must have been your primary residence for at least three of the previous five years. Under certain circumstances, nursing-home occupancy can be counted for this purpose. You also must have owned your home for at least three of the previous five years (although these need not be the same three of five years that you occupied it). Finally, you must be at least 55 years old on the day you sell your home. Turning 55 later in the same tax year will not qualify you for the exclusion.

> **SUGGESTION**
> If you are close to turning 55, stipulate a settlement date after your 55th birthday in the sales contract.

Some special rules apply to married couples who want to claim the exclusion. On the plus side, only one of the spouses needs to be 55 on the sale date in order to qualify for the exclusion. However, the younger spouse also will be considered to have used his or her exclusion and will be ineligible to claim it again after turning 55. On the other hand, since the exclusion is a once-in-a-lifetime opportunity, neither spouse can have claimed it previously. If either spouse was married before and the exclusion was claimed during the previous marriage, neither party to the current marriage is eligible to claim it. Further, if one spouse (spouse A) has never used his or her exclusion but is married to someone who has (spouse B), spouse A remains disqualified from using the exclusion for as long as he or she remains married to spouse B. If spouse B passes away or the couple subsequently divorces, spouse A again is eligible to use his or her exclusion. In short, married people only get one exclusion per couple, not one per person.

The Best of Both Worlds

Consider this final strategy: If you are selling a large family home to purchase a smaller residence, perhaps in a lower-cost area, it may make sense to combine the deferral of gain discussed above with the exclusion of gain explained here in order to maximize your tax savings.

> **EXAMPLE**
> You are 60 years old. You purchased your home many years ago for $25,000. You sell it for $200,000 and immediately purchase a condominium in the

Sun Belt for $100,000. Your gain on this transaction is $175,000 ($200,000 − $25,000), which can be reduced by the once-in-a-lifetime exclusion to $50,000 ($175,000 − $125,000). Since the adjusted sales price of the old residence ($200,000 − $125,000 (exclusion) = $75,000) is less than the purchase price of the new one ($100,000), you also qualify to roll over the $50,000 gain into the new condominium. If you had not used the exclusion, your taxable gain would have been $100,000.

OUR ISSUES

Tax Planning for Gay Couples

For lesbian and gay couples, the rules regarding the once-in-a-lifetime exclusion apply at the individual level, not at the couple level. This creates one possible planning opportunity and one potential pitfall.

First the pitfall: Unlike married couples, in a gay relationship *both* parties must be over the age of 55 in order for both to claim the exclusion. In other words, if one partner is 56 and the other is 54 when they decide to sell their townhouse and retire to Key West, the older partner will be eligible for the exclusion while the younger one will be unable to exclude his gain. Of course, the under-55 partner will still have the rollover provisions available to him if his share of the Florida house is at least equal to his share of the adjusted sales price of the townhouse. Also note that the over-55 partner is still comparatively young and may be better off using the rollover provisions now and saving his once-in-a-lifetime exclusion for the future. While decisions in this regard are always going to be highly fact-specific, this pitfall can be avoided through proper planning. Again, as the numbers in this area usually are very large, the advice of a tax pro quickly can pay for itself.

Now the opportunity: Through proper planning, lesbian and gay couples can turn the pitfall above on its head and exclude from income up to $250,000 (2 × $125,000) in gain from the sale of residences. Since the exclusion applies at the individual level, each partner is eligible to take advantage of it. Let's look at an example of how this might work.

EXAMPLE

Nelson and Peter are in their sixties. They purchased a home together 20 years ago for $100,000. They each contributed equally to the down payment on the home, as well as to the payment of the mortgage, property taxes, upkeep, and all other expenses. They have just sold their home for $350,000. The expenses of the sale were $25,000. Their combined gain on the sale is $225,000 ($350,000 – $100,000 – $25,000), or $112,500 each. However, each partner may use his once-in-a-lifetime exclusion to avoid paying tax on the entire gain.

Note that, in contrast, a married couple could only exclude $125,000 of the $225,000 gain, leaving them to pay tax on the remaining $100,000 unless they are eligible to roll it over into another home.

How these techniques play out for you and your partner will depend on your ages, how much gain you have built up in your home, and what your future plans are. A knowledgeable tax adviser will quickly earn his or her keep in putting these techniques to work for you.

RELATED TOPICS

You unknowingly could create serious gift tax problems if you gratuitously add a partner's name to (or remove a partner's name from) the deed to a house. See the "Gifts" section on page 321 before making such a move.

For some lesbian and gay couples, joint ownership of property can be an effective way to keep a home out of a messy probate court battle. However, this strategy won't always work, and it sometimes is not advisable for those with large taxable estates. The pros and cons are discussed in the "Wills and Will Substitutes" section on page 302.

When you die, your home could be the most valuable asset in your estate. If you think your estate (or the combined estates of you and your partner) could exceed $600,000, find out how to minimize taxes in the "Estate Tax Planning Techniques" section on page 328.

If you or your partner cannot prove to the IRS that each of you contributed equally toward a jointly owned home, part of that home may be subject to federal estate tax more than once. This trap is explained in the "Estate Planning Basics" section on page 287.

To understand the many tax advantages associated with home ownership, see the "Tax Deductions from Your Home" section on page 180.

Your house is likely to be one of your most significant investments. See the "Homeowner's Insurance" section on page 86 to learn how to protect that investment.

If you buy a home with a friend or domestic partner, seriously consider the many benefits described in the "Domestic Partnership Agreements" section on page 361.

5

CHAPTER

Retirement Planning

COMPUTING RETIREMENT NEEDS AND SAVINGS

THE STRAIGHT FACTS

Introduction

Many professionals involved in the retirement planning process refer to a "three-legged" stool supporting people in their golden years. One leg of the stool is the retirement plan provided by an individual's employer. Another leg comes from Social Security retirement benefits. The third leg is derived from an individual's own savings. The amount of retirement support provided by each leg of the stool varies considerably from person to person. Therefore, it is very important for you to understand what each leg is going to look like on your particular stool. To complete the analogy, if one leg is a little short, you need to begin compensating for it early in order to ensure a stable base of support when you retire.

This chapter is intended to help you understand how each leg of the stool works, to be certain that you know what to do with the leg you're responsible for, and finally to make sure you maximize the stool's support in your retirement years. The first step in this process is to compute your retirement needs. That's what we're going to do in this section.

Computing your retirement needs by yourself can be difficult. In addition to some advanced number crunching, you have to make difficult assumptions about how your savings will grow and what inflation will do (among other things) in order to get to the bottom line. You should consider seriously the benefits of disinterested professional assistance in computing your needs.

Another viable option is to use one of the software programs provided by the numerous investment companies and brokerage houses anxious to have you park your retirement savings with them. One word of caution if you choose this approach: Not surprisingly, these programs often tend to err on the side of computing the highest amount of money possible you should be saving. While there's nothing wrong with telling you to save as much as possible, make sure it's being done because it's in your best interest, and not someone else's.

In the event that neither of these excellent options appeals to you, we'll walk through the process the long way. On a gross level, the task at first seems simple. Most people need somewhere between 60 percent and 80 percent of their preretirement income in order to enjoy a comparable lifestyle in retirement. While this may sound high at first, research and experience show it's the way things usually work out. If you think about it for a second, retiring is a lot like going out on disability—at least from the perspective of what it does to your cash flow. If you're comfortable accepting the need to replace between 60 percent and 80 percent of your income in the event of disability, the same logic should persuade you that these numbers will apply in retirement. If your house is paid for when you retire, you'll be at the low end of this range. If you plan to travel a lot, figure on coming in near the top end.

On a more specific level, however, you need to know not just what your retirement income needs will be, but how much you have to save in order to meet those needs—to build your leg of the stool. Figuring this out is not easy, but it is possible. What makes it so complicated is the number of variables and assumptions that go into the process—when you'll retire, what impact inflation will have on your retirement income needs, what rate of return your nest egg will earn both before and after retirement, and how long you'll live in retirement. This is why the software and the expertise available from professionals and investment institutions can be so valuable. Nevertheless, it can be an instructive exercise to work through the process yourself.

Again, it's only possible to do this if several assumptions are made. If these assumptions prove to be wrong or inappropriate for you, the resulting numbers will be completely meaningless for you. As we work through the process, you'll be told the assumptions being made at each step along the way. While the assumptions we make here are common, if they're not right for you, ultimately you'll need a computer, an expert, or both. The figures used in this section have been rounded to keep them manageable. The rounding always has been done erring on the side of caution. In order to keep the computations as conservative as possible, sometimes a three or a four got rounded up instead of down, or a six or seven got rounded down instead of up. Nevertheless, be advised that rounding big numbers over long time frames can have a surprisingly significant impact on the final result. Note, too, that some of the numbers we'll be dealing with may seem surreally large. Many of us will be working with seven-digit figures (as in millions of dollars). No matter how absurd these numbers might seem, rest assured they are very real. Inflation and time are working against you in this regard. One final warning: Never skip any of the steps in this process. If you decide to change a figure or an assumption, always go back to Step 1 and start again. With this background, let's begin the process of computing retirement savings needs.

Step 1. Compute Annual Retirement Income Needs in Today's Dollars

As we learned above, most people will need between 60 percent and 80 percent of their preretirement income in retirement. This makes the first step in the process somewhat easy. Review your annual budget from Chapter 1 and analyze your levels of income and expenses. Consider which expenses are likely to increase and which are likely to decrease when you retire, and determine where you fall in the 60 percent to 80 percent range. There are a few considerations to bear in mind as you undertake this analysis. On the one hand, if your house is paid off, your expenses will tend to be lower. However, the other costs associated with home ownership (property taxes, repairs, homeowner's association fees) will go up over time. Next, be sure to factor in the likelihood that your expenditures for health care will increase substantially. Finally, think about the retirement lifestyle you aspire to. Are you the kind of person who will be satisfied with simple, quiet golden years? Or will retirement be the time for you to do all the things you've spent the last 30 years dreaming about? An active retirement will cost more.

EXAMPLE

We'll walk through the five steps for computing retirement savings needs with Joelle. Joelle is 32 years old and earns $40,000. She hopes to retire at age 62 (i.e., in 30 more years), and anticipates a very active retirement lifestyle. While her condo will be paid off by then, she knows she lives in a building with high condo fees. Because of her planned retirement lifestyle, as well as the slightly younger age at which she hopes to retire, Joelle estimates that her retirement income needs will be 75 percent of her current income level. In today's dollars, Joelle will need a $30,000 annual income in retirement ($40,000 × 75%).

Step 2. Subtract Annual Social Security Benefits Estimated in Today's Dollars

After you've determined your total annual income needs in retirement, the next step in computing your retirement savings needs is to account for Social Security's leg of the stool. We treat Social Security retirement benefits separately because they are adjusted each year for inflation (at least under current law). Other common sources of retirement income—employer pensions, annuities, and earnings on retirement savings already in place—tend to remain constant throughout retirement (i.e., they generally are not adjusted each year for inflation).

EXAMPLE

Joelle has received a statement from the Social Security Administration indicating that, in today's dollars, her monthly retirement benefits will be about $900, or $10,800 annually, if she starts collecting them at age 62. Therefore, her retirement income needs net of Social Security are $19,200 ($30,000 from Step 1 – $10,800 in annual Social Security retirement benefits).

Step 3. Grow Annual Net Needs for Inflation

After determining your annual net income needs in today's dollars, you must grow that figure for inflation. If, for example, you're 25 years old, you know that your income needs when you retire in 40 years will be significantly higher than they are right now due to inflation. Table 5–1 enables you to convert your current unmet annual net income needs into the approximate unmet needs at retirement.

T A B L E   5–1

Inflating Current Needs Into Future Needs

Current Needs	Years Until Retirement			
	40	30	20	10
$ 10,000	$ 48,000	$ 32,400	$ 21,900	$ 14,800
20,000	96,000	64,900	43,800	29,600
30,000	144,000	97,300	65,700	44,400
40,000	192,000	129,700	87,600	59,200
50,000	240,000	162,200	109,600	74,000
60,000	288,000	194,600	131,500	88,800
70,000	336,000	227,000	153,400	103,600
80,000	384,000	259,500	175,300	118,400
90,000	432,000	291,900	197,200	133,200
100,000	480,000	324,300	219,100	148,000

The table assumes that your current income will grow at 4 percent per year. If inflation turns out to average more than this amount over time, you will need to save more. The figures have been rounded to the nearest 100.

EXAMPLE
From Table 5–1, Joelle can see that her $19,200 in annual net income needs will have grown to about $64,900 in her first year of retirement! In theory, the $64,900 will buy her the same goods and services in her first year of retirement as $20,000 buys today.

Step 4. Compute Total Funds Needed at Retirement

The next step in the process of computing retirement savings requires you to determine what the size of your total retirement "pot" will need to be in order for it to generate the annual net retirement income needs computed in Step 3. In order to do this, you'll need to make a very critical assumption: how many years you expect to live in retirement. This is probably the hardest assumption in the retirement planning process—when you'll die. In addition to the obvious emotional and spiritual aspects of such an assumption, the financial consequences of outliving your savings must be taken into account. Err on the side of caution here by assuming that you'll live long and prosper. Once you determine your anticipated years in retirement and your future needs, refer to Table 5–2 to aid your calculation.

T A B L E 5–2

Total Funds Needed at Retirement

	Anticipated Years in Retirement				
Future Needs	15	20	25	30	35
$ 10,000	$ 129,200	$ 164,700	$ 197,000	$ 226,400	$ 253,000
20,000	258,500	329,500	394,000	452,700	506,100
30,000	387,700	494,200	591,000	679,100	759,100
40,000	516,900	658,900	788,000	905,400	1,012,100
50,000	646,200	823,700	985,000	1,131,800	1,265,200
60,000	775,400	988,400	1,182,100	1,358,100	1,518,200
70,000	904,600	1,153,100	1,379,100	1,584,500	1,771,200
80,000	1,033,900	1,317,900	1,576,100	1,810,800	2,024,300
90,000	1,163,100	1,482,600	1,773,100	2,037,200	2,277,300
100,000	1,292,400	1,647,400	1,970,100	2,263,500	2,530,300
110,000	1,421,600	1,812,100	2,167,100	2,489,900	2,783,400
120,000	1,550,900	1,976,800	2,364,100	2,716,300	3,036,400
130,000	1,680,100	2,141,600	2,561,200	2,942,600	3,289,400
140,000	1,809,300	2,306,300	2,758,200	3,169,000	3,542,500
150,000	1,938,500	2,471,000	2,955,200	3,395,300	3,795,500

There are quite a few things to note about this table. First, it assumes that inflation will grow at 4 percent, and that your investments in retirement will earn 6 percent. While 6 percent would be a conservative estimate if we were projecting preretirement returns, it reflects a rate of return consistent with a risk tolerance suitable for most individuals in retirement with current income needs. Nevertheless, if your actual rate of return is lower, you will need to start out with a larger amount in order to fund the same retirement income needs. Next, the figures in the table have been rounded to the nearest 100 (using the unconventional rounding convention explained in the beginning of this section). Most importantly, this table assumes that you will consume your savings over the time period you've chosen. In other words, it assumes that you will spend your principal down to zero over the time period chosen.

EXAMPLE

Joelle plans to retire at age 62 and she expects to live a full 30 years in retirement. Thus, from the table above, she can see that she will need about

$1,300,000 on the day she retires in order to provide the $64,900 in retirement income (from Step 3) she'll need each year.

Note how Joelle had to extrapolate from the table to get the $1.3 million, since her $64,900 is not represented on the table. This is a fairly good illustration of the risks involved in using this rough estimate approach to calculating retirement savings.

Step 5. Subtract Other Sources of Retirement Income

After you know what your total funds needed at retirement will be, you need to account for your employer's leg of the stool—assuming that it exists. In Step 5, we subtract from the total retirement funds computed in Step 4 an amount that approximates the value of the income stream you'll receive from other sources, such as an employer's noncontributory pension plan, an annuity, or savings already in place. We account for these items here because they tend to remain constant throughout retirement; that is, they do not increase each year for inflation.

If you know you will receive an inflation-adjusted pension from your employer (e.g., many government employees receive inflation-adjusted pensions), subtract the amount of your first year's payment under Step 2 (along with Social Security), and not here. Otherwise, consult the annual statement you receive from your employer to determine the amount of your annual pension benefit. Use Table 5–3 to convert that amount into a lump sum. (If, by chance, your employer's annual statement tells you what the lump-sum value of your pension will be at retirement, obviously you won't need to use the table to convert the annual payment into a lump sum. Most employers don't provide it, but if they do, use their lump-sum figure.) Subtract the lump sum from the result of Step 4 to determine how much you need to save personally for retirement.

Similarly, if you already own an annuity, use Table 5–3 to convert the annual annuity payment into a lump sum. (Again, if the insurance company provides you with a lump-sum value, use their figure, and not the one from the table.) Subtract the lump sum from the result of Step 4.

Likewise, if you already have some savings earmarked for retirement, you should subtract what those savings will be worth when you retire from the result of Step 4. If necessary, you can use Table 5–1 from Step 3 to help you figure out how your in-place savings will grow over time.

Sometimes it may be appropriate to treat anticipated inheritances and gifts the same as your in-place savings for purposes of this step, but

TABLE 5–3

Lump-Sum Value of Fixed Annual Payments

Annual Payment	Anticipated Years in Retirement				
	15	20	25	30	35
$ 2,500	$ 32,300	$ 41,200	$ 49,200	$ 56,600	$ 63,200
5,000	64,600	82,400	98,400	113,200	126,400
7,500	96,900	123,600	147,600	169,800	189,600
10,000	129,200	164,800	196,800	226,400	252,800
12,500	161,500	206,000	246,000	283,000	316,000
15,000	193,800	247,200	295,200	339,600	379,200
17,500	226,100	288,400	344,400	396,200	442,400
20,000	258,400	329,600	393,600	452,800	505,600
22,500	290,700	370,800	442,800	509,400	568,800
25,000	323,000	412,000	492,000	566,000	632,000
30,000	387,600	494,400	590,400	679,200	758,400
35,000	452,200	576,800	688,800	792,400	884,800
40,000	516,800	659,200	787,200	905,600	1,011,200
45,000	581,400	741,600	885,600	1,018,800	1,137,600
50,000	646,000	824,000	984,000	1,132,000	1,264,000
60,000	775,200	988,800	1,180,800	1,358,400	1,516,800
70,000	904,400	1,153,600	1,377,600	1,584,800	1,769,600
80,000	1,033,600	1,318,400	1,574,400	1,811,200	2,022,400
90,000	1,162,800	1,483,200	1,771,200	2,037,600	2,275,200
100,000	1,292,000	1,648,000	1,968,000	2,264,000	2,528,000

be very careful in doing so. If the gift or inheritance is not already in your possession, it's always risky—and sometimes a little ghoulish—to assume it's coming. Despite predictions in the popular press about an unprecedented intergenerational transfer of wealth coming to baby boomers from their parents, most of that wealth has not yet been transferred. More than one boomer will see (or already has seen) "their" inheritance depleted paying for doctors and nursing homes. In short, don't count on the kindness of strangers in your retirement planning.

Again, the table assumes inflation will run at 4 percent and your investment rate of return in retirement will be 6 percent. Also, the amounts in the table have been rounded to the most appropriate $100.

EXAMPLE

The annual statement Joelle received from her employer's pension plan indicates that her monthly pension will be approximately $1,500, or $18,000 annually when she retires. (Note that the annual statement indicates that this is the benefit she will receive if she works until age 62, and Joelle is comfortable making this assumption.) Joelle currently has about $20,000 in savings and investments already earmarked for retirement. Joelle does not expect to receive any large gifts or inheritances. Using Table 5–3, the $18,000 annual pension equates to an approximately $400,000 lump sum at retirement. Using Table 5–1, the $20,000 already committed to retirement savings will inflate to about $65,000 in 30 years when Joelle is ready to retire. Thus, the unfunded "nest egg" Joelle will need to have saved personally by retirement is approximately $835,000 ($1,300,000 from Step 4 – $400,000 lump-sum value of pension – $65,000 inflation-adjusted value of in-place savings).

Step 6. Compute Personal Monthly Savings Amount

After figuring the size of the leg of the stool you'll be responsible for at retirement, it only remains to be determined how much you will need to set aside each month to reach that goal. Another important assumption is necessary in order to do this: how much your investments will earn over time. If you assume your investments can earn 10 percent, you'll reach your goal faster than if you believe they'll only earn 6 percent. Choosing a rate of return largely is a function of your risk tolerance: The more risk you're willing to accept, the higher your potential return will be. This is discussed in the "Investment Risk and Risk Tolerance" section in Chapter 3. Review it before going on.

Once you've decided on an appropriate rate of return, Table 5–4 will quickly help you determine how much you need to set aside each month to accumulate the necessary nest egg you computed in Step 5. This table shows how much you will need to set aside each month for every $50,000 of nest egg you've figured you'll need. Thus, if in Step 4 your personal retirement savings needed to be $600,000, you would multiply the appropriate monthly payment below by 12 ($600,000/$50,000).

Several observations need to be made regarding this table. First, the figures were rounded to the next highest dollar. Next, note that these figures do not consider any income tax you would have to pay on your earnings. While taxes will lower your overall rate of return, people generally do not

TABLE 5-4

Monthly Savings Needed per $50,000 of "Nest Egg"

Years Until Retirement	Assumed Rate of Return								
	4%	5%	6%	7%	8%	9%	10%	11%	12%
40	$ 42	$ 33	$ 25	$ 19	$ 15	$ 11	$ 8	$ 6	$ 5
30	73	61	50	41	34	27	23	18	15
20	137	122	109	96	85	75	66	58	51
10	340	322	306	289	274	258	245	231	218

pay those taxes out of the funds they're saving for retirement. Since the taxes aren't coming out of the retirement "pot," they won't have an impact on how quickly it grows. Moreover, people frequently save for retirement on a tax-advantaged basis—through 401(k)s or other employer plans, IRAs, and annuities. Since taxes aren't paid on earnings from these investments until they're withdrawn, it's fair not to factor taxes into the table. However, if you're going to pay taxes on your retirement savings' earnings out of those earnings, you're going to need to save more. Finally, of greatest significance, if you do some comparisons, you will quickly see how important it is to start saving for retirement early. It's always going to be easier to set aside $20 a month for 40 years than $289 a month for 10 years, regardless of your income level. The reason for this striking disparity is the benefit of compounding: The income on your savings earns income of its own. The longer you let an investment compound, the more pronounced are compounding's effects. The table demonstrates this clearly.

EXAMPLE
Joelle has an average risk tolerance, so she assumes her investments will earn 10 percent over time. Since she has 30 years until retirement, she knows from the table that she'll need to save $23 per month for each $50,000 she's going to need at retirement. She rounds the $835,000 computed in Step 5 to $850,000. Joelle multiplies the $23 by 17 ($850,000/$50,000) to determine that she must save $391 per month (almost 12 percent of her salary) in order to meet her retirement savings goal.

Once you know how much more you need to save each month, it's time to determine where and how to save it. Generally, the procedures you follow for this are the same as for any other investment decision, and they are explained in detail in Chapter 3. There is one important point that bears exploring here, however. Because saving for retirement is such an important goal, the tax law provides many advantageous ways for you to go about it. Throughout the rest of this chapter we'll explore these options in detail. You need to understand how the options available to you work in order to know where best to put the monthly retirement savings computed above.

OUR ISSUES

Planning for a Gay Retirement

Although the AIDS epidemic has caused some in our community to adopt a somewhat fatalistic view of the future, the truth is that most of us are going to live to see our so-called golden years. And, whether or not these years really turn out to be golden depends largely on how well we prepare for them. As you read through this chapter, remember that we likely have more than the average amount of planning and saving to do for our old age. It is not likely that the usual paradigm of support from children and grandchildren (financial or otherwise) will be available to most of us. If nothing else, it therefore is likely we will have to pay more for care and living assistance when we're older. Accordingly, we will have to save more. It is critical that you factor these realities into your retirement planning. Because of the perspective on life we've developed in response to an oftentimes hostile world, many gay people take the "Peter Pan" approach to these matters: "I won't grow up!" As the last few sentences make clear, however, we will grow up, and we probably have more work to do in planning for our futures than most. So get on it, Tinkerbell!

Retirement Planning for Gay Couples

The process for computing retirement savings needs outlined in this section is designed for single individuals. If you are in a relationship, both you and your significant other should consider computing your retirement needs individually and planning for retirement individually. There are several reasons for this, some of which we'll discuss in detail later in this chapter. First, under current law, you will not be treated as spouses for purposes of receiving Social Security retirement benefits. Also, an employer's noncontributory retirement plan won't provide survivor's benefits to the domestic partner of an employee who dies before benefits begin. Finally, there is always the possibility that your relationship will have ended by the time you reach retirement. You need to plan for such a contingency. If it's any consolation, this last observation applies more and more to married straight couples as well, many of whom also are well advised to compute their retirement needs on an individual basis. The Ozzie and Harriet paradigm doesn't always work for them anymore, either. Besides, what's the worst that could happen: you and your other half save *too much* for retirement?

RELATED TOPICS

A detailed discussion of the role Social Security will play in funding your retirement, including information on how to obtain an estimate of your retirement benefits from the Social Security Administration, appears in the "Social Security Retirement Benefits" section on page 262.

The various types of retirement plans available to you are analyzed in these sections: "Employer-Sponsored Retirement Plans" on page 243, "Retirement Plans for the Self-Employed" on page 254, and "Individual Retirement Accounts" on page 257.

The portion of your retirement savings contained in an employer plan or other pretax savings vehicle (such as an IRA) comes with many tax strings attached. It is vital to understand the many restrictions the tax law places on the withdrawals and distributions from these plans. Failure to do so can result in some of the most serious unintended consequences contained in the tax law. The ins and outs of this complex area are detailed in the "Withdrawals and Distributions of Retirement Savings" section on page 266.

Many people with strong retirement savings habits are still underinvested for their golden years. Recent studies confirm that people are underallocating their retirement savings; that is, they are not allocating properly among cash, income, and growth investments. In order to avoid this situation, review the "Asset Allocation and Portfolio Structure" section on page 138, paying particular attention to the discussion of investing for long-term goals.

The last step in the process of computing how much you need to save each month in order to meet your retirement needs required you to assume a rate of return for your savings. Review the "Investment Risk and Risk Tolerance" section on page 106 in order to ensure that your assumption is appropriate for you.

Annuities are an important form of tax-advantaged retirement savings for many people. The details of these complex investments are outlined in the "Annuities" section on page 49. Their tax treatment is explained in the "Tax-Favored Investments" section on page 212.

If you can't remember what a marginal tax bracket is, it's explained in the "Income Tax Basics" section on page 161.

EMPLOYER-SPONSORED RETIREMENT PLANS

THE STRAIGHT FACTS

The retirement plan—or combination of plans—offered by an employer constitutes a central component of many people's retirement savings. Retirement plans come in an amazing variety of shapes and sizes, however, and they don't all work the same. Some promise to put in a certain amount, others to pay out a certain amount. Some allow you to defer part of your current salary, others are funded entirely by your employer. Some provide incomparable tax incentives, others significant tax incentives, and still others only nominal tax incentives. The purpose of this section is to provide a general explanation of the many types of employer plans. You'll need to understand the basics of the plan or plans available to you in order to maximize their impact on your overall retirement planning.

If your retirement plan does not allow you to contribute to the savings, as with many employers' pensions, one of its main tax advantages is the ability of plan assets to earn income on a pretax basis. The interest, dividends, and/or capital gains your retirement savings earn are not taxed until you receive them. (How they are taxed when you do receive them is explained later in this chapter in the "Withdrawals and Distributions of Retirement Savings" section). This means money that would otherwise go to pay taxes on the income earned by the plan's assets instead stays in the plan. This tax-free compounding increases the value of the plan dramatically over time.

EXAMPLE
If you invest $5,000 to earn 8 percent simple taxable interest for 20 years, at the end of that period you would have a total of $18,638 if you are in the 15 percent tax bracket and only $15,325 if you are in the 28 percent bracket. In contrast, a retirement plan containing $5,000 earning 8 percent would be worth $23,305 after 20 years.

Of even greater significance, if the plan is a "qualified" plan (and, for rank-and-file employees, most are), the money your employer sets aside on your behalf is not considered income to you until you withdraw it from your account. Meanwhile, your employer is allowed to claim an immediate deduction for the amounts it contributes. This is a major exception to traditional tax rules, which wouldn't allow an employer to claim a deduction for such contributions until its employee recognizes them in income. This makes qualified retirement plans very attractive for employers and employees.

If your retirement plan allows you to contribute, such as with a 401(k) plan, in addition to all of the benefits above, you have the opportunity to shelter some of your own income from taxation. Within limits, you can make contributions out of your own salary to such plans, and your income for the year is reduced by the amount of the contributions. These plans truly are among the best deals in the tax law.

Of course, in order to enjoy the benefits of tax-advantaged retirement savings, you must comply with a very complex set of rules. Experts make careers out of interpreting and explaining the rules relating to retirement plans, so only a broad outline can be presented here. However, the discussion that follows should provide you with enough information to understand the various types of retirement plans. One other thought before discussing specific plans: If you aren't sure which type of plan or plans your employer has, ask your human resources department. It's essential to know which types of plans you need to focus on.

Noncontributory Plans

Many retirement plans available to employees are noncontributory. That is, your employer makes a contribution based on your salary, and perhaps your age and/or years of employment. As discussed above, the advantage of these plans is that you receive tax-deferred income and that such income is growing on a tax-deferred basis. In exchange for these benefits, the tax law expects you to delay drawing on these assets until you retire.

Traditional Pension Plans

There are two traditional types of retirement plans. The first type promises to pay you a certain percentage of your salary when you retire. The company makes this promise to its workforce and then places as much or as little into its retirement plan as its actuaries say is needed to meet this promise. Since your employer is promising to pay you a specific benefit (i.e., *x* percent of your salary at retirement), this type of plan is called a *defined benefit plan.*

Under the other common type of retirement plan, your employer promises to place in its retirement account a certain percentage of your annual earnings. Since the employer commits to how much it will put in on your behalf and not to how much it will pay out, these plans are known as *defined contribution plans.* Defined contribution plans can be based on a fixed percentage of income, or they can vary each year depending on the firm's profits. The former type of plan is called a *money purchase* defined contribution plan, and the latter a *profit sharing* defined contribution plan. Annual contributions to a money purchase plan are mandatory. Profit sharing contributions are optional, but they must be made at least once every three or so years.

Under both defined benefit and defined contribution plans, there are limits as to how much your employer can pay into a retirement plan on your behalf. In the case of defined benefit plans, the most your employer can set aside each year is enough money to fund a retirement benefit equal to either $120,000 or 100 percent of your salary (averaged over its three highest years), whichever is lower. For defined contribution plans, each year your employer generally can set aside up to 25 percent of your salary (15 percent if it's a profit sharing plan), to a maximum of $30,000. Eventually, these limits will be indexed for inflation. Of course, in the case of any retirement plan, your employer can choose to provide lower benefits, and many do.

Your employer can require you to work for a certain period of time before the funds it sets aside on your behalf become your nonforfeitable property. This is called *vesting.* There are two different approaches to vesting, gradual and all-at-once. If your employer phases in your vesting gradually, it usually must start to do so by the time you complete three years of service and finish when you have completed seven years of service. If your employer chooses all-at-once vesting, it can wait until the completion of your fifth year of service to vest you in its plan. Sometimes vesting periods are even shorter when the plan covers too many highly compensated employees. Also, your employer can usually wait up to six months after you've completed one year of service before it starts covering you under its plan.

Employee Stock Ownership Plans (ESOPs)

Employee stock ownership plans (ESOPs) are more or less profit sharing plans that are paid in the form of shares of the employer's stock instead of cash. If you participate in an ESOP, the value of your account rises and falls in conjunction with the change in the price of your employer's stock. One of the advantages of an ESOP is that it enables you to defer paying tax on any gain until you actually sell your shares. Because ESOPs almost exclusively hold only employer's securities, there is little investment diversification in such plans. Therefore, employees over age 55 who have been with a company more than 10 years must be allowed to diversify the assets in their ESOP accounts. Because of this lack of diversification, most employers offer ESOPs in addition to some other form of retirement planning.

Simplified Employee Pensions (SEPs)

If you work for a small business, you may be covered by a streamlined form of retirement plan known as a *SEP*, or *Simplified Employee Pension.* SEPs allow small businesses to avoid the intricate rules just described by in essence making annual contributions to their employees' IRAs (individual retirement accounts). Among other things, SEPs dramatically lower the cost of administering retirement plans. This is a good part of the reason they are popular with small business owners. Additionally, an employer can decide on a year-by-year basis whether and how much to fund its SEP contributions. In this respect, they are somewhat akin to profit sharing plans.

In exchange for this simplicity, SEPs follow a fairly uniform set of rules. The maximum amount your employer can contribute to a SEP–IRA on your behalf is 15 percent of your salary (up to $22,500). Under the simplified vesting requirements applicable to SEPs, your employer can require you to work for three of the past five years before including you in its plan. However, if you are over 21, earn more than $400 annually (for 1996), and have met this service requirement, your employer must cover you in its SEP.

If you are covered by a SEP, it is important for you to understand that, once funds are placed in your SEP–IRA, they are your nonforfeitable property. They cannot be reclaimed at some later date by your employer. From that moment forward, the account is treated like any other IRA. The rules regarding IRAs are discussed later in this section.

Contributory Plans

The tax law provides for a number of plans under which employees can defer part of their current income, thus avoiding taxes on both the amounts deferred and on the earnings on those amounts until they are withdrawn from the plan. Clearly, there are substantial benefits to be found in tax-favored retirement savings. Therefore, it is in your interest to be socking away into retirement savings the maximum amount your budget can possibly afford. Putting aside the maximum amount possible (or allowable under the law) can save you hundreds or even thousands of dollars off your annual tax bill. At the same time, you'll be helping yourself prepare for an increasingly uncertain future.

401(k) Plans
401(k) plans, named after the section of the tax law that created them, are the most common form of employer-sponsored contributory retirement plan. These plans usually allow you to designate a certain percentage of each paycheck to be deposited into an investment account (or accounts) on your behalf. The salary on which you pay tax each year is reduced by the amount you put into your 401(k). The tax law allows you to defer a maximum of $9,500 in income each year. This 1996 figure is indexed for inflation every few years in $500 increments. Your plan may have lower limits.

> **EXAMPLE**
> You earn $48,000 per year, placing you in the 28 percent marginal tax bracket. You are paid $2,000 semimonthly. Your employer offers a 401(k) plan to its employees. If you were to elect to participate in the plan by deferring 5 percent of your income, $100 per pay period ($2,000 × 5%) would be placed in your 401(k) account. This would reduce your annual income by $2,400 ($100 × 24), saving you $672 in taxes ($2,400 × 28%). Moreover, because you're not paying tax on the amount being deferred, your actual take-home pay would only go down about $75 each pay period as a result of your $100 deferral (the actual amount depends on your withholding rate and some other factors).

The funds in your 401(k) account accumulate interest and dividends on a tax-deferred basis. This adds even further to the value of your savings.

Sometimes your employer will match all or part of the contributions you elect to defer. This means that, up to a certain percentage, for every dollar you contribute, your employer will fully or partially match your contribution. Over a period of time, through the vesting process described above, these matching contributions become your nonforfeitable property. Matching increases the value of your contributions in two ways. First, it is a tax-deferred source of additional income. Your employer is giving you more money, but you don't pay tax on it until it's withdrawn. Second, the amounts your employer contributes grow on a tax-deferred basis. At an absolute minimum, then, you should contribute to your employer's 401(k) plan as much as your employer will match. If you don't, you're basically turning down "free" money.

Tax-Sheltered Annuities (TSAs or 403(b) Plans)

403(b) plans are roughly comparable to 401(k) plans. They are available to employees of nonprofit organizations and public schools. If you are covered by a 403(b) plan, you generally may contribute up to $9,500 per year. This 1996 figure is indexed for inflation along with the figure for 401(k) plans. If you work for a health care, religious, or educational nonprofit, there also is a special provision in the law that lets you make so-called "catch-up" contributions to your 403(b) after 15 years of service to the same employer. If you qualify to make these contributions, you can add up to $15,000 extra to your 403(b) account, but only in $3,000 annual increments. This catch-up option probably won't be available to you if your regular contributions average more than $5,000 per year. For those who qualify, these catch-up contributions can provide an important way to increase your tax savings. More importantly, for people getting a late start in their retirement planning, they offer a unique opportunity to do exactly what the name suggests—to catch up. If you're eligible to take advantage of your 403(b) plan's catch-up rules, it's probably very much in your interest to do so.

457 Plans

457 plans also are somewhat akin to 401(k) plans, although 401(k) and 403(b) plans probably are closer relatives. 457 plans are available to employees of state and local governments and nonprofit organizations. Under a 457 plan, you may contribute as much as 25 percent of your salary, up to $7,500, to the plan each year. Note that this latter figure is one of the few numbers in the retirement world not indexed for inflation each year. 457 plans also come with catch-up provisions, although not the

same ones applicable to 403(b) plans. In each of the three years before your normal retirement age, you may contribute up to an additional $7,500 per year to your 457 plan, provided that you have deferred less than the maximum in earlier years. Again, these catch-up rules are important both as tax savings strategies and to help late starters boost their retirement nest eggs. If you can use the 457 catch-up rules, it's usually highly advisable to do so.

One word of caution with regard to 457 plans: Unlike most of the other retirement plans we've discussed so far, the assets in a 457 plan are subject to the claims of your employer's creditors. In practical terms, this means that if your employer declares bankruptcy, the salary you've deferred might not be protected.

Salary Reduction SEPs (SARSEPs)

If you work for a small business, the tax law provides a simplified mechanism for your employer to make available to you the option of deferring income. These plans are called SARSEPs (salary reduction SEPs). The mechanics of SARSEPs essentially track 401(k) plans in much the same way that SEPs parallel profit sharing plans. As an employee, you still enjoy all of the advantages of deferring income, up to the same limits as with 401(k) plans. Similarly, as with 401(k) plans, your employer has the option of matching your contributions. In order to offer a SARSEP, the business must have fewer than 25 eligible employees. Not many small businesses have taken advantage of SARSEPs. If yours hasn't, it should.

Supplemental Retirement Plans

In order to attract and retain key employees, such as senior managers and those with unique technical skills, some employers offer various types of supplemental retirement plans targeted to just these individuals. Because these plans are not offered on an equal basis to all employees (they "discriminate," in tax lingo), they don't enjoy all of the same tax benefits as the other plans described in this section. As we learned above, qualified plans provide a major exception to traditional tax principles, allowing employers to deduct contributions when they're made even if employees don't include them in income until years later. This exception doesn't apply to the supplemental plans under consideration here, and traditional tax principles apply: Your employer doesn't get a deduction for contributions to a nonqualified plan until you pay tax on them. This distinction is more important than it may sound at first because it drives how these plans are structured, what the tax consequences are to you, and what nontax risks come with these arrangements.

Supplemental Executive Retirement Plans

Supplemental executive retirement plans (SERPs), also sometimes referred to as "top hat" plans, are one of the more common forms of non-qualified supplemental plans. Under a SERP, an employer promises to pay you an additional amount of money when you leave or retire. Since the SERP is nothing more than the employer's promise, there are no tax consequences to you until the money actually is paid. Of course, since the SERP is nothing more than the employer's promise, you also have no guarantee you'll receive the money if your company is sued or goes bankrupt. Another risk with SERPs is that, if your employer doesn't actually invest funds on your behalf, but merely promises to pay out of the company's operating budget, you and the company may assume different rates of growth for the funds—and the company's rate probably will be lower than yours!

Other Supplemental Plans

There are a variety of other forms of nonqualified deferred compensation arrangements, from phantom stock plans to so-called "rabbi trusts." The important thing to remember with these plans is that, in order to defer taxes, the plans likely will be subject to the claims of your employer's creditors. The money generally cannot be set aside for you with no strings attached (or else you'd have to include it in your income now, defeating the goal of deferral), so there's always a risk involved. Sometimes, life insurance may be used to "informally" fund a deferred compensation arrangement, as with so-called split dollar insurance. These types of arrangements usually are negotiated in the context of an overall compensation package, and, as opposed to SERPs, frequently are structured on a case-by-case basis. If you're fortunate enough to be in a situation where you're negotiating one of these arrangements, you're foolish to attempt to do so without outside professional assistance.

Posttax 401(k) Contributions

There is another supplemental plan available to a broader range of employees: posttax contributions to a 401(k) plan. Under such a plan, you would continue making contributions to a 401(k) plan even after you've maxxed out on your pretax contributions (i.e., $9,500 in 1996). You can continue to do this as long as your total 401(k) contributions, pretax and posttax, don't exceed the plan's stated limits.

Posttax 401(k) contributions aren't for everybody. You probably have a six-figure income if posttax 401(k) contributions are an option. Moreover, not all employers who offer 401(k) plans include the posttax option. Nevertheless, if they do, they can be a valuable tool either for retirement savers getting a late start or for high-income earners who want the earnings on their investments to grow on a tax-advantaged basis. While contributions aren't deductible, the earnings on your contributions will grow without being taxed until you withdraw them. In this sense, they're roughly analogous to nondeductible IRA contributions (discussed later in this chapter).

One final thought regarding posttax contributions: As we know, 401(k) plans come with limited investment options. Your plan may not offer the investment diversification or the performance results appropriate for your goals, risk tolerance, and so on. While the benefits of pretax contributing may outweigh lackluster investment performance, the same cannot be said of posttax contributions. Before signing up to go over the $9,500 limit, be especially certain that the investment choices in your plan make sense for you.

OUR ISSUES

Spousal Rights in Employer Pensions

As we'll see in the "Withdrawals and Distributions of Retirement Savings" section later in this chapter, you will be allowed to choose how you want the vested benefits in your employer's noncontributory pension plan paid to you—all at once, for a period certain, over your life, or over the lives of both yourself and another person. However, what happens to your vested benefits in such a plan if you die before you begin receiving them? Unless you have a spouse, the answer to that question is that you lose them. The law gives a surviving spouse significant rights in a deceased spouse's noncontributory pension benefits. None of those legal rights are available to domestic partners—or, for that matter, any other alternative family members. Lesbians and gay men usually can provide for their significant others in structuring payouts from an employer plan in retirement, but not in the case of premature death.

This can create a significant problem for gay couples whenever they rely on an employer's noncontributory retirement plan to fund their retirement income needs. The risk is especially acute if the couple is depending heavily on one partner's employer plan for such needs. It may be possible to partially manage this risk by increasing your other sources of retirement savings. This is why gay couples were encouraged to compute retirement income needs individually in the first section of this chapter. However, if your planning relies heavily on an employer's pension, you also might consider life insurance as a way to manage this risk.

Note, too, that this same risk exists vis-à-vis Social Security retirement benefits. Actually, the problem here is even worse. The risk in the case of an employer pension can be eliminated once you reach retirement by arranging distributions that provide a survivorship benefit for the nonemployee partner. It's not possible to arrange Social Security benefits to provide survivorship rights for a domestic partner. Once you die, your benefits stop.

Finally, remember that this issue only arises in the context of noncontributory retirement plans. Your vested benefits in a contributory plan such as a 401(k) are distributed to the beneficiary or beneficiaries you designate.

Hiring a Partner

In Chapter 4 we discussed how hiring a partner as a tax planning strategy can allow some gay couples to move income from a higher-bracket business owner to a lower-bracket significant other. We also saw that this technique allows the business owner to provide a number of important fringe benefits to his or her employee-partner. Hiring a partner also can be a great way of providing him or her with retirement plan coverage. As we saw in the first section of this chapter, since lesbians and gay men may have comparatively more work to do in preparing for retirement than the dominant culture, this strategy should be considered by every gay person who owns a small business.

RELATED TOPICS

Contributory retirement plans like 401(k) plans offer you the opportunity to defer paying income tax on a portion of your wages until you withdraw the funds—presumably in retirement and presumably in a lower marginal tax bracket. This shifting of income constitutes one of the most important opportunities available to most taxpayers to engage in bracket arbitrage. The benefits of this technique are explained in the "Bracket Arbi-trage" section on page 206.

If you participate in a retirement plan that allows you to direct where the funds are invested, as is the case with many 401(k) plans, for all practical purposes these funds should be treated as part of your total portfolio. In order to be certain you invest this part of your portfolio in a manner consistent with your overall goals and your risk tolerance, and also that achieves proper diversification, carefully review the "Asset Allocation and Portfolio Structure" section on page 138.

It's one of the defining characteristics of the 1990s that people are leaving employers more frequently than ever. If you are covered by an employer's plan, it is important for you to understand how to treat dis-bursements you receive from such a plan when you leave your job—regardless of whether you're moving up, moving on, downsizing, or retir-ing. These disbursements are called *withdrawals* or *distributions,* and the penalties for doing the wrong thing with them can be very high. Carefully review the section on "Withdrawals and Distributions of Retirement Savings" on page 266 to avoid the pitfalls in this complicated area.

One of the more important goals of the estate planning process for many lesbians and gay men is to minimize the assets that pass through the probate process. Contributory retirement plans offer an important opportunity to help meet this goal, since they allow you to name a beneficiary who automatical-ly will receive assets remaining in your account when you die. Therefore, it is very important that you carefully consider the beneficiary designations you make on your retirement accounts. The benefits of avoiding probate are detailed in the "Wills and Will Substitutes" section on page 302.

Similarly, you should try to avoid having your estate be the benefi-ciary of a retirement account. This can happen if you fail to specify a ben-eficiary, if all your beneficiaries predecease you, or if you actually name your estate in the paperwork for your plan. Again, the logic for avoiding this is outlined in the "Wills and Will Substitutes" section on page 302.

If you and a partner are relying on a retirement income stream from an employer's noncontributory retirement plan, you might need to con-sider purchasing life insurance to protect against the risk of losing that benefit in the event of premature death. The ins and outs of life insurance are explained in the "Life Insurance" section on page 37.

The lack of a domestic partner's survivorship rights for Social Security benefits is discussed in the "Social Security Retirement Benefits" section on page 262.

RETIREMENT PLANS FOR THE SELF-EMPLOYED

THE STRAIGHT FACTS

If you are self-employed (i.e., a sole proprietor or a partner in a partnership), your retirement planning options are slightly more limited than those discussed in the last section. Most of the plans discussed there are only available to corporations, although the tax law allows for plans to benefit self-employed people that roughly parallel some of those options.

The major difference in self-employed retirement plans is that, at least with regard to the owner, they do not distinguish between employer and employee contributions. The tax law treats a self-employed person as both an employer and an employee for retirement plan purposes. The net effect of this restriction is to reduce the amount of money self-employed people can set aside for themselves in retirement savings each year. Note that, in contrast, if your sole proprietorship has employees, the plans available to you treat them roughly the same way they would be treated under the plans described in the last section.

The two types of retirement plans available to self-employed individuals are SEPs and Keogh plans, the latter named for the legislator who first introduced them.

Keoghs

Keogh plans essentially permit self-employed persons to establish and maintain defined benefit and defined contribution plans in much the same fashion as those discussed in the last section. The advantage to these plans is that they allow self-employed people to defer more of their income into retirement savings than SEPs do. The higher contribution limits applicable to money purchase defined contribution plans and to defined benefit plans can be used when establishing a Keogh (with some technical adjustments). The disadvantage is that they are more complex to administer and likely will require the assistance of a pension expert.

SEPs

Self-employed SEPs function in much the same way as the employer SEPs described in the last section, except that the maximum contribution percentage is lowered from 15 percent for employees to about 13.04 percent for the owner/employee. Once the funds are placed in a self-employed person's SEP–IRA, they are treated like any other IRA. In addition, as a self-employed person, you can establish a SARSEP for the benefit of your employees, but the total contribution for the year to your own account—SEP plus SARSEP—still cannot exceed 13.04 percent.

One other advantage to SEPs is that contributions can be made anytime up until the date the owner's tax return is due, including extensions. This provides you with the flexibility to do some late tax planning, deciding as late as April (or August if you extend your return) of 19X2 how much you want to contribute to a SEP for 19X1 and deduct on your 19X1 tax return. In contrast, Keoghs allow deductions up until the due date of the return (without extensions), but only if the plan was in existence before the tax year in question ended. In short, Keoghs provide more limited opportunities for after-the-fact tax planning than do SEPs.

If you are a high-income self-employed person with a mature business, consider consulting with a pension plan administrator to see if a Keogh can be of benefit to you. If you are still a struggling entrepreneur, the SEP probably is a better bet right now.

OUR ISSUES

SEPs for Moonlighters

Many lesbians and gay men engage in moonlighting or freelancing work. This work is often an important supplement to a regular paycheck. However, regardless of whether it pays for those little extras or is your main source of support, it's important to remember that this income is eligible for a SEP contribution. Contributing 13.04 percent of your net income from moonlighting or freelancing will lower your tax bill this year, help you generate tax-favored income on your SEP accounts in future years, and help you save for a secure retirement. SEPs are fairly low maintenance, especially if you don't have employees. Although you have to fill out a very short form, you don't even have to file it with the IRS—just keep it in your permanent records. What's more, you can vary the percentage of your SEP contribution each year as your financial circumstances dictate (although you're always well advised to contribute the maximum 13.04 percent). Even small amounts compound substantially when placed in a tax-favored account, so, if you're generating a little extra income on the side, don't overlook the SEP option!

Hire Your Partner

The tax and retirement advantages of hiring your partner apply even if your business isn't incorporated—that is, even if you're a sole proprietor or a partner in a partnership. As long as the employment relationship is bona fide and your significant other is paid reasonable compensation for work actually performed, you can lower your own taxes and increase your total household retirement savings by covering him or her under a Keogh or SEP. Again, keep in mind that, if you have more than one employee, you have to treat them all equally when it comes to retirement benefits.

RELATED TOPICS

The retirement scenario for members of the lesbian and gay community is not likely to follow the dominant paradigm. For many of us, there will not be a younger generation of family members to provide financial and other forms of support. Accordingly, we need to be more diligent than most in saving for retirement. This phenomenon is explored in more detail in the "Computing Retirement Needs and Savings" section on page 231.

While Keogh contributions are invested more or less subject to the same restrictions as qualified retirement plans, SEPs allow you to choose your own investment vehicles. In this sense, then, they become part of your overall investment portfolio. In order to be sure that your SEP is invested consistent with your time frame and risk tolerance, review the "Asset Allocation and Portfolio Structure" section on page 138.

At some point, the money going into your SEP or Keogh will need to come out. You may close your business and receive a distribution of your Keogh account balance, you may decide to move your SEP funds to a different investment, or it may simply be time to retire and start living off your nest egg. Regardless of the circumstances, you'll want to be certain you avoid the numerous withdrawal and distribution pitfalls in the tax law. They're all reviewed in the "Withdrawals and Distributions of Retirement Savings" section on page 266.

Making beneficiary designations on a Keogh or SEP is an essential part of estate planning for lesbians and gay men. It helps ensure that these assets pass to your intended beneficiary without the supervision—and potential interference—of the probate court. Similarly, naming your estate as the beneficiary of your SEP or Keogh account can cause those assets to pass through probate unnecessarily. The financial and nonfinancial incentives for lesbians and gay men to minimize probate are detailed in the "Wills and Will Substitutes" section on page 302.

INDIVIDUAL RETIREMENT ACCOUNTS

THE STRAIGHT FACTS

Individual retirement accounts (IRAs) are a familiar part of the financial planning landscape. Before the 1986 overhaul of the tax laws, IRAs were a wonderful form of both tax-deductible and tax-advantaged savings. The deduction is much more limited now, but there are still benefits in IRAs.

Since 1986, IRAs have come in two varieties: deductible and nondeductible. Whether or not you can deduct IRA contributions depends on whether you (or your spouse) are covered by an employer's plan, and, if so, how much you make. Regardless of whether or not you can deduct your IRA contributions, they still can grow in the account on a tax-deferred basis. This feature may make even nondeductible IRAs an attractive investment (more on this later).

Contribution Amounts

IRA contributions are limited to a maximum of $2,000 per person per year (you can contribute less). If you earn less than $2,000, you can only contribute up to the amount of your actual earnings. If you have any earnings that entitle you to make an IRA contribution, there is a $200 minimum on IRA contributions; if your earnings are less than $200, you still may contribute this minimum.

If you have a nonworking spouse, he or she also is entitled to make an IRA contribution, up to a maximum of $250. You and your spouse can divide your total contributions between your two accounts however you choose, but you cannot put more than $2,000 in one person's account in any year.

Note that, if you contribute more than the $2,000 allowed, there's a 6 percent excise tax imposed on the excess. If you find that you've somehow overcontributed, ask your IRA trustee or custodian to apply the overage to the next year's contributions; assuming you catch the overage in time, this usually avoids the penalty.

Deductibility

As we saw above, the deductibility of IRA contributions depends first on outside pension coverage and then on income. If you (or your spouse if you're married) are covered by an employer's pension, your contribution is only fully deductible if your income is beneath certain adjusted gross income (AGI) limits. Once your income crosses the applicable limit, your deduction gets phased out until it is eliminated for AGIs $10,000 or more over the limit. The AGI limit is $25,000 if you are a single filer or head of household, $40,000 if you file jointly with your spouse, and $0 if you and your spouse file separately. Thus, you cannot claim any IRA deduction if you (or your spouse) are covered by an employer plan and your AGI exceeds $35,000, $50,000, and $10,000, respectively. Note that, for purposes of determining eligibility to deduct IRA contributions, AGI is computed without taking any IRA contributions into account (technically this is called *modified AGI* or *MAGI*).

If you are within the $10,000 phase-out range, the amount of your IRA deduction is computed based on the amount by which your MAGI exceeds the lower limits of that range.

EXAMPLE

Jose is single and has MAGI of $31,000. Jose is covered by his employer's pension. This puts Jose's MAGI $6,000 over the $25,000 limit applicable to him ($31,000 – $25,000). This makes his maximum $2,000 IRA contribution 60 percent nondeductible ($6,000/$10,000), and 40 percent deductible. Thus, any amount Jose contributes up to $800 is deductible ($2,000 × 40%), but any contribution above $800 (and under the $2,000 maximum) is nondeductible.

You are considered covered by an employer's defined benefit plan if at any time during the year you or your spouse were eligible to participate in such a plan, whether you chose to do so or not. You are considered covered by a defined contribution plan if contributions were added to your account during the year. It doesn't matter whether or not your benefits have vested; once you're on the plan's books, you are considered covered. As a practical matter, the way to tell if you are covered by an employer's plan is to review your W-2. If either of the squares in Box 15 of that form labeled "Pension Plan" and "Deferred Compensation" are checked, you are covered by your employer's plan.

You may find the decision tree in Figure 5–1 helpful in determining the deductibility of your IRA contributions.

IRAs and the Self-Employed

For self-employed persons, you are subject to the rules limiting deductibility of IRA contributions if you've established a Keogh plan or if you make a SEP contribution for the year in question. Since SEP contributions are based on net income, a self-employed person with low net income may be better off forgoing a SEP for the year and claiming an

FIGURE 5–1

Determining the Deductibility of your IRA Contribution

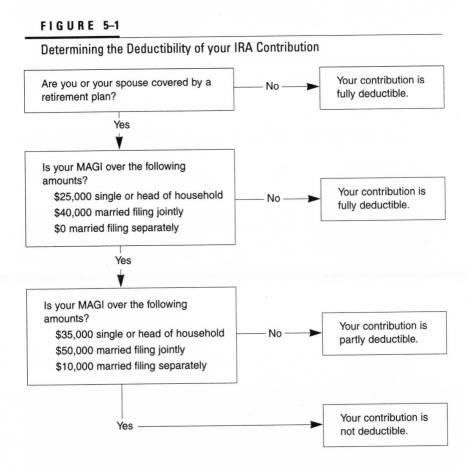

IRA instead. Of course, you must meet all the usual IRA requirements in order to qualify for the deduction. More importantly, you must be able to afford the contribution.

EXAMPLE

Michelle began a computer consulting business this year. Her net income for the year was only $2,000. She would be entitled to make a maximum SEP contribution of approximately $240 (the actual formula for determining SEP contributions requires subtracting from AGI one-half of FICA tax paid, making the computation a little complex). Michelle is in the 15 percent tax bracket, so her SEP would result in a tax savings of only $36 ($240 × 15%). Alternatively, Michelle could make an IRA contribution of $2,000, which would produce a tax savings of $300. Assuming she cannot afford to fund both a SEP and an IRA, the IRA is the better choice for Michelle this year.

Sometimes it may be advantageous to combine a SEP and a deductible IRA contribution in order to maximize tax savings (assuming you have the resources to pay for such contributions).

EXAMPLE

Maggie is a self-employed electrician. She just started her business last year, so her net business income for the year is only $5,000. Maggie has no other sources of income. Maggie has several options in this situation. First, she could make a SEP contribution of approximately $600. Since she is in the 15 percent tax bracket, this saves her $90 in taxes ($600 × 15%). Alternatively, she could forgo the SEP and make the maximum allowable IRA contribution. A contribution of $2,000 would net Maggie a tax savings of $300. Finally, assuming she could afford it, Maggie could make both a deductible SEP and a deductible IRA contribution since she qualifies for both. This would give her a combined tax savings of $390 ($90 + $300).

Nondeductible IRAs

If you don't qualify to make deductible IRA contributions, this does not automatically mean you should dismiss the IRA option. If you choose to make a nondeductible contribution, your IRA continues to earn income on a tax-deferred basis. Many financial planners therefore think nondeductible IRAs are a good deal.

However, some professionals believe that the restrictions placed on IRA accounts outweigh their benefits once the ability to deduct contributions is lost. For example, unless you're willing to pay a 10 percent penalty tax in addition to federal and state income taxes, you can't withdraw your IRA funds until age 59½. In contrast, if you took those IRA funds and invested them in a tax-free municipal bond fund, you would achieve the same tax results and still have access to your money whenever you needed it.

There is something to be said for this latter argument. There's also something to be said for "locking up" your funds until retirement in an IRA, especially if you're not a strong saver. Also, IRAs give you more diverse investment choices than municipal bond funds. This can be a close call, and you should weigh both arguments to decide which fits better with your spending habits, financial discipline, and overall goals.

Due Dates

IRA contributions must be deposited by the due date of your return without extensions. If you file early, you still have until April 15th to get the money in the account, though.

OUR ISSUES

Spousal IRAs

Lesbian and gay couples cannot make spousal IRA contributions for their domestic partners. Although the amount of the spousal IRA—$250—is small, the ability to divide the total IRA "pot"—$2,000 regular IRA + $250 spousal IRA—between spouses would prove a helpful benefit for some lesbian and gay couples were it available. On the other hand, one domestic partner's ability to deduct IRA contributions does not hinge in part on whether or not the other partner is covered by an employer's pension. This so-called spousal tainting rule proves to be a significant headache for married couples trying to save for retirement.

RELATED TOPICS

If you're having trouble remembering how your AGI—the starting point for determining the deductibility of your IRA contributions—is computed, review the discussion in the "Income Tax Basics" section on page 161.

Lesbians and gay men have unique needs when it comes to planning for retirement. Although it may seem counterintuitive to some, we actually may need to save more than average in order to ensure a secure old age. To meet our unique needs, perhaps IRAs deserve a second or third look. The many factors that must be considered when planning for your golden years are drawn together in the "Computing Retirement Needs and Savings" section on page 231.

To get a sense of how best to invest your IRA funds as an integrated part of your total portfolio, review the "Asset Allocation and Portfolio Structure" section on page 138.

If you want to transfer funds from one IRA account to another, there are definite hoops you must jump through in order to avoid serious tax consequences. This is explained in the "Rollover Distributions" section on page 270.

It is essential that you designate beneficiaries for your IRAs in order to ensure they pass the way you want without the supervision of the probate court. Similarly, generally you should not name your estate as a beneficiary of your IRA. This, too, could cause your IRA funds to pass through probate unnecessarily. The logic for avoiding this is outlined in the "Wills and Will Substitutes" section on page 302.

SOCIAL SECURITY RETIREMENT BENEFITS

THE STRAIGHT FACTS

Social Security currently is the most important leg of the three-legged stool supporting many Americans in their retirement years. Monthly Social Security benefits mean the difference between poverty and relative comfort for a wide variety of recipients. For those of us in the planning stages, it is very important to understand the role Social Security benefits are likely to play in our retirement finances.

One important disclaimer before we dive into this topic: Social Security is a massive and intricate system, and volumes could be written about how it works—and have been. While the next several pages provide a broad overview of the major features of the system in order to help you know where Social Security will fit in your retirement planning, they cannot and do not purport to offer a comprehensive treatment of the topic.

Qualifying for Coverage

To qualify for Social Security retirement benefits, you must earn what's known as *40 quarters of coverage* (you need fewer than 40 quarters if you were born before 1928). A quarter of coverage is equal to about $640 in quarterly earnings (this 1996 figure is indexed for inflation). However, you can only earn four quarters of coverage per year, regardless of how high your income is.

Your Social Security coverage also is based on the amount of your earnings and the taxes you pay into the system. These taxes are withheld by your employer, who also is required to pay into the system the same amount you do. If you're self-employed, you report your Social Security taxes when you file your annual income tax return, paying both the employer's and employee's portions yourself. There are two components to the Social Security taxes you (and your employer) pay. The main component pays for Social Security's retirement benefits, as well as some disability benefits. It's known as OASDI (Old Age, Survivors, and Disability Insurance). It's equal to a flat 6.2 percent of your wages up to $62,700 in 1996. This figure is inflation-adjusted. The tax you pay for the other component of Social Security benefits—Medicare—is 1.45 percent of your wages, with no upper limit. Thus, the total rate of taxation on the first $62,700 in 1996 wages is 7.65 percent (6.2% + 1.45%).

The Social Security Administration keeps track of the wages you receive. This is very important information, because it is used to compute your level of retirement benefits. It therefore is a good idea to doublecheck Social Security's records—in fact, the agency encourages it. Paperwork mistakes in the records it receives from employers are not uncommon, and of course the government is not above a computer error or two of its own. Since Social Security's records become final after three years, you're well advised to request a copy of your record periodically. This can be done by submitting to the Social Security Administration (SSA) a Form SSA-7004-SM. You can get this form by visiting your local Social Security office or calling 1-800-772-1213. When you submit the form, the SSA will send you a Personal Earnings and Benefits Statement. This form often goes by its acronym, PEBES. Your PEBES will contain a complete printout of SSA's records regarding your annual earnings history. If there is a discrepancy between your records and the government's, the PEBES will tell you how to correct it.

Estimating Social Security Retirement Benefits

There are two ways to estimate your Social Security retirement benefits: the simple way, and the hard way. The simple way is to request from Social Security a PEBES, discussed above. In addition to your earnings record, the PEBES provides an estimate of your retirement benefits, based on your current level of earnings.

The hard way to estimate your Social Security benefits involves trying to do so yourself. Unfortunately, this process isn't just hard, it's numbingly so. Nevertheless, in summary form, the Social Security Administration estimates your *primary insurance amount (PIA)*—that is, your benefit—something like this:

1. They index your earnings before age 60 for inflation.
2. They compute your average monthly earnings for your highest 35 years of indexed wages (called the *average indexed monthly earnings (AIME))*.
3. They compute your PIA by giving you 90 percent of the first $400 in AIME, 32 percent for the next $1,900, and 15 percent for the balance (these figures are indexed each year for inflation).

There is one important thing to note about Social Security benefits: The percentage of your retirement income needs met by Social Security benefits decreases as your preretirement earned income increases.

EXAMPLE

A retiree with average preretirement earnings of $30,000 will see Social Security benefits replace about 60 percent of his income, whereas a retiree with average preretirement earnings of $50,000 will have only about 27 percent of her income replaced by Social Security.

There's a clear implication here for retirement planning: the higher your retirement income needs, the smaller the portion of those needs that will be met by Social Security. This means that you will need to save even more yourself.

The earliest you can claim your Social Security benefits is age 62, but your benefits are reduced if you claim them before your "normal retirement age." This age currently is 65, but it gradually is being raised for people born after 1937, and reaches age 67 for those born after 1959. The reduction in benefits for "early claimers" is computed on a sliding scale that reaches 20 percent of your normal benefit if you start right at age 62. Traditionally, then, people were advised not to start collecting benefits before reaching their normal retirement age unless they absolutely had to. However, if you retire early, it may be advantageous to begin receiving Social Security benefits as soon as you qualify for them. One recent study concluded that it's not until you've been collecting benefits for about 12 years (i.e., not until age 77) that you come out ahead by having waited until age 65 to start. This can be a complicated decision, with taxes and other factors coming into play, so you're well advised to consult a professional for advice.

Benefits for Family Members and Survivors

When you retire, Social Security retirement benefits aren't just paid to you. Your spouse can choose to claim either her or his own benefits or a spousal retirement benefit, usually 50 percent of yours. What's more, your spouse can change the option he or she chooses each year, ensuring that he or she always will receive the larger benefit. The Social Security Administration can provide the paperwork to help your spouse switch from receiving his or her own benefits to receiving your spousal benefits, or vice versa. Moreover, if you have minor children when you retire, they can receive benefits, usually until they reach age 18. Note that the total benefits paid to your family generally can't exceed between 150 percent and 188 percent of the amount paid to you individually.

When you die, Social Security also provides survivors benefits for your spouse and dependent children. These benefits may be available regardless of how old you are when you die.

Social Security into the Future

One of the fundamental premises underlying Social Security is that it is a "compact between the generations." In other words, each working generation of Americans compacts to support through Social Security taxes the generation currently in retirement. In return, when the current working generation retires, it will receive the support of the next working generation. This system has served the nation well since 1935. However, some of the basic demographic assumptions underlying the system are showing signs of stress. More people are living longer and fewer babies are being born. These changes suggest that the current system cannot continue indefinitely. Under current projections, Social Security will begin paying out in benefits more than it takes in through payroll taxes in 2013. Right now, there are huge surpluses in Social Security's "account," but the net outflow occurring after 2013 suggests that the system will run out of money around 2030.

Notwithstanding the predictions of doom and gloom currently popular in some quarters, it seems unlikely that the Social Security system will ever be allowed to go broke. However, the system will need to be changed, and it's important for those who have many years to go before retirement to factor these potential changes into their retirement planning.

One possibility is that Social Security will be "means-tested"—that is, wealthy retirees may see their benefits reduced or even eliminated. Another possibility is that all Social Security benefits will be subject to income tax (currently, only between 50 percent and 85 percent of the benefits of certain high income retirees are subject to tax). Social Security's annual cost of living adjustments also could be reduced. Yet another possible change to bring the system back into balance would be to raise the Social Security tax rate on either employers, employees, or both. Some policymakers also suggest "privatizing" Social Security. Under such a plan, the Social Security taxes you pay would be placed into a private account similar to an IRA. You would own the account, and you would direct the investment. While it has a fair amount of appeal, this proposal currently seems a longshot. One very likely change is an increase in the Social Security retirement age for younger workers.

OUR ISSUES

Spousal Benefits

Social Security's spousal retirement benefits are one of the best deals going for married couples in retirement. Lesbian and gay couples are not eligible to claim such benefits. More importantly, they are not entitled to survivors benefits if one of them dies. This means that lesbian and gay couples who are counting on Social Security retirement benefits to help meet their retirement income needs run the risk that a premature death—or even a death early in retirement—could undermine their retirement planning. As with the lack of survivor rights for domestic partners in non-contributory employer plans, this risk may have to be managed through a combination of increased savings and life insurance. Again, as we saw in the first section of this chapter, it often is advisable for gay couples to compute their retirement income needs individually, even if they save toward them jointly.

RELATED TOPICS

To understand how Social Security benefits tie into your overall retirement planning, review the "Computing Retirement Needs and Savings" section on page 231.

The taxation of Social Security benefits is outlined in the "Income Tax Basics" section on page 161.

The Social Security taxes paid by sole proprietors and partners in partnerships are explained in the "Other Taxes" section on page 201.

Social Security disability benefits are detailed in the "Disability Insurance" section on page 56.

Gay couples who count on each other's Social Security benefits in computing their joint retirement needs risk a shortfall in retirement income in the event a partner dies sooner than expected. See the "Life Insurance" section on page 37, which may be helpful in managing this risk. The similar risk associated with relying on a partner's noncontributory employer plan if that partner dies prematurely is explained in the "Employer-Sponsored Retirement Plans" section on page 243.

WITHDRAWALS AND DISTRIBUTIONS OF RETIREMENT SAVINGS

THE STRAIGHT FACTS

If you have been participating in some form of tax-deferred retirement plan—such as an IRA, SEP, 401(k), Keogh, or employer plan—you eventually will begin making withdrawals from your plan. These withdrawals may be voluntary, as when you make a distribution from your IRA at age 68 to help meet your retirement income needs, or they may be involuntary, as when your employer "downsizes" you at age 56 and in the process informs you that something must be done with the $127,000 balance in your profit sharing plan. Regardless of the circumstances, you are going to have to decide—sometimes fairly quickly—what to do with very large sums of money.

These decisions cannot be made without reference to their tax implications. When it comes to your retirement savings, remember that if the funds in a retirement account were not taxed going in, they will be taxed coming out. Since most retirement savings occur on a pretax basis, this is an issue for most of us. Unfortunately, the stakes are higher than most people realize, and the margin of error is slim. If you make the wrong move, or through ignorance miss a tax-deferral opportunity, you could lose a hefty chunk of your retirement nest egg to unnecessary taxes. It therefore is important for you to learn the ways to minimize the tax bite on your retirement plan withdrawals and distributions.

The strategies available to you to minimize taxes on retirement plan withdrawals vary based on your age, how long you've been participating in the plan, how much you're taking out, and what type of plan it is. The following general discussion should help you determine which approach will save you the most money. However, if after reading this section you're still not confident about what to do with your retirement savings, hire a number cruncher. You have tens, or perhaps hundreds, of thousands of dollars in your plan, so the amounts at stake are too high to risk a mistake. A good financial planner or tax adviser will more than earn his or her fee in the amount of taxes they save you.

As a general proposition, you are well advised to keep money in tax-deferred retirement plans for as long as possible. As we saw earlier in this chapter, your retirement accounts grow without paying tax until they're withdrawn. This means that interest, dividends, and capital gains earned by your retirement assets can grow for years and years free of income tax. If you're tempted to withdraw money from a plan to meet short-term cash needs, or to finance current spending, think long and hard first. As we'll see in a moment, the price for doing so usually is prohibitively high.

Some employer plans, particularly 401(k) plans, allow participants to take loans against their cash balances. If you need money and this option is available to you, it is preferable to a withdrawal. Essentially, you're making a loan to yourself, and the interest you pay on the funds you borrow gets credited back to your account. Be forewarned, however, that even the 401(k) loan strategy is not without its drawbacks. You lose the advantage of tax-deferred compounding on the amounts you've borrowed from your account, and if you retire or leave your employer with a loan balance, you have to pay it back or it is considered a withdrawal. Nevertheless, if your financial back is against the wall, and it's either a loan or a withdrawal, go for the loan. Note, too, that loans are not available from IRAs and SEPs.

Premature Distributions and Penalties

10 Percent Penalty Tax on Premature Distributions

Regardless of the reason, it's almost always advisable to wait until you're at least age 59½ before withdrawing funds from any type of retirement account. If you take anything out before then, you may be subject to a 10 percent penalty tax in addition to any income tax you owe.

> **EXAMPLE**
>
> At age 40, you withdraw $10,000 from your IRA account to purchase a new car. You are in the 28 percent bracket. When you file your next tax return, you will pay $2,800 in federal income tax ($10,000 × 28%), plus $1,000 in penalty tax ($10,000 × 10%). This leaves you with a net of $6,200 on this transaction before you pay any applicable state income taxes ($10,000 − $2,800 − $1,000).

Clearly, the approach in this example was not a good way to purchase your new car. You've only realized about 60 cents on the dollar from the amount you've withdrawn.

The 10 percent penalty tax also will be applied to most distributions you receive from an employer's plan before age 59½, if you decide to keep them. These distributions usually occur either when you leave your job or when your employer terminates its plan. Strategies for handling these distributions and avoiding the penalty tax are discussed below.

Exceptions

There are some exceptions to the 10 percent penalty tax. If you die before age 59½, your beneficiaries won't be required to pay the tax when they withdraw your retirement plan proceeds. Similarly, if you are disabled before 59½, you can withdraw from retirement accounts free of the 10 percent penalty. Finally, if you receive a so-called lump-sum distribution (discussed below) from an employer's plan after age 55 because your employment has been terminated (regardless of whether you or your employer did the terminating), the penalty won't apply. Of course, in all these situations, the regular income tax due on the withdrawal still must be paid.

Annuitized Distributions

IRAs

There is a way to take money out of your IRAs before 59½ without incurring the 10 percent penalty, but it's only a practical technique in a small number of cases. The tax law allows you to avoid the 10 percent penalty if you make a "series of substantially equal periodic payments" from your account. This means that, if you annuitize your account balance and make equal withdrawals over your life expectancy, your withdrawals will be free of the penalty tax.

Keep in mind, too, that your IRAs can be funded from a variety of sources: your pretax contributions, your posttax contributions, SEPs, SARSEPs, and rollovers of distributions from an employer's plan (we'll discuss rollover distributions next). For simplicity's sake, we'll assume in this discussion that your IRAs are funded exclusively with pretax contributions (i.e., none of your contributions were included in income on previous tax returns). If you made any nondeductible contributions to your IRA accounts, the portion of any distribution attributable to those contributions (but not to any earnings on them) are not taxed.

While this "annuity exception" to the penalty rule may seem like a golden opportunity, it has two very serious practical drawbacks. First, you must keep making withdrawals at least every year until you reach 59½ (or for at least five years, if that's a later date). Second, you must have a very large account balance to make this technique worthwhile.

EXAMPLE 1

You are 45 years old with a $10,000 IRA account balance. Your life expectancy is 40 more years according to applicable IRS tables. In order to withdraw the funds from your IRA without being subject to the 10 percent penalty, you would have to withdraw $250 from your account each year until you reach age 59½ ($10,000/40).

EXAMPLE 2

Change the circumstances in Example 1 somewhat. Assume that your IRA account balance is $200,000. Now you can withdraw $5,000 each year without paying the penalty tax ($200,000/40).

Clearly, the tiny amount of money you would realize in Example 1 isn't going to do you very much good. And, while you've avoided the penalty tax, you still have to pay regular income taxes on the $250. Annuitized distributions thus don't make a lot of sense for small account balances. Depending on your overall circumstances and the purposes for which you seek to withdraw the money, however, the approach in Example 2 may be beneficial for you. For example, depending on the availability of other assets, it may be helpful in meeting the costs of a child's college education. Or, if it fits in with your overall financial and personal goals, perhaps it can help you pay off a mortgage in time for early retirement.

This technique is not for everyone. In fact, it's only going to work for the exceptional few. Not many people have high enough IRA balances to make this approach viable. Also, there's a downside to it that you must factor into your computations: It has the effect of drawing on your retirement savings about 10 to 20 years earlier than "normal." You probably will need to adjust your retirement income expectations if you decide to use this approach. However, if you're one of the lucky few for whom it will work, it provides a nice way to supplement your current income or perhaps even expand your financial goals.

Employer Plans

When you retire, you usually are given the option of receiving assets from an employer's plan either in the form of a lump sum or an annuity. There often are tax and nontax advantages to opt for the lump sum, and we'll discuss them later in this section. If you do choose to have your employer annuitize your pension, you have several options for receiving monthly payments, just like with any other annuity: over your life expectancy, over the joint life expectancy of yourself and a beneficiary, or over a life expectancy with some guaranteed payment period. Note that, for purposes of the joint life expectancy, your beneficiary need not be a spouse.

Rollover Distributions

Employer Plans

So far, our discussion largely has focused on minimizing the impact of voluntary retirement plan withdrawals. What happens, however, when you receive a distribution involuntarily—when you leave an employer or the employer terminates its plan? Sometimes nothing happens. Some employer plans, particularly defined benefit plans, don't always distribute your vested pension assets to you before retirement. Instead, they hold the funds and pay them out only when you reach normal retirement age. Other times, if the plan is administered through an investment firm or brokerage house, that firm or brokerage may let you keep your account with them even if you are no longer part of your employer's plan. Occasionally, a new employer will allow you to transfer your savings directly from your old employer's plan into theirs. In each of these instances, you don't actually receive a distribution, so you don't have to worry about what to do with it. Accordingly, if one of these options is available to you, by all means take advantage of it—assuming that you like how and where the plan's assets are being invested.

Many times, however, you don't have the flexibility to avoid receiving retirement funds. A distribution from an employer's plan (or former employer's plan) often requires you to do a little planning and spend some time with paperwork in order to avoid big tax headaches. The guiding principle here is clear: You should try to roll your distribution over into another retirement account—another employer's plan or an IRA—in order to avoid paying income tax on it, along with the 10 percent penalty tax if you're under 59½.

First, the general rule: If you receive a lump-sum distribution from a retirement plan, you can avoid taxation on it by redepositing the funds—rolling them over—into another retirement plan within 60 days. The rollover can be either into another employer's plan or into an IRA, but it must be done within 60 days to avoid tax. The time clock starts running the day the funds are disbursed to you. This rollover option is not available for annuitized distributions from an employer's retirement plan. That is, once you retire and you start receiving your monthly pension check, you cannot roll it over to avoid paying taxes on it.

EXAMPLE
On March 1, 19X1, you quit your job to start a new one. On May 1, 19X1, your former employer notifies you that your pension plan account contains $10,000. On June 1, 19X1, you open an IRA account with a local brokerage firm and authorize your former employer to deposit the funds in your new account. Your former employer does this on June 15, 19X1. You have successfully rolled over your retirement plan balance without any adverse tax consequences.

In this example, notice that you asked your employer to deposit the funds directly into your IRA account. That's because, if you had taken the distribution yourself, the tax law would require your employer to impose income tax withholding of 20 percent on the funds, leaving you with only 80 percent of your account balance to deposit in the IRA. This withholding requirement applies even if you plan to roll over 100 percent of the account balance. Thus, in order to avoid adverse tax consequences, you would have to deposit the other 20 percent of the distribution using your own funds, and then claim a credit for the 20 percent withheld on the following year's tax return. Otherwise, the 20 percent your employer withheld wouldn't be considered rolled over, and you'd pay income and penalty taxes on it. Thus, even though the money washes out after taxes, the impact on your cash flow makes direct distributions an unattractive option.

EXAMPLE

On March 1, 19X1, you quit your job to start a new one. On May 1, 19X1, your former employer notifies you that your pension plan account contains $50,000. In order to avoid income tax and the 10 percent penalty, you decide to roll over the funds into an IRA account. You ask your employer to remit the funds to you for this purpose. The check arrives dated May 15, 19X1, in the amount of $40,000 ($50,000 − 20%). If you only deposit the $40,000 into an IRA, you will still owe income tax (and penalty tax if you are under 59½) on the $10,000 your employer was required to withhold. In order to avoid this outcome, you will have to take the additional $10,000 from your own savings and deposit it into your new IRA by July 14, 19X1 (60 days after May 15, 19X1). Of course, when you file your income taxes on April 15, 19X2, you will be able to claim a $10,000 credit for the withheld taxes on your return.

As you can see, the out-of-pocket expense of rolling over retirement plan distributions yourself can be prohibitive. In order to avoid the pitfalls and vagaries of retirement distributions, then, you need to remember two simple rules: Always roll over your lump-sum distributions to avoid income tax and the 10 percent penalty tax, and always do a direct plan-to-plan or plan-to-IRA rollover to avoid 20 percent tax withholding.

Conduit IRAs

A final warning with regard to employer plan rollovers: If you're rolling over funds from an employer's plan into an IRA, be sure to keep the funds in a separate account. This technique creates what is known as a *conduit IRA*. Putting the funds from a company plan into a conduit IRA gives you the flexibility to roll them over into another employer's plan down the road (many employers' plans permit this). There's a definite advantage to doing this: Funds in an employer's plan are eligible for *forward averaging,* a favorable form of tax treatment we'll discuss later in this section. Funds in IRAs don't qualify for forward averaging. If you mix employer funds and your own funds into a single IRA account, you lose the ability to roll over the old employer's funds into some new employer's plan. This in turn means that, eventually, you also lose the option of using forward averaging on the old employer's funds.

Rolling Over IRAs

In the typical preretirement scenario, you'll probably be thinking about withdrawing IRA funds in order to move them from one investment to another with the expectation of improved investment performance. As with the other rollover distributions we've discussed, ideally you never want to receive the funds yourself. Instead, use what's called a *trustee-to-trustee transfer.* Under this arrangement, the folks administering IRAs for your new investment contact the trustee holding your current IRA and, based on your written authorization, instruct the old trustee to transfer your IRA funds to the new trustee directly. The funds never pass through your hands, and neither the 60-day rule for redepositing funds nor a 12-month rule limiting IRA withdrawals (discussed below) ever comes into play. Doing a trustee-to-trustee transfer sometimes takes a little longer because of the paperwork involved, but it usually is the better way to go. Of course, if for whatever reason you decide to withdraw the funds directly and redeposit them in a new account yourself, you have to abide by the 60-day and 12-month rules. Otherwise, the withdrawals are treated as distributions subject to income tax, and perhaps the 10 percent penalty tax on premature distributions.

Note that the 20 percent withholding rule discussed earlier applies only to distributions from employer plans, and not to IRA distributions. Because of this distinction, there's one other strategy involving IRA rollovers you should be aware of. It can provide you with a short-term, interest-free loan if you use it properly. If you withdraw funds from an IRA and redeposit them within 60 days, there are no tax consequences to the transaction. The purpose of this rule is to give you time to move your IRA assets from one investment to another. But, the law imposes no restrictions on what you can do with the money for the 60 days you have it. Thus, these funds can be a source of short-term loans. This can be especially helpful for small businesses with uneven cash flows (although anybody can use the technique).

EXAMPLE

It is January 15th, and your fourth quarter estimated taxes are due. You must pay $4,000, but you don't have the funds available. You know a $6,000 commission check will be issued to you on February 1. If you choose, you can withdraw the $4,000 you owe from your IRA and use it to pay your estimated taxes. When you receive your commission check in early February, simply deposit $4,000 of it into your IRA.

Note in this example that you didn't pay yourself interest on the money you borrowed. Not only is that not required, it's not allowed. The loan is, in effect, interest-free. Of course, since you're borrowing from yourself, you are also losing the benefit of tax-deferred interest compounding while your funds are withdrawn. That's the first of several reasons why you should always redeposit borrowed IRA funds as quickly as possible.

A few other critical warnings apply if you use this technique. First, be absolutely positive you will be able to replace the funds within 60 days. There is no flexibility here; 9:00 am on the morning of the sixty-first day is too late. You will owe income tax on the distribution, and the 10 percent penalty tax if you're under 59½. Also remember that the law says 60 days, not two months. If one of the two months in question has 31 days in it, you have one less calendar day in the next month to redeposit your funds.

EXAMPLE

You withdraw funds from an IRA on July 15th to finance a short-term loan. You have only until September 13th to redeposit the funds you've withdrawn into your old IRA (or to open a new one).

Second, you can only use this strategy once every 12 months, regardless of how many IRAs you own. Notice, too, that's once every 12 months and not once every calendar year. Plan ahead, because a second withdrawal will be taxable!

Lump-Sum Distributions and Forward Averaging

As we suggested earlier, many times you have to take retirement funds with you when you leave an employer. When your employer distributes to you all of your plan assets at one time, it's called a *lump-sum distribution.* We also suggested earlier that it's usually best to roll over lump-sum distributions, either into another employer's plan or into an IRA. However, if you're at or near retirement, there's a special rule (actually a set of rules) that can make it more advantageous for you to pay tax on the assets now.

Forward Averaging

The *lump-sum averaging* or *forward averaging* rules allow you to pay tax on a lump-sum pension distribution as if it were received over a number of years instead of all at once. You're allowed to "average" the payments over five years if you're 59½ when you receive the lump sum. Even better, if you were born before 1936, you're allowed to average the payments over 10 years.

The method for computing the tax works something like this: Divide the lump sum by 5 (or 10), apply the single filer tax table to the result (even if you're married), and then multiply the result by 5 (or 10) again. Even though you actually pay the tax all in one year, these rules allow you to take advantage of the lower bracket 5 (or 10) times. The actual rules for computing forward averaging are a bit more complicated than this, and you likely will need the help of a tax adviser. To give you some idea of the benefits of averaging, however, consider the following simplified examples.

EXAMPLE 1

You received a taxable $150,000 lump sum in 1996. You are single. The tax due on this sum would be at least $43,071. It could be more if you had other sources of income. However, the tax on $30,000, one-fifth of $150,000, would only be $5,280. Multiplied by five, the tax due if the $150,000 is forward-averaged over five years is only $26,400 ($5,280 × 5). This represents a savings of $16,671 ($43,071 − $26,400).

EXAMPLE 2

Use the same facts as above, except now assume that you qualify to average the lump sum over 10 years. The tax due on $15,000 (one-tenth of $150,000) is $2,250. Thus, the total tax due is $22,500 ($2,250 × 10). This represents a savings of $20,571 over the original tax of $43,071, and $3,900 over the five-year-averaged tax of $26,400.

There are, of course, restrictions applicable to forward averaging. The 10-year rule, in particular, can be tricky. It requires some special computations to be made regarding any pre-1974 capital gains included in your lump-sum distribution and is only available once in your lifetime. Both rules require that you be a plan participant for at least five years before receiving your lump sum in order to qualify for averaging. Again, this is an area where expert assistance quickly can pay for itself.

A final note: Lump-sum forward averaging is not available for retirement savings contained in IRAs or 457 plans. It is available on a somewhat limited basis for funds in a Keogh plan.

Lump Sum versus Annuity

If you're at or near retirement, you generally should either roll over a lump-sum distribution or elect to receive your pension in the form of an annuity, unless the income tax benefits of forward averaging dictate otherwise. However, there's an important nontax reason it may make sense to opt for the lump-sum/IRA rollover combination, rather than the annuity. When your employer's plan pays you in the form of an annuity, it must assume the risk that you (or some portion of its retirees) will live longer than the actuarial tables say you will. Accordingly, it must reduce slightly your payment in order to account for this actuarial risk. Therefore, you can increase your return by taking a lump-sum distribution and investing it, with the assistance of a trusted financial adviser. This way, you avoid paying the plan's actuarial and administrative costs. Note this may not be a good idea for you if you are poor at managing money or are very concerned about outliving your savings.

Minimum Distributions and Penalties

Again, as we've seen throughout this chapter, in general the longer you allow your retirement assets to enjoy the benefits of tax-deferred compounding, the better. However, eventually the tax law requires you to begin making withdrawals from your retirement accounts or face yet another penalty for failing to do so. Worse yet, the penalty is equal to a whopping 50 percent of the amount you were supposed to withdraw. It therefore is critically important to understand the minimum distribution rules. Since your employer usually has made you decide what to do with funds in its plan(s) either when you leave or at age 65, this issue most often arises in the context of IRAs. Again, keep in mind that, by 70½, your IRA accounts can include substantial sums from a variety of sources.

Required Distributions

By April 1st of the year after you reach age 70½, you must begin withdrawing from your IRA in order to avoid the 50 percent penalty. The rules require you to withdraw the money over your life expectancy, which you can find by consulting IRS tables. For instance, at age 70, according to recent IRS tables, a person's life expectancy is 16 years. The net effect of this rule is to require you to turn your IRAs into annuities shortly after you reach age 70½.

EXAMPLE 1

You were born on June 1, 1926. You have $80,000 in an IRA account. You turn 70½ on December 1, 1996, and by April 1, 1997, must begin to make withdrawals from your IRA. Since IRS tables say your life expectancy is 16 years, your first withdrawal must be at least $5,000 ($80,000/16). This amount must be included in your 1997 income.

Even if you've already started tapping into your IRAs before age 70½, it nevertheless is a good idea to compute your required minimum distribution to be certain you're taking out enough each year to avoid the 50 percent penalty tax.

Minimizing the Tax Impact of Required Distributions

There are a few things you can do to soften the sting of the minimum distribution rules, assuming your financial circumstances are such that you don't need to withdraw and pay tax on your retirement funds on the government's timetable. First, you can recompute the amount of your required minimum distribution each year. Since average life expectancies increase a little every year, this may lower slightly your minimum distribution for subsequent years.

Next, if you designate a beneficiary for your IRA account(s), you can use either your own life expectancy or the joint life expectancy of you and your beneficiary to compute your minimum distribution. Under the latter option, special rules apply if your life expectancy and your beneficiary's are not within 10 years of each other and your beneficiary is not your spouse. Using a younger beneficiary results in greater life expectancy rates and thus smaller minimum distributions. Again, this is a good area in which to seek the assistance of a tax adviser.

EXAMPLE 2

The same facts apply as in Example 1, but you have named your 67-year-old brother as your beneficiary. According to the IRS, your joint life expectancy is 22 years, so now you must withdraw only a minimum of $3,637 ($80,000/22) and include that amount in your 19X2 income. This lowers your taxable income by $1,363 ($5,000 – $3,637).

EXAMPLE 3

The same facts apply as in Example 2, but your brother is 55. Because he is more than 10 years younger than you and is not your spouse, you are required to use a so-called *minimum distribution divisor* of 26.2, found in IRS tables. Now you must withdraw a minimum of $3,054 ($80,000/26.2) in 19X2. By way of comparison, if your 55-year-old beneficiary were your spouse, you could have used the IRS joint life expectancy tables, and your minimum distribution would have been $2,676.

Finally, remember that the 50 percent penalty only applies to the difference between what you were supposed to withdraw and what you actually did withdraw.

EXAMPLE

Your required minimum distribution for 19X1 was $5,500. Because of a math error you made when computing your minimum distribution, you took out only $5,400. The 50 percent penalty tax must be paid only on the $100 difference between the amount you were supposed to withdraw and the amount you actually withdrew.

Note that, if you can make a strong case to the IRS that your error was inadvertent, you may be able to convince them to waive the penalty. Not surprisingly, of course, the IRS doesn't like to waive this penalty, and you need a very good reason for asking them to do so. It's not clear that the simple math error in the last example would be good enough for the IRS. Therefore, you always are better off avoiding the mistake on the front end, even if it means paying for expert assistance. After all, math errors aren't always for (comparatively) small sums like $100!

Other Retirement Penalty Taxes

So far in this section, we've seen examples of two penalty taxes that are intended to encourage you to treat your retirement accounts as funding vehicles for your golden years: the 10 percent penalty tax on premature distributions and the 50 percent penalty tax for failing to make minimum distributions. Now we're going to look at two penalty excise taxes that seem to be intended to prevent people from enjoying too much of a good thing. They apply only when you've "overstuffed" your retirement accounts. For this reason, some professionals refer to them as "success taxes." Fortunately, this is one of the few areas where the tax law takes a generous view of what constitutes "too much." Whereas the 10 percent penalty tax on premature distributions and the 50 percent penalty tax for failing to make minimum distributions can affect anyone, the penalty taxes we'll look at now will affect only a very few taxpayers. However, because they can be so severe when they do hit, everybody should understand how to avoid them.

Excess Distributions Penalty Tax

The first success penalty tax—a flat 15 percent excise tax—applies if you withdraw too much from your account at once. The good news is that the amounts involved are very high—the tax kicks in above $155,000 in regular withdrawals during any year and above $775,000 in lump-sum distributions. These are 1996 figures and are indexed for inflation in $5,000 increments.

> **EXAMPLE 1**
> You retire at age 65 with a $250,000 balance in your 401(k) plan. You decide to withdraw $180,000 from the plan in order to purchase a new residence in a retirement community. In addition to paying income tax on the amount you withdraw, you will owe a $3,750 penalty tax on the $25,000 in excess of the $155,000 annual limit on withdrawals ($25,000 × 15%).

> **EXAMPLE 2**
> You retire at age 65 with an $825,000 balance in your defined benefit retirement plan. Rather than receiving an annuity from your employer or rolling the funds over into an IRA, you elect a lump-sum distribution of the entire accrued benefit. In addition to the income tax on the $825,000, you will owe a $7,500 penalty tax on the $50,000 by which you've exceeded the $775,000 "limit" on lump-sum distributions ($50,000 × 15%).

Note that, in the second example, it may still be beneficial to take the lump-sum distribution and pay the penalty. This is because the benefits of forward averaging available for lump-sum distributions may outweigh the amount of the penalty tax you will be required to pay. This will depend on your overall financial and tax picture. So, if either of these taxes applies to you, spend some time with a tax adviser or financial planner working the math before deciding what to do with your pension.

Excess Accumulations Penalty Tax

The second success penalty tax—another excise tax with a 15 percent rate—applies to excess retirement plan accumulations in your estate when you die. The threshold for imposing the penalty on these accumulations varies with your life expectancy, and the tax is only levied on the excess of what an annuity would pay over that expectancy.

EXAMPLE

You are a 70-year-old male. According to the IRS, a hypothetical annuity currently is paying 10 percent. The IRS tables indicate your actuarial life expectancy is a little less than 6½ years. If you were to die today, your applicable threshold would be about $961,400. Any money in your retirement plans above that amount if you died today would be hit with the 15 percent penalty tax.

This example gives you a good idea of the "price range" involved. As a rough rule of thumb, multiply your life expectancy by $155,000 (the inflation-indexed figure from the excess distributions penalty tax; that is your applicable threshold. Remember, however, that it's only the excess in your accounts when you die that gets taxed. Since your life expectancy goes down as you get older, so will your threshold. The tax, of course, is paid by your estate, but it is in addition to any other estate taxes you may owe.

Keep in mind this tax is applied at the aggregate level. That is, it applies to all of your retirement plans combined—IRAs, Keoghs, 401(k)s, and company pension plans all must be considered when determining if you've accumulated too much.

Avoiding Success Taxes

To reiterate, because of the very high dollar amounts involved, the two excise penalty taxes discussed in this section will affect only a small minority of taxpayers. If you fall within this select group, however, the taxes can be more than a small annoyance. Fortunately, there are a couple of things you can do to avoid, or at least minimize, these taxes.

First, try not to make withdrawals in excess of the withdrawal limits to which the 15 percent excise tax applies. If there's anyway to avoid it, don't take a periodic distribution in excess of $155,000 in any one year. Similarly, keep track of your account balances and, assuming that it's consistent with your age and retirement goals, try not to let those balances rise above the $775,000 limit. If you sense you're getting close, you might want to stop making discretionary contributions.

EXAMPLE

You are 55 years old and employed by a large company that offers both a pension plan and a 401(k) plan. You contribute the maximum amount allowed by law to the latter. You also own a few IRA accounts from the days when contributions to them were fully tax deductible. The combined balances in all of your accounts are $715,000. You should consider ending or reducing the elective contributions to your 401(k) plan in order to stay below the $775,000 limit.

You very well may need to save beyond this $775,000 limit in order to meet your retirement goals. Accordingly, the strategy just described won't work for you. There's a second—and probably better—technique available if you think you are going to be affected by one or both of the penalty excise taxes. If you are over the $775,000 limit, consider making withdrawals as soon as you hit age 59½. This allows you to avoid the 10 percent penalty on premature distributions (discussed in the last section) and also helps you avoid the 15 percent penalty tax on excess accumulations.

EXAMPLE

You are 60 years old, with $60,000 in your IRA accounts and an accrued benefit of $675,000 in your employer's retirement plan. You conservatively estimate that your employer will accrue $15,000 per year more to your benefit in each of the next five years before you reach age 65. If you withdraw $12,000 from your IRA in each of the next five years, your total retirement accumulations will fall just short of the $750,000 threshold. This will enable you to elect a lump sum on your pension and forward average the income without incurring the 15 percent penalty tax, should you choose to do so. Remember, though, you will have to pay income tax (but not the 10 percent penalty tax on premature withdrawals) on the $12,000.

In this example, you were encouraged to take five smaller distributions from your IRA in each of the next five years instead of just liquidating the account in the fifth year. By spreading the withdrawals out over a period of time, you minimize the chances that the extra income will put you in a higher income tax bracket. In fact, you'll want to keep a careful eye on your tax bracket if you use this strategy. If you know your marginal bracket is going to go down in the near future (e.g., you're going to retire), you should wait until you're in the lower bracket to start using this technique. Figuring out exactly how much to withdraw and when will depend on your overall circumstances, and can be tricky, so you're well advised to get professional help in crunching your particular numbers.

Try to keep some perspective when planning for these two taxes. If you're relatively young and still in good health, it makes good sense for you to accumulate more than the proscribed amounts. It is likely that you will spend your retirement balances below the penalty tax thresholds.

Discretionary Withdrawals in Retirement

Now that we've gotten a sense of the landscape in which tax-favored retirement plans operate, it's time to look at the bigger picture. Those of us living in retirement, and perhaps living off our tax-favored retirement savings, need to know how much we *should* withdraw from our accounts. Amazingly, the answer to this question is frighteningly simple: As long as you operate within the rules we've discussed in this section, it's entirely up to you how much to withdraw from your retirement accounts and when. Of course, as we've seen, the applicable rules are significant. There are penalties if you take out too much, others if you take out not enough, penalties if you withdraw too soon, and penalties if you start too late. Nevertheless, within these constraints, making withdrawals to fund retirement needs can be dictated by nontax considerations: how much you've saved (both tax-favored and otherwise), what your retirement needs are, what your other resources are, what your life expectancy is, and so on.

Some retirees annuitize their retirement account balances and make periodic withdrawals (monthly or quarterly) over their life expectancies or over the joint life expectancy of themselves and their beneficiaries. Frequently, the institution holding your IRA will allow you to arrange for this option automatically. Note that, while there may be a small administrative fee for this service, it does not entail the same actuarial costs discussed under lump-sum distributions. It is not necessarily the same as converting your account into an annuity, so your payout normally is not reduced to account for actuarial costs. Of course, if you choose to convert your IRA to an annuity with a guaranteed payout, the institution's actuarial costs—the risk you'll outlive the principal—gets factored into the payout amount, as does the institution's administrative expenses. Accordingly, this may not be a good option.

More often, however, retirees withdraw funds from their accounts only on an as-needed (or as-required-by-the-tax-law) basis. Again, as long as you're tax smart about how you do it, it's up to your discretion what to take out and when. Is it finally time to take that 'round the world cruise? Go for it! After all, this is why you've been saving your whole life.

However, because outliving available resources is such a large concern for most retirees, you'll want to review your portfolio, your retirement goals, and your retirement needs before taking any large distributions. Get out your calculator, and, if necessary, get disinterested professional advice before making any large withdrawals. One good rule of thumb for retirement withdrawals: As much as possible, avoid withdrawing principal from your accounts. Ideally, you should try to live off the income your nest egg generates, at least until the very last years of retirement.

One additional tip for making discretionary withdrawals in retirement: If you've got both tax-favored retirement savings and other "post-tax" retirement savings, make your discretionary withdrawals from post-tax accounts first. That way, you continue to defer the income tax on the pretax savings. You also continue to enjoy the full advantages of tax-favored compounding of interest, dividends, and capital gains on your pretax balances. Of course, this strategy is only valid up to the point you have to worry about the various penalty taxes.

By way of summary, then, the short answer to the question, "How much should I withdraw from my retirement account?" is, "As little as you have to, consistent with the tax law and your financial needs." This section covered the tax law, and much of this book has been designed to help you cover your needs. If you've done your retirement planning properly, computed your retirement needs accurately, sought professional advice where necessary, periodically monitored your investments to ensure they were on track to meet your retirement goals, and made changes along the way as appropriate, you're well prepared to meet those needs.

A Quick Recap

We've covered a lot of ground in this section, so let's review quickly the broad rules that you should keep in mind when handling retirement withdrawals and distributions. You can go back and drill down for the details when and where you need them.

1. If you're not at or near retirement, lump-sum distributions from an employer's plan should be rolled over directly by your employer into either a conduit IRA or another employer's plan. IRAs should be rolled over directly from an old account to a new one via a trustee-to-trustee transfer.

2. If you're at or near retirement, you'll need to choose between a lump-sum and an annuitized distribution for assets in an employer's plan. If you take the lump sum, you'll want to arrange for your employer to roll over the distribution directly into an IRA, unless the income tax benefits of forward averaging dictate that you receive the assets yourself and pay tax on them at that point.

3. IRA distributions can be made on your schedule, as long as you start by age 70½ and meet the minimum distribution rules.

OUR ISSUES

Lump-Sum Distributions May Benefit Gay Couples

Usually, an employer's plan permits you to opt for an annuity that pays out over the joint lives of yourself and any other beneficiary you choose—often including a domestic partner. Sometimes, however, an employer's plan limits the joint annuity option to a legal spouse. If your employer's plan is restrictive in this way, and you are retiring and must decide how to receive your pension, the lump-sum/IRA rollover combination may make more sense for you and your partner. (Again, this assumes that the tax benefits of forward averaging don't dictate otherwise.) That way, you can provide for your joint financial security on a timetable that makes sense for you, using the strategies outlined in the "Discretionary Withdrawals in Retirement" section. Even if you subsequently decide to purchase an annuity yourselves covering your joint lives, you at least will have the peace of mind that comes from working with an institution that respects your preferences and accommodates your needs.

Minimizing Minimum Distributions—Our Way

Usually, people who have been saving for retirement need to draw on the funds in their IRAs in order to support themselves during retirement years. Again, these IRAs may contain substantial sums comprised both of their savings and of amounts rolled over from an employer's plan. For these people, the minimum distribution rules usually do not impose an undue burden. Others, however, are fortunate enough not to need the money when the tax law says they have to take it. For them, the minimum distribution requirements force them to recognize and pay tax on income before they really want to.

The ability to annuitize distributions over a beneficiary's life expectancy or your joint life expectancies provides an important opportunity to minimize the impact of the minimum distribution rules. It's significant to note that the tax law does not require you to be related to your beneficiary. This means the tax planning opportunity we've been discussing is equally available to lesbian and gay couples or to any alternative family in which one member designates another as beneficiary for his or her retirement accounts.

EXAMPLE
Go back and reread Examples 2 and 3 in the "Minimum Distributions and Penalties" section, substituting the word *partner* for the word *brother.*

RELATED TOPICS

Designating beneficiaries for your retirement accounts is an excellent way to direct the disposition of your assets without subjecting them to the jurisdiction of the probate court—an important goal for lesbians and gay men. The reasons for this are detailed in the "Wills and Will Substitutes" section on page 302.

Similarly, one of the fundamental rules of estate planning is that you should avoid naming your estate as a beneficiary on a retirement account, life insurance policy, and so on. This, too, can cause assets to pass through your probate estate unnecessarily. Again, the logic for avoiding this is explained in the "Wills and Will Substitutes" section on page 302.

In order to make sure your retirement planning is on track, it might be helpful to review the "Computing Retirement Needs and Savings" section on page 231 In order to make sure you're handling your retirement investments the best way possible, revisit the "Asset Allocation and Portfolio Structure" section on page 138.

If you choose to take a payout from an employer's pension in the form of an annuity, you usually are given several payment options. The option you choose can have very important consequences both for you and your partner if you're in a relationship. To see which option makes sense for you, review the discussion of payout options the "Annuities" section on page 49.

For the small number of taxpayers affected by the retirement excise penalty taxes, it can be difficult to balance saving for retirement with planning to avoid the taxes. It might be helpful to review the "Computing Retirement Needs and Savings" section on page 231 to get a broader perspective on establishing priorities in planning for both retirement savings and excise taxes.

6

CHAPTER

Estate Planning

ESTATE PLANNING BASICS

THE STRAIGHT FACTS

When a person dies (a *decedent*), a byzantine set of rules kicks in to govern the distribution of the assets he or she owned at death (an *estate*). How these rules affect a particular decedent's estate depends on a number of variables—the size (i.e., value) of the estate, whether and which estate planning documents were in place when he or she died, and the laws in the particular state or states having jurisdiction over the distribution of the decedent's estate. We'll spend this chapter fleshing out the details of these variables. The important point here is that, although the word estate sounds like it only applies to rich people, if you own any assets when you die, you will leave behind an estate. Whether the distribution of that estate is smooth or bumpy—as well as whether it is expensive or economical—largely depends on how well you understand the process and plan for it.

There are two major areas of the law with which virtually all decedents' estates must contend: the state laws governing the distribution of a decedent's property (probate laws), and the federal and state laws taxing the transfer of a decedent's property (estate and inheritance taxes). While there's often a good bit of overlap between these two areas of the law, it's important to understand that they play separate roles in the estate planning process. It's also important to remember that what is included in your estate for purposes of one area of the law may not be included for the other. For example, the estate subject to the jurisdiction of the local probate court often contains fewer assets than the estate subject to estate and inheritance taxes.

If this seems confusing, hopefully it will be clearer by the end of this section. Our goal is to become acquainted with the broad concepts relevant to estate planning. Then, throughout the rest of this chapter we'll drill down and explore the more important concepts in greater detail. By the end of this section, you should understand the basics of what goes into your estate, know the fundamentals of how property is distributed and of the probate process, have a broad understanding of the federal estate tax, and be familiar with the issues surrounding state taxation of a decedent's estate.

A word of caution before we proceed: Estate planning is *not* a field for do-it-yourselfers. Of all the topics we've covered in this book, this is the very worst one in which to try going it alone. Relying on the self-help books or software programs widely available at the local superstore to create estate planning documents is a recipe for disaster. Admittedly, the estate planning process is expensive, probably more expensive for average folks than it needs to be. However, the only thing more expensive than engaging professional help is *not* engaging professional help. The rules are so numerous and so complex, the mistakes are so irreversible and their price is so high, that no mass-produced book or software program can give the level of assurance specific to your needs that you deserve. For example, by the end of this chapter, you should be convinced that there's no such thing as a "simple" will and no way to cut corners in estate planning. So, let's be blunt: You're a fool if you try to do your estate planning yourself.

What's in Your Estate

When you die, your estate is made up of all the property you leave behind. To give you a sense of how broad this definition is, consider the following list of assets included in your estate:

- All the real estate you own.
- Houses, boats, and other vehicles.

- The entire contents of your house(s), including clothing, jewelry, furniture, rugs, china, crystal, silver, artwork, electronics, and so on.
- Bank accounts.
- Stocks, bonds, mutual funds, and other investments.
- The value of life insurance policies you own (if you are the person insured, then the full death benefit).
- Annuities.
- Retirement account and pension plan balances.
- Money owed to you at the time of your death, from unpaid interest and dividends to income tax refunds and legal claims arising from the cause of your death.
- Debts you owe that are forgiven when you die.
- Gifts you've given within three years of your death, but only if they were made with certain "strings" attached (for example, you retained some interest in the gift or some right to control what happened to the gift).
- The death benefit from any policies insuring your life that someone else owns if you used to own them and transferred them within three years of your death.
- If you own a small business:
  All assets of the business if it's a sole proprietorship.
  Your proportional share of the business if it's a partnership.
  Your shares of stock if it's a corporation or limited liability company.

With a definition this broad, then, estates aren't just a concern for the wealthy. Just about all of us will leave one when we die. Read on to find out what happens to your estate when you die. Then, throughout the rest of this chapter, we'll discuss ways to maximize the outcome when you plan your estate.

Distributions of Property and the Probate Process

When you die, the assets you leave behind legally pass to others in one of four ways:

1. Automatically ("by operation of law" in legalese) because you owned a particular asset jointly with another person and the title

to the property included a right of survivorship, as with a house or a bank account.

2. Through the designation of another person as a beneficiary in the documents governing the ownership of the asset, as with a beneficiary designation on a life insurance policy or a retirement account.

3. Through the provisions of a valid trust.

4. Through the probate laws of the state having jurisdiction over your property. If property doesn't pass as a result of survivorship, beneficiary designation, or trust, it has to pass through probate.

If you die with a valid will in place, your probate assets usually pass under the terms of the will, subject only to the supervision of the probate court. If you die without a valid will in place, your probate assets still pass subject to court supervision, but they also pass according to the provisions of a state law known as the *intestacy statute,* which determines to whom those assets go. Intestacy statutes vary by state, but there is a general pattern to them: First, the statute usually leaves everything to a spouse while providing for the needs of minor children. If there's no spouse, the assets go to children; if there's no children, then to parents; if there's no parent, then to grandchildren; and so on. The important thing to note is that, in any intestacy statute, it is your state legislature, and not you, deciding who gets what. There's no flexibility to provide for a best friend, a favorite niece, a destitute cousin, or a respected charity, unless by chance it all goes to them in the statutory pecking order—and many of these potential recipients never even make it into that pecking order. In an effort to create a uniform system that suits most people's needs, the intestacy laws produce a sort of one-size-fits-all will drafted by a committee! In practice, then, intestacy statutes create an inflexible, unappealable, and one-size-fits-none approach to probate. The bottom line: Don't die intestate—execute a will or other combination of estate planning documents to make sure your property goes where you want it to.

One other thing to note about probate: We said above that probate assets pass subject to the supervision of the court having jurisdiction over them. The court in the state where you are a resident has jurisdiction over all of your probate assets with one exception: real estate. Real estate is subject to the jurisdiction of the court where it is located. So, if you live in one state and have a vacation house in another, and if your vacation house is part of your probate estate when you die, the person administering your estate has to probate the vacation house in the courts of the other state. This is called *ancillary probate,* and it means an additional probate proceeding.

Assets in your estate subject to the jurisdiction of the probate court—that is, your probate estate—are regulated by a strict set of laws intended to ensure that they pass in an orderly and appropriate manner. Most often the probate process appears as little more than an unnecessary burden on a decedent's family, but for some it serves as a safeguard to prevent unscrupulous or emotionally distressed people from misappropriating property. This would be a good place to mention for the first of what will be many times that the emotional strain of losing a loved one causes even good people to behave strangely. One function of the probate process is to help minimize confusion, uncertainty, and the possibility of property falling into unintended hands.

Contrary to popular belief, there generally is no need to race to a lawyer's office when someone dies. The first order of business really should be for friends and loved ones to tend to their emotional and spiritual needs. This is not to suggest that the next of kin will not need to attend to certain affairs as they arise. Utility bills and property taxes for the decedent's residence must still be paid, along with a mortgage if there was one. Other recurring debts (e.g., car payments, credit card bills) also must continue to be paid timely. While the personal representative eventually will open a checking account in the estate's name in order to handle such expenses, bills should not be allowed to fall into arrears in the interim. Usually, either the will or state law authorizes the estate to reimburse next of kin for any advances of this sort made on the estate's behalf.

In order to begin the process of administering probate assets, the person named in a decedent's will as the *personal representative* for an estate (also known in some states either as the executor/executrix or administrator/administratrix) must file a probate petition with the local probate court. This generally requires the professional assistance of a lawyer. As soon as it is practical after death, but generally not more than 30 days afterwards, the personal representative will need to contact an attorney to begin the probate process. The attorney will assist the personal representative through the steps of the probate process. While these steps vary from state to state, there are a number of common features.

Generally, in order to distribute a decedent's assets, a personal representative must:

1. File a petition for probate with the appropriate court to "open" the estate and to be appointed as its personal representative.

2. Obtain a taxpayer identification number for the estate from the IRS.

3. Contact any potential creditors who may have claims against the estate.

4. Notify any person named in a will as a beneficiary that the estate is being probated, and, in most states, also notify anyone else who would have a right to a portion of a decedent's estate under the intestacy statute (called *interested parties* under most state laws).

5. Publish the required newspaper notices.

6. Open a checking account to pay the estate's ongoing expenses.

7. Prepare for the court an inventory of all the assets in the decedent's probate estate.

8. Collect all amounts owed the decedent at the time of his or her death, including any outstanding debts, life insurance proceeds, medical insurance claims, and legal claims that may be related to the cause of death.

9. Sell any assets as directed by the will and approved by the court.

10. File any federal or state income and estate/inheritance tax returns required of the estate.

11. Pay out of the estate's assets all federal and state taxes owed by the estate.

12. File with the court all papers necessary to gain approval for distribution of the estate's assets, generally including an accounting of all the money and other property collected and disbursed during the period of administration.

13. Pursuant to the court's order, pay all of the decedent's debts and the expenses of administering the estate (fees for the services of the attorney and/or the personal representative usually must be submitted to the court and approved separately).

14. Distribute the assets of the estate pursuant to the court's order (usually—but not always—in accordance with the terms of the decedent's will if there was one).

15. File a final petition with the court to "close out" the estate.

This entire process can take as little as six months, but generally it requires approximately one to two years to complete. While it is not as daunting an enterprise as it may first sound, there are no short cuts in estate administration. In most states, there are procedures for *informal probate* or *abbreviated probate* where the size of the estate is under a specified amount.

As you may have surmised, the assistance a lawyer provides in guiding an estate through the many steps of this process will not come cheap. The expense is the first of many reasons people seek ways to minimize the portion of their estates subject to the jurisdiction of the probate court. Other reasons people try to avoid probate include:

- Probate proceedings are a matter of public record—anybody can know your business.
- Probate can tie assets up for months or years.
- Probate gives your creditors easy access to your assets.
- There is a strong incentive to avoid having to go through the trouble and expense of ancillary probate (discussed above).
- Probate increases the possibility that a court might try to second-guess your wishes if those wishes are unclear or unusual.

As we saw above, there are three other ways a person can pass on property when they die—survivorship, beneficiary designation, or through a trust. Properly used, each of these techniques can offer a way to keep all or part of your assets outside of the probate process. In the next section we'll explore the pros and cons of each.

The Unified Estate and Gift Tax System

Although probate is a significant concern in the estate planning process, it usually applies to only a portion of your estate. Taxes—the other focus of the estate planning process—are more comprehensive: They usually apply to your entire estate, regardless of whether or not it passes through probate. Death taxes are imposed at both the federal and state levels. By far, the most significant of these death taxes is the federal estate and gift tax.

If you read the last four words carefully, you noticed that the federal tax impacts both your estate when you die and certain gifts you make while you're alive. Many years ago, Congress realized that people were getting around the estate tax by simply giving away all of their property shortly before they died. To prevent this, the tax laws over time were revised to create a combined system that now taxes both your estate when you die as well as some lifetime gifts. While these changes made good sense as a matter of tax policy, it made understanding the system even more complicated for taxpayers.As with the income tax, there's a formula used to compute the federal estate tax. The formula works like this:

> Gross Estate
> − Debts
> − Administration Expenses
> − Marital Deduction
> − Charitable Deduction
> Taxable Estate
> + Taxable Gifts after 1976
> Tax Base
> × Rates from Rate Table
> Tentative Tax
> − Unified Credit
> − Gift Tax Paid since 1976
> − State Death Tax Credit
> Net Estate Tax

As with the income tax formula, each of the components of the estate tax formula is a term of art under the tax law. While we'll devote considerable time later in this chapter to the various techniques you can use to minimize your federal estate tax, let's concentrate on the important components of this formula.

Gross Estate

Your *gross estate* includes all of the assets you own at the time of your death—houses, cars, investments, retirement accounts, annuities, life insurance, small businesses, and so on. The list provided earlier gives you a good sense of how comprehensive the definition can be. All of the items on the list are part of your estate if you own them (or the tax law deems you to own them) when you die. One of the most important ways for people with very large estates to minimize estate taxes, then, is to whittle down the size of their estates while they are still alive. Of course, this means giving up all control of the assets in question, which can be a scary proposition for some people. Giving away assets also means you have to watch out for potential gift tax issues. Careful planning is required if you want to shrink your gross estate properly. We'll get a broad sense of how to do this later in the chapter.

One particular asset included in the total value of many estates deserves special mention here: life insurance. If you own a life insurance policy, the value of that policy is included in your estate when you die. (Remember that there are three key players in any life insurance policy: the owner(s), the person(s) insured, and the beneficiary(ies). While we usually think of the owner and the person insured as one and the same, this isn't always the case. In fact, as we'll see, the estate tax rules discourage it.) If you are both the owner and the insured, this means the entire death benefit paid by the policy is included in your estate—a potentially sizable sum. Because of this, people who have estate tax liability exposure often will try to relinquish ownership of the policy; frequently, they establish a trust for this purpose. As we said earlier, generally, once you give an asset away it's no longer counted in your gross estate. Not so for life insurance. If you give away a policy you own insuring your life, either to another person or to a trust, the proceeds are included in your gross estate if you die in the first three years after the transfer. It's important to keep this in mind when doing your estate tax planning. If you know you're going to have estate tax problems, get life insurance out of your estate as soon as possible. Better yet, when buying life insurance, never title it in your name at all; have it purchased by a trust or another person. That way, the three-year rule won't apply.

You also should note that a few types of gifts are included in your gross estate if you make them within three years of your death. These gifts with "strings" include (1) gifts in which you retain some interest, such as the right to use property for the rest of your life; (2) gifts that don't take affect until you die; and (3) gifts that you retain the right to alter, amend, or revoke.

A common problem in determining the amount of a person's gross estate is assigning a value to the assets in it. Obviously, it's easy to value cash, but other assets, such as real estate, artwork, or a small business, can be much trickier. Your gross estate must be computed using the fair market value of the assets in it, but reasonable people can differ about the value of a unique item. From your estate's perspective, the lower the value, the better; it means less estate tax will have to be paid. The IRS audits a very high number of estate tax returns, and disagreement over the value of assets is a very common problem in these audits. There are even special penalties the IRS can assess if assets are too undervalued on the estate tax return. Therefore, it's very important that objective and realistic appraisals of the value of property are used when computing your gross estate.

Marital Deduction

In computing its estate tax, your estate is entitled to a *marital deduction* for whatever property you leave to your spouse when you die. The purpose of this provision is to ensure that no estate tax is levied on assets transferred between spouses. The marital deduction doesn't eliminate estate taxes; it only defers them. When the second spouse dies, all of the property remaining from both spouses gets included in the estate. The marital deduction creates some important estate tax planning opportunities that we'll touch on later.

Charitable Deduction

In computing its estate tax, your estate also is entitled to claim a *charitable deduction* for any charitable contributions you make upon your death, either through your will, trust, or beneficiary designation. The purpose of this provision is to ensure that charitable bequests pass free of any estate tax. The charitable deduction also provides significant estate tax planning opportunities, as we'll also see later.

Rate Table

Estate tax rates are *very* steep. Technically, they start at 18 percent and increase a few percentage points at a time until they reach a whooping maximum of 55 percent (or sometimes even 60 percent). However, because of the impact of the unified credit (discussed below), no one actually pays tax in the lower brackets, and people therefore generally talk about estate taxes ranging from 37 percent (on estates over $600,000) to 55 percent (on estates over $3 million).

Unified Credit

The *unified credit* is the primary way that the tax law attempts to protect small- to average-size estates from the bite of the federal estate tax. The credit is $192,800. This amount translates into an exemption equivalent of $600,000, meaning that the first $600,000 of your taxable estate usually is not subject to the federal estate tax. This $600,000 is one of the most important figures in estate tax planning, and you will see it referred to frequently.

Hopefully, your eyes perked up when you saw the word "usually" in the last paragraph. Sometimes your exemption can be less than $600,000. You may recall earlier we said that the estate and gift tax systems were combined many years ago. That's why the credit we're discussing here is called a *unified* credit. It is a credit used for purposes of both the estate tax and the gift tax. We'll talk about gift taxes in detail later, but for now you need to know the general rule regarding gifts. You can give $10,000 per recipient per year without any gift tax consequences. Any amount over $10,000 is treated as a taxable gift. However, before you really start paying taxes on the gifts you give, you first "use up" your $600,000 exemption. While the actual rules are more complex, the following simplified example gives a sense of how all this works:

EXAMPLE
You die at age 70. Three years before your death you gave your favorite niece a $50,000 cash gift. That gift was $40,000 above the amount you are allowed to give to any one person in a single year without gift tax consequences. When computing your estate taxes, your $600,000 exemption is reduced by the $40,000 to $560,000.

As we'll see later, the $10,000 gift tax annual exclusion presents many planning opportunities. It also can create problems if we forget it exists. Remember the $10,000 limit when making gifts of cash or other property.

There is some good news in all of this: The $192,800 unified credit, combined with proper estate tax planning, insulates the vast majority of Americans from federal estate tax liability.

Net Estate Tax

Your estate must pay its *net estate tax* to the IRS within nine months of your death. Your estate can request a six-month extension for filing its return, but not for paying the tax. Interest and penalties accrue if the tax is not paid on time. Special rules permit people to pay over as much as 14 years the portion of the total federal estate tax bill that's attributable to the value of a small business or family farm.

If your estate is very large, nine months is not much time in which to come up with money to pay estate taxes. And remember, while only a few estates have federal estate tax bills, those that do usually owe substantial sums of money. Sometimes an estate has trouble liquidating enough assets to pay the liability in this short time frame. This is often the case when the bulk of an estate is made up of one hard-to-sell asset, like a small business, large house, or farm. This can create serious hardships for a decedent's surviving family. Life insurance is a common way to solve this liquidity problem. Your estate planning should include a projection of your estate's liquidity needs for paying taxes (and other expenses), and whether there is likely to be enough cash on hand when you die to meet those needs.

The legal burden for paying estate taxes falls on the decedent's estate and usually is satisfied from the assets in the estate. However, if for whatever reason the estate has not paid the taxes due, there are provisions in the law that allow the IRS to collect what's owed from the beneficiaries who received property from the estate.

State Taxation of a Decedent's Estate

It's not just Uncle Sam who wants a piece of the action when you die. Virtually every state imposes some form of transfer tax on your estate. While the generalities here are a little harder to come by, these taxes usually take one of two broad forms: an estate tax that "piggybacks" on the federal tax, or an inheritance tax levied on the value of your total estate. A handful of states impose both types of death taxes. As of this writing, the following states impose inheritance taxes (a few call them estate taxes, but they've set them up like inheritance taxes): Connecticut, Delaware, Indiana, Iowa, Kansas, Kentucky, Louisiana, Maryland, Massachusetts (until 1997), Mississippi, Montana, New Hampshire, Nebraska, New Jersey, New York, North Carolina, Ohio, Oklahoma, South Dakota, Pennsylvania, and Tennessee.

Unlike the federal estate tax (and the state piggyback estate tax), state inheritance taxes technically are imposed on the person receiving the property, although you can specify in your will that your estate will pay the taxes, and people often do. Inheritance tax rates generally are much lower than estate tax rates, but, since the tax is levied on your entire estate, the amount subject to the tax generally is much higher. Inheritance tax schemes often impose different rates of tax depending on the relationship between the person who dies and the person who receives the property. For example, a state may impose a 3 percent tax on inheritances from a parent or grandparent (sometimes called a *lineal transfer*), but 10 percent taxes on inheritances from anyone else (sometimes called a *col-*

lateral transfer). Inheritance tax rates aren't always flat. Sometimes they're graduated with the size of the estate. In addition, a few states tax real estate differently from other property. Also, while the federal tax generally only applies to estates worth over $600,000, state inheritance taxes usually aren't so generous. If there is any exemption at all, it's generally a modest amount, often somewhere around $20,000 to $50,000. Again, these figures vary by state and sometimes also by the relationship of the recipient to the decedent. In addition, modest exemptions often are provided for a surviving spouse or minor children. In short, the general principle is fairly clear: While estate taxes affect only the very wealthy, inheritance taxes hit most people who live in the states that impose them.

While we'll spend a lot of time talking about planning around federal estate taxes throughout this chapter, we'll pretty much end our discussion of state transfer taxes here. There are two reasons for this. First, the laws are different in each state, so it's hard to give specific advice. More importantly, there are fewer opportunities for state transfer tax planning. Inheritance taxes generally are so broad that they're hard to plan around, and state estate taxes usually are covered by your federal planning. Accordingly, when it comes to estate tax planning, the focus usually is on federal taxes. Nevertheless, you should ask your estate planner if there's anything you can do to lower your state transfer tax bite. If nothing else, this will be a good way to gauge whether he or she is on the ball!

OUR ISSUES

The Big Picture

Of all the aspects of financial planning, nowhere are our issues more profound than in the area of estate planning. Whether single or part of a couple, gay people face an enormous set of challenges in planning their affairs around an insensitive to downright homophobic probate system and a generally unfriendly tax regime. While our community has made tremendous progress in the past several decades in at least persuading most probate courts to respect our preferences when we articulate them clearly and properly (there was a time not very long ago when any bequest from one gay partner to another risked invalidation by a probate court as the product of "undue influence"), we still have to work twice as hard as straight people do to get the same results.

Even so, the stories are legion of people who didn't do their leg-work, having surviving lovers thrown out of houses, or sizable estates donated by misguided parents to the First Bible Church of Intolerance, or oral assurances that "we'll make sure your friend Steve gets the baby grand" abjectly ignored. We've said it before, and we'll say it again: Even good people act strangely when confronted with death; people seldom behave predictably, and they often do the exact opposite of what they said they would do. You cannot take anything for granted. If you take nothing else away from this book, then please let it be this: Regardless of your cir-cumstances, get your estate plan in order. It doesn't matter whether or not you're in a relationship or how modest your means. Every lesbian and gay man should have a will and/or will substitutes. You are precious, your loves and friendships are precious, your assets are precious, and your wishes are precious. They all deserve to be respected, and you cannot afford to leave any of them to chance.

Choosing a Sensitive Estate Planner

Because this area of financial planning presents so many unique issues for lesbians and gay men, it is essential that you select an estate planner who is sensitive to our needs and well versed in our issues. He or she need not be gay; competence should always be your main criterion. Nevertheless, being gay certainly gives superior insight as to what we're up against. Referrals are always an excellent starting point in finding an estate plan-ner suited to your needs. If you don't have the option of engaging estate planning services within the community, be sure to probe the person you're considering very carefully to be certain he or she understands our issues. Be as up-front, even "in-your-face," as possible. You're paying this person good money, and you do yourself a grave disservice if you pussyfoot around such a central issue.

State Inheritance Taxes

Lesbians and gay men face yet another challenge under state inheritance tax regimes: Bequests made to friends and lovers are likely to be treated as col-lateral bequests, as opposed to lineal bequests. This usually means that the rate of taxation imposed on them is higher, in some states markedly so.

This could create a burden of potentially significant proportions for some gay couples. Whereas in most states transfers between spouses either are fully or partially exempt from tax or taxed at the lower lineal rate, transfers to a domestic partner are taxed at the higher collateral rate.

In some states, this means inheritance taxes of 10 percent or 15 percent imposed on assets transferred to the survivor when the first partner dies. Rates this high may be hard to pay from available assets, especially if the bulk of an estate is made up of illiquid assets (e.g., a house).

Keep in mind, too, that unlike the federal estate tax, most state inheritance taxes don't offer whopping $600,000 exemptions, especially not for collateral bequests. It's quite likely that the tax is going to be imposed on the first dollar transferred, not the 600,001st. In short, depending on your state's tax structure, your surviving partner may receive only 85 percent to 90 percent of what you leave him or her—and that's without considering any federal estate tax!

Since the rules are different in every state, planning generalizations are difficult to make. However, you should discuss this issue with your estate planner to be sure you understand what you're up against. It's not likely, but you may be able to plan around the tax in your state. If not, you (or you and your partner) need to plan ahead for the extra tax. You'll want to make sure your estate is sufficiently liquid (i.e., has enough cash) to pay state transfer taxes. Depending on your circumstances, you might need to do a little extra saving, especially if you're in a relationship; this issue tends to hit surviving partners hardest. Another possible approach, as we'll discuss later in the "Estate Tax Planning Techniques" section, is using life insurance to help pay transfer tax bills. If the people you want to leave your assets to are facing steep state inheritance tax collateral rates, you might consider using insurance to help pay state taxes, as well as federal.

Also remember that if you own real property in another state, that property will be taxed by that state. If you're fortunate enough to be a multistate land baron, you need to check this issue out every place you own property.

RELATED TOPICS

Because of the unique needs of our community in relation to an often hostile world, every gay person needs to do some basic estate planning, regardless of the size of his or her estate. This should include a will and/or one or more will substitutes, which are explained in the "Wills and Will Substitutes" section on page 302.

If you think you (or you and your significant other if you're in a relationship) may have gross estates large enough to present potential estate tax problems, there are specific techniques you can employ to minimize the estate tax bite. These strategies, including ways to take advantage of the annual gift tax exclusion, the marital deduction, and the charitable deduction, are described in the "Estate Tax Planning Techniques" section on page 328.

In addition to the basic set of estate planning documents most people need, lesbians and gays have a unique set of needs for several related documents: powers of attorney, living wills, directives regarding the disposition of one's remains, and/or domestic partnership agreements. You probably need to have some or all of these collateral documents in your planning arsenal, and it's often a good idea to see to them while you're doing your estate planning. The ins and outs of these various documents are explained in the chapter on Other Planning Issues beginning on page 347.

To understand how insurance can help you to in essence "prepay" a transfer tax bill, sometimes for a fraction of the total cost, see the "Using Life Insurance to Pay Estate Taxes" section on page 335.

WILLS AND WILL SUBSTITUTES

THE STRAIGHT FACTS

Will Basics

A *will* is a document that provides for the legal transfer of your assets after you die, names a person to settle your estate, and names a guardian for your minor children. Wills are fundamental estate planning documents, and it is highly unlikely that you will emerge from the planning process without one. Let's take some time, then, to review some of the basic features of a good will. Will requirements vary by state, but the rules here apply broadly.

Final Arrangements

In most states, there's a law that sets limits on how much your estate can pay for your final arrangements. Therefore, your will must authorize your estate to pay all such expenses without regard to this limitation, or it can only disburse up to the amount set by law. Failure to authorize full payment of final expenses may have the effect of lowering the amount of the inheritance of any next of kin who pays such expenses on your behalf (assuming they're inheriting anything).

Payment of Debts

Your will should authorize your estate to pay all of your debts, although it probably would have to do that anyway. You should give some thought as to whether you want this to include any mortgages or liens against property you own. In other words, do you want the house to pass clear of the mortgage, or do you want Junior to pay it off himself? You can do it either way, but you have to specify which you prefer. Otherwise, the state law (whatever it is) will decide for you.

Shipping Expenses

If you leave personal property to someone, that person usually is responsible for paying for the costs of transporting the property from wherever it's located to wherever they want it. While this may not seem like a very big deal, it can be if the property is, say, a baby grand piano. You should decide whether you want your estate to pay the shipping costs or not, and draft language into your will if you do. Also note that this same logic applies to any storage and insurance expenses for personal property.

Bequests and Beneficiaries

Provisions regarding the assets you leave and the people you leave them to are the meat of most wills. You can leave the assets in your probate estate largely to whomever you want and in whatever amount you want, so you need to have a good idea of who gets what early in the planning process. Here are a few pointers as you consider these weighty matters.

1. When you name a particular beneficiary, you have to decide what you want to happen to the property you're bequeathing to her if she dies first. You may want it to go to someone else, but it's fairly typical for people to want that property to pass on to the named beneficiary's next of kin, particularly if the named beneficiary was a family member. However, when there's more than one family member involved, there's more than one way to provide for the next generation. You'll need to understand two important terms if you want bequests to pass on to a predeceasing beneficiary's next of kin: *per stirpes* and *per capita.* If you make a bequest per stirpes and the beneficiary dies before you do, that beneficiary's heirs share equally in her share. If you make a bequest per capita, all surviving beneficiaries share equally in the bequest.

> **EXAMPLE 1**
> You have two daughters, each of whom has two sons. You own a beach house you wish to leave to them. If you leave the beach house per stirpes, and both of your daughters are living when you die, each gets half. However, if one daughter dies, her two sons would share in her half of the house. In other words, your surviving daughter would receive one-half of the house, and your deceased daughter's surviving sons would each receive one-quarter of the house.

EXAMPLE 2

The same facts apply as above, but you leave the house per capita. Everybody who survives you gets an equal share in the house. If your daughters were both alive when you died, each person would receive one-sixth of the house (2 daughters + 4 grandsons = 6 shares). If one of your daughters dies before you, each person would receive one-fifth of the house (1 daughter + 4 grandsons = 5 shares).

As these two examples make clear, there is a large difference between the two ways of bequeathing property down through a family tree. You'll want to think carefully about whether you want an asset to pass to a beneficiary only if he or she survives you, whether you want them to receive it per stirpes, or whether you want them to receive it per capita.

2. A *specific bequest* leaves a specified piece of property to a particular person (e.g., "Great Uncle Beauregard's Civil War sword to Scarlett"). It's the best way to treat items of unique or sentimental value. It's generally a good idea to make real estate a separate specific bequest if it's to pass under your will.

3. A *residuary bequest* is a way to dispose of all the property in your will that you haven't specifically bequeathed elsewhere. Among other things, the residuary is a catchall intended to make sure that none of your assets gets missed. If an asset "falls through" your will, it passes under the intestacy statute. A residuary clause prevents this from happening. If you're concerned that a residuary beneficiary might predecease you, residuary bequests to one or more charities sometimes can be a good way to prevent partial intestacy—especially if you really want to be sure the people who would receive property under the intestacy statute don't get anything.

4. If there are not enough assets in your probate estate to satisfy the bequests made in your will, there can be problems. This sometimes happens when you make a specific bequest of a flat dollar amount, and that amount is more than is available when you die. Usually, the residuary bequests get trimmed back first and the specific bequests generally are given priority as much as possible, but the probate law in your state has a sort of reverse pecking order for abating the bequests you make. In order to satisfy the specific bequests, other people you really hoped to benefit may get cut out. To avoid this, consider leaving percentages instead of dollar amounts.

EXAMPLE

Your estate currently is worth $100,000, and you want to leave $10,000 to Cousin Anne. Instead of drafting a specified dollar amount into your will, consider leaving Cousin Anne 10 percent of your estate. If it turns out your estate is worth more than $100,000, and you really want Cousin Anne to get no more than the $10,000 you initially had in mind, limit the bequest to *the lesser* of 10 percent or $10,000.

Tax Clause

If you want your estate to pay any state inheritance taxes on the assets you leave behind, you need to say so. Without your authorization, these taxes usually need to be paid by the people receiving the property. You'll probably want to mention any other taxes your estate will owe, as well. If you've left someone cash, paying the inheritance taxes on that cash may not seem like a very big deal, but, how does one get money for taxes out of a baby grand? Often, deciding how to pay taxes is an integral part of the overall estate planning process, so it's very likely that you and your planner will give considerable attention to this matter. One other thing you need to decide: Where does the cash to pay the taxes come from? From the specific bequests? From the residuary estate? From a trust? If it's coming out of the probate estate, you need to specify where.

Personal Representatives and Their Powers

Your will must name someone to serve as the personal representative of your estate. This nomination is subject to the acceptance of the probate court. Assuming that you choose intelligently, this almost always is a formality. The many considerations that go into choosing a personal representative, as well as the many duties he or she must undertake, are outlined later in this chapter. There are restrictions on who may serve as a personal representative, and these restrictions also are discussed in that section. You should note here, however, that the probate statutes in most states place severe limits on the things a personal representative is empowered to do with the assets in his or her charge. It therefore is quite likely that your estate planner will recommend that you add a list of additional powers to your will to enable your personal representative to discharge his or her duties more effectively. Although extensive grants of power are quite common, review carefully the list your estate planner recommends, and take the powers listed seriously—they may be more than just legal "boilerplate."

Guardianship of Minors

Your will also is the place to name the person or people you want to serve as guardians of your minor children. Note again, however, that your choice may be subject to court approval.

Bequests to Minors

If you make a bequest to a minor, you will either need to draft a trust with-in your will to hold that property, or nominate a custodian to hold that property on their behalf. Minors cannot own property on their own. The ins and outs of gifting to minors are discussed later in this chapter.

Simultaneous Deaths

If someone dies at the same time you do, does a bequest you've made to him still count? The answer to this question could be very important to you, to your beneficiaries (as well as the other person's), and maybe even to the tax man. Accordingly, most wills are drafted with a provision spec-ifying that anybody who does not survive you by 30 days will be deemed to predecease you for purposes of the bequests made in your will. This way, your property passes to the alternate beneficiaries you name, rather than to the beneficiaries named by a person who more or less dies at the same time you do.

Things You Can't Do in A Will

There are a surprisingly small number of things the probate law will not permit you to do in your will. For example, there are a very few people you simply cannot disinherit through a will. All states have laws to pre-vent you from disinheriting a spouse, and some states also make it diffi-cult to disinherit children; usually you cannot do so if they're minors. Also, you can't ask your beneficiaries to do something that's illegal or against "public policy" in order to receive their bequest (for example, get married or join a certain club). In some states, it's either difficult or not possible to persuade a court to enforce an *in terrorem* clause in your will (i.e, a clause that says challengers to a will get nothing). In other states it's not a problem to do so. If any of these issues concern you, ask your estate planner how the rules work in your state.

    Within these constraints, you pretty much can do whatever you want in your will—including disinheriting anyone you want. If you want to disinherit a close family member, however, you're probably better off mentioning their name and your decision not to provide for them. Don't be mean-spirited or vindictive, but don't equivocate either. The disinher-ited person is a prime candidate to ask the probate judge to second-guess your intentions, and you don't want to give the judge any reason to won-der what was going through your mind when you made your decision.

Execution Formalities

The formalities for validly executing a will vary by state, but it is critical that you comply with the rules in your state. Failure to do so could result in having your will invalidated. In virtually all circumstances, laws require witnesses (sometimes two, sometimes three) for a will to be valid. A few states permit *holographic wills* (i.e., wills written in longhand by the person making them). Others forbid them completely or severely restrict them. Even if you believe a holographic will is valid in your state, try to avoid relying on one if at all possible—especially if there's a chance of a will contest. Be sure your planner understands the execution requirements in your state and any unique requirements that may apply in any other state in which you own real property.

In a fair number of states, you can execute what's known as a self-proving will. In addition to the normal execution formalities, this feature requires your witnesses to sign a notarized affidavit attached to the will. The affidavit basically is the same one they'd be asked to sign when your will is admitted to probate, expediting that process by seeing to it in advance. If the option is available in your state, it's smart to take advantage of it.

Codicils

If you want to change a will after you've executed it, one economical way to do so is through a *codicil*. A codicil contains specific instructions about the changes you want to make to your original will—sort of line-by-line instructions about how to amend the original document. You must follow all of the same execution formalities for a codicil that you need for a will. Moreover, if the changes you want to make to your will are extensive, you may be better off simply drafting a new one. After a certain point, the amending instructions contained in a codicil can become confusing.

Protecting Your Will

Once your will is executed, you need to keep it in a safe place. A safe deposit box, or even your estate planner's safe, are good choices for this. Be sure your personal representative knows where the original will is stored, and that he or she will have quick and certain access to it when you die. If you are concerned about an unscrupulous family member doing something untoward with your will after you die, you definitely should go the estate-planner's-safe route. Better yet, in some states you are allowed to record a copy of your will with the local court. If this option is available to you, it's a wonderful way to make sure everybody remains on the up-and-up.

Will Challenges

Generally, if someone wants to challenge your will, they must prove a defect in the execution, that you were not of sound mind when you made it, that you were under duress or undue influence, or that it was a product of fraud. The burden of proof is on the person challenging the will, and will challenges are expensive and hard to win, so they tend to be rare. Nevertheless, since your estate's already in court when it enters the probate process, the mere threat of a will challenge sometimes can be sufficient to prompt the beneficiaries to agree to alternate arrangements. If this is a concern for you, be sure to alert your estate planner to the possibility. Also give extra consideration to the various will substitutes we'll discuss below.

What If You Change States?

Generally, if the will you executed was valid in the state you executed it, it should be valid if you move to another state. There are sometimes exceptions to this. For example, if you move to a state that does not recognize holographic wills, even if your holographic will was valid in your old state, there's a chance you may have a problem in the new one. You are well advised to consult an attorney in your new state for a quick review of your will to make sure it's still OK. Be certain to find a professional who's more interested in giving good advice than in talking you into new documents you don't really need.

Beneficiary Designations

When you purchase a life insurance policy or place assets into a retirement account, you are required to name a beneficiary or beneficiaries to receive the proceeds from the policy or account when you die. You generally can name more than one person as a beneficiary (e.g., 50 percent to A and 50 percent to B, 60 percent to A and 40 percent to B, or whatever). You also usually are allowed to name a contingent beneficiary or beneficiaries, in case your primary beneficiaries die before you do. If you fail to name a beneficiary where one is asked for, or if all your beneficiaries die before you do, the proceeds are paid to your estate.

There's not a lot of sophisticated planning surrounding beneficiary designations; they're a clean, simple way to keep assets out of probate. The most important tip to keep in mind is that you should never name your estate as a beneficiary. Besides needlessly exposing assets to the time, expense, and delay of probate, naming an estate as your beneficiary has some potentially nasty tax consequences that can be easily avoided. It also exposes those assets to any claims your creditors may have against your estate. Avoid this trap by keeping your beneficiary designations up-to-date and out of your estate!

One final thought regarding beneficiary designations: You can always designate a charity as a beneficiary to an insurance policy or retirement account. If charitable giving is part of your estate planning anyway, this may be a clean way to go about it. This option is far too underutilized, so be sure it's considered when you do your planning.

Joint Ownership of Property

There are four different ways to own property.

1. As a sole owner.
2. As a *tenant in common* with one or more other people.
3. As a *joint tenant with a right of survivorship* with one (usually) or more (rarely) other people.
4. As a *tenant by the entirety* with your spouse.

Two of these ownership methods are self-explanatory. Sole ownership means what it says, and when you die this property gets distributed under your will or trust. Tenants by the entirety is available only to married couples, and when one spouse dies the other spouse automatically owns the entire property.

Let's focus for a moment on the other two forms of property ownership: joint tenancy with right of survivorship and tenancy in common. The main difference between these two methods is the *right of survivorship.* When a tenant in common dies, her interest in the property is distributed under her will or trust. The person or people to whom she leaves this property become new tenants in common with the original surviving tenant(s). Tenants in common are sort of "co-sole owners" then. In contrast, under a joint tenancy with right of survivorship, when one owner dies, the surviving owner automatically owns the entire property by operation of law. No court proceeding or order is necessary to transfer title. In fact, even if a joint tenant willed the property to another person, such an action would probably be of no consequence, and the surviving joint tenant still would own the entire property. The survivorship provision in the deed takes precedence over the bequest in the will. Usually, a certified copy of the deceased co-tenant's death certificate is sufficient to get the title changed over to the survivor's individual name. In this respect, joint tenants with a right of survivorship functions sort of like a tenancy by the entirety.

Joint tenancy with a right of survivorship can be an effective way to keep assets out of probate. Since the property passes by operation of law, it's never subject to probate court jurisdiction or even administration under a trust. It's usually a quick and painless way to pass on property, and for this reason it sometimes is referred to as "the poor man's will."

Although people usually first think of their house as a candidate for joint tenancy with right of survivorship, virtually any asset that requires titling is eligible for this technique. Cars, boats, bank accounts, stocks, bonds, or mutual funds all are fair game for the *JTWROS* designation.

There are a few minor risks associated with the JTWROS option. First, some state courts and/or legislatures have a history of being reluctant to believe that two unrelated people could really mean to create survivorship rights in each other for property they jointly own. Consequently, in a few states the language in the title has to be very specific. While many states accept just the designation "joint tenants" (versus "tenants in common") to establish the survivorship right, some require the complete legal description "joint tenants with right of survivorship" to appear in the title in order for the survivorship aspect to be effective. Worse yet, a handful require the cumbersome "joint tenants with right of survivorship and not as tenants in common" in order to adequately create the survivorship right. Be certain you know the requirements in your state, and *insist* that whoever is titling your documents follow them to the letter. Otherwise, you run the very real risk that your wishes will not be respected.

Also, it is possible under the laws of most states for joint tenants to convert their ownership to tenants in common by acting in a way that is inconsistent with joint tenancy (i.e, without ever changing the designation on the title, but just by acting like tenants in common). It is extremely rare, but it is theoretically possible for a disgruntled family member to try to persuade a court that a deceased joint tenant converted his interest to tenancy in common, thereby destroying the co-owner's survivorship rights. It is even rarer for these claims to succeed, but they can be a headache when they do arise. If you think this may be an issue for you, ask your estate planner what you need to do to avoid it in your state.

One good way to get around both these problems is by putting a provision in your will that (1) confirms your intention that joint property pass to your co-owner and (2) bequeaths your interest in that property to that co-owner if for whatever reason the right of survivorship is no longer recognized. This should short-circuit potential troublemakers.

There's one other reason joint ownership sometimes won't work: estate tax planning. If assets need to be retitled as part of a plan to minimize estate taxes, or passed from a decedent through a trust to another person, it's very likely that the survivorship right will be inconsistent with the estate plan. Similarly, as we'll see in the section on "Estate Planning Techniques," sometime your estate plan will require you and your partner to "equalize" the values of your respective estates. Depending on what else you own, you may need to title a particular asset unequally to do so. In these circumstances, property will need to be owned either individually or as tenants in common. Your estate planner will let you know if this is an issue for you.

A final thought on joint ownership: Not all assets can or should be jointly titled, and it's not likely that joint ownership can solve all of even the proverbial "poor man's" estate planning needs in the 1990s. For example, you may recall from our discussion of automobile insurance that, for liability reasons, it was never a good strategy to jointly title ownership of an automobile. While joint ownership has a place in your estate planning, it can never be a complete substitute for other estate planning documents.

Trusts

Trust Basics

Trusts have a long and distinguished history in assisting people in transferring and managing their property. Their flexibility and largely self-directed nature makes them an important tool in the financial and estate planning arsenal. Before we learn the various uses to which planners put these wonderful documents, however, we need to become familiar with some of the terminology surrounding trusts.

First, you should know that there are three main players in any trust. The *settlor* (also referred to as the *grantor* or the *donor*—the three terms usually can be used interchangeably) is the person who places assets into the trust. The *trustee* is the person or institution that agrees to hold the assets and administer them in accordance with the terms of the trust. The *beneficiary* (or beneficiaries) is the person (or persons) entitled to receive some benefit from the trust—either income generated by the assets the trust holds, or distributions of those assets under conditions specified in the trust document, or both. These beneficiaries, called an income beneficiary and a residuary beneficiary, respectively, need not be the same person. Indeed, as we'll see, oftentimes there are very good reasons for a settlor to give one person an interest in a trust's income and another person an interest in the trust's assets.

EXAMPLE

In order to avoid having his assets included in his wife's estate when she dies, a husband may place those assets in a trust (called a Q-TIP trust) that provides her with income for her life and their children with the assets when she dies.

The assets in a trust sometimes are referred to as the *corpus* or the *res,* but we'll just call them the trust assets.

Now that you've met the main characters, let's look at some of the important characteristics used to identify every trust's story line: when the trust is created, and whether or not the trust is permanent. Combining these characteristics in different ways produces trusts suited for different uses and also can create very different tax results.

Trusts can become operative at one of two points in time. *Living trusts* (also known as *inter vivos trusts*) are established while you are alive. Assets are transferred into the trust at the time it is created, and the trust operates during your lifetime. *Testamentary trusts* are created in your will (as in "last will and *testament*"), are funded by bequests made in your will, only operate after your death, and are administered by a trustee you name in your will. Note that this trustee need not be the same person as the personal representative named in your will to administer your estate. *Pour-over* trusts are created while you're alive but funded when you die. They often are used to receive and distribute life insurance proceeds, retirement benefits, or residuary bequests from your will.

The other important characteristic for any trust is whether or not it is permanent. In legalese, trusts are said to be either *revocable* or *irrevocable.* As the name suggests, in a revocable trust the settlor reserves the right to amend or revoke the trust, change the conditions under which the assets are held, or reclaim the assets for his or her own use. Because assets in a revocable trust are distributed in accordance with the terms of the trust, they are not subject to the jurisdiction of the probate court when you die (as we'll see below). This makes revocable trusts an important estate planning tool for people whose goal is to avoid probate. In an irrevocable trust, the settlor relinquishes all rights to the assets in the trust. He or she cannot later have a change of heart and try to alter the terms of the trust or reclaim some or all of the assets for his or her own use. Because the transfer is irrevocable, assets placed into these trusts not only avoid the jurisdiction of the probate court, but they usually are removed from your gross estate. This makes irrevocable trusts valuable tools for estate tax planning.

One other thing you should be aware of with regard to trusts is that they may be separate taxpaying entities. The general rule of thumb here is that revocable trusts are not separate taxpaying entities; the income they earn is taxed to the settlor of the trust. Irrevocable trusts usually are separate taxpaying entities, and the trustee must file an income tax return for the trust and pay any tax due out of the trust's assets. There are some important exceptions to this general rule (i.e., sometimes revocable trusts are separate taxpaying entities), so be sure to ask your estate planner who pays the taxes on your trust's income. Another aspect of trusts and income taxes is that, when Congress tinkered with the tax law in 1993, it severely compressed the bracket structure used to compute trusts' taxes. Trusts now find themselves in the top income tax bracket—39.6 percent—when their income exceeds $7,900. A single person, in contrast, doesn't reach this rate until her income is over $263,750 (these 1996 figures are adjusted annually for inflation). Trusts always had more compact rate structures than people, and this isn't necessarily wrong in theory, but the 1993 change was downright harsh and has made planning very difficult. If your trust is going to have to pay taxes, this is another issue you should explore in depth with your planner.

Revocable Living Trusts as Will Substitutes

One of the most common uses of the revocable living trust is as a probate avoidance device. Here's how the technique works: You create a revocable living trust, name yourself and a friend, loved one, or trusted advisor as co-trustees, and transfer all of the assets you own into it. The trust specifies that all of the income is to be paid to you for your life, and further specifies what is to be done with all of the trust assets when you die. In other words, you are the income beneficiary, and the people to whom you would leave your assets under a will are the residuary beneficiaries. In fact, the operative clauses in a revocable trust for disposing of its assets after you die often are the same as those used in a will. Since the trust is revocable, there are no current income or gift tax consequences to its creation. You continue to file income tax returns under your own name and Social Security number. When you die, your co-trustee distributes the trust assets to the residuary beneficiaries—without the supervision of the probate court. The process is much quicker, much more private (unlike probate, it's not a matter of public record), and much harder to contest.

Revocable living trusts can be an excellent way to avoid ancillary probate when you own out-of-state property. Even some estate planners who generally are leery of revocable trusts find them effective for this purpose. If you own real estate in another state, look carefully into this option.

There is one other advantage to revocable living trusts: If you become incapacitated, they allow your co-trustee to act as a sort of attorney-in-fact for you, at least with respect to those assets contained in the trust. This power of attorney feature is an important consideration for some people.

So, with all this going for them, why hasn't everybody gone the living trust route? There are several reasons. First, in a few states, it's not clear that the law governing these documents is sufficiently settled to make malpractice-weary attorneys comfortable recommending them. Probate laws have been around a long time, and experienced lawyers generally know what to expect when they write a will. In contrast, the use of revocable trusts to avoid probate is a fairly recent phenomenon.

Next, trusts cost more money to set up than wills. They also sometimes cost money to administer on an ongoing basis. For modest estates, some estate planners question whether the cost-benefit analysis works out favorably for trusts. On the other hand, trusts cost a lot less on the distribution end than probate does, and most people really do come out ahead with a living trust in the long run.

A major downside to revocable trusts is that they require ongoing care and maintenance. There's a constant danger that one or more of your assets could fall outside of the trust. All of your assets must be retitled in the trust's name when you set up the trust, and you must subsequently remember to title all new assets you acquire thereafter in the trust's name. Over time, almost all people forget to do this with one or more assets—a car, a boat, or a mutual fund acquired well after the trust was set up. This results in a risk of what's called *partial intestacy:* If the asset's not in the trust and you don't have a will, the asset passes under your state's intestacy statute when you die. There's a simple way around this problem, however: Execute a pour-over will that gives any assets outside the trust to the trust when you die. It's a simple and effective way to close the loop in most states, and it would be very risky to create a revocable living trust without such a backup.

Finally, many people operate under the mistaken assumption that a revocable trust can save taxes. This is simply not true. These trusts do lower probate expenses (probate fees usually are tied to the size of the probate estate, and the probate estate is nominal at best when there's a properly maintained living trust involved). However, all of the assets in the trust are taxed when you die. After all, the trust is revocable, meaning you have the right to take back the assets in it, right? Then, as far as the tax law is concerned, you still own those assets.

In the end, deciding whether or not to use a revocable trust with a backup will to minimize or (ideally) avoid probate depends on your personal circumstances, your willingness to try something a little new, the nature and bent of the professional advice you receive, and any particular quirks of law in your state. You need to discuss the issues involved in this decision with your estate planner, since no one knows the situation in your area better than she. If she's open-minded in discussing the pros and cons, you've found someone who will give you the advice you need to make a good decision. If, on the other hand, she will not even discuss the option, maybe you need to find someone a little more flexible and attuned to your needs to work with. Revocable living trusts are a wonderful estate planning tool, and they deserve fair consideration in every situation.

Other Common Uses of Trusts

In addition to probate minimization, there are several other important uses of trusts in the estate planning process. Let's take a look at a few of the more common ones.

1. Minimizing Estate Taxes. Certain testamentary trusts are an important tool used by married couples to minimize their estate taxes. Under a *credit shelter trust,* the first spouse to die leaves part of his estate in a trust for the couple's heirs, thereby ensuring that the trust's assets are not included in the gross estate of the surviving spouse when she dies. In a *Q-TIP trust,* a surviving spouse receives only a special right to lifetime income and support from the trust's assets, thereby also avoiding the inclusion of those assets in her gross estate. These techniques are detailed in the "Marital Deduction" section later in this chapter.

2. Holding Property for Minors. Since minors are not permitted to own property in their own names, trusts can be an excellent way to hold and manage property for them. Such trusts generally are testamentary, having been created under a family member's will, but they can be inter vivos as well. In most states, trusts are not subject to the same restrictions as custodial accounts (i.e., Uniform Transfer to Minors Act (UTMA) accounts or Uniform Gifts to Minors Act (UGMA) accounts). One key difference between trusts for minors and custodial accounts is that minors can claim the assets in a custodial account once they reach the age of majority, whereas the settlor decides at what age they get the assets in a trust. On the flip side, trusts entail both set-up and ongoing administration expenses. Also, the tax burden on a trust may be higher than the tax burden on a custodial account. It may not be higher, too, depending on how the kiddie tax rules apply. The various aspects of gifts to minors are outlined in the "Gifts" section later in this chapter. The bottom line is that, if the gift is nominal, go the UTMA or UGMA route. If a substantial sum is involved, consider the trust option.

3. Protecting Beneficiaries. If you are concerned that one or more of your beneficiaries may not be responsible with the assets you want to give them, consider placing those assets in a trust with a *spendthrift clause.* Such a clause prohibits a beneficiary from borrowing against the trust's assets or future income, and protects the trust from the beneficiary's creditors. Of course, once money goes out of the trust and to the beneficiary, creditors have complete access to it. However, since spendthrift provisions usually give the trustee discretion regarding whether, when, how much, or to whom to pay a beneficiary's share of the trust's income, they are very effective in protecting irresponsible people from themselves.

4. Holding a Life Insurance Policy. Irrevocable trusts can be established to hold a life insurance policy, the proceeds from which are intended to be used to pay the estate taxes of the person insured by the policy. By having the trust own the policy, the amount of the death benefit is not included in the gross estate of the insured when he or she dies. (Remember, the owner of a policy and the insured don't have to be the same person.) These trusts therefore are very popular estate tax planning vehicles for high-net-worth individuals who are certain to owe estate taxes. Uses of this technique are more fully explained in the "Using Life Insurance to Pay Estate Taxes" section later in this chapter.

5. Qualifying for Medicaid. In order to insure that the costs of long-term nursing care services do not deplete a person's estate, a Medicaid qualifying trust can be established to hold those assets that create a net worth too high to qualify for Medicaid. There are several important requirements in order to successfully implement this controversial strategy. They are explained in the "Health Insurance after 65" section in the Risk Management and Insurance chapter.

OUR ISSUES

Will Challenges

A challenge to one's will by hostile family members is a major concern for many people in our community, particularly for those of us who want to provide for our alternative families (of whatever stripe). Again, it should be emphasized that will challenges are rare, and successful ones are even rarer, but the *threat* of a will challenge can be a real hassle for your beneficiaries.

If a potential will challenge is a serious concern for you, there are steps you can take to minimize the risk. First, fully explore all the will alternatives discussed above—beneficiary designations, joint ownership, and trusts. A will challenge only threatens the assets in your probate estate, so if there's not much there, there's not much risk. Next, be certain your will mentions each and every member of your family, even if it's to politely disinherit them. As we said above, don't be bitchy, but don't mince words, either. This is serious business, and it's no place for a curtain call as either a drama queen or a co-dependent. Third, if you face AIDS or some other life-threatening illness, be certain to execute your will early. The "sound mind and body" standard is not hard to meet. If you're sound enough to be worried about estate planning, you're sound enough to execute a will. Nevertheless, the earlier you get the paperwork done, the less likely it is someone can convince a judge that you had lost it before the will was executed. Fourth, make sure everyone observes the formality of the execution "ceremony." As stupid as this sounds, it can be very persuasive if the documents look "official," and the witnesses, the notary, and the estate planner all can say you seemed sound to them. Finally, if you are leaving the bulk of your estate to a significant other, be certain that he or she is not in the room when you execute the will, that your witnesses take note of his or her absence, and that you tell them you are under no duress or undue influence from him or her to execute the will. If your witnesses believe you were of sound mind and not under undue influence, it will be very hard for someone else to convince a judge otherwise. In combination, this formidable arsenal of defenses ought to discourage most people from wasting their own money in pursuit of vengeance (or whatever).

Share Your Plans with Your Family

Regardless of how serious the threat of a will challenge is, it's a sometimes painful but always good practice to let family members—or at least one trusted family member—know of your intentions in advance. Surprise can be a big factor in sending people off the deep end when you die, so if they know what's coming, they should be less surprised. As soon as it's finalized, discuss your estate planning with your family. Unfortunately, too few people—especially gay people who aren't out to their families—find the strength to explain their decisions while they're still around to do so. Even if you're only out to one member of your family, you should explain your decisions to him or her at the earliest opportunity. It's not possible to overstate the value of communicating your plans in advance. It can and will preempt many potential problems down the road.

Joint Tenancy with Right of Survivorship

Like any other technique that has the potential to keep gay assets out of straight courts, the JTWROS option deserves extra consideration within our community. However, the estate tax drawbacks mentioned above apply equally in our circumstances, and perhaps even more so since some of us have to work harder than our straight counterparts to avoid the sting of these high taxes. This issue is explored in the "Estate Tax Planning Techniques" section later in this chapter.

To the extent you are able to use the joint tenancy option, take to heart the admonition above to restate your survivorship intentions in your will. It would be extremely odd for someone to successfully drag joint assets back into your probate estate, but it's so easy to plan around such a risk that there's no reason not to.

Jointly Owned Property and Estate Taxes

When a gay couple, or even two friends, jointly own a piece of property, they generally assume that they each own one-half of the property. If they thought about it, they also likely would assume that therefore half of the value of their property would be included in the gross estate of the first one to die. The property would pass by right of survivorship to the other owner, whose gross estate would then include the full value of the property. Logical, no?

Unfortunately, the tax law doesn't make quite the same assumptions that most normal people would when it comes to the joint ownership of property by unmarried co-tenants. The IRS assumes that the first person to die owned 100 percent of the property and includes all 100 percent in the first owner's gross estate. Of course, when the second owner dies, all 100 percent also is included in his or her estate. This creates a nice little windfall for the government, which gets to tax half the property one extra time.

It is possible to rebut this presumption, but the burden of proof is on you—not the government—to do it. To prevail, you must be able to demonstrate that both owners contributed equally to the purchase and upkeep of the property in question. The paperwork burden here should not be underestimated. Years, perhaps decades, of account statements and canceled checks may be required. Moreover, these can't just be any canceled checks; they have to specifically prove each person's separate contribution. You should be thinking now about how to create and maintain an adequate paper trail. It will be too late to try to reconstruct one when you die. Of course, if you and a co-owner have been allocating income tax deductions from your house (mortgage interest, property taxes) other than 50/50, its likely that your income tax allocation will apply for estate tax purposes—if you can persuade the IRS to use it instead of the 100/0 allocation it assumes.

While in the initial instance, how hard it is to prevail in these matters depends on the reasonableness of the estate tax auditor assigned to your case, your estate could be in for a real fight. It's not unusual for these issues to have to be appealed within the IRS before the agency gets it right—again, assuming that your paperwork is in good shape.

The truly charming aspect of all this, of course, is that the law doesn't make this assumption when dealing with a married couple. Common sense prevails in the case of a married decedent, and only half the value of jointly owned property is included in the first-to-die's estate.

A final thought on gay jointly owned property and transfer taxes: If the presumption on jointly owned property we've just discussed also applies to your state's inheritance taxes, you have an added reason to keep good paperwork. As we saw above, the rule creates a real risk that half of the same asset could be subject to taxes twice. Moreover, since state inheritance taxes often kick in for collateral property without any exemptions, the joint ownership issue could create state inheritance tax problems for you even if you don't expect to owe federal estate tax. And, as we saw in the last section, collateral inheritance tax rates can be high. Once again, you should take steps now to make sure your estate can document equal contribution on jointly owned property.

Revocable Trusts

Although there is not uniform agreement within the legal community as to the preferability of revocable living trusts over traditional wills, they deserve careful consideration within the gay community. In addition to all the other benefits these trusts offer, the ability to keep assets out of a homophobic court system cannot be lightly discounted. Most of the concerns about these trusts can be satisfied with a backup will, as described earlier. Unless there is a specific legal problem with these documents in your state—and there are such problems in a few states—the burden really ought to be on your estate planner to demonstrate why you shouldn't use one. Probate avoidance is an important goal for lesbians and gays, so if the revocable trust option won't work for you, pay extra attention to the possibilities offered by joint ownership and beneficiary designations.

RELATED TOPICS

If you want to be certain that none of your assets will pass to family members under your state's intestacy statute, charities can be a good option for residuary bequests under a will or trust, as well as alternate beneficiary designations under a life insurance policy or retirement account. To understand the role charitable contributions can play in estate tax planning, see the "Charitable Deductions" section on page 333.

Automobiles are an important exception to the general rule that lesbian and gay couples should use joint ownership of property as an estate planning tool. The reasons for this are outlined in the "Automobile Insurance" section on page 92.

For the number of things you will need to think about if you want to make a gift to a minor, see the "Gifts" section on page 321. The income tax aspects of gifts to certain minors are explained in the discussion of the kiddie tax rules in the "Bracket Arbitrage" section on page 206.

Irrevocable life insurance trusts are an important estate planning tool for high-net-worth individuals and couples. They are discussed in the "Using Life Insurance to Pay Estate Taxes" section on page 335.

Medicaid qualifying trusts can be an effective way to ensure that the cost of long-term nursing home care does not deplete your assets before you die. The pros and cons of this technique are discussed in the "Health Insurance after 65" section on page 76.

Although revocable trusts can be an important tool in planning for incapacity, they cannot fully replace powers of attorney. The various aspects of powers are detailed in the "Powers of Attorney" section on page 348, and in the "Advance Directives (Living Wills) and Health Care Powers" section on page 354.

For a thorough understanding of the responsibilities imposed on personal representatives and trustees, as well as some of the considerations that should go into who you choose for this important role, read the "Choosing a Trustee and/or Personal Representative" section on page 340.

GIFTS

THE STRAIGHT FACTS

Federal Gift Tax

In general, the tax law allows each person to give away up to $10,000 dollars (cash or property) per recipient per year free of federal gift tax. This amount is called the *annual exclusion.* It's important to remember that you have an unlimited number of annual exclusions—it's just that they're only worth $10,000 each. Another way of saying this is that you can give gifts to an unlimited number of different people, but you can't give more than $10,000 worth of cash or property to any one person each year without having to worry about federal gift taxes.

If you are married, you and your spouse each can give away $10,000 to any one person each year free of federal tax (i.e., up to $20,000). In fact, the tax law allows married couples to combine their annual exclusions, so that either spouse can give away up to the full $20,000 tax free (assuming the other spouse doesn't use his or her $10,000 exclusion him- or herself). This is called *gift-splitting.*

If you do give more than $10,000 to one person in a year (or more than a total of $20,000 if you are married), the excess theoretically is taxable. In practice, however, as we saw in "The Unified Estate and Gift Tax System" section earlier in this chapter, your $600,000 estate tax exemption in effect is reduced by the amount the gift exceeds the annual exclusion. In essence, it's only once you've completely used up your $600,000 estate tax exemption that you actually pay tax on the gifts you make in excess of the annual exclusion.

EXAMPLE
You are single and give your niece $15,000 in 19X1. You must file a gift tax return by April 15, 19X2. This in effect will reduce your estate tax exemption by $5,000 (the excess over the $10,000 annual allowance), to $595,000 (assuming that this is your first taxable gift).

SUGGESTION
To avoid this problem, give your niece $10,000 in 19X1 and the other $5,000 on January 1, 19X2.

Note also that not every gift qualifies for the annual exclusion. You must give what the law calls a *present interest* in property in order for it to qualify. A gift of a *future interest* is not sufficient. Gifts of future interests usually are proposed as part of a complex estate plan. The issue often arises in the context of a trust or a gift of real estate (or real estate in a trust). It's likely that any gift you give on your own will be of a present interest that qualifies for the annual exclusion. Nevertheless, you need to be familiar with the concept in case your estate planning requires this level of complexity.

EXAMPLE
Howie creates an irrevocable trust giving his cabin to his sister Ellen for her life, and then to her son Drew. Howie has given Drew a future interest, and that gift does not qualify for the annual exclusion.

The law takes a very broad view of what constitutes a gift. Generally, anytime you transfer an asset to another person without receiving something of equal value from them in return, you've made a gift to that person. Of course, if you do receive something of value in return, the law treats the transaction as a sale and there are income tax consequences to it. So, there's really no way to avoid the tax issue completely. In fact, if you sell something to somebody for less than what it's worth, the tax law treats the transaction as a part sale/part gift, and both sets of rules come into play.

Stop and think for a second about what's being said here—people make gifts all the time, and usually they do so completely oblivious to the potential gift tax consequences. You buy a friend dinner, you treat your sister to a new outfit, and you've made a gift under the law. Similarly, if you "loan" a relative or close friend money, but never establish any terms for the loan or a repayment schedule, the IRS could make a pretty convincing argument that what you've really made is a gift. Sometimes, the distinction is a little more subtle. Suppose you loan your son $50,000 interest-free. Is the forgone interest a gift? The answer here is not certain, but at least one Supreme Court case suggests it may well be.

Of course, most gifts made without regard to their tax consequences usually fall in the category of "no harm, no foul," because the majority of them are well under the $10,000 annual exclusion. Nevertheless, the potential for gift tax liability certainly exists, at least in theory. Moreover, a series of gifts over a period of months within the same year can turn theory into practice for a lot more people than probably realize it.

These rules aren't a problem for married couples, because the law allows them to make unlimited transfers to and from each other without any gift tax consequences. There are, of course, estate planning opportunities—and pitfalls—associated with this exception, and we'll explore them later in this chapter.

None of the federal gift tax rules applies to gifts made to a recognized charity. There are no limits on the amount you can contribute to one or more charities, and those gifts are never subject to the federal gift tax. There are limits on the amount of charitable contributions you can claim as an itemized deduction for income tax purposes, but that's a different matter.

The law places the burden of paying any gift tax on the person who made the gift. However, if the IRS can't collect from the donor, there are provisions in the law enabling them to go after the person who received the gift for the tax due.

Payments for Health Care and Educational Expenses

There's one tax-free gift-giving opportunity hidden in the law that many people are not aware of: gifts of educational or medical payments. You may directly pay the medical expenses of another person, including medical insurance premiums, without limit, with no gift tax consequences. The same rule applies for expenses paid directly to an educational organization for tuition (but not room and board). You don't have to worry about the $10,000 limit. It doesn't apply, and the amount you pay isn't counted against it. In fact, you don't even have to file a gift tax return. Just be sure to pay the institution or provider directly. If instead you were to give the money to the person you're helping out so he or she can forward it to the school or health care provider, you would lose the advantage of this special rule, and all the normal gift tax rules would apply.

State Gift Taxes

State gift taxes vary tremendously, even more so than state income or inheritance taxes. Not all states impose them. For those that do, some follow the federal rules, others create their own. Because of this variation, it's impossible to discuss state gift taxes in any detail. Nevertheless, it's important to be mindful of the possibility that these taxes could be an issue for you. If you are planning a substantial gift, you might consider checking for any state gift tax consequences before proceeding.

Gifts to Minors

Under the laws in every state, minors are not allowed to own property in their own names. Property must either be held for them in a trust or in a custodial account. In most states, custodial accounts are created under a law called either the Uniform Gifts to Minors Act (UGMA) or the Uniform Transfers to Minors Act (UTMA). All states have enacted either UGMA or UTMA, and a few have both. When you make a gift to a minor, you must use either a trust, an UGMA account, or an UTMA account to make the gift.

Trusts generally offer greater flexibility than UGMAs or UTMAs, both in terms of the assets they can hold and the powers that can be granted to the person holding them (i.e., the trustee). Since UGMAs and UTMAs are created by state laws, the custodian holding the assets can only exercise those powers granted by the statute. The disadvantage associated with trusts is that they cost money to set up and administer. In contrast, there usually is no fee to set up or administer UGMAs and UTMAs. UTMA accounts can hold most any type of property, but usually UGMAs can hold only cash, securities, or life insurance. The rules, of course, vary slightly from state to state.

There are some other things to consider when making gifts to minors. First, a minor is entitled to claim all of the assets in an UGMA or UTMA account when he or she reaches the age of majority (18 or 21, depending on the state). If this idea makes you nervous, a trust may be a better route to take. In a trust, *you* get to specify the age at which the gift actually comes into the recipient's control.

Next, if you name yourself as the UGMA or UTMA custodian and die while the child is still a minor, the assets are included in your gross estate for federal estate tax purposes. Obviously, if the gift is part of your estate tax planning, this rule would defeat your intentions. You should consider naming someone else as custodian if this is an issue for you.

Finally, keep the kiddie tax rules in mind. Investment income in excess of $1,300 (this 1996 figure is indexed for inflation) of a child under 14 gets taxed at his or her parents' marginal tax rate. Make sure you aren't shifting income into a higher bracket when you make a gift to a minor. One great way to minimize this problem is to give assets to minors under 14 that emphasize growth rather than income. While income from an asset is taxed every year as it's earned, the growth isn't taxed until the asset is sold. As long as the asset isn't sold until after the minor turns 14, there are no kiddie tax problems.

OUR ISSUES

Gifts between Lovers

The federal gift tax rules threaten to create some serious burdens for lesbian and gay couples. In theory, here's the issue: If living expenses aren't split equally, it's quite likely that one partner is making a gift to another. This can arise in a number of ways. For example, suppose one partner makes more than the other, and the couple pools its income. The partner earning more probably has made a gift to the partner earning less. Similarly, suppose one partner owns a house, and the other lives there rent-free. The owner probably has made a gift in the amount of the fair market rent to her other half. It may even be possible that couples who maintain separate finances make gifts to each other if they don't contribute equally to all joint expenses. (This last example actually would be the hardest case for the government to win, as long as the contributions were in proportion to the ownership interests, the couple was scrupulous about each person paying in the proper amount for each joint expenditure, and they kept meticulous records.)

As is often the case with these issues, we should note here that this problem is not confined to couple relationships. Any alternative family structure in which the parties are not legally related faces the possible exposure described here.

This is an issue with very serious potential for our community. If you've started to process the implications of all this and you're beginning to get a little nervous, let's step back and get some perspective. First, remember the $10,000 annual exclusion. There has to be a significant disparity in income, assets, or contributions between partners before they exceed this amount. For example, for couples who pool their funds, it's not even possible for the pooling to create a taxable gift as long as their incomes are within $20,000 of each other. (Why $20,000? Following the logic of the premise all the way through, only half of the difference in a couple's pooled incomes is "given away"; the other half is kept for oneself. Since the annual exclusion is $10,000, the gift tax only becomes an issue when the difference in earnings is more than twice that amount.)

Next, remember that, before you actually pay any gift tax, you first essentially reduce your $600,000 estate tax exemption to zero. While this is small comfort for people who need their full $600,000 for estate tax planning purposes, it does mean it likely would be many years before you actually had to start paying any tax.

Finally, if you think this is a concern for you and your other half, there are things you can do to ensure that you're treated fairly. First, as was suggested above, be scrupulous about the paper trail. Make sure that you can document what each of you contributed to joint expenditures, so there's no possibility of the IRS arguing that a gift was made when none was.

It's important to note this theory has never been put to the test. There is no record of the IRS ever trying to enforce the rules in this way nor any record of someone asking for the IRS's opinion on the matter. Gift tax compliance and enforcement in general are comparatively low, and most gift tax issues only get raised when the IRS audits a decedent's estate tax return. For what it's worth, if your estate isn't going to be required to file a tax return, the situation probably won't come to the IRS's attention. Further, even if it does, it's not clear that the IRS is inclined to do anything about it. Nevertheless, this book is supposed to be about planning for people who want to comply with the tax law, and "don't worry about it, you'll never get caught" is lousy tax advice. The logic is pretty clear for many situations, at least on a theoretical level. The issue is lurking out there, and somewhere, someday, some unfortunate couple could be the IRS's test case. Until Congress amends the tax law to accommodate our relationships, gay couples remain at least theoretically exposed to a potential gift tax nightmare.

Adding a Partner to a Deed

You've met the woman of your dreams, you've fallen in love, she's moved into your townhouse, and you've exchanged rings and vows during a Holy Union ceremony. The two of you have decided she should co-own your house, in case something happens to you. Here's the problem: If she pays you for half your interest in the house, you've made a sale and you have to pay income tax on any gain. On the other hand, if in a grand gesture of Sapphic love you simply add her name to the deed, you've made a potentially taxable gift. It's likely that the value of the gift is one-half of your equity in the house. As long as that half is under $10,000, there are no problems. But, if your total equity is over $20,000 (and hence her half would be over $10,000), it's gift tax return time!

All this doesn't mean you should automatically veto the idea of changing the deed. There often are compeling nontax reasons for lesbian and gay couples to hold property as joint tenants with a right of survivorship. These issues were discussed in the "Wills and Will Substitutes" section earlier in this chapter. It may well be that the most prudent course of action in your circumstances is simply to make the gift, file the gift tax return, and in effect lower your $600,000 estate tax exemption.

This is just one possible strategy. Annual gifts of $10,000 worth of house until you each own half, followed by a retitling of the property as joint tenants with right of survivorship, is another. Even better, you also might consider using a trust to get a lover's name onto the title of a house. You can structure the trust in such a way that the ownership is transferred gradually over a number of years, taking advantage of each year's annual gift tax exclusion without going over it and triggering any adverse tax consequences. Of course, trusts cost money to set up, so you'll have to weigh the costs against the benefits for your situation.

One additional caution: You may have even more gift tax problems if your partner assumes part of your mortgage—she's made a gift to you for the amount of debt she's assumed! (By the way, did you get your lender's permission to add a name to the deed?)

Hopefully, by now you've gotten the message loud and clear: Don't change the title to an asset without getting competent advice from a professional who is well versed in these particular issues.

RELATED TOPICS

If you're having trouble remembering the interplay between estate and gift taxes, review "The Unified Estate and Gift Tax System" section on page 293.

When you transfer money to another person, or when someone else transfers money to you, the general rule is that the transfer is either a gift (with possible gift tax consequences) or some sort of compensation (with possible income tax consequences). This rule is discussed in the "Income Tax Basics" section on page 161.

A structured program of annual gifting to family members can be an effective way to lower the size of your gross estate, thereby lowering your estate tax bill. To understand how this strategy might fit into your estate planning, see the "Lifetime Gifts" section on page 329.

Joint ownership of property can be an important estate planning technique for gay couples. It is detailed in the "Wills and Will Substitutes" section on page 302.

Trusts can be an effective mechanism for adding a name to the deed to a house without triggering gift tax consequences. They also are an important planning tool when making gifts to minor children. The various aspects of these unique instruments are explained in the "Wills and Will Substitutes" section on page 302.

The kiddie tax rules are explained in the "Bracket Arbitrage" section on page 206.

ESTATE TAX PLANNING TECHNIQUES

THE STRAIGHT FACTS

The old saw regarding death and taxes gets a new lease on life when discussion turns to the federal estate tax. As we saw in the "Estate Planning Basics" section at the beginning of this chapter, if your gross estate—or your combined gross estates if you are married—exceeds $600,000, or if it is likely to reach that threshold before you die, you probably need to be concerned about the federal estate tax. Also as we saw in that discussion, a very broad range of items goes into computing your gross estate, too—things many people wouldn't expect. Take a moment now to review the list of what's included in your gross estate, and try to think of something not on this list. You'll quickly get a sense of how all-encompassing the federal estate tax is. When you add these assets together, it is not hard to see that more people than expected have to worry about the federal estate tax. A house that's paid off, some life insurance, a solid pension plan, a little nest egg in the bank, and that magical $600,000 figure can quickly start closing in!

> **EXAMPLE**
>
> Clay has just entered his retirement years. He has lived in the same home for almost 30 years and has seen inflation increase its value to approximately $240,000. Clay's mortgage has been paid off for a couple of years now. Clay owns an $80,000 paid-up life insurance policy. He keeps $5,000 in a checking account, $25,000 in a savings account, and owns a $50,000 CD. He also has $60,000 invested in mutual funds. Clay participated for many years in a company-sponsored pension plan, and the value of his account currently is almost $140,000. Additionally, Clay has a total of about $30,000 in IRA accounts. Without taking into account the value of any personal property or collectibles he owns, Clay's net worth for federal estate tax purposes is $630,000. Clay very well may "spend down" that net worth below the $600,000 estate tax threshold (he also may see the value of his house and invested assets increase sufficiently to keep him hovering around the $600,000 mark for a number of years). In any event, if Clay were to pass away unexpectedly tomorrow, his estate could owe up to $11,100 in federal taxes. Through proper estate planning, these taxes can be avoided at a fraction of that cost.

Although the individual combination of assets will vary considerably from person to person, Clay's "big picture" is not atypical for many older Americans. However, there are steps you can take to minimize or even eliminate the federal estate tax bite. For example, married people with combined gross estates worth less than $1.2 million, but still over the $600,000 threshold, can eliminate federal estate taxes altogether. The rest of this section will be devoted to this and other techniques for handling estate taxes.

Lifetime Gifts

One technique for minimizing estate taxes involves annual gifting. When you give money or other property away, it's obviously no longer yours. Therefore, in most situations, it's not considered part of the equation for federal estate tax purposes. Within the gift tax limits discussed in the last section, there are some very effective gifting strategies you can deploy to minimize estate taxes by making lifetime gifts. The $10,000 gift tax annual exclusion is often an ideal solution to potential estate tax problems for people whose net worth is right on the border of the $600,000 threshold.

EXAMPLE

Consider the example above, where Clay's gross estate was $630,000. By making a gift of $6,000 to each of his five nieces, for example, Clay can bring his gross estate down to $600,000 and avoid federal estate taxes.

SUGGESTION

Clay should periodically review his finances to see if he again creeps over the $600,000 threshold. If he does, gifts may again be the solution to his estate tax problems.

Even if your high net worth puts you well within the estate tax regime, you can still make good use of the $10,000 annual allowance to minimize your problems. Consider these examples:

EXAMPLE 1

Fam and Lee Values have two married children, Tolerance and Harmony. In one year, if they so desired, Fam and Lee could remove $80,000 from their gross estates free of federal gift tax simply by both giving $10,000 each to Tolerance, Harmony, and their two spouses (2 parents × $10,000 × 4 "children").

EXAMPLE 2

The same facts apply as above, but Tolerance and Harmony each have two children of their own. Now, if Fam and Lee wanted to, in one year they could shrink the size of their gross estates by $160,000 (2 parents × $10,000 × 8 children/grandchildren).

EXAMPLE 3

Suppose Fam and Lee want to use the gift tax annual exclusion to reduce their gross estates and minimize estate taxes but are reluctant to make the drastic adjustments in Example 2 above all at once. After all, they may yet need that money at some point. They still can set up an annual gifting program, but use a more gradual approach. For example, they might give each of their four grandchildren $2,500 a year. After five years, they will have incrementally removed $50,000 from their gross estates (4 grandchildren × $2,500 × 5 years).

SUGGESTION

If you adopt an annual gifting program like the one discussed in Example 3, don't be afraid to change it as circumstances dictate. If you decide finances are becoming tight, pull back to $1,000 or $2,000 per grandchild per year. If you realize you may have been too conservative in your original projections, you can always raise the gifts to $5,000 or $6,000 per year. Just don't go over that magical $10,000 figure!

WARNING

If you decide to adopt an annual gifting program, remember to plan carefully for your future needs. Even though your net worth may be over $600,000, a large percentage of that may be in illiquid assets—your house, life insurance, retirement plans. Your gifts probably will have to come from your liquid assets, such as savings accounts, money markets, CDs. Be sure you don't end up cash poor making annual gifts.

Once you have some idea how much to give and when to give it, you still must decide what to give. Cash? Stocks? Bonds? A favorite auto? As was suggested above, it is important that you retain enough cash to keep yourself liquid throughout your golden years. However, it's usually better to have most noncash property—stocks, bonds, real estate, vintage autos—transferred when you die rather than through lifetime gifts. The tax laws provide a strong preference for transferring appreciated property at death: Any appreciation you've accumulated in them is erased when you die. Your beneficiaries receive them at their full market value, wiping out all the capital gains that built up while you owned the assets. This powerful incentive does not apply to lifetime gifts. Your appreciation in such transfers "carries over" to the recipient, and he or she must pay income tax on all that gain when the asset is subsequently sold.

EXAMPLE

You own stock worth $10,000. You bought the stock many years ago for only $1,000. If you were to sell the stock, there would be a $9,000 taxable gain. If you give this stock to your nephew, and he sells it, there would still be a $9,000 taxable gain. However, if you left the stock to him in your will, that $9,000 gain would be erased upon your death.

On the other hand, in some situations it actually can be advantageous to give away property instead of cash. This technique works well for people who own assets they know are going to appreciate considerably in value before they die, like certain real estate or stock in a family-owned business. If the math works, it can make more tax sense to transfer the asset sooner rather than later. Doing so removes the appreciation from one's gross estate.

EXAMPLE

You own stock in a family-owned company that consistently appreciates in value at an average rate of 10 percent per year. Your investment in this company is currently worth $500,000. If you live another 15 years, this stock should be worth $2.1 million (based on its past performance). By gifting the stock to your heirs now, the $1.6 million in anticipated appreciation over the next 15 years is removed from your estate when you die, saving you hundreds of thousands in federal estate taxes.

Keep in mind, however, that this technique almost always applies to people with very high gross estates who are already certain of paying estate taxes. Moreover, using this approach is always part of a carefully (and professionally) drafted estate plan. For most people who do not have a high net worth, the general rule should be: Whenever possible, give cash instead of property, and always seek professional advice before giving away during your lifetime property that already has substantially appreciated in value.

Marital Deduction

Another essential estate planning tool, available only to married couples (as its name implies), is known as the *marital deduction*. The marital deduction is unlimited, which means that you can give as much as you want to your spouse, while you're living or when you die, and not pay gift or estate tax on it.

EXAMPLE

Consider once again the tale of those wholesome Americans, Fam and Lee Values. However, the plot has taken a turn for the worse: Fam has just gone on to that big country club in the sky, leaving a gross estate of $700,000. In his will, Fam leaves $500,000 to his spouse Lee, and $200,000 to be

divided between his daughters Tolerance and Harmony. Since the first
$500,000 goes to Lee tax-free (thanks to the unlimited marital deduction),
the amount of Fam's taxable estate is reduced to $200,000. Since the estate
tax threshold is $600,000, Fam's estate does not owe any federal estate
taxes. In contrast, if Fam had left all $700,000 to Lee, her gross estate
would have been $700,000, or $100,000 above the threshold, creating the
real possibility of an estate tax problem for Tolerance and Harmony when
Lee joins Fam at the Last Cotillion. Using the approach outlined in this
example, the Values' estate planning ultimately saved their beneficiaries as
much as $37,000 in federal estate taxes!

This example illustrates the beauty of the unlimited marital deduction: Through careful planning and use, it can allow married couples to
double their estate tax threshold from $600,000 to $1.2 million.

EXAMPLE

The same facts apply as above, except Fam's net worth is $1.2 million. He
leaves $600,000 to Lee, and $600,000 in equal shares to Tolerance and
Harmony. The first $600,000 passes to Lee free of federal estate tax, and
the next $600,000 just misses the estate tax threshold. Fam has saved his
beneficiaries as much as $235,000 in federal estate taxes!

This technique is not without its difficulties, however. Consider the
last example as a case in point. Lee received $600,000 from Fam; howev-
er, Lee probably individually owns some assets of her own. She now has a
gross estate worth over $600,000, and no spouse with which to take advan-
tage of the marital deduction. If the elder Values' combined gross estates are
(or will be) over $1.2 million, they cannot completely avoid estate taxes
through the use of the marital deduction. They will need to consider a combination of estate planning techniques to deal with their situation.

However, many couples who have estate tax problems fall within the
$600,000 to $1.2 million range. With a little planning, they can avoid federal estate taxes altogether. It may require retitling some assets from one
spouse to another, or into or out of joint ownership, and will definitely
require carefully prepared estate planning documents. Among other concerns, such couples often need to be sure that their individual gross estates
are roughly equivalent, so that the second spouse to pass away does not
leave too large an estate. As the examples above make clear, however, the
tax savings for these efforts will pay for themselves many times over.

If there is a concern that giving a large portion of a first-to-die-
spouse's estate to the couple's children will financially strap the surviving

spouse, the couple could consider placing the children's share in a trust. Under one special type of trust, called a *qualified terminable interest property trust,* or *Q-TIP trust* for short, the surviving spouse receives both all the income the trust earns each year along with limited rights to assets from the trust in case of "hardship"; the remaining trust assets are distributed to the couple's children upon the second spouse's death. If it's drafted properly, the Q-TIP trust protects a surviving spouse in an emergency but still gets the assets in the trust out of both spouses' estates without estate tax.

Finally, if a married couple has a combined net worth over $1.2 million, they might consider combining the marital deduction with annual gifts to minimize estate taxes. If these two techniques together won't solve their problems, they should discuss with their estate planner what other options may be available to them. One approach he or she might suggest is the tax-smart use of charitable giving.

Charitable Deductions

The use of charitable giving can be an important part of every estate plan. For certain high-net-worth people, it is an option that must be given serious consideration. Beyond the obvious altruistic and societal benefits of charitable giving, certain provisions of the tax law make such gifts a financially attractive option.

First, any amounts you leave to a qualified charity are deducted from your gross estate for federal estate tax purposes. Thus, outright charitable gifts made in a will sometimes can solve all of one's estate tax problems.

> **EXAMPLE**
> Again consider the case of Clay from the beginning of this section, whose $630,000 gross estate was just over the exemption limit. If Clay made a bequest of, say, $35,000 to charity in his will, he would avoid federal estate taxes altogether.

Charitable bequests work well in a good number of situations. However, if your gross estate is high enough that you can't afford or don't want to make the large outright gifts necessary to come down under $600,000, there is a family of charitable trusts that may help solve your problems. Charitable trusts are complex mechanisms that should only be established with the assistance of a competent professional, but, in the right circumstances, they can be a perfect way to beat the estate tax rap.

There are three kinds of charitable trusts: the charitable lead trust, the charitable remainder unitrust, and the charitable remainder annuity trust. Of these, the two *charitable remainder trusts (CRTs)* seem to be the more popular estate planning tools.

The mechanics of the CRT are fairly straightforward. You place money or other property into a trust; the trust pays you income for a specified period of time or for your life, and then gives the remaining trust assets to the charity you designated when you created the trust. The assets you placed in the trust are no longer yours, so they're not counted as part of your gross estate. You've lowered your estate tax bite correspondingly. (You still pay income tax on some of the money you receive from the trust, of course.)

Part of what makes CRTs such an appealing planning technique is their income tax treatment: They give rise to an immediate charitable deduction for income tax purposes. The amount of the deduction is based on the present value of the trust assets that eventually will be distributed to the charity; this is determined using the IRS life expectancy tables. As you may recall from the discussion of charitable contributions in the chapter on Tax Planning, your total charitable deductions, including the deduction generated by a CRT, cannot exceed 50 percent of your adjusted gross income (AGI) for any year. The percentage can be even lower when property other than cash is donated. However, any unused amounts can be carried forward for up to five years.

In the somewhat less common charitable lead trust, the mechanics are merely reversed. The income interest is given to a qualifying charity for a specified number of years, and the remainder passes to the beneficiaries you designate in the trust agreement (e.g., your children).

One other estate planning technique akin to charitable trusts you might consider is the *pooled income fund (PIF)*. A PIF is a common investment fund established by a charity. You make a contribution to the PIF, and the PIF provides you with an income stream based on your contribution, either for life or for a set number of years. Again, the amount you contribute gives rise to a partial charitable contribution, and the gift lowers the size of your gross estate. Because there are expenses involved in operating a PIF, it's usually only large charitable institutions like universities that offer them.

Remember, charitable giving is an important part of estate planning, but it is not a panacea. You still end up giving away a chunk of your assets to charity, so make sure you're motivated at least in part by charitable purposes. Don't be fooled into thinking charitable trusts always result in a wash (although, in the right circumstances, they do). Nevertheless, most people want to include charitable giving in their estate plans, and charitable trusts can make such generosity pay off.

Using Life Insurance to Pay Estate Taxes

What happens if you just can't avoid having your estate pay taxes? In most cases, the government expects its money within nine months of your death. There are, however, steps you can take to assure that your estate is liquid at that critical and difficult time.

First, if your estate consists largely of a small business or family farm, the tax law includes an extended payment plan of sorts, which lets you stretch out the estate tax bill over a 14-year period. The rules for qualifying for this option are complex, so check with your estate planner to see if extended payments will be available to your estate.

If you don't qualify for extended payments (or even if you do), there may be another way to help fund your estate tax liability: *survivorship life insurance.* Also called *second-to-die* insurance, these policies insure two lives, and as the name suggests, they don't pay any benefit until the second insured dies. Such insurance usually is purchased by a husband and wife, and the estate of the second spouse to die is the beneficiary. In essence, purchasing such insurance allows you to "prepay" your estate tax liability through the insurance company—often for pennies on the dollar.

> **EXAMPLE**
>
> The Cleavers, a couple in their mid-sixties, anticipate an estate tax liability of $290,000. They purchase a $500,000 survivorship policy for seven $10,000 annual premiums. The Cleavers have purchased $500,000 in estate tax payments for $70,000.

In this example, the Cleavers' estate tax liability was only $290,000, yet they purchased $500,000 in insurance. Why? Because, as with all other forms of insurance owned by a decedent, the proceeds from a second-to-die policy are included in the gross estate of the second spouse. Estate tax must be paid on those proceeds, so the total amount insured has to be "grossed up" to account for this. Your estate planner or insurance representative should be able to help you gross up your figures accordingly.

EXAMPLE

In the last example, based on the Cleavers' estate tax bracket, the additional $500,000 in net worth added another $210,000 to their estate tax bill. This additional amount also had to be funded with insurance. Even with this additional tax, the insurance is still a good deal. The Cleavers funded their federal estate tax obligation for about 24 cents on the dollar ($70,000 total premiums/$290,000 original estate tax liability).

It's even possible to improve on this technique. To save more money, the Cleavers could ask their estate planner about setting up a trust to own and pay for the survivorship insurance. If the trust is structured properly (i.e., if the Cleavers have no control over the trust after they set it up), the proceeds won't be included in June Cleaver's gross estate (assuming Ward goes first).

As with any insurance purchase, the Cleavers—and you—should shop around carefully when buying a survivorship policy. Be skeptical when reviewing insurance company policy illustrations; not surprisingly, they try to put a good spin on things. They seldom forecast a worst case scenario (for example, what happens to premium prices if one spouse dies shortly after the policy's inception), and the illustrations are rarely if ever guaranteed. Make sure you're working with a broker or agent you trust and that he or she is representing a highly rated insurance company. Make sure you've gotten all the facts up front. And, make sure you're getting the best possible value for your insurance dollar.

OUR ISSUES

A Gay Gifting Program

The discussion of using lifetime gifts to lower estate taxes largely presumed the typical "family values" scenario of a husband and wife, children, and grandchildren. Even though this mold doesn't fit most of our community, it doesn't mean that those of us with estate tax concerns should ignore the benefits of a gifting program. Annual gifts can be made to virtually any-one—friends, relatives, or partners, although there are some unique considerations for gay couples that we'll discuss next. Anyone you might want to name as a beneficiary under a will or trust is fair game for a lifetime gift if you need to get assets out of your estate before you die.

Lesbian and gay couples have some extra thinking to do when it comes to lifetime gifting for estate tax planning purposes. Presumably, gay couples will want first and foremost to provide financial security for a surviving partner. For those couples whose high net worth suggests potential estate tax problems, this means planning to ensure that assets from the first partner to die go to a surviving partner and not to paying estate taxes. If the couple has adopted this dominant paradigm, (avoiding estate tax liabilities at least until the death of the second partner), then gifts from one partner to another may be no more effective in removing assets from their combined estates than gifts between spouses. In "joint" estate tax planning, the goal is to get assets outside of *both* gross estates, so the gifts may need to be to other people, not to each other. (As we'll see when we talk about the lack of a marital deduction next, achieving this goal is harder for gay couples than for married straight couples.)

This is not to suggest that high net worth gay couples shouldn't make lifetime gifts to each other; it's just that doing so may not help their estate tax planning. There is at least one situation in which gifting between partners makes good sense: to equalize gross estates. As we saw in the discussion of the marital deduction above, in order to take maximum advantage of the $600,000 estate tax exclusion, spouses often need to transfer property to "equalize" the values of their estates. While gay couples can only transfer $10,000 per year, the same logic applies.

Marital Deduction

Obviously, the marital deduction isn't available to lesbian and gay couples. This makes our estate planning work much harder. It increases the risk that, when the first partner dies, money will have to go to estate taxes instead of to his or her surviving partner. At a minimum, the unlimited marital deduction allows heterosexual couples to put off altogether the estate tax bite until after they're both gone, regardless of the size of their gross estates. Moreover, as we saw with Fam and Lee Values above, through proper planning, legally married couples can double from $600,000 to $1.2 million the amount of assets ultimately sheltered from the federal estate tax through the marital deduction. Gay couples don't have that luxury.

EXAMPLE 1
Eldra and Diane are a couple in their early 60s. They have been together for 30 years, and own (equally) a home worth $180,000. The mortgage has been paid off for many years. Each owns a $75,000 paid-up life insurance policy. They have $5,000 in a joint checking account, $30,000 in a joint savings account, and $95,000 in various jointly owned mutual funds. Eldra and Diane were both teachers employed by the local school district, so they

each receive a comfortable pension. In order to obtain the highest possible monthly payments, the couple decided not to draw their pensions over their joint lives, so neither partner has a survivorship interest in the other's pension. The couple's only other assets are personal property and household furnishings (owned equally) worth a total of $40,000. The couple has adequate documentation to prove that each contributed equally to the jointly owned assets, so only half of each asset will be included in the gross estate of the first to die. Eldra and Diane each have a gross estate of $250,000, and the couple has combined gross estates of $500,000. If Eldra passed away tomorrow, she would not owe any federal estate tax on her $250,000 gross estate. Moreover, assuming that all of Eldra's assets passed to Diane, if Diane were to die shortly thereafter, her gross estate would be $500,000, and she would not owe any federal estate tax.

EXAMPLE 2

Let's add to the facts in the last example. Assume all of the information above, but now Eldra also owns a piece of land she inherited from her great aunt worth $200,000. She promised her aunt that when she died, if she still owned the land, it would go to her two nephews. Now if Eldra passes away, her estate is worth $450,000. She still has no estate tax problems, however, since her estate is under the $600,000 threshold. Similarly, Diane's gross estate will still be only $500,000 (Eldra having given the land to her nephews), so Diane's estate escapes federal taxation as well.

EXAMPLE 3

Now let's alter the facts from Example 2 slightly, and you should be able to see how the loss of the marital deduction hurts gay couples. What if Diane dies first? Her $250,000 estate passes to Eldra free of federal estate tax. However, Eldra now has a gross estate worth $700,000. When she dies, her estate is going to pay tax on that last $100,000 to the tune of $37,000.

EXAMPLE 4

Finally, let's tweak the facts in Example 3 some more, and make the problem crystal clear. Assume that Eldra's gross estate is $1.2 million and that she leaves half of it to her nephews and half to Diane. One-half of Eldra's estate passes free of tax (thanks to the $600,000 exemption). However, without the benefit of the marital deduction for the property passing to Diane, Eldra's estate must pay $235,000 in federal estate tax on the second $600,000 of her gross estate.

If you were paying close attention, you noticed that the size of the combined gross estates in Examples 2, 3, and 4 we just reviewed were the same as those of Fam and Lee Values in the "Marital Deduction" section.

However, the results in Examples 3 and 4 here are quite different—the Values never paid any estate tax, but Eldra and/or Diane did. As these examples demonstrate, the unavailability of the marital deduction can have some fairly significant consequences for high-net-worth gay couples. Whereas married couples can use the deduction to shelter up to $1.2 million from tax, gay couples are stuck with the usual $600,000 threshold. This is a significant burden for a long-term, two-earner couple, where the odds are quite good that their combined gross estates will be over this amount. This means that the use of lifetime gifting programs, charitable contributions, and life insurance becomes even more important in the estate tax planning of gay couples.

Charitable Contributions

Lesbians and gay men tend to be more community oriented than many, and this orientation generally results in above-average philanthropic intentions. For those in our community with estate tax problems, the charitable deduction should not be overlooked as a way to "do good while doing well." Remember, your estate starts paying federal estate taxes at 37 percent; can't you think of a charity—perhaps an organization within our community—that could put that money to better use than the government? Sometimes, the charitable trusts discussed above can make this a truly painless way to be generous. The rules work equally well for us, so be certain to consider charities in your estate planning, especially if you're going to have estate tax problems.

Life Insurance

Regardless of whether or not it's a survivorship policy, life insurance can be an excellent way to prepay your estate taxes for a fraction of their eventual cost. The same math that the Cleavers used above to pay their estate tax bill for 24 cents on the dollar works for us. Of course, the actual numbers will be different in every case, depending on factors such as your age (or ages if you and your other half go the survivorship route) when you buy the policy, the type of policy you buy, your health, whether or not you smoke, and so on. For example, survivorship policies usually cost less than single life policies, since the insurance company doesn't have to pay out any money until after two people die. Using life insurance to prepay estate taxes frees up more money to be left to significant others, friends, family, gay causes, and so on. To borrow a phrase: "life insurance . . . it isn't just for breeders anymore."

RELATED TOPICS

Before considering an annual gifting program to reduce estate taxes, review the various tax and nontax aspects of making gifts in the "Gifts" section on page 321.

The "Charitable Contributions" section on page 188 explains the income tax aspects of claiming these deductions.

In many respects, purchasing a survivorship policy is like buying any other life insurance product. If life insurance is part of your estate tax planning, you probably should revisit the "Life Insurance" section on page 37 in order to be sure you understand what you're buying and what to look for in a policy.

Separate and apart from regular estate taxes, some estates have to pay a so-called success tax on excess accumulations in a decedent's retirement accounts. This tax is explained in the "Other Retirement Penalty Taxes" section on page 278.

If you and your significant other adopt a gifting program as part of your estate tax planning, or if you make gifts to each other as part of your planning, it is critical that you factor these gifts into your domestic partnership agreement. Various approaches to these agreements, along with essential considerations when hammering one out, are reviewed in the "Domestic Partnership Agreements" section on page 361.

CHOOSING A TRUSTEE AND/OR PERSONAL REPRESENTATIVE

THE STRAIGHT FACTS

Trustees and personal representatives both serve similar functions. Trustees have what the law calls a *fiduciary responsibility* for assets placed in their care through a trust, and personal representatives have this same responsibility for assets entrusted to them through a will (or through a court if there is no will). In order to protect ourselves from tripping over a lot of extra words, for the rest of this section we'll refer to both trustees and personal representatives as *fiduciaries*. Similarly, for convenience' sake, we'll use the term *donor* to refer to the person who's giving assets to a fiduciary to care for, whether via will or via trust.

What exactly is a *fiduciary?* The dictionary defines fiduciary as "a person who stands in a special relation of trust, confidence, or responsibility in his obligations to others." The "others" in this case are the beneficiaries named by the donor. The law requires a fiduciary to place the interests of the beneficiaries ahead of his own interests in dealing with the assets entrusted to him, to act prudently to conserve and protect those assets, and to confine his actions to the scope of the authority granted him by law or by the will or trust appointing him.

Thus, a fiduciary's powers—the things she can or cannot do with the assets under her control, such as buying, selling, lending, gifting, and so on—are limited by law in every state. The limits vary from state to state, and sometimes there are different restrictions placed on personal representatives than on trustees. While these restrictions are intended to protect beneficiaries' interests in their assets, they sometimes prove to be a little too restrictive. Donors therefore usually are allowed to grant their fiduciaries broader powers than those authorized under state law, and this is fairly standard practice in most wills and trusts. The power granted has to be specific and unambiguous, however. Be sure to discuss with your estate planner the powers you want to give to your fiduciary.

EXAMPLE

In some states, a fiduciary can only invest assets through federally insured institutions (e.g., banks or credit unions). While the logic behind this restriction is fairly understandable, it unnecessarily makes for inferior returns in many situations. Consequently, many people authorize their fiduciaries to invest in publicly traded stocks, bonds, or mutual funds.

Traditionally, a fiduciary's responsibility was to *conserve* the assets entrusted to him or her, as the example above suggests. However, a more modern reading of the fiduciary's role is to *manage* those assets. This suggests that there can be a role for prudent risk-taking in the fiduciary process. Of course, there's a difference between investing in blue-chip stocks and cattle futures (Hillary Clinton, call your broker), but that's where the "prudence" part comes in. Fiduciaries need to have excellent judgment, and they should be authorized to engage the services of competent professionals to augment and inform that judgment.

Fiduciaries have other responsibilities besides managing assets. Generally, they must keep good records and periodically provide an accounting of the assets they manage to the beneficiaries, and sometimes to the donor. They must file returns and pay any taxes that are imposed on the assets and income of the trust or estate. They must carry out all of the instructions in the will or trust that appointed them regarding whether, when, how, and to whom to distribute the assets they manage or the income from those assets. Finally, if the fiduciary is a personal representative, he or she also is responsible for seeing to it that all the steps explained in distributions of property and the probate process in the "Estate Planning Basics" section are undertaken—petitioning the court to open the estate and to serve as personal representative, marshaling the decedent's assets and notifying all creditors and beneficiaries, paying taxes, providing the court and the beneficiaries with an accounting, selling and distributing assets, and closing out the estate.

Note that personal representatives must petition the court for approval to serve. The court can reject that request if the beneficiaries raise strong and valid objections or if the proposed fiduciary fails to qualify under the state's laws or the court's rules. Courts prefer to have clear jurisdiction over the people they appoint as personal representatives, so it usually is a good idea to name someone who resides in the state where the will is to be probated. This problem can be overcome in many states if the fiduciary designates a local agent to receive court orders (called *service of process* in legalese). But, if you think your choice for personal representative is going to be controversial, why give the court one more thing to be concerned about? Name a local as your fiduciary if at all possible. Some states require that your personal representative be a U.S. citizen, and will not approve him or her to serve if there is a criminal record involved. As is so often the case in the estate planning process, these rules can vary from state to state, so be sure to ask your estate planner about the specifics in your state. You also should note that some of these restrictions don't apply to trustees, providing yet another reason to opt for trusts over wills in your estate planning.

From the brief discussion so far, you can see that the law takes the role of a fiduciary very seriously, and with good reason. So should you. The person you name as a fiduciary is entrusted with considerable responsibility and considerable power over your assets. You therefore need to choose carefully who will serve as your fiduciary.

People generally tend to turn to a spouse, other loved one, or friend to serve as their fiduciary. This usually is an appropriate choice. However, if an estate is particularly complicated, or if a will or trust contains provisions that are likely to be unexpected or unpopular among the beneficiaries, it may be wise to consider the services of a disinterested third party. Banks, brokerage houses, attorneys, and accountants usually all are willing to take on this role—for a fee, of course. If your estate planning is complex or nontraditional, however, these professional fees can be money well spent. Professionals bring a certain distance and objectivity to their role, making it harder for emotional responses from beneficiaries to prevail. This is a good time to point out one more time that death causes even good people to behave strangely. In dealing with death and money, bizarre accusations can and do fly, and even the best of families sometimes suspect the worst of each other. It is far less likely that a disgruntled beneficiary will be able to claim that a professional serving in a fiduciary capacity has a conflict of interest impairing his performance—a claim not altogether unheard of when the fiduciary is close to the donor, but not necessarily to one or more of the beneficiaries. Do the names Cain and Abel ring any bells?

If your estate planning is complex or nontraditional, some professionals recommend that you consider naming a professional as a joint fiduciary along with a family member or friend. This approach sometimes can combine the best of both worlds, offering both detached objectivity and familial comfort in tense situations. Other professionals, however, are strongly opposed to the co-fiduciary concept. If the co-fiduciaries disagree, your affairs quickly can become bogged down by the disagreement. This is a real risk, and one you should take seriously. At a minimum, you should discuss the co-fiduciary concept with both the professional and the friend or loved one you have in mind, and ask them to discuss it with each other. If you sense any possibility of difficulty, err on the side of caution. If your estate planning requires a professional fiduciary, drop the idea of the friend or loved one serving jointly. Remember, this isn't a popularity contest, it's a job—and a critical one, at that. Anyway, you have a much better chance of making people feel good about you if you name them as beneficiaries, not fiduciaries!

One other thing: Don't be afraid to shop around for professional fiduciary services. Accountants in particular sometimes make wonderfully objective and prudent fiduciaries, often at a fee far more reasonable than some of the other professional options. Ask several people what they charge, and don't assume that the professional drafting your estate plan or its supporting documents has to be the fiduciary. In fact, if one of them tries to tell you they do need to be named as fiduciary, you need to find a new advisor—fast!

OUR ISSUES

Whom to Choose?

Naming fiduciaries can be a risky proposition for lesbians and gay men who expect their estate planning wishes to be questioned by homophobic family members. And, once again, even if you think your family is supportive, that premise is nowhere put to the test quite like it is when you die. The stakes are even higher for a gay couple, who presumably would be inclined to name each other as their fiduciaries.

Historically, courts took a dim view of this, and sometimes would not allow domestic partners to serve as fiduciaries. The situation got particularly tricky if the partner/fiduciary also was a beneficiary, which of course was generally the case. It became very easy to read "conflicts of interest" and "undue influence" into such arrangements, and courts could use these arguments to remove partners as fiduciaries—or worse yet, as beneficiaries. Things have been better for most of our community for several years now, but you should discuss the issue with your estate planner to see if there are any potential problems with the rules or the courts where you live. Be certain that your estate planner is well versed not only with how these issues apply in theory in your state, but, more importantly, how they're applied in practice by local courts. If you have an unusual situation and there is a concern that you may be faced with a homophobic probate court, there are steps you can take to minimize the risks. Truth to tell, these steps should be prudent components of the estate plans of most lesbians and gay men, anyway.

First, revisit the will-versus-trust issue one more time. If you know local judges won't be sympathetic, use a trust or other will substitute to minimize the potential damage they can do. Next, name an alternate fiduciary to serve in the event a court does disallow or remove your first choice. A professional fiduciary is a real good idea here; it would be very hard for a judge to question a professional's objectivity. Finally, you might consider including language in your estate planning documents indicating that, if there's a conflict between having a friend or lover as both a fiduciary and a beneficiary, that the beneficiary role take precedence. Taken together, these steps usually should ensure that no one can do any lasting damage no matter how hard they try.

If you've become unduly concerned about all of this, let's step back and gain some perspective. It is the 1990s, after all, and even ignorant judges are only going to go so far to upset the apple cart. If your estate planning documents are tightly drafted and properly executed, the odds of the issue ever even arising are remote, and the odds of a judge ruling against you are only slightly less so. Even the most unenlightened judge dislikes getting overturned on appeal more than he dislikes homosexuals. Of course, court battles—even successful ones—are expensive. It's the job of the estate planning process to prepare for the million-to-one shots, however, and that's really the point of this discussion. All of this also highlights the need to be certain the lawyer responsible for your documents is a tight drafter and a proper executor.

RELATED TOPICS

To gain a big picture perspective on the role fiduciaries play in wills and trusts, review the discussion of each in the "Wills and Will Substitutes" section on page 302.

Powers of attorney grant fiduciary powers to the person they name as attorney-in-fact, and most of the guidelines above can be helpful when selecting an attorney-in-fact. (One important exception: Co-fiduciaries are rarely a good idea for powers of attorney. The comparatively "urgent" nature of powers militates in favor of a single decision maker.) Powers of attorney can be granted for any purpose, but they most often are used today to enable people to designate someone to make financial and health care decisions for them in the event of their incapacity. The mechanics of powers are explained in the "Powers of Attorney" section on page 348, and the "Advance Directives (Living Wills) and Health Care Powers" section on page 354.

7

CHAPTER

Other Planning Issues

INTRODUCTION: THE NEED FOR COLLATERAL DOCUMENTS

In addition to traditional estate planning documents, the uncertain legal status of lesbians, gay men, and their relationships forces many of us to consider the need for a number of so-called collateral planning documents. Many of these documents increase our ability to ensure that our preferences and relationships are respected in the event of our illness or death: powers of attorney for financial matters, health care powers of attorney, advance medical directives, living wills, and directives regarding the disposition of our remains when we die. For some of us, circumstances also dictate a need to plan for the contingency that a relationship will end. Domestic partnership agreements are as much a reality for our community as prenuptial agreements are for the dominant culture.

While our community tends to perceive many of these planning issues in terms of significant others cruelly shut out from the decision-making process in times of crisis by a partner's hostile relatives, it is important to remember that gay people have built families of many kinds. Even if you are not part of a "couple," it is possible there are people in your life you trust more than your family to make important decisions in times of crisis. The law will not honor your priorities unless you articulate them clearly and properly in advance. Don't think that just because you haven't found Prince Charming yet, nothing in this chapter applies to you.

It also is important to remember that the documents we are going to discuss are largely creatures of state law. Whether these documents are available in your state, and the extent to which they will be respected by a potentially homophobic legal system, vary widely. It is critical that you seek competent and well-informed legal advice when you do planning in this area.

GENERAL POWERS OF ATTORNEY

THE STRAIGHT FACTS

A *power of attorney* is a document that authorizes another person to act on your behalf. There is a unique syntax to the world of powers of attorney, so some initial definitions are in order. The person granting the power of attorney to another is called the *principal.* The person receiving the power is called the *attorney-in-fact* (some people refer to this person as the *agent,* but attorney-in-fact is more precise). Although the document is known as a power of attorney, we'll refer to it as the *power* or the *powers* for short. Powers can be as broad or narrow as the principal desires. They can take effect immediately upon execution of the document, or they can be triggered by the principal's incapacity or incompetence. How broad the powers should be, and when they should be effective, depend on what they're to be used for and to whom you're granting them. We'll look at these issues in detail throughout this section.

Granting Powers

A general power of attorney gives another person the authority to transact business on your behalf. It usually gives your attorney-in-fact access to your bank and brokerage accounts, the authority to sell property on your behalf, the authority to deal with insurance companies, and generally the authority to handle any other aspect of your financial affairs on your behalf. The process for drafting powers is becoming increasingly technical and sophisticated, so lawyers now frequently include detailed lists of the powers a principal is granting. A principal gives an attorney-in-fact extraordinary powers, so it is critical that you choose your attorney-in-fact carefully.

While most principals choose to grant broad powers to their attorneys-in-fact, nothing requires you to do so. You can limit a power to a specific asset or group of assets, exclude a particular asset or group of assets from a broad delegation of powers, or even execute a power limited to one specific transaction. If the purpose of your power of attorney is to provide for the management of your financial affairs in the event you are unable to do so yourself, limiting your powers may not make very good sense. However, in unique circumstances, it is helpful to know you have the flexibility to draft powers to suit your needs.

EXAMPLE

Maxine and Dianna are life partners. Maxine is the sole proprietor of a landscaping business; Will is her key employee. Dianna, a gastroenterologist, knows little about landscaping, and, beyond being generally supportive of her life partner, has shown little interest in acquiring such knowledge. After consulting with Dianna, Will, and her lawyer, Maxine decides to give Will a power of attorney with regard to her business, and Dianna a power for all other financial matters.

Watch out for this potential gift tax trap, though: If a power of attorney is not drafted properly, the IRS might try to reclassify it as a gift from the principal to the attorney-in-fact. To avoid this possibility, make sure your attorney-in-fact is prohibited from exercising the powers you grant her in favor of herself or her creditors.

When Powers Are Effective

Unless your document specifies otherwise, a power of attorney is effective upon execution. Historically, powers were used to enable principals to have business transacted at a distance. An attorney-in-fact could act on behalf of a faraway principal, or he could serve in the event of a principal's extended absence. While modern transportation and communications largely have vitiated this use of the power of attorney, the properly drafted power remains a very effective way to ensure that your finances are seen to in the event of your illness, incapacity, or disability. Since the purpose of most modern powers is to plan ahead for incapacity, it usually makes little sense to have them become effective prior to one's incapacity. Most powers with this delayed effective date contain a provision requiring certification by the principal's health care provider that the principal is incapacitated before the powers can come into effect. Since obtaining such a certification can raise difficulties of its own, couples designating each other as their attorneys-in-fact for whom there are no trustworthiness concerns may choose to make the powers effective immediately upon execution as a matter of convenience. You should discuss this matter thoroughly with the lawyer drafting your power of attorney early in the process.

Duration

Historically, powers of attorney only were valid while the principal was of sound mind; they did not "survive" her incapacity. While this limitation made sense when powers were used to facilitate the business transactions of distant principals, it doesn't help modern principals whose goal is to plan for their incapacity. All states now permit powers to survive a principal's incapacity, provided that the document specifically states that the principal intends this result. This is called a *durable power of attorney,* and it is the form that most powers take when drafted as a tool for incapacity planning.

Execution Formalities

Powers of attorney are governed by state law, and what the law requires in order for a power to be valid varies widely from state to state. It is important that your power of attorney be executed in compliance with your state's legal requirements. These execution formalities usually cover witness or notarization requirements, but it is important that you comply with all requirements regardless of the form they take. Also, if you routinely reside in more than one state, ideally you should execute separate powers in and for each state. At a realistic minimum, however, make sure your power of attorney satisfies the execution formalities of the stricter state.

Revoking Powers

If for whatever reason you decide to revoke a power you've granted, be sure your efforts to do so are thorough. First, destroy the original. Next, retrieve and destroy all copies, or at least all copies for which it is feasible to do so. Finally, communicate your revocation to all third parties who should know about it, especially those you previously told about the powers, keeping copies of those letters for your permanent files. If your revocation is motivated by a change of heart as to the trustworthiness of your attorney-in-fact, you probably should communicate the revocation to all third parties you reasonably believe might be presented with the document, regardless of whether you informed them of the powers' original existence.

OUR ISSUES

Substitute "I Do's"

For lesbian and gay couples, a power of attorney is an important thread in the patchwork of legal protections we must build for ourselves. These protections come automatically for married couples. Presumably, one's life partner would be one's preferred decision maker in times of crisis, but that only can happen if it's planned for ahead of time. You've read it before, and you'll probably read it again before you finish this book: A crisis can cause the best, most supportive family members to behave irrationally. The law will not respect our relationships unless we force it to. Combined with the other documents and techniques discussed in this book, the durable power of attorney for financial matters is designed to ensure that respect.

Everybody Needs Somebody Sometime

Single lesbians and gay men often share the same need for an attorney-in-fact as their "coupled" counterparts. The specter of illness is, of course, a very real issue for many in our community. Beyond that, however, lies the real risk for many of us that, if we suddenly found ourselves incapacitated, our financial decisions might not be made in accordance with our wishes or by people who respect our priorities. It is quite likely that, absent a power of attorney, family members who may or may not be supportive of our lifestyles and sensitive to our needs will be called on to handle our finances in the event of an emergency. All lesbians and gay men should consider carefully the need for a power of attorney. While it is essential for those of us with significant others, it likely is equally critical for many of the rest of us. Appointing a trusted friend or business adviser as our attorney-in-fact may better serve our needs than relying on the judgment of family members.

Having Your Powers Honored

One of the potentially most frustrating aspects of being an attorney-in-fact is that, when you really need it, any power of attorney is only as good as the person or institution you're asking to honor it believes it to be. Not infrequently, for example, an attorney-in-fact will present her power to a bank in an attempt to transact some business regarding her principal's account only to be told that the power "must be on the bank's form." While this requirement seldom proves to be ironclad, it does illustrate a serious limitation of powers of attorney. Even the most comprehensive, tightly drafted document does not offer 100 percent assurance of acceptance by the third parties to whom it is presented. Fortunately, as we'll see shortly, there are concrete steps you can take to minimize this problem, but it's important to understand ahead of time that there are no guarantees.

Before we get into specific techniques you can employ to minimize the risk that your powers won't be honored, it's helpful to know why this is an issue. In this way, we can make intelligent choices about how to prevent it from happening in the first place. The overwhelming reason third parties refuse to honor powers of attorney is a fear of being sued by the principal if something goes wrong. Frequently, the third party has no way of knowing whether a power is valid. The principal could have revoked it, it may have been obtained under fraud or duress, or it may contain language an institution's lawyers are unfamiliar or uncomfortable with. If someone honors an invalid power, or acts beyond its scope, and the principal loses money or other property as a result, there is a real risk that the third party will be sued by the principal. Third parties therefore are understandably cautious in honoring powers of attorney.

What can you do to allay the concerns of those who will be asked by your attorney-in-fact to honor your power of attorney? First, send copies of your executed powers to all your bankers, brokers, insurance agents, and other financial advisers. Ask them to put the copy in your file. This way, those third parties who you know will be asked to deal with your attorney-in-fact are put on early notice as to your true intentions.

Next, be sure there's language in your power promising to "hold harmless" any individual or institution who acts in reliance on the power. Essentially, this is your promise not to sue anybody who acts within the scope of the written document. It's another level of assurance for third parties that they aren't risking a lawsuit if they honor your powers.

Another good way to ease a third party's mind with regard to the legitimacy of your power of attorney is to include a sample of your attorney-in-fact's signature in the document. This sample is called an *exemplar.* In this way, the third party can compare the sample signature in the document with the signature of the person presenting it, gaining a high level of confidence that he or she is dealing with the person you've designated to act on your behalf.

You also should keep your power of attorney "fresh" by reexecuting it periodically. A dated power is likely to make third parties nervous, whereas a recently executed power gives greater assurance that it remains in effect. Ideally, don't let your power get more than five years old without reexecuting it.

Finally, if you've done all these things and your attorney-in-fact still is having difficulty getting a power honored, it may be necessary for him or her to do some delicate negotiating. First, an attorney-in-fact should never take an initial "no" as an institution's final answer. It is quite likely that a front-line employee who declines to honor a power either is afraid to or is prohibited from accepting responsibility for acting otherwise. If you are an attorney-in-fact who finds herself in this situation, politely ask to speak to the employee's supervisor. If necessary, ask the supervisor to contact the legal department. If your principal has followed the steps above, and you remind the supervisor that the principal has done so, they will be hard-pressed to maintain their position. If there are significant assets involved, you also might try to gently remind the third parties you are dealing with that those assets are in your control, and that if they can't find a way to work with you, you ultimately will find an institution that can.

RELATED TOPICS

Joint ownership of assets can eliminate the need for powers of attorney, at least for those assets and accounts owned jointly. While this planning technique can't work for everybody or for all situations, and needs to be used carefully, it is an important tool. The pros, cons, and pitfalls of joint ownership are explained in the "Joint Ownership of Property" section on page 309.

Choosing an attorney-in-fact is very similar to choosing any other fiduciary. See the "Choosing a Trustee and/or Personal Representative" discussion on page 340 for some thoughts on this important decision.

Advance directives and health care powers of attorney are also critical components in planning for disability or incapacity. These documents should be drafted independently of the general power of attorney for financial matters. They are explained in the "Advance Directives (Living Wills) and Health Care Powers" section on page 354.

ADVANCE DIRECTIVES (LIVING WILLS) AND HEALTH CARE POWERS

THE STRAIGHT FACTS

Financial matters aren't the only concerns a person can have in the event of incapacity. Interacting with the health care behemoth becomes a major concern for those within its grasp. Decisions regarding medical treatment, termination of medical treatment, and the use of life-sustaining measures need to be made routinely in a health care emergency. In the event you are unable to make these decisions, it is critical that you express your preferences clearly and correctly while you are healthy, and that, if you wish to designate someone else to make medical decisions for you, you do so in advance. In the absence of such documents, it is a patient's next of kin or the system itself that will make all health care decisions.

There are different documents to accomplish different purposes within the health care system, and we'll take a look at each. It's important to remember, however, that as with so many of these documents, the form and content of anything you sign will be determined largely by the laws of your state. Be sure you're working with a well-informed planner in order to get the combination of documents right for you. Another point to keep in mind regarding state laws: In many states, the statutes authorizing these documents provide recommended language for health care powers or living wills. In a few states, however, the law provides mandatory language you must use in order for your document to be valid. Be sure your lawyer knows the score in your state.

Health Care Powers of Attorney

A durable power of attorney for health care matters functions in the medical realm in about the same way general powers of attorney function in the financial realm. A principal grants powers to an attorney-in-fact to make health care decisions in the event the principal is unable to do so for herself. Accordingly, many of the same rules and techniques we discussed in the last section are applicable here. The rules regarding durability, execution, and revocation of health care powers usually are identical to those for financial powers. The powers granted to an attorney-in-fact for health care decisions can be broad or limited, although it is almost always advisable to grant the broadest possible powers. Health care providers are understandably litigation-shy, and the more assurances you can give them in your document, the better.

As with financial powers, the list of specific powers granted in a health care power of attorney is ever-increasing. At a minimum, your powers should specifically authorize your attorney-in-fact to consent to treatment, to refuse treatment, to withdraw treatment, to take these actions even if the medical establishment advises to the contrary, to discharge any health care provider, and to discharge you from a health care facility, even if doing so is contrary to medical advice.

When you consider this list of powers, it once again becomes clear that you are placing paramount confidence in your attorney-in-fact, perhaps more so even than in financial matters. You may be quite literally trusting this person with your life. Clearly, you should have a great deal of faith in the person you designate as your attorney-in-fact. More than that, however, you should take the time to ensure that you make this person intimately familiar with your wishes, preferences, and priorities in health care matters.

As with other financial powers of attorney, health care powers also need to be drafted so they are durable. They must be written to state your intention that they survive your incapacity. After all, a health care power will do you and your attorney-in-fact little good if it's not valid when you're incapacitated.

Keep in mind that a health care power is not the same thing as an advance medical directive or so-called living will. However, there can be an overlap between health care powers and advance medical directives. We'll look at this after we cover the basics of living wills.

Advance Medical Directives (Living Wills)

Many people have a basic understanding of advance medical directives, more generally known as *living wills,* as documents that tell doctors and hospitals not to prolong their lives by using artificial means in the event they become terminally or incurably ill or injured, or lapse into what the medical profession sometimes refers to as a "chronic vegetative state." When you can't speak for yourself, the living will tells the health care system what treatments you do not consent to. While this is more or less accurate, there is a lot more to living wills than meets the eye. For example, which medical procedures are "artificial" and which ones aren't? When are you terminally ill, or when is your vegetative state "chronic"? These are hard questions, and the ethical—and legal—implications of answering them incorrectly are profound.

A key aspect of a good living will is a clear statement of what procedures you want withheld and under what circumstances. Within the confines of your state's laws, your living will should spell out specifically which procedures you wish withheld in the event you are terminally ill and incapable of granting or withholding consent. These include such procedures as artificial respiration or ventilation, heart pumps, dialysis, the administration of food and water, and the administration of pain-killing medications. In many states, if you fail to specify your preferences, there is a "default" preference the health care provider will be required to follow. This default may be at odds with your personal wishes, so it is best to be as specific as possible.

EXAMPLE

In some states, you must specify that food and water are to be withheld or they will automatically be administered. If you live in such a state and would not want your life "artificially" prolonged by the mechanical administration of food and water, your living will would need to be drafted to indicate such a preference. Otherwise, a hospital in your state would be required to administer food and water to you.

It is important to understand that your state's laws may not permit you to prohibit certain acts that in your view artificially prolong your life. To continue with the example above, in some states it may be a violation of "public policy" for a hospital to withhold food and water, regardless of what your living will stipulates. Your attorney should be able to help you nail down what you can and cannot direct in advance under the laws of your state with regard to life-sustaining procedures.

There also are likely to be provisions in your state's laws regarding how it is determined that your condition is "terminal," "incurable," or "chronic." These provisions usually specify how many physicians have to make what kind of determination regarding your medical condition before the provisions of your living will come into play. It's likely that you'll include these provisions in the language of your document, anyway, but be sure what your living will says is consistent with applicable laws in your state.

Because of the obvious gravity of the decisions contained in a living will, each state usually prescribes a set of execution formalities that must be followed for a living will to be valid. Usually, in addition to clearly articulating what procedures you do not want performed on you, these formalities require a certain number of witnesses. The law in most states also requires that these witnesses not be related to you by blood or marriage, that they not work for any of your health care providers, that they are not your creditors or employees of your creditors, and that they have no financial interest in your death. In short, as with all estate planning documents, it is critical that your witnesses be totally disinterested parties.

Combining Living Wills and Health Care Powers

It's important to understand that there are no ironclad guarantees that a living will is going to be honored in all situations. In some states, living wills are only "advisory" or a "guide" for your health care providers. Occasionally, a health care provider will determine that some circumstance prevents the living will from coming into operation. He, she, or they may be unsure as to the incurability of your condition, or the legal implications of honoring your living will and, in effect, ending your life. This is rare, but it can happen, and usually with tragic consequences. The best way to minimize the possibility of such an unfortunate outcome is to execute both a living will and a health care power. That way, if the medical establishment cannot or will not honor your wishes, your power-of-attorney can use his or her authority to either litigate the issue or change your health care providers. In some states, the durable health care power of attorney is the "stronger" of the two documents. Thus, the combination of a living will and a health care power is about as close as one gets to a guarantee in these matters.

Having Your Wishes Respected

As we discussed in connection with financial powers of attorney, in a crisis, health care powers and advance directives, even if expertly drafted, only will be as valid as the person presented with them believes them to be. Accordingly, most of the tips provided in the last section of this chapter apply here. Once you execute a health care power or living will, it is critical that you send copies to all your health care providers and ask them to place them in your file. Next, keep these documents "fresh" by reexecuting them periodically. Also, a "hold harmless" clause is a very good idea, as is an exemplar of your attorney-in-fact's signature. Keep in mind, however, that you should not include either of these provisions in your documents if doing so runs contrary to mandatory language in your state's laws. If there's a required format in your state, always follow it.

OUR ISSUES

Lesbian and gay people need to prepare for three particular contingencies with regard to health care.

1. Providing instructions regarding life-sustaining procedures.
2. Designating who will make health care decisions for us in the event of our incapacity.
3. Ensuring that those individuals important to us have access to us while we are incapacitated.

We'll look at each of these issues separately.

Living Wills

The lesbian and gay community faces more or less the same issue with regard to living wills as the dominant culture: attempting to stop the medical juggernaut from overriding our preferences regarding quality of life and life-sustaining measures. In the absence of a valid living will, the health care establishment sometimes sees fit to ignore the decisions of even biological next of kin in these matters. It therefore is critical that any person who does not wish to receive extraordinary life-sustaining measures properly executes the necessary paperwork.

Designating an Attorney-in-Fact for Health Care Decisions

If you are incapable of making medical decisions for yourself, your next of kin usually are authorized to make these decisions for you. This means your spouse if you're married, your parents or children if you're not. (Of course, as we just discussed, the medical establishment may not always honor the "pull-the-plug" decisions of even biological families. This is why it is so important to have both an advance directive and a health care power.) Note that, as we've seen to our dismay so many times throughout this book, if you are in a gay relationship, your partner is not your next of kin for these purposes. Therefore, it's critical for couples to execute durable powers of attorney for health care naming each other as their attorneys-in-fact. Single gays, however, also should consider naming an individual of their own choosing to make health care decisions if they can't. This is particularly true for lesbians and gay men who may be estranged from their birth families and/or who have established alternative families of their own.

Priority of Visitation

There's one other aspect of interacting with the health care system that is of critical importance to gay people and unique to our circumstances. When one is in a hospital or other in-patient facility, it traditionally is one's biological next of kin who decides who gets to visit and when (within medical limits, of course). Lesbians and gay men can find themselves cut off from their life partners in devastating ways by family members who have barred them from hospital rooms and so on. If the horror of this is not real for you, recall the case of Sharon Kowalski and Karen Thompson, who were separated for years during a medical crisis by homophobic parents and a homophobic court system, despite medical evidence that their visits were therapeutic. Sharon and Karen were reunited, but only after a protracted, emotionally draining, and expensive legal battle. It's very likely this could have been avoided through the use of health care powers. Sharon and Karen didn't know this, but now you do!

Although there can be no ironclad guarantee that it will be honored, it is critical that your health care powers grant to your attorney-in-fact what's known as a *priority of visitation*. A priority of visitation basically says that your attorney-in-fact gets to see you before anyone else, including biological family members. It usually also gives your attorney-in-fact the power to decide who else can—and cannot—visit you. It's important that the wording of this power be brutally direct. Language such as "in preference over my blood relatives" is not out of line.

If you think about it for a second, you'll see that a priority of visitation gives your attorney-in-fact a tremendous tool to help control a tense family situation. It also flies in the face of the most sacred of conventions—the family. So you can't mince words to spare a relative's feelings, no matter how tempted you may be to do so. After all, if you think about it for another second, you'll also realize this is the same power straight couples get just by saying "I Do."

There may be one or two judges out there who would construe a priority of visitation granted to a gay partner as a "violation of public policy" and therefore unenforceable. You should discuss this possibility with the lawyer drafting your documents. In the long run, however, you still are immeasurably better off planning ahead.

RELATED TOPICS

Choosing an attorney-in-fact is a very serious decision. Lesbian and gay couples presumably will name each other to serve as their attorneys-in-fact. For others, the decision can be a lot more complicated. Many of the concepts explored in the "Choosing a Trustee and/or Personal Representative" section on page 340 are applicable here.

The many similarities between health care powers and financial powers were noted in this section. Financial powers are explained in detail in the "General Powers of Attorney" section on page 348.

DIRECTIVES REGARDING DISPOSITION OF REMAINS

THE STRAIGHT FACTS

In all states, decisions regarding a decedent's final arrangements are made by the person's next of kin. At the same time, although durable powers of attorney survive a person's incapacity, they do not survive his or her death. To put it more bluntly, they expire when the principal does. Accordingly, a power of attorney cannot be used to direct the disposition of a principal's remains. In some states, a person can execute a document directing the disposition of their remains or authorizing another person to make those arrangements for them. Usually, final arrangements are also discussed (and paid for) through a person's will and/or living trust.

OUR ISSUES

Under no state laws are lesbian or gay life partners considered next of kin for purposes of making a partner's final arrangements. This limitation can combine with the circumstances outlined above to create a critical gap in the ability of lesbians and gay men to plan their final affairs. In the absence of an "advance directive" for final arrangements, it may be difficult for a gay person to have respected his or her wishes regarding burial, cremation, memorial services, and so on. This creates a clear problem for the surviving partner in a lesbian or gay couple, but it also can present difficulties for any gay person whose family may not respect his or her wishes. It even is possible for a distraught or homophobic family to exclude altogether a surviving partner from his or her deceased partner's final arrangements.

There are a limited number of strategies for minimizing the impact of this situation. Of course, if you live in a state that recognizes documents to designate an agent or otherwise leave instructions for disposing of your final remains, you should by all means execute one. If you do not, it may be possible to "preplan" your final arrangements, to use the terminology of the funeral industry folks. In preplanning, you essentially make all your funeral arrangements yourself—in advance, of course. You should enlist the assistance of a local gay-friendly funeral director if this approach makes sense for you.

Alternatively, if it is not possible or practical for you to isolate your biological family from the process, there are ways in which you can attempt to influence their behavior through the power of your purse strings. Your will and/or living trust usually will contain provisions regarding the payment of your funeral expenses. It is possible in most states to stipulate the circumstances under which your final arrangements will be paid out of your estate. Unless your next of kin are independently wealthy, the prospect of having to pay by themselves the significant sums associated with even modest funerals should they fail to comply with your wishes usually encourages them to do things your way (or your partner's). Whether or not this technique will work for you depends largely on the laws in your state. Be sure and discuss this with your estate planner.

This may seem like a ghoulish topic to some, but the consequences of failing to prepare for it ahead of time can be even more frightening. Again, at the risk of being repetitive, death causes even good people to behave badly. You cannot guarantee that your family will honor your wishes and include your alternative family unless you do everything possible ahead of time to force them to do so. You certainly can't ignore this reality if your family has already demonstrated it is less than supportive. If you are in a relationship, you presumably want to minimize the additional sources of grief for your life partner by making your preferences in this sensitive area as clear and ironclad as possible.

RELATED TOPICS

Most wills contain a clause regarding the payment of funeral expenses. As was suggested above, this may provide you with an indirect opportunity to ensure that your birth family honors your wishes and includes your significant other in making your final arrangements. The mechanics of such a clause are discussed in the "Wills" section on page 302.

Because they offer your trustee greater discretion and invite less court supervision, revocable living trusts may provide even more flexibility than wills in dealing with the issue of your final arrangements. They are explained in the "Revocable Living Trusts as Will Substitutes" section on page 313.

DOMESTIC PARTNERSHIP AGREEMENTS

THE STRAIGHT FACTS

When a couple gets married, the state hands them a domestic partnership agreement in the form of the various laws governing the sharing of assets, income, and expenses. For an unmarried couple, however, there are few, if any, laws governing the sharing of assets, income, and expenses. Such a couple needs a domestic partnership agreement in order to set adequate ground rules for such matters.

OUR ISSUES

Should We or Shouldn't We?

Whether or not to enter into a domestic partnership agreement is probably one of the most difficult choices a lesbian or gay couple must make. This is not to suggest that the decision to actually form the domestic partnership will be difficult. It's just that writing down how it should end can prove delicate, to say the least. First, it's likely the two partners will not approach the project with the same level of enthusiasm. Put another way, one is likely to be more keen on the idea than the other. This will quickly raise suspicions, questions of trust and commitment, and a host of similar emotions poorly suited to the nesting phase of any relationship. Next, it is likely to bring to the surface any economic disparities between partners (assuming that these issues haven't arisen already). Lastly comes the inevitable objection: A domestic partnership agreement is like admitting in advance that the relationship isn't going to work.

It's likely the therapists among us would note that the existence of these issues suggests the exercise of hammering out a domestic partnership agreement is an ideal way to work them out. Even if you're not a therapy groupie, however, the response to these objections is compelling. There are no rules when it comes to lesbian and gay relationships, so at every step of the way we have to write our own. The end of a relationship, while not a pleasant possibility to contemplate, is no exception—we must once again write our own rules. This being the case, when is the better time to write them: when the parties are on good terms or on bad terms? Moreover, who's more qualified to write them: you and your significant other or a judge?

It may be helpful to keep a little perspective here. In some sense, the decision regarding the domestic partnership agreement is not altogether unlike the prenuptial agreements many heterosexuals enter into shortly before the "I Do's." If these agreements make sense for people who receive all the legal trimmings that come with marriage, doesn't it seem reasonable to assume that we need them at least as much?

Income and Expenses

Of course, some couples don't need much convincing with regard to the advisability of a domestic partnership agreement. They're ready to proceed right on to the next phase of the process: deciding what approach to take with an agreement. Is the domestic partnership a Ward and June

Cleaver marriage, where all financial resources are pooled and all expenses paid from these common funds? Or, will each partner contribute from separate accounts to pay only for joint expenses—rent, utilities, food, vacations? Will all joint assets be owned equally or in proportion to each partner's contributions? These issues need to be resolved and spelled out clearly in the agreement.

What Assets to Cover

There are three categories of property that you'll want to cover in your agreement. You may decide to treat each category differently, so you'll want to discuss them separately in the agreement. The first category is the property you each bring into the relationship. Usually, the domestic partnership agreement would stipulate that such assets are the separate property of the individual partner who owned them. The second category of property is assets received by inheritance or gift during the relationship. Usually, these assets also remain the separate property of the receiving partner. The third category is assets acquired during the relationship. Usually, domestic partnership agreements specify either that these assets are owned equally or in proportion to each partner's contribution toward them.

A Quick Word about What Not to Cover

Again, you're writing your own rules here, so your domestic partnership agreement can be as detailed and flexible as you both want. However, as a general rule, only the financial arrangements will be enforceable. Accordingly, morally binding provisions—who does the dishes, who walks the dog, and so on—usually should only be spelled out, if at all, in a separate document. And never, never, never include provisions governing sexual matters in your documents. There's a name for such an arrangement and it usually comes with a fine or prison time.

You're Never Too Old

People usually think of domestic partnership agreements as coming in the early stages of a relationship. But, in truth, you usually can draft an agreement at any point in the relationship. Sometimes, a change in life circumstances can trigger a need on the part of one or both partners that never was felt before. Don't read too much into such a need, but don't suppress it, either. It's never too late to execute a domestic partnership agreement. More than one couple has found the exercise to be just what the doctor ordered to clarify many aspects of long-standing relationships.

Buying a House Together

For many lesbian and gay couples, the joint purchase of a home is the most significant financial decision the two make together. There are a few things to consider before you take this plunge, however. First, remember real estate is an illiquid investment. If the relationship is still young, there is a real risk that you will not be able to sell a house quickly if things don't work out. Moreover, in an era of stagnant real estate values, it is quite likely that, only a year or two later, you will be unable to sell your house for much more than you paid for it. These stagnant prices, combined with the high selling costs associated with real estate, easily could turn the transaction into a significant net loss. If the relationship is still new, or not as stable as you might like, think long and hard before you plunge into the housing market—there'll be plenty of houses to choose from next year.

Going It Alone

There are self-help books on the market that maintain it is possible, indeed easy, for lesbian and gay couples to draft their own domestic partnership agreements. While this point of view may or may not be correct, the laws governing these issues vary so much from state to state that it is hard to imagine "one-size-fits-all" advice is going to be right in all cases. If financial resources are an issue, at a minimum you should elicit the assistance of a sympathetic attorney to review the agreement you've drafted; the fees for that should be doable. At the other extreme, in theory each partner should have his or her own separate counsel for the process. It technically can be a "conflict of interest" for an attorney to represent both sides to such a document, and the issues can be more than just technicalities for high-net-worth partners. In practice, most people likely will work with one good lawyer throughout the process. If you go this route, it is a good idea to be certain that the attorney you choose is well versed in how these agreements work in your state and that he or she comes with excellent references.

RELATED TOPICS

The many issues raised by the joint ownership of property are explored in the "Wills and Will Substitutes" section on page 302.

When unmarried couples change their ownership interest in property, which sometimes occurs in the context of organizing a domestic partnership, the tax law says that such a change is either a sale or a gift. If the transaction is a sale, any gain or loss must be reported on the selling party's tax return. The rules for this are highlighted in the "Income Tax Basics" section on page 161 If, on the other hand, the transfer is a gift motivated by love or emotion, see the gift tax rules discussed in the "Gifts" section on page 321.

A house or condo often is the most significant investment a domestic partnership makes. While there are unique aspects to lesbian and gay couples becoming co-mortgagors, the financial fundamentals are no different for us than for anyone else. The basics of buying a house are discussed in the "Managing Debt" section on page 19. The tax advantages are reviewed in the "Tax Deductions from Your Home" section on page 180.

CONCLUSION

Ten Key Financial Planning Strategies for Lesbians and Gay Men

Over the past several hundred pages, we've surveyed the major aspects of the financial planning process. More importantly, we've learned in detail the unique considerations lesbians and gay men (and their advisers) must bring to the planning process. While the details are complex and variable, a few broad themes emerged.

- We could be a little better about managing our money.
- The insurance industry doesn't really understand us.
- We need to do some extra planning for the financial challenges we're likely to face in retirement.
- We need to execute an arsenal of legal documents to ensure that our wishes are respected in the event of our incapacity or death.

We also saw that some of these themes take on an added dimension when we are in a relationship.

When you consider the breadth and depth of all that we've explored in this book, it's impossible to summarize succinctly all of "our issues" in the financial planning process. Nevertheless, if we reflect on the themes we've just articulated, it is possible to create a "Top 10 List" that highlights the most important financial planning strategies for lesbians and gay men. You should use this list as a reality check to be certain you haven't missed anything important, either in identifying goals or in developing planning strategies to meet those goals. So, direct from the home office in Provincetown, Massachusetts, here are the top 10 financial planning strategies for lesbians and gay men.

1. Pay Savings First (Part I)—The Emergency Fund

As we saw in the "Constructing Your Balance Sheet" section, the conventional wisdom holds that gay people aren't strong savers. To the extent this generalization is true, its first consequence is likely to be insufficient savings in the form of an emergency fund. If you do not have an emergency fund sufficient to cover four to six months' worth of your fixed and variable outflows, you are unnecessarily risking disaster. We're talking unsafe finances here, and the emergency fund is your protection—use it.

2. Pay Savings First (Part II)—Retirement Planning

At several points throughout this book, we learned that lesbians and gay men may have a little extra work to do when it comes to saving for retirement. It's likely that many of us will not have access to the support system that comes from children and grandchildren to assist in our care and other needs. This means we may need more money in retirement than other folks. For those of us in relationships, the lack of survivorship rights in noncontributory employer pensions and Social Security benefits also means we may have some extra planning to do. If any of this rings true for you, the time to start planning (and saving) for these extra needs is now. Remember, too, studies have shown that many people do not allocate enough of their portfolios to the growth vehicles that are necessary to adequately fund their long-term retirement needs. Don't "underinvest" your retirement savings.

3. Make Sure You Have Adequate Disability Insurance

Regardless of sexual orientation, people tend to underestimate the risk associated with the loss of ability to earn an income. As we saw in the "Disability Insurance" section, the chances of becoming disabled often can be greater for younger people than the chances of dying. For our community, this issue may be even more significant—especially for those of us who are not in long-term relationships. If an illness or injury were to leave you unable to work, you very well may not be able to turn to family for financial or other support. You'll have to provide for yourself whatever assistance you don't get from your family. While this added dimension to the risk exists for all gay people, it may be even more acute for single gays, who won't have the resources of a life partner to draw on—financial and otherwise (and maybe especially otherwise). Adequate disability insurance therefore is essential to protect one of your most critical assets: your income stream.

4. Don't Ignore The Paperwork (Part I)—Estate Planning Documents

As we heard loudly and clearly in the "Wills and Will Substitutes" section, no gay person should be without the proper estate planning documents—a will and/or a revocable living trust. The risks associated with relying on a homophobic court system and an always unpredictable family reaction are simply too high. Throughout the discussion of estate planning, it was emphasized that death causes erratic and unpredictable behavior among even the most supportive family members. No matter how well you think you know your family, you simply do not know how they'll react to your death. You don't know how they'll treat the alternative family you leave behind, and you don't know if they'll respect your wishes regarding the distribution of your property. You can avoid this uncertainty through proper estate planning, and you really need to do it.

5. Don't Ignore The Paperwork (Part II)—A Living Will

Similarly, an advance medical directive (living will) is essential if you want the system to respect your priorities when it comes to making fundamental decisions about prolonging your life. The gay community is probably more sensitive to the issues involved in this difficult decision than society at large. Nevertheless, many of us have not followed through on our hard-learned convictions by seeing to the necessary paperwork. If you don't have a valid living will, by all means execute one.

6. Don't Ignore The Paperwork (Part III)—Powers of Attorney

In trying to identify who to allow to make important decisions for us when we can't make them ourselves, the courts, the health care system, and financial services providers all adhere to an historical definition of family that has little relevance to the lives of many lesbians and gay men. Until something better comes along to guide these institutions, it's up to each of us to spoon-feed them our individual answers in order for them to be responsive to our needs. This is done through a power of attorney, and it's the best hope you have for making sure that the people you want are calling the shots when you can't. Powers of attorney are especially critical for couples, and every couple should execute them.

7. Don't Ignore The Paperwork (Couples Version)—Domestic Partnership Agreements

Lesbian and gay couples who own property together or otherwise combine their finances face a more serious dilemma than they may realize. If the relationship ends, there is no established legal pattern for unraveling its financially interwoven lives. In a worst case scenario, it could fall to a judge who doesn't even respect our relationships to try to find an equitable way to untangle them. In order to avoid this, we are forced to establish the ground rules ourselves in advance. This is done through a domestic partnership agreement. It is essential that every couple who does not enjoy the benefit of the legal infrastructure that comes with marriage carefully consider the need for such a document.

8. Tell Your Family about Your Estate Plan

As awkward and difficult as it may be, it is essential that you identify at least one family member to explain your estate plan to in advance. There's a good chance your preferences will be met with a reaction of anger and surprise when they're revealed after your death. Remember, as we've heard (and heard and heard), even good people get weirded out by the death of a loved one. Briefing at least one family member on your decisions while you're still alive and well makes it harder for such a reaction to carry much weight—within the family or within the courts. This is a critical step to take for gay men and lesbians in relationships, where the potential for conflict over your estate planning decisions is high (and almost certainly higher than you think).

9. Avoid an Estate Tax Trap: Keep a Paper Trail on Jointly Owned Property

Keeping assets out of the probate court is an important estate planning goal for most lesbians and gay men, and titling assets jointly with a right of survivorship often can be a good technique for achieving this goal.

However, there is an important estate tax trap to beware of when using this technique: If joint owners aren't married, the tax law assumes that the entire property was owned by the first joint owner to die. This means 100 percent—not 50 percent—of the property's value is subject to estate taxes on the first owner's death, and then again on the second owner's death. In effect, the government gets to tax half the property an extra time, just because the joint owners aren't married. The only way to avoid this result is to keep detailed and meticulous records that prove each person contributed equally to the purchase and upkeep of the property. The paperwork burden imposed by these rules is enormous, but with estate tax rates starting at 37 percent, it's worth the effort.

10. Come Out

At first blush, it may seem like bizarre advice for a book on financial planning, but in fact one of the most important things you can do to help achieve your financial goals is to come out of the closet. Until you come out, you cannot ask your employer for domestic partner benefits, you cannot ask your state legislature to provide the infrastructure that comes with legal sanction for your relationship, you cannot attack homophobic practices in the insurance industry, you cannot ask a bank or a hospital to honor your partner's power of attorney, and you cannot explain your estate plan to your family. That's just a smattering of the broad range of financial planning objectives that you'll have trouble achieving until you're out. Most important of all, however, you cannot achieve fully the desired peace of mind that brought you to the financial planning process in general and this book in particular until you never again are forced to hide who you are. Come out!

INDEX

Other books of interest from Irwin Professional Publishing . . .

CHARITABLE REMAINDER TRUSTS

A Proven Strategy for Reducing Estate and Income Taxes Through Charitable Giving

Peter Fagan

Outlines the information that enables people to make clear decisions about the disposition of their wealth. Coverage includes:

- The dynamics of charitable giving in the United States.
- Planned giving techniques through business and personal applications.
- Income and estate tax considerations in the gift process.

200 pp. ISBN: 0-7863-0229-1 $50.00 ©1996

ASSET ALLOCATION

Balancing Financial Risk
Second Edition

Roger C. Gibson

This classic resource has been revised and updated to reflect the latest data affecting asset allocation. Provides a thorough review of the capital market theory behind asset allocation, plus step-by-step guidelines for designing and implementing appropriate investment strategies. Also includes:

- An up-to-date review of capital market investment performance.
- Thorough discussion of the critical dimensions of asset allocation: risk, return, time, and the diversification effect.
- A disciplined framework for making asset allocation decisions throughout the investor's life.
- Guidelines for managing investor expectations and encouraging commitment to an investing strategy.

300 pp. ISBN: 1-55623-799-5 $50.00 ©1996

(continued)

THE SEVEN SECRETS OF FINANCIAL SUCCESS
Applying the Time Tested Principles of Creating, Managing and Building Personal Wealth
Jack B. Root, Sr. and Douglas L. Mortensen

A practical, easy-to-read guide to the basic principles of personal money management, insurance and investments. Moves readers step by step up the "Success Triangle"—a road map to building a secure lifestyle and peace of mind by retirement. Educates readers on the foundations of financial fitness, and helps them think and plan like financial winners to define personal financial goals and develop a financial strategy to achieve them.
275 pp. ISBN: 0-7863-0459-6 $25.00 ©1996

STOCKS FOR THE LONG RUN
A Guide to Selecting Markets for Long-Term Growth
Jeremy J. Siegel

This unique and substantive guide gives investors essential background on the stock market by explaining the historical returns on stocks and bonds over the past two centuries. Discusses the risk and return profile on financial assets that makes stocks safer and more productive long-term investments.
250 pp. ISBN: 1-55623-804-5 $27.50 ©1994

THE VEST POCKET INVESTOR
Everything You Need to Know to Invest Successfully
Jae K. Shim and Joel G. Siegal

An authoritative, easy-to-understand overview of every aspect of investment. Describes the instruments, strategies and principles of successful investing in clear, straightforward language. Covers everything from mutual funds to options to sources of investment information. Specific topics include:

- Advantages and disadvantages of stocks, bonds, CDs, mutual funds, real estate, annuities, futures and options.
- Understanding risk and return.
- Building an investment portfolio.

300 pp. ISBN: 1-55738-813-X $16.95 ©1996

THE HUMAN RIGHTS CAMPAIGN FOUNDATION

Social progress and civil rights are driven by knowledge and fueled by solid research that honestly tells the important place lesbian and gay Americans hold in our society. Established in 1985, the Human Rights Campaign Foundation works with the Human Rights Campaign (HRC) to promote the visibility of gay and lesbian issues and to advance understanding among all Americans. Through publishing, public policy research and other outreach programs, the Foundation provides vital support to educate the public and to create an America in which it's safe to be honest about who you are.

The National Coming Out Project sponsored by the Foundation is a year-round effort to show the diversity of lesbian and gay Americans and their place in our society. Those efforts culminate on National Coming Out Day, which is held annually on October 11 and is a nationwide event that honors and encourages people in the coming out process.

The Human Rights Campaign Foundation is tax-exempt under Section 501(c)3 of the Internal Revenue Code and is a co-publisher of *Personal Financial Planning for Gays & Lesbians: Our Guide to Prudent Decision Making.*

For more information, write or call

The Human Rights Campaign Foundation
1101 Fourteenth Street, NW
Washington, DC 20005
phone (202) 628-4160
fax (202) 347-5323

THE HUMAN RIGHTS CAMPAIGN (HRC)

The Human Rights Campaign envisions an America where Lesbian and gay people are ensured of their basic equal rights—and can be open, honest and safe at home, at work and in the community

The Human Rights Campaign is America's largest national lesbian and gay membership organization. With more than 150,000 members, HRC pursues its mission through a combination of nonpartisan political action, advocacy, education and grassroots mobilization. The Campaign leads the fight for lesbian and gay equality at the federal level and works with state and local organizations on a coordinated basis.

HRC fights for laws that protect lesbian, gay, and bisexual people from discrimination. In these efforts we combat anti-gay legislation, conduct vital polling research, take active positions on issues, lobby the Congress and Administration and educate communities across this country about the issues that face gay Americans. Chief among legislative priorities is the Employment Non-Discrimination Act which would make it illegal to fire someone solely for being gay.

HRC safeguards the health and welfare of lesbian and gay Americans. We have worked to craft a sound federal policy on the AIDS epidemic that includes care, prevention, education, research and housing. Working with a coalition of national organizations, HRC leads the efforts to ensure Congress lives up to its responsibility. The Human Rights Campaign is also putting lesbian health issues on the national agenda by working to educate the public, build coalitions and promote health care reform that addresses the unique needs of lesbians. HRC helps to secure increased funding for breast and cervical cancer care, research and screening.

HRC mobilizes communities to stop bigotry. As intolerance sweeps the nation, anti-gay initiatives have been introduced in a number of states. With financial backing and campaign resources from HRC, every anti-gay initiative since Colorado's Amendment Two has been successfully defeated. We have also committed significant resources to the courtroom battle to overturn Amendment Two before the Supreme Court.

The Human Rights Campaign is your voice in Washington, DC. Our action programs empower you to make change happen. As a member and activist with the Human Rights Campaign, you'll help broaden minds, create laws, defeat hateful agendas, and build communities where we can all live free from discrimination.

Join us today. Please write or call

The Human Rights Campaign
1101 Fourteenth Street, NW
Washington, DC 20005
phone (202) 628-4160 fax (202) 347-5323
email hrc@hrcusa.org http://www.hrcusa.org

YES

I support lesbian and gay Americans' struggle for basic rights, health, safety and dignity. That's why I'm supporting the Human Rights Campaign with a contribution in the amount of:

- ☐ **$20** ☐ **$35** ☐ **$50**
- ☐ **$100** ☐ **$250** ☐ **Other $_____**

When you join us as a member of HRC, we'll send you a free subscription to HRC Quarterly magazine.

Your name & address:

_____

_____

_____

_____

Your phone number: _____

I would like to make my contribution by credit card:

VISA   MasterCard   American Express   Discover

Card # _____ Exp. Date _____

Authorized Signature _____

Would you provide us with your e-mail address?

_____

HUMAN
RIGHTS
CAMPAIGN

Visit us at our Website: http://www.hrcusa.org
MP6BT1